INSIDE THE
MIRAGE

ALSO BY THOMAS W. LIPPMAN

Understanding Islam

Egypt After Nasser

*Madeleine Albright and
the New American Diplomacy*

INSIDE THE MIRAGE

America's Fragile Partnership
with Saudi Arabia

THOMAS W. LIPPMAN

Westview
PRESS

A Member of the Perseus Books Group

All rights reserved. Printed in the United States of America. No part of this publication may be reproduced or transmitted in any form or by any means, electronic or mechanical, including photocopy, recording, or any information storage and retrieval system, without permission in writing from the publisher.

Copyright © 2004 by Thomas W. Lippman

Hardcover edition first published in 2004 by Westview Press, A Member of Perseus Books Group. Paperback edition first published in 2005 by Westview Press.

Find us on the world wide web at www.westviewpress.com.

Westview Press books are available at special discounts for bulk purchases in the United States by corporations, institutions, and other organizations. For more information, please contact the Special Markets Department at the Perseus Books Group, 11 Cambridge Center, Cambridge, MA 02142, or call (617) 252-5298, (800) 255-1514 or email specialmarkets@ perseusbooks.com.

The Library of Congress has cataloged the hardcover edition as follows:

Lippman, Thomas W.
    Inside the mirage : America's fragile partnership with Saudi Arabia /Thomas W. Lippman.— 1st ed.
        p.   cm.
    Includes bibliographical references and index.
    ISBN 0-8133-4052-7 (hc)
        1. United States—Relations—Saudi Arabia.   2. Saudi Arabia—Relations—United States.
    3. Persian Gulf War, 1991.   4. September 11 Terrorist Attacks, 2001—Influence.   I. Title.
    E183.8.S25L57 2004
    303.48'2538073—dc22

2003017526

ISBN 0-8133-4313-5 (pbk)

Text set in 12-pt AGaramond

The paper used in this publication meets the requirements of the American National Standard for Permanence of Paper for Printed Library Materials Z39.48–1984.

10   9   8   7   6   5   4   3   2

CONTENTS

ACKNOWLEDGMENTS

Any author of a work of nonfiction needs help from many people. I am profoundly grateful to the many scores of Americans and Saudis who gave generously of their time, their recollections, their documents, and their advice. In particular, I owe debts that cannot be repaid to Rick Weintraub, Jonathan Green, Brian Hannon, Elizabeth Brown, Bobbye Pratt, Bob Norberg, Bill Nash, David Mack, Leonard Garment, Daniel Wolf, Medlej Al-Medlej, Susanne Lendman, Saud Al-Suwaileh, Elizabeth Colton, David Hamod, Dave Walker, Nimah Ismail Nawwab, and Nicholas Scheetz. The staffs of the special collections department of the Lauinger Library at Georgetown University and of the Middle East Institute in Washington responded generously and courteously to every request, and the U.S.–Saudi Arabian Business Council provided crucial assistance. I thank them all.

A NOTE ON ARABIC WORDS AND NAMES

THERE IS NO UNIVERSALLY ACCEPTED form of transliteration of Arabic words and names into English. I have used the versions commonly found in American newspapers and magazines. No attempt has been made to reproduce the diacritical marks, glottal stops, long vowelings, and unique consonants of the original, except where they are part of the standard transliteration. In quotations of writings by others, I have retained the transliterations used by them. Thus Muhammad may sometimes appear as Mohammed, Jeddah as Jidda or Jiddah, Faisal as Feysal.

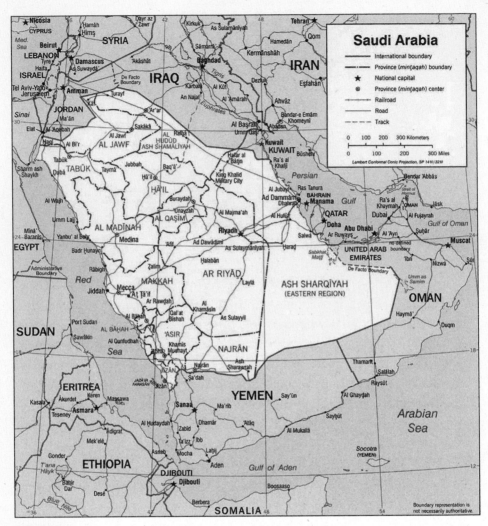

Saudi Arabia

PROLOGUE

AN AMERICAN SHOPPER WOULD FEEL right at home at the Azizia supermarket on Mecca Road in Riyadh, the capital city of Saudi Arabia. The immense, brightly lighted store looks like a Wal-Mart and features aisle after aisle of familiar products with familiar brand names: Uncle Ben's, Libby's, Green Giant, Tide, Spaghetti Os, Pepsi, Heinz, Kal-Kan. The store sells fresh and processed vegetables, fruit, meat, pasta, spices, and dairy products as well as household goods, stationery, compact discs, film, electrical connectors and extension cords, books and magazines, cosmetics, toys, and hundreds of other everyday products that would be on similar display in Dallas or Buffalo or Charlotte. Prices are fixed, as in America; the bargaining of the Arab *souk*, or traditional market, has been eliminated. The sense of familiarity is enhanced by the twenty-four-hour McDonald's restaurant next door and the Dunkin' Donuts a few steps away.

And yet it's not exactly just like America. All the Saudi Arab women shopping at Azizya are veiled, their faces invisible behind shields of black chiffon. Even the many Americans and other foreign women pushing carts along the bustling aisles wear the *abaya,* the black cloak that covers the torso, legs, and arms. No men wear shorts, however hot it may be. No pork products or alcoholic beverages are sold. And the store closes, dousing the lights and expelling its customers, when the call to prayer rises from a nearby mosque.

This is a microcosm of Saudi Arabia in the twenty-first century. Seven decades after the first handful of Americans arrived in the wastelands along the Persian Gulf coast to explore for oil, the desert kingdom has taken on many of the material characteristics of the land Saudis love to emulate. In one lifetime, Americans have reshaped a vast, bleak landscape of nomads' tents and farmers' mud huts in their own image, right down to Starbucks on the corner and the wheelchair-accessible ramps in the newest public buildings. Saudi Arabia today is a country of expressways, computers, air conditioned malls filled with the same glossy shops found in prosperous American suburbs, elegant hotels, fast-food restaurants, satellite television, up-to-date hospitals, high-rise office towers, and amusement parks featuring whirling rides.

Riyadh's newest lavish skyscraper is Kingdom Centre, an architectural oddity that splits into a V, like a giant tuning fork, on the upper floors. Westerners in Riyadh joke grimly that the building's design would let a plane fly through it instead of into it. On its lower floors is the city's trendiest shopping mall, its ambience entirely American—store layouts, lighting, English signs, and window displays. The anchor store is Saks Fifth Avenue. The mall has a Planet Hollywood as well as Van Cleef & Arpels, McDonalds, Coach, and Starbucks. The mall is so American that the veiled women look out of place in their own country. As I wandered among the upscale shops in the fall of 2002, I marveled at how the consumer environment had been upgraded since I first visited the Kingdom in the mid-1970s. Yet Saudi rules still prevail. The mall's third floor is reserved for women; there they can unveil and try on garments out of the sight of men. These shops also close at prayer times. The restaurants have two entrances: one for families, one for single men. Saudi women shop only in pairs or in groups, never alone. A sign posted outside the mall's drive-up entrance reflects the reality that women are not permitted to drive and must be chauffeured: "All drivers must wait at drivers rest room, at level 3. No exceptions. They can be contacted by intercom at concierge desks."

Kingdom Centre's glitter and Azizia supermarket's consumer cornucopia are the external realities of life in contemporary Saudi Arabia. Internally, the people of Saudi Arabia have retained their proud cultural and religious identity and the cherished traditions that make theirs a society like no other, utterly different from America. In the words of David Long, who spent many years in Saudi Arabia as an American diplomat and learned the language, "The two peoples remain very foreign to each other. Very few westerners really understand the Saudi mentality, and very few Saudis become as western in thought as they do in manner."[1]

For all its physical transformation, Saudi Arabia remains a socially conservative monarchy and a closed, inner-directed society, one where urban families live behind high walls, sequestered from passers-by and even neighbors. Its organizing principle is the family, its national document and spiritual beacon the Koran, its political cement Islam. The state and the royal family, the House of Saud, are one. The king's official title is "Custodian of the Two Holy Mosques" at Mecca and Medina, where the Prophet Muhammad promulgated Islam in the seventh century.

Individual Saudi citizens, if they are men, enjoy substantial personal freedom. They can travel at will, choose their professions, live where they wish, own businesses, possess foreign currencies, and speak their minds in private. At the same time, there are well-understood limits on personal, social, and political behavior, and the consequences of going beyond them can be severe. All important decisions are made by a small circle of powerful men who haggle their way invisibly toward consensus. There is no forum other than the king's favor in which they can be held accountable. Dissent is tolerated only within the narrowest of limits. There is no parliament and there are no labor unions. All Saudi citizens must be Muslims.

Never colonized or subjugated, the Saudis enjoy—or did until September 11, 2001—a serene self-confidence that theirs is the right way, at least for them. Although they are willing to explain customs that run counter to deeply held American beliefs about the value of individuals and the consent of the governed, they do not apologize for them. Americans have succeeded and prospered in Saudi Arabia because they have mostly respected Saudi traditions and accommodated themselves to the habits and preferences of their hosts; indeed, the strong bond that has formed between Saudis and Americans has benefited both countries for decades.

The Americans who waded ashore to prospect for oil in 1933 were entering a different universe from the one that sent them. Technologically they traveled back in time, to the era before the Industrial Revolution. In the first years of American involvement there, it was not surprising that the Saudi Arab people and the Americans would have different ways of thinking about life.

The Saudis knew virtually nothing of modern technology or life outside their community. Most of them were illiterate, except perhaps for knowing the Koran. Features of everyday life that were common even in African cities—electricity, buses, movies, aircraft, paved roads, flush toilets, telephones, restaurants, refrigeration, radio, wristwatches—were all but unknown to them. The scruffy port city of Jeddah was relatively cosmopolitan because of its contact with pilgrims going to Mecca, but it was on the other side of the country from the oil fields. Outside Jeddah and its environs, Saudis knew little other than the tribe, the family, the herd, the desert, and the faith. In that sense, when the American oil pioneers stormed into the backward lands of people who were isolated and powerless to resist, they were like European colonizers of centuries past. But there was a crucial difference this time: The Americans did not enter the Kingdom at gunpoint and they were not seeking religious converts. They entered with the assent and the high hopes of the monarch, and they were committed to respect the society over which he ruled and the traditions of his people.

Now, seventy years later, the country is up-to-date physically, to the point where Saudi doctors are doing experimental organ transplants, a Saudi pilot has flown in space, and automated teller machines perform functions still not available in the United States. The entire country is computerized.

In those seven decades, hundreds of thousands of Americans have worked and lived in Saudi Arabia. For those who are there today, the full array of worldly creature comforts is available; yet there is less sharing of the indigenous experience than there was in the early years because Americans are no longer dependent on the locals for camel transport, native food, or navigational guidance. Nobody needs to share a kerosene-lighted tent in the desert with armed bedouin, as the early oil geologists did all the time. Even in the earliest days of enforced desert intimacy, there were secrets of tribe and family to which Americans were not going to be privy; but the shared experiences of exploration, discovery, and mutual dependence created a closeness now hard to match. As Saudi Arabia evolved into a country of air conditioning, superhighways, up-to-date medicine, and English-speaking engineers, it became harder for Americans to understand, let alone accept, that the Saudis still have a completely different and often unfathomable decisionmaking process. The Saudis still live within the material and metaphorical walls of their family compounds, which Americans enter only by invitation. There is no reason to assume, as Americans tend to do, that as the people of Saudi Arabia achieve greater familiarity and contact with the Western world they will reduce the influence of Islam in their lives and adapt to Western ways socially and politically, as they have physically. The traditional verities of their lives, and especially Islam, became for many Saudis their shield against the inevitable social disruption that came with modernization. Saudis accept change, but only if the change is compatible with their faith. The Saudis have become fully modern in the physical sense without opening the doors to the inner sanctum of their lives. And they have learned much more about Americans than Americans have about them.

As different as the two societies were and remain, the relationship between the United States and Saudi Arabia has been the ultimate marriage of convenience. The Saudis wanted money and technology; the Americans wanted oil and a reliable ally in the global struggle against communism. By and large both countries got what they wanted and the relationship survived all crises, at least until September 11, 2001. The virulent strain of Saudi anti-Americanism revealed by that day's events has many causes, but it cannot rationally be justified by the behavior of Americans in the Kingdom. The people of Saudi Arabia have benefited, not suffered, from the American presence.

The story of America's role in Saudi Arabia begins with oil, but it hardly ends there. Over seven decades, hundreds of thousands of Americans have lived and worked in Saudi Arabia. They brought the country industrialization, electricity and telephones, modern medicine, mechanized agriculture, air conditioning, and jet aviation. One way or another, Americans have had a formative influence on almost every aspect of contemporary Saudi life except religion. By and large, the

Americans' behavior has been honorable and the results of their work beneficial to the Saudi people. The Saudi zealots consumed by hatred of America, whose existence became all too evident with the events of September 11, 2001, cannot argue persuasively that their compatriots have been exploited or diminished by the American presence. At all times in the stunning transformation of their country, the Saudis have benefited from American investment capital, American technological capability, and the American gift for efficient organization, but they never surrendered their freedom to choose or their independence of spirit. This is the story of how two cultures from opposite poles of human experience came together to the benefit of both.

CHAPTER 1

The Pioneers

THE LANDSCAPE OF EASTERN Saudi Arabia gives off a stark white glare, the color of sun-bleached bones. The featureless terrain between oases is an unforgiving expanse of sand and rock, offering none of the natural bounty that invites human habitation. A migrant homesteader would keep going. For Krug Henry and Bert Miller, the arid bleakness of the land mattered little; their interest lay beneath the surface. They were oil men, accustomed to harsh environments.

It was September 23, 1933, dark times at home in America as the Great Depression tightened its grip but the first light of a new dawn of promise and prosperity in the Kingdom of Saudi Arabia. Miller and Henry were the first geologists dispatched by Standard Oil Company of California, which had won an exclusive concession from His Majesty King Abdul Aziz ibn Saud to explore for oil in a territory bigger than Texas.

Arriving by boat from Bahrain, the nearby island in the Persian Gulf from which oil was already flowing, they landed in Jubail, a coastal village. The next day they were joined by Karl Twitchell, an industrious Vermonter who had ingratiated himself with the king by undertaking a country-wide search for water and minerals the preceding year. Twitchell traveled overland from Jeddah, at the opposite end of the vast country, with two cars provided by the monarch—a remarkable feat in itself, since there were no roads. All three men wore beards and Arab headdress to avoid giving offense to whatever local population they might encounter.

Thus began what would turn out to be the greatest oil bonanza in history. Saudi Arabia, one of the world's poorest countries at the time, would reap unimaginable wealth from its unpromising soil. King Abdul Aziz, whose kingdom was but one year old, would acquire the money and power to ensure his family's rule, which continues today. And the United States would gain guaranteed access to the world's most extensive pool of oil, which would fuel decades of American consumption and prosperity after World War II.

Hundreds of thousands of Americans would follow Twitchell, Miller, and Henry to work in Saudi Arabia in a melding of alien cultures probably without parallel in modern times. Only if green creatures with antennae had arrived from another galaxy could there have been a greater gap in culture, language, religion, education, diet, technology, and knowledge about the world than existed between the Americans and their Arab hosts. It is a credit to the flexibility and good humor of both societies that they made the relationship work, to their mutual benefit.

Within a few years, Saudi Arab men who had never heard of such things would learn how to use power tools, hook up generators, drive trucks, and communicate by two-way radio. Arab women—those mysterious, sequestered creatures who covered themselves with black veils— would meet American women who introduced them to the brassière and the baby stroller. Americans learned, too, about serenity in the face of privation, about the dexterity and intelligence of their Arab hosts, and about coming to terms with a culture that would not submit. Improvising as they went, and with no grand strategic plan, the American oil pioneers and a handful of early diplomats laid the groundwork for an economic and strategic partnership of astonishing durability.

⌇

Before the Standard of California concession, Britain was the primary economic power in the Persian Gulf region. The British were the colonial masters of the small coastal sheikhdoms and British companies controlled the oil fields of Iran and Iraq. King Abdul Aziz, who was a wily negotiator and shrewd evaluator of motivations despite his lack of contact with the outside world, did not want the British to have dominion over whatever oil might be found in his country. The British were colonizers, and more than anything else the zealously Muslim king feared infidel interference with his country's affairs. Moreover, because the British already had abundant oil from the neighboring countries, the king suspected they would be in no hurry to begin production in Saudi Arabia, and he needed money quickly.[1]

Never vanquished in battle and never manipulated by a colonial power, Abdul Aziz ibn Saud is a monumental figure in Arab history; but in 1933 he was not really a king at all in the sense of the monarchy as it is in Europe, where, amid lavish ceremony, a hereditary monarch is crowned and installed on his throne. Abdul Aziz was a desert warrior, a clan chief, who overpowered or bought off the other clans of Arabia to establish his family's rule. It was as if a chief of the Sioux had vanquished the other tribes of the American Great Plains and extracted their allegiance.

In partnership with an austere and xenophobic Muslim group, Abdul Aziz's clan, the House of Saud, had ruled Arabia twice previously, but had been overthrown by rival families and then banished to exile in Kuwait by the Ottoman Turks. In 1902, Abdul Aziz rode back in from Kuwait with forty followers, seized Riyadh in a daring raid, and reasserted the reign of the al-Saud. It took him more than twenty years to establish unquestioned authority over the rest of what is now Saudi Arabia. On September 22, 1932, having subdued all rivals and crushed the fanatic Islamic warriors who had been the instrument of his conquests, Abdul Aziz proclaimed the country unified as the Kingdom of Saudi Arabia.

ᘯ

By the standards of the industrialized world, his domain was a prize of dubious value. Although vast—larger than France, Germany, Spain, and Sweden combined—it was sparsely populated and lacked the resources essential to development, including water. About two thirds of Saudi Arabia's territory is uninhabitable desert; when the first oil men arrived, much of it had never been explored by outsiders. The country's principal source of revenue, taxes on Muslims making the pilgrimage to Mecca, was dwindling as the worldwide Depression reduced travel. Only in the western region known as the Hijaz, where the port city of Jeddah was the traditional point of entry for pilgrims, was there a small cosmopolitan population of Arabs familiar with the outside world. The king's most loyal followers, from the clans of the Riyadh region and the central part of the country known as Nejd, were almost entirely illiterate and had virtually no contact with outsiders.

The king's fateful decision to award the oil concession to an American concern rather than to the British was based on more than financial considerations. It was attributable in part to an affinity for Americans that can be traced back more than two decades before the full unification of his country and the granting of the oil concession. In 1911, ten of his soldiers who had been wounded in a gun battle over pearl-fishing proceeds went to Bahrain to seek medical treatment because they had heard about a mission hospital that had been established there by the Reformed Church in America. Patched up, the soldiers quickly carried the story of their care back across the water to Qatif and other oasis towns, where modern medical care was nonexistent.

The mission doctors were Arabic-speaking members of the Reformed Church. Their assignment was to provide medical treatment to all Arabs who sought it in the principalities along the Persian Gulf and, to the extent that they could gain access, in the interior of the Arabian peninsula. From their base in Bahrain, they fanned out through the region to treat the numerous chronic diseases that afflicted the population. They gained few converts but won many friends.

Their first foray into what would become Saudi Arabia came in 1913, when the local potentate in the Qatif oasis invited the mission to send a doctor. Dr. Paul Harrison, a medical graduate of Johns Hopkins University who had studied Arabic in Iraq for two years, spent six weeks in Qatif ministering to the local citizens, many of whom suffered from tuberculosis and trachoma, as well as malaria.

Word of the American doctors' work soon reached Riyadh. In 1914, Abdul Aziz rounded up a group of his men who were suffering from malaria and transported them to Kuwait, where he asked the ruler to summon help from the American hospital he had heard about. The

physician who made that trip, Dr. C. Stanley Mylrea, appears to h;
been the first American the king ever met.

"He was indeed a notable personality, of commanding height—well
over six feet—and beautifully yet simply dressed in a long white robe over
which he wore a brown cloak heavily embroidered with gold thread,"
Mylrea wrote of Abdul Aziz. "On his head was the regulation kerchief
and double rope. His feet were bare, for he had left his sandals at the
threshold as we came in. He appeared to be in perfect health and I
guessed his age to be about thirty-five. He impressed me immensely.
Every line of him, face and figure, told of intelligence, energy, determination, and reserves of compelling power. It was a good face, too, which
bore witness to his reputation as a man of deep piety and devotion. It was
not the face of a profligate upstart, but the face of a man who had disciplined himself and knew what it was to fast and to pray."[2] Mylrea's min-
istrations and Harrison's work among the people of Qatif inspired
confidence in Abdul Aziz that these Americans could and would help his
people. In 1917 he invited Harrison to his primitive capital, Riyadh—a
rare and possibly unprecedented honor for a foreign infidel—and arranged for a house there be used as a makeshift hospital.

"I know you are a Christian," he told Harrison, "but honorable men
are friends though they differ in religion."

Harrison and his aides remained in Riyadh for three weeks, leaving
only when their supply of medicines ran out. He returned in 1919
when the worldwide influenza epidemic struck Riyadh.

Physicians from the mission hospital roamed eastern and central
Saudi Arabia during the next several years, offering medical care to people who were desperate for it and asking nothing in return. Such was
their reputation that when the king himself fell ill in 1923, he sought
help from the Bahrain hospital. Sensing the urgency of the king's condition, Dr. Louis Dame traveled more than thirty hours across the
desert by racing camel to reach Riyadh.

"I found him suffering from a cellulitis of the face," Dame reported.
"His face was tremendously swollen, his eye was the size of a baseball,
and his lips were so swollen he could hardly speak. I barely recognized
him." Dame lanced the infection and the king was himself again within
a few days.

Dame's account, he stayed in Riyadh about a month, am provided treatment to several thousand of the local y-seven actual working days we made 3,374 treatments 1,306 were new cases and 1,978 were re-treatments and 90 outcalls," he reported. "We performed 36 major operations and 101 minor operations and gave 15 intravenous injections. We were very well received and have been very well treated."

Such was Abdul Aziz's admiration for the American doctors and so great was his people's need of care that he authorized extended visits by the missionary teams throughout his long life. The missionaries were never permitted to establish a permanent facility or take up residence, nor were they allowed to proselytize, but their selfless performance left an indelibly positive impression upon the king that would have consequences far beyond medicine.

The king's favorable assessment of Americans was reinforced by the personal diplomacy of Charles R. Crane, a plumbing fixtures heir from Chicago. Not much interested in his family's bathtub and toilet business, Crane found adventure in the Middle East in 1919 when President Woodrow Wilson sent him, along with Henry King, president of Oberlin College, to Palestine and Syria.

The work of their delegation, known as the King-Crane Commission, was an intense but ultimately irrelevant chapter in the immensely tangled story of how France and Britain carved up the Middle East after the collapse of the Ottoman Empire. The commission concluded that the Zionist proposal to create a Jewish homeland in Palestine could be carried out only at gunpoint, would impose "the gravest trespass upon the civil and religious rights of existing non-Jewish communities in Palestine," and "must be greatly modified."[3] These findings were ignored by the United States, Britain, and France; as Robert Lacey wrote in his monumental history of Saudi Arabia, "The recommendations of the King-Crane Commission were dropped into the maelstrom of the Versailles Peace Conference to vanish without a trace."[4] The more durable outcome lay in the esteem in which Arabs held Crane because of his views on Palestine and in the affection Crane developed for the Arab people, whom he selected as worthy beneficiaries of his commitment to use his wealth for the betterment of humanity.

By all accounts Crane was a thoughtful and generous person, and, save for his desire to acquire the best Arabian horses, his motivations were entirely philanthropic. He financed a translation of the Koran into English. He visited Yemen and provided the ruler with a technical team to look for water; he also supplied pumps and drilling equipment and paid for the construction of Yemen's first steel highway bridge. He toured the Hijaz before it came under the rule of Abdul Aziz. In 1930, while visiting Cairo in search of good horses, he encountered Sheikh Fawzan al-Sabik, Abdul Aziz's representative in Egypt, who had a renowned stable of the finest Arabians.

Through Sheikh Fawzan, Crane made an offer to the king: He would send a geologist or engineer to tour Arabia in search of water and mineral resources. Abdul Aziz, who had heard of Crane's affection for the Arabs and of his generosity in Yemen, invited Crane to visit him in Jeddah, which Crane did in February 1931. It was a measure of the high esteem in which Crane was held by the Arabs that the king traveled to the humid, foul-smelling Jeddah, which he disliked, to receive him.

Their momentous encounter was a truly Arab event in that it was punctuated by elaborate courtesies, exchanges of gifts, lavish meals, and elliptical conversations. Discussions that Americans could have completed in four hours required four days. Crane did not offer the king any cash, as the monarch apparently hoped he would, but indicated he would be willing to help the Kingdom exploit whatever resources it might have for its own development. The outcome was that Crane dispatched a mining engineer who had represented him in Yemen to tour Abdul Aziz's realm in search of water, gold, and other prospects for mining. That engineer was Karl Twitchell, who thus became the first American to work in Saudi Arabia.[5]

Crane represented the same phenomenon the king had encountered in the American doctors: an infidel foreigner who was willing to help him and asked nothing in return. From that time onward, the king inclined toward American interests in economic and strategic decisions. Not even American support for Jewish migration to Palestine and the creation of Israel, both of which the king strongly opposed, would undo this bond.

Twitchell arrived in Jeddah on April 15, 1931, and began his exploratory trek through the Arabian hinterlands. Amazingly, he was accompanied by his wife, Nona—quite a social innovation in Saudi Arabia. "The trip was arduous and Mrs. Twitchell was ill part of the time," Twitchell observed laconically in his account of this expedition.

The Twitchells traveled more than fifteen hundred miles through the Hijaz. Unhappily, they found "no geological evidence to justify the hope for flowing artesian wells. A pessimistic report therefore had to be made on the water question. Though a number of possibilities could be pointed out regarding the development of water in small units, reclamation projects on a large scale were entirely precluded."[6]

This, of course, came as a disappointment to the king and to his finance minister and chief adviser, Abdullah Sulaiman, who asked Twitchell whether he could "suggest other practical sources of income" to offset the decline in pilgrimage revenue. Twitchell said there could well be good prospects for mining, but that an extensive geological survey of the country would be required to assess them. Before going back to the United States to report to Crane, he presented to Sulaiman "a plan for engaging competent engineers and geologists to examine Saudi Arabia for minerals and do sufficient clearing and development work in order to obtain a fair idea as to a reasonably valuable estimate and make a competent report on each property that might interest foreign capital." Crane agreed to finance such an expedition, but told Twitchell that it would be the last he could support because the Depression was eroding the value of his investments.

Upon returning to the Kingdom in the fall of 1931, Twitchell set up teams to explore for gold near Taif, in the mountains southeast of Jeddah, and almost as an afterthought he undertook to improve Jeddah's primitive water supply. He and an Arab engineer employed by the king built a windmill with a 16-foot blade diameter. This contraption, used with an auxiliary diesel-powered pump, "raised an average of 40 gallons a minute into the water tunnel" that served the city, seven miles away, "making an appreciable addition to the water supply," Twitchell noted.

The king not only appreciated Twitchell's forthrightness in evaluating the Kingdom's water prospects but came to trust his judgment and rely on his advice. While Twitchell was supervising the search for gold, the king summoned him to his encampment near Riyadh to talk about the possibility of finding oil along the country's eastern coast. The terrain there was similar to that of Bahrain, where Standard of California, or SoCal, was already prospecting.

"Although this would be a thousand-mile trip over rough country, where no American had ever been, the invitation was readily accepted," Twitchell recalled of the trek to his rendezvous with the king. He left his wife in charge of a team looking for more water outside Jeddah. By his account, "She did a very capable job and had the unique experience of directing a crew of twenty to thirty devout Moslem Najdis, who served her with great courtesy."

The king would have preferred not to import foreigners to look for oil, or to do anything else. The people over whom he reigned were hostile to innovation and largely opposed any foreign presence; his own mistrust of outsiders had been heightened by an earlier oil-drilling scheme put forward by a buccaneering New Zealander named Frank Holmes, whose shell company never sank a well. But Abdul Aziz was desperate for cash, and he respected Twitchell. At their meeting, the king accepted Twitchell's advice to wait for the outcome of the oil drilling then underway on Bahrain. If test wells there were dry, it was unlikely oil would be found on the Saudi side because of the geological similarities. "On the other hand," Twitchell wrote, "if the Bahrain well proved a success, it was logical that commercial oil would be found in Hasa [eastern Saudi Arabia] but in greater quantities because of its much greater area."

Twitchell spent months looking for possible sites to mine for gold and other valuable minerals. At the king's request, and with Crane's permission, he returned to the United States to approach American corporations about their interest in such projects. All the mining companies he talked to turned him down, for various reasons, but oil companies were interested. The most interested was SoCal (later known as Chevron), which was "crude short," or lacking in proven reserves of crude oil to which it would have guaranteed access.

The well-established, British-controlled Iraq Petroleum Company was SoCal's nominal competition for the Saudi Arabia concession. King Abdul Aziz, however, wanted Americans, a preference endorsed by none other than his English friend and adviser, the legendary H. St. John Philby, who for his own reasons was undermining the British bid. Accompanied by Twitchell, a SoCal lawyer and negotiator named Lloyd N. Hamilton traveled to Jeddah in February 1933 to begin negotiations with Abdullah Sulaiman. After more than three months of talks, the agreement was signed on May 29. Thanks to Crane and Twitchell, and to the willingness of SoCal to commit extensive resources to an untested prospect halfway around the world at a time of industrial retrenchment, the king put the future of his throne and his country into American hands.

In the agreement, according to a history compiled by SoCal and the partners it later took on, the oil company "committed itself to loans totaling £50,000 gold (about $250,000 at that time), yearly rentals of £5,000 (about $25,000), and royalties of 4 shillings gold (about $1.00) per ton of oil produced. It also undertook to provide the government with an advance of £50,000 gold once oil was found in commercial quantities." Exploration was to begin immediately. The agreement was to run for sixty years, during which time SoCal enjoyed exclusive rights to produce and market all the oil found in the vast concession area as well as the right to match offers for drilling rights elsewhere in the Kingdom. The concession agreement required that SoCal employ local workers whenever possible, a condition that would result in the education and training of thousands of Arabs.[7]

Having cowed Saudi Arabia's reactionary religious leaders into accepting the prospect of infidels' taking up residence in their midst, Abdul Aziz thus weathered his immediate cash crisis. The United States and Saudi Arabia were in business together. Both were entering uncharted territory and they would make up the rules as they went along.

"Saudi Arabia," Twitchell wrote later, "is presumably the only country in the world whose development of oil and mining resulted from purely philanthropic sentiment."[8] He meant the sentiment of Charles Crane, not of SoCal, whose interest was strictly business. Crane and Twitchell had planted a seed of cooperation between Saudi Arabia and the United States that grew beyond their imagination and is still bearing fruit. Twitchell dedicated his book "To the memory of Charles C. Crane, the great American whose practical philanthropy was the foundation of the present development of the kingdom of his esteemed friend, King Abdul Aziz ibn Saud."

Upon arriving at Jubail, Robert P. Miller, known as Bert, and Schuyler B. "Krug" Henry wanted to meet up with Twitchell and go to work right away, but they were surprised to find a crowd of local people waiting on shore to give the newcomers a welcoming ceremony. Among the Arabs were the local emir (meaning prince or, in the context of a village or oasis, mayor or leader), and a squad of soldiers sent by the king to protect the Americans. The presence of the Arabs required a polite response, and the Americans drank many cups of cardamom-scented coffee. This was a crucial moment because it signaled to the population that the infidels were there with the consent of the king and for the good of the country. Unaccustomed to strangers and hostile to unbelievers as they often were, the local people not only welcomed these outsiders but offered them guides to lead the way and camels to transport them when their cars sank into the sand, as cars invariably did.

The orchestrator of the welcome and the supplier of the guides and other local workers was the most powerful man in that part of Saudi Arabia, Abdullah bin Jiluwi, the emir of Hasa and a cousin of the king's. On most matters, bin Jiluwi held the king's proxy to make decisions about what the Americans could and could not do. It was he who conveyed to the local people the king's desire that these outlandish-looking foreigners with their noisy machines be aided in their work, not impeded. This was not a colonial relationship. The king, Abdullah Sulaiman, and Abdullah bin Jiluwi were tough negotiators; they understood they needed to work with the Americans but at the same time never allowed them to forget who held the ultimate authority. Indeed, the Arabs had insisted on including in the concession agreement a provision specifying that "the Company or anyone connected with it shall have no right to interfere with the administrative, political, or religious affairs within Arabia." Nonetheless, the oil company would become deeply involved in such matters because it became the de facto government of Saudi Arabia's Eastern Province; but company officials always kept the king and bin Jiluwi informed and deferred to their authority.

As the welcoming party demonstrated, the eastern part of Saudi Arabia was not uninhabited. Bedouins roamed the desert with their herds, and there were settled populations in a few large oases, harvesting dates from the palms. Along the coast were small villages of fishermen and pearl divers. These communities lacked electricity and telephones; hospitals and schools were unknown, and there were no grocery or hardware stores. The Americans were like nineteenth-century pioneers heading into the western wilderness in their covered wagons—what they had was what they carried with them—except that the natives were mostly friendly once they understood that the foreigners were under the king's protection. The geologists set up temporary headquarters in a small housing compound in Jubail, a relatively cool and breezy settlement compared to the malarial oases, and commenced their explorations.

In another part of the world, the arrival of foreign oil-drilling teams would have ignited supporting activity by the government and by entrepreneurs, either local or imported. The government would have run some telephone lines, built a pier and an airstrip, perhaps paved some roads. Merchants and tradesmen would have appeared to sell clothing, cigarettes, food, and other basic commodities. Someone would have opened a hotel, a laundry, a barber shop. None of that happened in Saudi Arabia, at least not in the early years, because the government had no resources, the local people had no access to imported goods, and foreign merchants—from India, perhaps, or Lebanon—were not encouraged. It took a corporation with very deep pockets to begin the oil enterprise in Saudi Arabia because everything, from drinking water to trucks to prefabricated dwellings, had to be imported; the company was on its own for whatever services the workers required, from haircuts to medical care.

By default, the oil company—known at first as CASOC, for California Arabian Standard Oil Company, and later, after SoCal took on Texaco, Mobil, and Standard of New Jersey as partners, as Aramco, for Arabian American Oil Company—became the engine of commerce and the center of community life for the Americans and their Arab neighbors in the eastern region. For many years, the situation was a source of some tension between the oil company and the Saudis, who expected the oil company to provide essential public services such as water, schools, and hospitals for the local people. Aramco often resisted because it did not want to undertake costly ventures unrelated to its mission of finding oil, but it usually yielded in the end rather than risk losing its concession. Staying in the king's good graces was a powerful motivator of American behavior, and doing so required responding, however reluctantly, to the overwhelming needs of the local population.

Even such a cynical British chronicler of Western relations with the Arab Gulf states as J. B. Kelly acknowledged that Aramco delivered these services to the benefit of the local Arabs:

> It not only made itself responsible for such obvious matters as the training, safety, health, housing, and proper remuneration of its workers, but it extended its responsibility to the people of Hasa in general. It built and maintained a modern road network; it encouraged local commercial enterprises by assisting in the establishing of service industries to meet its own many needs; it improved the general health of the population of Hasa by eradicating malaria and reducing the incidence of fly-borne and water-borne diseases; and it developed a comprehensive system of hospitals, clinics and dispensaries to care not just for its own workers and their families but for thousands of Hasawis as well.[9]

Photographs from CASOC's earliest days show dusty men with dusty beards in dusty tent encampments, often in Arab garb, sometimes in the company of bedouin guides. As the little band of explorers grew, the company erected a rudimentary headquarters community consisting of prefabricated buildings with a crude form of air conditioning; but the exploration still required treks into the unmapped wilderness, where the geologists and their indispensable mechanics camped out with Arab guides. Sandstorms and intense heat often interrupted their exploration and calculations. Their vehicles bogged down in the sand or in salty marshes near the coast. The work was arduous, but there was no point in taking time off because there was nothing else to do. Three years elapsed from the time Miller and Henry landed until oil was found in commercial quantities, and only after that did SoCal commit itself to a permanent settlement where wives and children could join the men.

Within a year of the first arrivals, the CASOC band of pioneers had grown to thirteen Americans. They had imported steel girders, mosquito-repellent guns, portable toilets, generators, electric fans,

By January 1934, four months after the oil concession agreement was signed, these Americans had taken up residence at the coastal village of Jubail, where they wore Arab garb out of deference to their hosts. The first Americans to arrive were Schuyler B. "Krug" Henry, second from right, and Robert P. "Bert" Miller, third from right.

PHOTOGRAPHER UNKNOWN. COURTESY ARAMCO SERVICES CO.

wrenches, pulleys, pumps, trucks, and pipes. As the British journalist David Holden wrote in his history of the House of Saud, "By and by a whole new civilization had been created where, but a few months previously, there had been nothing but a few mud huts, the camels and the sea for as long as men had been there."[10] The Americans' equipment included a single-engine airplane for photographing and mapping the trackless expanse of the Hasa region. The plane and the motor vehicles, of course, were novelties to the local people. Their unfamiliarity with the internal combustion engine and the generation of electricity caused some bewilderment about exactly what it was the Americans were looking for beneath the surface of the land.

The most extensive personal account of this early period comes from the letters of Thomas C. Barger, who arrived in 1937, stayed thirty-two years, and rose to become chief executive of Aramco. He was a young mining engineer from North Dakota who signed up to work in Saudi

Arabia because he wanted to marry his hometown sweetheart and needed a job. "I was madly in love with Kathleen Ray, a young woman from Medora, North Dakota, and until I could earn a living wage, I couldn't ask her to marry me," he wrote years later.[11]

Once hired, he married Kathleen on November 18, 1937. Their honeymoon was a trip to New York, where Tom would embark on a passenger liner across the Atlantic. Two weeks after the wedding, he set sail for Saudi Arabia, about which he knew nothing.

The year of his arrival was momentous for Aramco for another reason: The first two wives arrived at the oil settlement. One of them was Mrs. Krug Henry, described by the novelist Wallace Stegner (who was commissioned by Aramco to write the official history of this period) as "the lovely Annette whom Krug Henry had seen, courted and won in an uproarious few weeks in Lebanon." Their quarters were to be two-bedroom portables that SoCal had shipped out after it became apparent that oil would be found and the workers would stay. These units, Stegner wrote, "squatted baldly on the stone and sand, without a bush, a spear of grass, a weed even, around them. Their view was of a lone derrick among bare *jabals* [hills], a fence enclosing an acreage of scorched earth, a cluster of gaunt power poles. But there were never two women more appreciated, respected and revered. The schoolteacher in a Wyoming cow town was a social outcast by comparison."[12] Their arrival began the transformation of a roughneck oil camp into the city known as Dhahran, destined to become a permanent fixture on the Saudi Arabian landscape.

Scruffy as it was when Barger got there, it had advanced considerably since Miller and Henry landed in 1933. He found a community of about sixty men: geologists, drilling crews, mechanics, engineers, Indian clerks, and "a young Army of Arabs," duties unspecified. There were five wives. "The food is fine," and there was rice and fresh vegetables, he wrote to Kathleen.[13]

Barger's letters describe the geologists' long hot days of driving around in the uncharted desert with their equipment and their local guides, who navigated by landmarks imperceptible to the Americans. Their vehicle was a four-wheel-drive Ford station wagon into which they loaded "two geologists, a cook, a mechanic and three soldiers, as well as a radio, the chronometer, a transit with tripod, four goatskins of water, spare parts and springs, a drum of gasoline and another of distilled water, food, bedrolls and tents for seven men." Before the arrival of the Ford, this entire apparatus was transported by camel, which the Americans had to learn how to ride, often to the great amusement of the Arabs.[14] The exploration teams passed entire days without encountering other human beings. Distances were measured by how far a camel could travel in a day. Always they were looking for water, not so much for themselves as for the Ford's radiator. They assigned place names to hills and *wadis* (gullies) and marked them on their rudimentary maps.

Barger and his colleagues went to places where no foreigners had ever been. They explored the oasis of Jibrin, 250 miles from Dhahran, and found it so malarial that it was inhabited only a few months a year. Mosquito larvae wriggled in the waters of the oasis. On a mapping expedition and search for water in a community called Laila, south of Riyadh and outside the CASOC concession area, they encountered a local population so hostile that no one would greet them. The people of Laila "refused to sell meat to the 'servants of infidels.'"[15] That was the only such incident recorded in Barger's letters; he attributed it to "fanatical bigotry."

At night the explorers camped around a fire, like cowboys in the American West. Mostly they ate canned food; the Arabs kept the empty cans, which had some unknown value for them. After the meal, the Americans and the Arabs entertained each other with stories—the Arabs telling tales of piracy, adventure, and tribal rivalry, the Americans recounting the fables of Aesop and the Homeric legends. "We sure got our money's worth out of Homer and Aesop," Barger wrote to Kathleen.[16] The Arabs—who referred to themselves as Hijazis or Nejdis, not yet as Saudis—were also fascinated by stories about the American Indians, to whom they sometimes likened themselves. In these exploration parties, Americans and Arabs achieved a level of fraternal camaraderie based on adventure and shared hardship that would soon be lost as production supplanted exploration and permanent buildings replaced the tent. During the months Barger spent on these explorations, construction was transforming the Dhahran base camp into an American town. Family housing was built, along with a dining hall, a swimming pool, and tennis courts. More wives arrived, but not yet Kathleen because housing was still scarce and other, more senior employees had precedence. As a geologist, Barger was expected to be out in the field most of the time and thus he was low on the list for permanent housing in Dhahran. Kathleen Barger did not arrive until February 1945, more than seven years after she and Tom were married.

"Some people ask, 'What do you do with your spare time in Arabia?'" Barger wrote. "We tell them we fix radios, take generators apart, repair cars, see that the camp has water, make sure there is enough gasoline, write reports on geology, servants' time, and food expenditures, and keep radio schedules. In between we work, and if there are no letters to write, we sleep."[17]

As he learned Arabic and became familiar with the culture and folk-ways of his hosts, Barger sprinkled his letters with observations about them and about how to get along with them: Always take time for the rituals of greeting, salutation, tea, and coffee; don't show the sole of your shoe to an Arab; it's polite to slurp your tea, to show your appreciation; if your host fills your coffee cup it is "a sign of high disfavor, the implication being that you should drink up and be gone."

One day the explorers encountered a young Arab woman. Their cook, Nasir, was smitten, but his hope of courtship ran into the objections of the woman's brother, who visited the camp and saw Nasir cooking. "The occupation of cook is scorned by the proud Bedouin," Barger reported, "who will cook for themselves on a raiding party but would rather die than cook for a living." Faced with this reality, Nasir quit.[18]

Barger won favor with the Arabs by shooting a wolf. Just as in the American West, the wolves killed sheep and the Arabs were happy to be rid of them. From time to time, Barger and his companions would encounter a herd of Arabian oryx. The reaction of the exploration party was always the same: Shoot the adults and capture the young to take back to base camp for food. When this pursuit took place on camelback, the oryx had a chance to escape; with the arrival of the Ford they were doomed.

The Americans were completely dependent upon their bedouin guides (assigned to them by Abdullah bin Jiluwi) not only for navigation but also for talking to local people, friendly or otherwise. Their favorite guide was a former pearl diver named Khamis ibn Rimthan, described in a company profile as "a great guide and a great man."[19] He was with Aramco's geologists when they picked the site of the first well to be drilled; he also accompanied chief geologist Max Steineke on his field expeditions.

Renowned for his sense of direction, Khamis became one of the first Arabs hired as a regular employee of the oil company, and he learned to read. "He was a walking encyclopedia with a built in navigational device," the Aramco profile said. An oil field was named for him, the only one named after a person.[20]

Young Arabs such as Khamis who were able to break out of their illiteracy and deprived backgrounds to seize opportunities offered by the oil company were to form a cadre of Saudi Arabs who admired and respected Americans and sought to emulate their work habits. Many of these early Arab employees became prominent in Saudi government and business and formed a strong constituency in support of the House of Saud's alliance with the United States.

∽

CASOC drilled six dry holes, inspiring doubt and hand-wringing at SoCal headquarters in San Francisco, before the Saudi Arabia venture produced its first big oil strike. On March 3, 1938, the well known as Dammam Number 7 delivered oil in commercial quantities; that is, there was enough oil to recoup the cost of developing the field and turn a profit. Corporate morale soared as it became apparent that CASOC had tapped into an oil reservoir of global importance. CASOC formally notified the king that Dammam was a viable commercial field and paid the £50,000 advance.

Dammam Number 7 would produce more than 32 million barrels of oil before it was taken out of service in 1982. Even today, visitors to the oil company headquarters in Dhahran have their photographs taken in front of this landmark, which still stands as part of an Aramco museum.

"The discovery of oil in commercial quantities in Dammam No. 7 was a turning point," according to the oil company's official history. "Until then the Saudi Arabian venture had been a risky and costly proposition. Now, as a commercially sound operation, it needed large transfusions of

Max Steineke, left, chief geologist of the oil exploration team sent to Saudi Arabia by Standard Oil Company of California, with Arab guides and four Arabian oryx they killed in the desert west of Ain Talha, 1936. The Arab in white, center, is Khamis ibn Rimthan, the Americans' favorite guide.
PHOTOGRAPHER UNKNOWN. COURTESY ARAMCO SERVICES CO.

money to expand some facilities and to build others. . . . CASOC now had the go-ahead for more housing, for enlargement of the pier at al-Khobar [a nearby town on the Gulf], for pipelines and storage tanks, for a stabilizer plant to remove poisonous hydrogen sulfide gas from the oil before shipment, for a small refinery, and for a marine terminal for tankers."[21] The boom was on in earnest—or would have been but for the outbreak of World War II. By the time King Abdul Aziz turned the ceremonial first valve to load the first tanker of oil for export it was May 1, 1939. Four months later, Germany invaded Poland.

The war marked a period of retrenchment rather than expansion for the oil company. The maritime supply lines upon which the Americans depended for food and equipment were disrupted. Steel for pipes, industrial equipment, vehicles, and spare parts were hard to get. With German troops in Egypt, Saudi Arabia's security was shaky, and the Americans' concern grew when an Italian warplane aiming at British installations on Bahrain mistakenly dropped ordnance on Dhahran. Damage was minor, but the reality of the war unsettled the community. The American workforce dropped from more than three hundred to a caretaker contingent known in company history as "The Hundred Men." All the women left except two nurses.

Having watched most of their colleagues sail away, the remaining Americans had little to do but work and drink, according to Aramco's chronicler of this period, Phil McConnell. In those early days, the oil company had the king's permission to import alcohol for its non-Muslim workers, so "the bar at the club became the setting for many awesome drinking contests."[22]

Paradoxically, this hiatus in the expansion of the oil operation coincided with a the first expressions of interest in Saudi Arabia in Washington, which before the war had been content to leave political management of the Arabian peninsula to the British. For the United States, access to Arab oil was not the strategic imperative it is now.

CASOC had installed its first resident representative in Jeddah, the diplomatic capital, in 1933; there was no official American government presence for nine years after that. When the king and his advisers wanted to talk to the United States, they did so through the oil company. The United States formally recognized the government of King Abdul Aziz and the two countries had nominal diplomatic relations, but until the war the U.S. government was officially represented in Saudi Arabia by a diplomat who resided in Cairo and rarely visited the Kingdom. The first resident American diplomat was James S. Moose Jr., whose title was chargé d'affaires. At the height of the war, he opened the first American legation in Jeddah, the base for all foreign diplomats in Saudi Arabia. They were permitted to visit Riyadh only by royal invitation.

The royal treasury was virtually empty in the middle of the war because few pilgrims came to Saudi Arabia and oil exports, which had barely started when the war broke out, were cut off. Starvation was reported in the hinterlands; CASOC lent the king money and ran convoys of relief trucks to remote parts of the country. The oil company also asked Washington to provide direct economic assistance to Saudi Arabia, which at first the administration of President Franklin D. Roosevelt declined to do. To the distress of the oil interests, Britain provided more than $40 million, raising the possibility that the king's favor—and the oil concession—would be shifted to the British.[23]

By 1943, however, Washington's attitude was changing. Saudi Arabia had taken on new importance as a transit point between theaters of war, and Washington was beginning to appreciate its potential as a source of oil. In February 1943, President Roosevelt declared Saudi Arabia strategically important to the United States and thus eligible for direct "Lend-Lease" economic assistance, even though Saudi Arabia was a noncombatant. This action opened the door to a whole new set of official arrangements between the United States and Saudi Arabia, including the first military contacts. The status of the Jeddah legation was upgraded and Moose was promoted to "minister resident." No longer would the United States government deal with the House of Saud from Cairo.

To the rest of the world, Saudi Arabia was still largely unknown and the Middle East a sideshow in the great war against the Axis powers, but Americans were soon to see how the country's profile had been elevated in official Washington. On February 14, 1945, Abdul Aziz met President Roosevelt aboard the USS *Quincy* in Egypt's Great Bitter Lake. Photographs of that encounter—the king in his robes, laughing as he talked, and Roosevelt, listening intently, only two months from death, his famous cloak over his shoulders—were published around the world.

The arrangements for that meeting were as complicated as the two cultures were different. The king wanted to bring his own sheep, for example, because he believed that good Muslims eat only freshly killed meat. When the USS *Murphy* arrived at Jeddah to ferry the royal party to Egypt, the king appeared with forty-eight traveling companions, although the Americans had said they could accommodate no more than ten. The Arabs insisted on sleeping in tents pitched on deck rather than in cabins. Yet the two leaders appreciated each other and developed a

mutual respect in their conversations, a rapport that papered over ir-
reconcilable views about Palestine. The king, a large man who used a
cane because he had difficulty walking, was grateful for a spontaneous
gift from the president: the spare wheelchair that traveled with him.

The impresario of that meeting was Colonel William A. Eddy, who
had succeeded Moose as resident U.S. minister in the summer of 1944.
Eddy was born in Lebanon in 1896, a son and grandson of Presbyterian
missionaries. He grew up speaking Arabic, and was the interpreter at the
meeting between Roosevelt and Abdul Aziz. In the photographs, he is
the tall man in U.S. Marine Corps uniform, his face turned away from
the camera.

Eddy, a decorated combat veteran of World War I, held a doctorate
from Princeton. In the 1920s, he lived in Egypt, where he taught at
the American University in Cairo. He is said to have introduced basketball to Egypt. He rejoined the Marines during World War II and
was posted to Cairo as naval attaché. According to an Aramco biographical sketch, he later "became one of General William J. 'Wild Bill'
Donovan's most energetic and gifted OSS intelligence agents.'"[24] Most
of what we know about the meeting of Roosevelt and Abdul Aziz is
drawn from Eddy's account *F.D.R. Meets Ibn Saud,* a monograph published in 1954.

In his opening paragraph, Eddy describes the king as "one of the great
men of the twentieth century. He won his kingdom and united his people by his personal leadership. He possessed those epic qualities of the
leader which Samuel recognized in Saul; he excelled in the common
tasks which all must perform. He was taller, his shoulders were broader,
he was a better hunter, a braver warrior, more skillful in wielding a knife
whether in personal combat or in skinning a sheep; he excelled in following the tracks of camels and finding his way in the desert."

Eddy's account of the voyage from Jeddah harbor to Great Bitter
Lake aboard the *Murphy* is quite droll: "A good time was had by all except me," he wrote, because it was his responsibility to sort out the culture clashes. Not only did the king insist on bringing his sheep but he
demanded that the American sailors join him in eating them, in accordance with the laws of Arab hospitality. He was deterred only when informed that the crew was prohibited by Navy regulations from eating

anything except the military rations provided for them: Surely he did not wish to see these fine young men sent to the brig!

The king inspected with interest the ship's armaments and navigational devices. His sons and others in his party had more frivolous interests: They were fascinated by a movie shown in the crew quarters that featured Lucille Ball "loose in a college men's dormitory late at night, barely surviving escapades in which her dress is ripped off."

In his talks with Roosevelt, Eddy wrote, the king did not even hint at any desire for financial assistance. "He traveled to the meeting seeking friends and not funds," and that is what he got, despite the arguments about Palestine and Jewish immigration. The king's view was that if the suffering of the Jews had been caused by the Germans, Germans should pay the price for it; let the Jews build their homeland on the best lands in Germany, not on the territory of Arabs who had nothing to do with what happened to them. The most he could get from Roosevelt was a promise that the president would "do nothing to assist the Jews against the Arabs and would make no move hostile to the Arab people."[25] The king, taking this as a commitment from the United States and not just from Roosevelt personally, was furious to discover three years later that Harry Truman did not consider himself bound by it.

✦

Bill Eddy and the few other Americans posted to Jeddah in that period faced a wholly different set of hardships from those in the oil camp on the other side of the country. Jeddah was a settled community, but it was hot, dirty, and smelly, and communications were primitive.

"It didn't have a single paved street, but it did have a black-top road to Mecca," recalled Parker "Pete" Hart, an American foreign service officer who arrived in Jeddah during the war and later became ambassador. "Camels wandered right through the town. There were no public utilities of any kind—no electric lights, running water or sewage system." The American legation got electricity from a generator operated by CASOC, whose office was nearby.[26]

CASOC, renamed Aramco in 1944, maintained a full-time staff in Jeddah because that was its point of contact with the Saudi Arabian government. Administrative and disciplinary matters that did not rise to cabinet-level attention could be handled in Dhahran through Abdullah bin Jiluwi, but discussions of money and policy were conducted through the office in Jeddah, where the ministries of Finance and Foreign Affairs operated.

The first CASOC resident representative, Bill Lenahan, set up shop in 1933 in a rambling seaside villa known as Bayt Baghdadi (Baghdad House), which had belonged to Philby. According to company archives, "He didn't like it, even though it had an electric generator and a number of marble-floored, domed bathrooms. Lenahan scouted around and found a building in the handsome Jiddah style under construction for a local merchant, whom he talked into making some modifications." That became Bayt Amrikani, or America House, "the first building in Jiddah with flush toilets."[27]

When Harry Mayhorn arrived to work at the American diplomatic mission during the war, he found "a walled city of about 30,000 population. . . . There were about 35 Europeans in Jiddah, made up of the diplomatic corps and employees of the few banks and other business firms. Except for our sleeping quarters and the American Legation, air conditioning was almost nonexistent. Aramco and the American legation had flush toilets, but some other foreign establishments used sand boxes that had to be emptied each day. Drinking water was hauled in small donkey carts to each residence from a sea-water distillation plant."[28]

"At all times," Wallace Stegner wrote, "the city clamored and howled and brayed and snarled with a bedlam of animal noises, with once in a while a midnight shot as some irritated Englishman potted a prowling pariah dog."[29] And this was by far the most developed and sophisticated community in Saudi Arabia.

J. Rives Childs, who arrived in Jeddah in 1946 as the first U.S. ambassador, recorded his dismay: "The evening of my arrival I stood on the balcony of the embassy fronting the Red Sea and recalled with a sinking heart that I had agreed to remain two years in this inferno." As for amusement, "the sole distractions were weekly movies organized for the foreign community on the terrace of the embassy, swimming in the shark-infested waters of the Red Sea with a temperature comparable to that of a tepid soup, and trolling in the embassy motor launch for fish."

When he offered to bring in an airplane for spraying "to rid the city of the intolerable swarms of mosquitoes and flies drawn by the filth," his Saudi hosts delayed a decision while seeking the approval of religious authorities, who feared spraying would interfere with "the inscrutable ways of Allah as manifested through the lowly fly."[30]

⟿

Discomfort and boredom were not the only problems confronting American diplomats in Jeddah. Their duties included reporting to Washington about important political and economic developments in the Kingdom, and looking after the welfare of American citizens who lived in Saudi Arabia; but the most interesting economic developments, and the majority of American residents, were nearly eight hundred miles away, at the opposite end of an undeveloped country that had no highways, airline, or cross-country telephone lines. Unless they wanted to emulate Karl Twitchell and travel overland for several days, camping out as they went, the Americans in Jeddah had no way of keeping posted on developments over in Dhahran. Traveling there meant flying first to Cairo, then to Baghdad, then to Basra in southern Iraq, and finally to Bahrain; from there, Dhahran was reachable by boat.

The obvious solution to this was to open a consulate, which is a U.S. diplomatic mission enjoying full diplomatic status and protection in a community overseas where there is no embassy. Britain refused to allow the United States to open a consulate in Bahrain, from which Dhahran was within easy reach, so James Moose formally asked the king's permission to put one on the Saudi Arabian side of the water, in Dhahran itself.

"The royal reaction was sharply and surprisingly negative," Parker Hart recalled. "To the king and his advisors, it was a matter of setting a precedent, of opening a Pandora's box, and of jeopardizing Saudi security. To Moose's practiced eye, it was obvious that neither the king nor his principal counselors had any notion of what a modern consul's duties were." The king feared he was being asked for Ottoman-style "capitulations" that would compromise Saudi sovereignty. He relented only after the Roosevelt administration importuned Prince Faisal, the foreign minister and one of the king's favorite sons, about this request during a visit

Dhahran in 1937, the year before the first big oil strike.

ARAMCO PHOTO FROM THE WILLIAM E. MULLIGAN COLLECTION, COURTESY GEORGETOWN UNIVERSITY LIBRARY.

to Washington in 1943. The Americans prevailed by arguing that because no other country was interested in establishing a diplomatic mission in eastern Saudi Arabia, a U.S. consulate would not set a precedent.[31]

The U.S. flag went up over the new Dhahran consulate on September 1, 1944, in temporary quarters lent by Aramco. The address was 1635 Gazelle Circle, a street known as "Easter Egg Row" because each house had been painted a different pastel color in a test of the paint's durability.[32] The first resident American diplomat was Parker "Pete" Hart, a classic State Department patrician who had degrees from Dartmouth and Harvard. Stopping first in Jeddah to fill in for an ailing colleague, Hart then made the tedious roundabout journey through Cairo, Baghdad, and Bahrain to reach Dhahran. In Cairo he was delayed by a lung ailment that required a stay in a U.S. Army field hospital, but this turned out to be a happy accident because he met another patient, Jane Smiley, who five years later would become his wife.

The consulate staff consisted of himself and one deputy, Clarence McIntosh. "Coming from Jeddah, we were in heaven. There was air conditioning," Hart recalled.[33] Two months later, he sent a status report to his boss, Secretary of State Edward R. Stettinius. "Arab circles in al-Hasa have so far extended to the consulate every courtesy and mark of respect," Hart wrote. "Apparently upon direct orders from the King, but largely as a result of natural friendliness and good spade work by Aramco, local authorities have shown a degree of amiability and will-ingness to cooperate which would be hard to equal anywhere. . . . Full marks must be given to Aramco for a remarkable achievement in the development of a pro-American bias." He said the local people regarded oil company personnel as friends, and he found "no antagonism based on religious and political differences."[34]

Hart was consul in Dhahran until 1946, returned there as consul general after the mission's status was upgraded in 1949, stayed three years on that tour, and later became ambassador in the early 1960s. His wife, Jane, whom he met in that Cairo hospital, accompanied him to Dhahran when he was assigned as consul general, and their first child was born in the Aramco hospital.

Every morning, Hart worked at his Arabic lessons. His instructor was a bright young man sent to him by Aramco named Sulaiman Olayan. Hart paid him three riyals an hour. Years later, when Olayan was one of the most successful businessmen in Saudi Arabia, Hart was with him at a social event and mentioned to another guest that he had studied with Olayan for three riyals an hour. "You could have had me for two," Olayan interjected.[35]

The end of the war and the opening of the consulate began a new pe-riod of rapidly expanding relations between the United States and Saudi Arabia. Washington now saw Saudi Arabia in strategic terms. State Department officers and other U.S. officials broke out of the Jeddah diplomatic ghetto and ventured into new areas. Aramco emerged from its wartime mothballs into a new phase of rapid expansion and construction. American corporations, among them Bechtel Corporation, a giant San Francisco–based construction and engineering firm, scooped up con-tracts for projects that brought a surge of foreign workers, Americans and otherwise. Jane Smiley and other American women began to penetrate the closed world of Saudi Arabian women. And a direct military relationship developed when the king acceded to an American request for permission to construct an airfield in Dhahran.

The idea behind the airfield was to give American military planes access to the Asian theater during the war against the Axis powers. The war ended before the base could be completed, but work proceeded anyway because of the obvious need for an airfield that would serve the rapidly growing foreign community and the needs of commerce in eastern Saudi Arabia. As the Cold War developed, the field became an important strategic outpost for the U.S. Air Force.

In a letter to acting foreign minister Yusuf Yassin, Bill Eddy detailed American commitments and understandings under the airfield agreement.

The base would include housing for up to five hundred members of the U.S. armed forces, and provisions for expansion to 2,000. "These Army [air corps] personnel, representatives and employees of the United States government, will not be subject to the jurisdiction of the civil or criminal courts of Saudi Arabia for unlawful acts committed within the boundaries of the airbase," Eddy's memo said. Such clauses are standard for U.S. "status of forces" agreements around the world, but this was a breakthrough in Saudi Arabia. It was the first time the king had agreed to allow the entry of foreign personnel who would be outside the legal jurisdiction of his government.

There was another innovation as well. "It being mutually agreed that mechanics, artisans, and labor are not available in sufficient quantities among Saudi Arabia subjects to prosecute the construction of the airbase within the time allotted," Eddy's memo said, the Saudi Arabian government will allow the United States government to import into Saudi Arabia, during the construction period, "approximately 500 Americans, 1,500 Italians, 500 Iraqis and Iranians, 1,000 from Aden protectorate [in Yemen], and 25 Egyptians of European descent for the construction work on the airbase." This, too, represented a relaxation of Saudi control.[36]

Aramco archives include a detailed agreement for the oil company to provide fuel, vehicles, and laundry service to the military, complete with rates: Bathrobes, 8 cents; aprons, 4 cents; dish towels, 2 cents; pillow cases, 3 cents. There is a similar list for medical services at the company's hospital: Amputation of limbs, $16.50 for the doctor, another

$16.50 for the hospital, total $33; anaesthetic, including tooth extractions, $11.50; appendectomy, $76.35.[37]

~~

Up to this point, all the American money invested in Saudi Arabia was private capital. Now, with a consulate and an air base under construction, Congress was putting taxpayers' funds into this new relationship. Could the first congressional inspection tour be far behind?

Right after the war, a delegation from the House Foreign Affairs Committee, led by Representative Karl Mundt, traveled to the Kingdom and met Abdul Aziz. Among the travelers was a woman, Representative Frances Bolton of Ohio, whose account provides one of the earliest reports of a meeting between the king and a foreign woman and one of the first accounts we have of activity in the female quarters of the palace, known as the *hareem* (harem).

The king told the Americans that he wanted Bolton to be included in their audience with him. The morning after the group's arrival in Jeddah, they all flew to Riyadh in a twin-engine Douglas DC-3 passenger plane, which President Roosevelt had presented to Abdul Aziz as a gift at their meeting in Egypt.

"It was very picturesque," Bolton reported. "The King had a cordon of soldiers, who were wearing green veils on their heads and scarves. Going up some very steep stairs, they were just like characters out of a book—with their scimitars and white things which waved around them." During the conversation, "The King held Mr. Mundt's hand all the time, which embarrassed him quite a bit." (It is customary for Arab men to hold the hands of other men with whom they are on good terms.)

The first session with the king "was occupied almost entirely by an argument between Mr. Mundt and the King relative to Arab hospitality," Bolton reported. "The custom is that anyone who goes to see the King goes for a 3-day period. We did not have 3 days; the arrangement had been made for us to stay for lunch and go back, so of course nobody had a toothbrush or razor. The argument was that we had to spend the night. Well, Mr. Mundt lost the argument. We were told that the king never lunched, he only dined. The result was that we spent the night."

The Americans were taken to a guest palace to while away the afternoon in rooms cooled by electric fans. Servants appeared constantly bearing tea and coffee. Mundt ate a slice of watermelon, which made him sick.

They were invited to swim in a pool at the nearby villa of Crown Prince Saud. The water, Bolton noted, "was brought up from wells run by little donkeys. The wells all squeak." (Tom Barger had noted this same sound on his first visit to Riyadh seven years earlier. The donkeys pulled water up from wells in goatskin bags tied to ropes that traveled over pulleys. "All night long the pulleys of the wells creak. It sounds like distant factory whistles," as he described it to Kathleen.)[38]

When the heat of the afternoon had passed, the members of Congress were taken back to rejoin Abdul Aziz. When the conversation turned serious, the king asked Bolton "if I would be good enough to go and call upon the queen." Her account of what followed is worth quoting at length because she saw things that no other American had seen.

I accompanied this delightful little man, who spoke French. I went back into the corridor, through doorways, up and down stairs, until finally I got to the harem. There was a lot of gold brocade, blue brocade with gold leaves in it, and along the walls were these pads, about 3 feet high, that could be taken down. They are Bedouins, you see, and everything is movable. These pads could be taken down quickly and moved on. There were these awful Grand Rapids chairs, all beautifully done in gold brocade, but uncomfortable. Then there were sofas and a lot of clocks. The king likes clocks; he has a special engineer for making clocks all the time. . . .

Finally in came four women trailing yards of black muslin and holding their shawls over their faces because, of course, there was a man. They could only speak Arabic, so for a while he translated the formalities. Then finally came a fifth woman, who turned out to be a very charming medical officer. She had been trained outside Arabia and also speaks French, so the minute she came in the man left and all the veils went. We took down our hair and we talked. It was most interesting.

Alas, Bolton neglected to record what they talked about that was so interesting, but she observed that "these women are out of another world. They are not in our lives at all."

When she rejoined her colleagues, she learned that they had been invited to dine with the king and his sons on the roof of the palace, but she was expected to dine with the women. Moose advised her that it would be rude to object to this segregation, so she complied and rejoined the royal females.

We sat at a Grand Rapids mahogany table with rather heavy Chippendale chairs all around. There were a great many children and a great many servants, they were continually in and out. It was the most confused meal I have ever had. On the table was just one great bowl of rice. . . . The whole sheep gets on top of this bowl of rice, which is very beautifully done in little lines of saffron and little hard boiled eggs put into the rice. The entire table was covered with food in little dishes. I could not quite make out whether they ate with forks except with guests, or just what. They were a little awkward with their forks. . . . It was quite a treat and exciting for the children to be anywhere around me. Various sons of the king came wandering down from upstairs to see this woman. It was an interesting experience for me because these women do not do anything; they are harem women.

At the women's request, she donned one of their dresses and went upstairs to show herself to the king and the princes. Her account unfortunately does not record their reaction, or that of her fellow travelers.[39]

∽

For Saudi Arabian women, such encounters were voyages of exploration into a world of which they had no knowledge—the world of American women who dress as they please, travel without their husbands, have responsibilities outside the home, leave their faces uncovered in the presence of men, know how to read, and visit foreign countries. When Saudi women first began to visit American homes, they would search uninvited through drawers and closets, not out of rudeness but out of simple curiosity. The Americans had gadgets and garments that were outside their experience.

Pete Hart's wife, Jane, said that when she persuaded Saudi women to visit her, she would leave fashion magazines such as *Vogue* out on the table where her guests could peruse them. "By the time I left they were all unbelievably chic under those robes, way past me, you know? These lovely jewels and everything," she recalled. She said the Arab women "want to be up to date, and they're smart. They know they were living the way they were because they had no alternative."[40]

The Harts were newly married when Pete returned to Dhahran in 1949 to take up the post of consul general. (The diplomatic status of the U.S. mission had been upgraded from consulate to consulate general, as had the title of its chief officer.) Shortly after they arrived, Abdullah bin Jiluwi invited them to visit him at his compound in the Hofuf oasis, about seventy-five miles southwest of Dhahran. Jane Hart said she could not tell whether the emir looked directly at her because he was cross-eyed, but he did not speak to her directly. He spoke to her in the third person, through her husband: "I hope you wife enjoys our country."

At dinner time she was made an "honorary man" and allowed to sit with the men, but only briefly. After ten minutes, she was dispatched to the *hareem.*

"So I got up and left," she recalled.

And my first trip to the *hareem* in Hofuf was largely about the brassière. They had heard of it, but they had never seen one, and ultimately I had to show them one. All the older ladies had bosoms coming down to here, because they had done so much work bending over this way, you know, their breasts had gone way down to their waists. And it's uncomfortable, that's why they weren't doing anything physical. The reason people have brassières is to so they can be active, you know? Well, anyway, they were intrigued by this and you can be sure they found ways to get their husbands to buy brassières after I was there. They had no money, they had no access, they had been totally tucked away, but they were wanting to learn.[41]

This was cultural interaction between Americans and Arabs that Charles Crane had never envisioned.

CHAPTER 2

Into the Wilderness

PAUL ARNOT AND ELIZABETH ZERBE came from similar all-American backgrounds. Both were born in small mid-country towns, he in Missouri, she in Colorado. Both moved to California with migrating parents and attended college at the University of California at Berkeley. She was five years younger than he, so they did not meet as students; they met some years later in Dhahran, where both arrived as Aramco employees, by very different routes.

Graduating with a degree in mine engineering in 1932, Paul Arnot was hired by Standard Oil Company of California. He spent some time in the California oil fields and was moving up through the company's management training program when Dammam Number 7 struck oil in far-off Saudi Arabia. SoCal transferred him to CASOC and sent him to Dhahran in 1938. He was one of the "Hundred Men" who kept the enterprise alive through World War II.

Elizabeth Zerbe earned a master's degree in nursing education; in 1944, she was working as a surgical nursing supervisor at the University of California School of Nursing when an oil company recruiter came looking for nurses willing to go to Saudi Arabia. She was ready for an overseas adventure—any adventure. Earlier she had accepted an offer to establish a nursing school in Greece after it was liberated from the Nazis, but she was forced to forgo the opportunity because the short-staffed nursing school in California would not release her from her contract. Now that wartime personnel restrictions had eased, off she went.

As the war neared its conclusion and Aramco resumed hiring in anticipation of postwar growth, Elizabeth Zerbe was one of the first women to arrive in Dhahran. There were very few American women in Dhahran during the last months of the war, and most of those who were there were the nonworking wives of Aramco men. As an unattached female, Elizabeth Zerbe had scores of bachelors to choose from. Paul Arnot was the one.

Elizabeth Zerbe and Paul Arnot were married on February 1, 1945, in the Dutch Reformed Mission in Bahrain. Not having planned to get married so soon and so far from home, she had no wedding finery. She wore her best dress, which was black. A local metalsmith forged their rings out of a British gold sovereign.

The Arnots' time as a two-job Aramco couple did not last long. Aramco management quickly forced Elizabeth to resign because female workers who got married were regarded as "unreliable"—that is, they might become pregnant. Since Paul by that time had made a long-term commitment to Aramco, the couple could not just pack up and go home; Elizabeth accepted her new status as a nonworking company wife and they stayed on, for twenty-four years. Their daughter, Mehala Anne, was born in Dhahran in December 1946, and six weeks later the Arnot family moved to a new Aramco settlement at Abqaiq, about forty miles southwest of Dhahran.[1]

"There was at this time no road across the sands to Abqaiq," Aramco's company history notes. "One proceeded there across the desert by driving from target to target placed on the highest dunes."[2] The Arabs there "were absolutely astounded" by their arrival, Elizabeth Arnot recalled. "Many of the Arabs had never seen a white woman, much less one with her face completely uncovered, and I had Anne in a wooden Dutch Cleanser box" (the box was an improvisation she used to tote the baby around).[3]

Abqaiq was the boondocks the way Dhahran itself had been a decade earlier. Their house was still under construction as the Arnots moved in.

Once a week, Paul Arnot drove back across the dunes to Dhahran for groceries and water. Electricity service from portable generators was spasmodic. When Elizabeth hung diapers to dry on the clothesline, goats nibbled at them. When she wheeled Anne around in her stroller on the one short patch of sidewalk, local Arabs would gather just to watch this remarkable spectacle.

The Arnots were sent to Abqaiq because Aramco had dug new wells there and needed American workers to operate them and the related storage and gas-separation facilities, and also to supervise Arab workers. The oil company's rapid expansion outward from its base in Dhahran meant running roads and pipelines and establishing facilities along the Gulf coast as well as inland. The first refinery went into operation as Ras Tanura, north of Dhahran, two weeks after Japan's surrender ended the war. The company built a new shipping terminal and a submarine pipeline to Bahrain. By December 1945, construction companies under contract to Aramco had six hundred Americans working in Ras Tanura alone, in addition to Aramco's own personnel. In the growth spurt that followed the war, Aramco was transformed from a lone oil-drilling out-post into an industrial octopus that spread across eastern Saudi Arabia, drawing more and more Arabs into its employment and its sphere of economic influence. At the company's first formal school for Arab boys and young men, enrollment tripled between 1944 and 1947.

Suddenly it seemed as if Aramco geologists were finding oil wherever they looked. The Abqaiq field, discovered in 1944, was followed by dis-coveries at Qatif, Ain Dar, and Fadhili. Safaniya, the first giant offshore reservoir, was found in 1951. Even before the world's largest onshore field at Ghawar was confirmed in the early 1950s, its was obvious that oil production would be a permanent operation in Saudi Arabia and that Aramco would be around indefinitely.

As production rose from wartime trickle to postwar flood, the prob-lem facing the oil companies was not finding oil but transporting it to consumers. It was expensive and time-consuming to send crude oil by tanker all the way around the Arabian peninsula and through the Suez Canal to refineries in Europe. The canal toll for one tanker was almost $40,000.[4] In July 1945, Aramco's parent companies agreed on a solution: a giant pipeline from Dhahran to the Mediterranean Sea. To develop it they created a subsidiary corporation, the Trans-Arabian Pipeline Company, or Tapline.

Building the pipeline was a mammoth undertaking. At the time it was the world's largest privately financed construction project, but money was not the only issue. The Middle East's turbulent politics and the creation of Israel required payoffs to the government of Syria for transit rights and a change in the destination port on the Mediterranean. Instead of Haifa, which by the time construction started was destined to be part of independent Israel, the pipeline went to Sidon, in Lebanon, 1,040 miles from Dhahran.

"Most of the line crossed desert lands where there were no roads, no water, and no permanent habitations," Aramco's company history recounts. "The terrain included rolling sand dunes, gravel plains, rocky lava belts, and the rugged mountains of Lebanon. . . . More than 350,000 tons of pipe, equipment and materials had to be shipped halfway around the world, then trucked long distances overland. At the peak of construction more than sixteen thousand men were employed and over three thousand pieces of automotive and construction equipment were in operation."[5] Building the line required "the movement of greater tonnages and more men for longer distances than had ever been undertaken in peacetime."[6]

In the first years after World War II, few if any companies outside the United States were capable of pulling off such a feat of engineering, logistics, and politics. One that could do it was the Bechtel Corporation, which had built Boulder Dam and the San Francisco–Oakland Bay Bridge. To build Tapline, Bechtel transported Americans and American technology into remote corners of Saudi Arabia not yet touched by Aramco; in the process, it created a lucrative and seemingly permanent market for itself in Saudi Arabia.

Bechtel, a well-established construction and engineering company, had enjoyed a long relationship with Standard Oil of California. As a family-owned concern with no public stockholders to worry about, it was in a position to take risks in pursuit of new opportunities. The head of the company, Steve Bechtel, met Prince Faisal, the foreign minister and future king, when the prince visited San Francisco in 1943, hit it off

Bedouin camel caravan crossing "sand bridge" over the Trans-Arabian Pipeline in the early 1950s. Built by American construction firms, Tapline, as the pipeline was called, carried oil from the Saudi Arabian fields to a port on the Mediterranean in Lebanon.

PHOTOGRAPHER UNKNOWN. COURTESY ARAMCO SERVICES CO.

with him, and sensed an opportunity in a vast and undeveloped country. When SoCal asked for help in a crash program to construct the new facilities it would need in the postwar buildup, Bechtel was ready.

Its first project was Aramco's refinery at Ras Tanura. "That too was the beginning of something new," Wallace Stegner wrote. "Up to now, Aramco had done its own construction work. From here on, and increasingly, it would contract out its heavy construction, generally to Bechtel; and from here on the Saudi Arab government, wanting some industrial job done, would have another string to its bow."[7]

Indeed, the Ras Tanura refinery and the Trans-Arabian Pipeline contract turned on a gusher of projects for Bechtel that is still flowing. King Abdul Aziz, who had heard a favorable report about Steve Bechtel from Faisal, invited him to Riyadh. The two "got along so splendidly," Laton

McCartney wrote in his history of the company, "that by the end of the audience, the king, helped along by an offer of a $10 million loan Bechtel had promised to secure through the U.S. Export-Import Bank, had commissioned [the company] to build not only the railroad [from Dammam, the grungy Arab town adjacent to Dhahran, to Riyadh] but a port facility at Dammam, a modern pier at Jeddah and the electrification of the entire city of Riyadh as well."[8]

During the next half-century, Bechtel would undertake one giant project after another in Saudi Arabia. The company has built airports, hospitals, power plants, highways, office buildings, water desalination plants, petrochemical factories, and the entire "industrial city" of Jubail, on the Persian Gulf coast north of Dhahran. "Over the course of these activities," the company said about itself, "thousands of Saudis have received training from Bechtel, both in the Kingdom and in the United States, in a broad range of disciplines and skills, including: engineering, architecture, construction management, business management, accounting, human resources development, marketing, public relations and many other subjects. Saudis trained by Bechtel now occupy responsible managerial positions in scores of businesses and organizations throughout the Kingdom and abroad."[9] Not surprisingly, Bechtel has been a strong corporate advocate of Saudi Arabian interests in the United States over these decades; it has also made its personnel and facilities available to the U.S. and Saudi government for operations that it did not wish to reveal to the public, including intelligence gathering on behalf of the CIA, as McCartney's book recounts in detail.

Michael Cheney, who worked on Tapline as it was being built across the wilderness, was stationed in a construction base camp at Ras al Mishab, 180 miles from Dhahran over terrain "that grew flatter, hotter and more barren as we went along." The camp "consisted entirely of a rectangle of sand enclosed by a wire fence, holding a huddle of tin-roofed workshops and warehouses and four long rows of barracks. They held forty-eight men apiece, in twenty-four rooms each roughly the size of a tandem outhouse. The buildings were split in the middle by showers and toilets that worked in good weather, as well as an air conditioning unit whose noise carried to both ends of the building but whose cooler air never got past the first two rooms on each side. Mine was an end room, a tin oven in which I found a roommate about medium-well done."[10] The route of the pipeline, he wrote, ran "through the heart of the Bedu belt, a treeless, waterless waste with a climate like a blast furnace and a shifting population that traditionally took a jaundiced view of all outsiders. Long stretches of the route had never been seen by a foreigner."[11]

All food and supplies, of course, had to be trucked in from the Persian Gulf coast, which was farther away with each mile of pipe laid westward toward Jordan. Hauling the 90-foot lengths of 30-inch- and 31-inch-diameter pipe required 150 specially outfitted trucks. Although the permanent Aramco community in Dhahran had by then inspired local entrepreneurs to open shops and laundries in nearby towns, that did not happen along the Tapline route because there were no nearby towns.

When the construction crews departed upon completion of the pipeline, they left behind only small communities of maintenance workers at its four pumping stations; a gravel road connected the communities to each other and to the pipeline's entry in Dhahran and its terminus in faraway Lebanon. (Peter Speers, an Aramco Arabist who was assigned to one of these pumping stations for three months as a sort of diplomat, responsible for smoothing over any unpleasantness that might be caused by "rough construction workers," said he was glad to get back to the "big city," Dhahran, when his tour ended.)[12] Small and isolated as the pumping station settlements were, they nonetheless transformed the lives of the region's nomads. As an Aramco history recounted, "The road, the pump stations and the availability of water and medical care provided the stimulus for the development and growth of the northern area of Saudi Arabia."[13] Because of their water wells, which provided water to all who sought it, these little pumping-station villages had a permanent impact on the bedouin. No longer was it necessary for the tribes and their herds to fight each other for water at the scattered oases, or to migrate all the way north to the Euphrates River in Iraq in dry season. Some of them settled permanently around the pumping stations; soon, they began acquiring motor vehicles, which they could drive on the road paralleling the pipeline. The transformation of bedouin life, which had begun with the first oil drilling, was accelerated by the Trans-Arabian Pipeline.

Tapline was completed in September 1950, just when Aramco was finding vast new fields of oil. It added 320,000 barrels to the company's daily export capacity; the government's revenue also increased because it charged the Tapline partners a fee for every barrel sent through the pipeline. Total crude oil production, which was 58,000 barrels a day at the end of the war, surged to 761,000 by 1951 and surpassed 1 million barrels a day by 1958.[14] The company's Saudi Arab work force grew to more than 14,000.

Indeed, by the early 1950s, Aramco had become such a powerful influence on the development and economy of Saudi Arabia, and so critical to world energy supplies, that it became a policy issue for the State Department.

"The influence of Aramco on the Saudi Arabia economy and on our political relations with that country is so great that Aramco's policies and actions must be carefully watched and, if need be, guided," the State Department said in a classified memorandum to overseas posts in February 1951. "It can do a great deal to preserve American prestige and interests in the area and to combat communism. For example, Saudi Arabia's labor policy toward its 14,500 Arab workers is not only of nation-wide importance in Saudi Arabia, but is a critical factor in the development of western orientation and democratic processes. The department should, therefore, encourage Aramco to pursue progressive and enlightened policies in connection with wages, housing for Arab employees, training and education, and to shift responsibilities to Saudi Arabians as fully and rapidly as possible."[15]

The idea that Aramco could be "guided" by the State Department, which had sent only a handful of diplomats to Saudi Arabia, would have seemed absurd to anyone familiar with the inner workings of the company. Hermann F. Eilts, who was economic officer at the embassy in the late 1940s and later ambassador, recalled that Aramco's specialists in Arab affairs, with their greater experience and resources, paid little heed to the diplomats.[16] Raymond A. Hare, who arrived in Jeddah as U.S. ambassador in 1950 expecting to find that oil issues took up much of his time, quickly discovered instead that Aramco lived in its own universe and he had little involvement with it. "They became sort of an autonomous entity and did their own negotiating with the Saudis, which in many ways

Burgis Burkha, a member of an Aramco drilling crew, is splattered with mud after the sinking of a "structure drill," or geological exploratory drill, in the trackless desert known as the Empty Quarter, early 1950s.

PHOTO BY T. F. WALTERS, COURTESY ARAMCO SERVICES CO.

was good," he said. "There were many things that they were able to do, a lot of good things such as helping the Saudis with sanitation problems and things like that which would have been awkward for the American government to do."[17] Conversely, Aramco was happy to let the embassy deal with the Saudis' anger over U.S. recognition of Israel.

Aramco was an entrenched economic juggernaut, but more than that. Aramco had assumed an amazing number of governmental functions and social welfare responsibilities that the government of Saudi Arabia was not capable of performing on its own. Some of these functions, such as training workers and building roads between the oil installations, were directly or indirectly related to the production and shipment of oil. Others had nothing to do with oil. They were done because Aramco thought they would be useful or valuable to a ruler to whom the company wished to be indispensable, or because the company believed that knowledge was power, or both.

As Wallace Stegner put it, "In Saudi Arabia, the conditions of remoteness and the exclusive concession left everything to be done by the company, and if that gave them the advantage of greater control, it also left them with the responsibility for greater foresight."[18]

Aramco's official histories and internal memoranda are replete with accounts of the company's prodigious construction work and public service programs, including not only oil-related facilities but hospitals and clinics, schools, roads, water wells, and radio transmitters. All these were projects that the Saudi Arab public could see and benefit from. Less visible were Aramco's political and public relations and intelligence-gathering activities, which combined some of the functions of government with those of embassy political reporting.

Aramco supplied the maps used by the Saudi government in boundary disputes with neighboring countries, and sometimes participated in the negotiations. On a few occasions when the Saudis deployed troops in these disputes, Aramco provided the transport vehicles. The oil company planted concrete markers on eighteen small islands in the Gulf to demarcate Saudi Arabian territorial claims. (This was not a geographical abstraction; if a patch of earth or water belonged to Saudi Arabia, Aramco had exclusive rights to drill for oil on it. If it belonged to a neighboring country, Aramco was excluded.) Inside Saudi Arabia, Aramco was a virtual government. Company geologists analyzed rock samples from an explosion on a mountain near Medina to help the Saudis determine the cause. Frozen meat and other food for the royal entourage was imported by Aramco and stored at oil company facilities. Aramco supplied the chairs for a royal reception for the visiting king of Iraq. Aramco linguists and graphic designers produced Saudi Arabia's first "No Parking" signs, a task that was not so simple as it sounds because, as a company official noted, "there was no exact or well-established Arabic equivalent for the English phrase." When Crown Prince Saud and his entourage visited the United States in 1947, Aramco paid for the trip—a mere $682,000. Aramco's staff translated government documents into English and company documents into Arabic. As schools opened, the company supplied textbooks and other materials about Arabian history and culture. Aramco health teams carried out mosquito control programs to eradicate malaria in the eastern region and later in Riyadh. By company figures, the malaria morbidity rate for its Arab employees was 2,677.8 per 10,000 in 1947; a decade later, it was 97.3 per 10,000.[19] By Wallace Stegner's account, the malaria program was adopted over the opposition of some Saudis, who did not believe mosquitoes were responsible for transmitting the disease. Among the skeptics was Khamis ibn Rimthan, the geologists' favorite guide.[20]

Aramco provided more than 4,000 tons of free asphalt a year to the government and its contractors for road paving. An internal memo notes that in December 1957 the company supplied 992 tons to "Moh'd ibn Ladin Associates," the construction company in which Osama bin Laden's father made his fortune.[21]

The oil company made it its business to know as much as possible about how the country functioned, a prodigious task in the absence of statistics, reliable media, and competent government organizations. In the quest for information, Aramco's Government Relations Department, headed at the time by Tom Barger, was aided by a semiorganized cadre of bedouins who were known as "relators" because they related what they knew. John W. Pendleton, who led the company's Arabian Research Division in the 1950s, gave this description of the relators:

> This source consists of the bedouins who frequent the offices in Dammam. . . . A few of them are on the regular payroll; the majority are casuals. They come from various parts of the kingdom, and are what I might call homespun authorities in general on the areas which they represent. Some of them are expert guides and are used as such by the exploration department. Others are content to lead a more sedentary existence, answering countless questions about the geography and sociology of a particular area under study. Some are especially useful in establishing the names of remote places as actually pronounced by the local Arabs. All of them are colorful and friendly, and they have become a vital source of information.[22]

Pete Speers described the work of the relators as an extension of a centuries-old Arab tradition of oral narrative in which men who had witnessed great events or traveled to faraway places would recount what they had seen. George Rentz, Aramco's chief specialist in Arab language and culture, presided at meetings during which these men told their tales about tribes and people and described places the Americans had not visited; all the while, Aramco scholars recorded what they were hearing.[23]

This network of informants kept the company posted on local personalities and village disputes that would not otherwise have come to its attention. The Government Relations files for one year contain a report about a dispute over payment of blood money to the family of a boy who had died in a truck accident that went unresolved because both sides were bribing the local officials; an account of an argument then in its fourth year over the boundary between two palm groves in which the owners "spent more money in *baksheesh* than the groves were worth"; and a report on an argument between two villages over a road-building project. The project was planned by the *baladiyah* government of one of the villages, that is, by an official government-sponsored organization. The other village, which had no *baladiyah* government, opposed the plan because it "would involve an extension of *baladiyah* government into their village and interference in their affairs."[24]

Using information from the relators and from its own extensive contacts with Saudi government officials and the growing ranks of Saudi merchants and contractors, Aramco compiled biographical files on everyone who was anyone in the Kingdom, as well as a comprehensive directory of government officials. This was the only reliable list of who did what in the Saudi Arabian government—the royal government itself depended on it. Because the roster of government employees changed constantly, with no public notice, as people rose and fell in royal favor, the Aramco directory was kept in loose-leaf form. Two Aramco employees, Harry Alter and Saad Afifi, would go from ministry to ministry, office to office, updating these files. The officials they talked to cooperated because they hoped to learn something themselves. Alter distributed internal memos reporting his discoveries: a new department established here, a new deputy minister appointed there, eight university graduates hired as trainees.

"Growing out of these 'Who's Who' files," John Pendleton said, "is a published directory of members of the Royal Family and public officials. This volume contains genealogical tables of the Royal family and lists the names, titles and positions of members of the government and other public officials. . . . The collection of correct who's who information is tedious and frustrating because there is no one repository for such information and it must be gleaned piecemeal from newspapers, radio broadcasts and casual acquaintances."[25]

In 1942, the royal government promulgated regulations requiring Aramco to provide free medical care for its Arab workers for all illnesses except venereal diseases. Later, the requirement was expanded to cover the workers' families. Aramco constructed and equipped a full-service general hospital and two clinics, and hired a medical staff of eight hundred doctors, nurses, and technicians. In a typically deft political move, the oil company hired as a resident physician Dr. Louis Dame, the Bahrain mission hospital doctor who had successfully treated the king in 1923. The annual cost of this operation peaked at $13.4 million in 1968.

An internal company memorandum noted that "as the local population became more and more conscious of the benefits of modern medicine, the Company was increasingly called on to treat members of the general public"—Arabs who had no relationship with Aramco—until the government began to provide medical care. The company had little choice about this because the king let it be known that he expected it. Aramco also provided funds to the developers of private hospitals and paid part of the cost of a joint Saudi Government–World Health Organization project to train the staff of a 250-bed hospital in Dammam.[26]

The medical program made Aramco the custodian of the medical records and histories of its Arab patients. Evidently the privacy of this information was not sacrosanct. A Government Relations internal memorandum from early 1958 contains this notation: "The Eastern Province Representative, Ministry of Health, has agreed that his staff will review records at the Company's Medical Liason Office, Dhahran, to obtain information needed by the government concerning some patients treated in Company medical facilities. This eliminates the need for the Company to prepare voluminous reports and translated correspondence and expedites Ministry of Health reports needed by Government agencies, particularly the Police." The company was sharing its patients' medical histories with the cops. Its memo does not specify what the police were looking for.[27]

~⌐

By the time of the State Department's 1951 memo suggesting that Aramco be "guided" constructively in its dealings with the Kingdom, the influence of American big business was also beginning to transform conditions in Jeddah. Bechtel had established a headquarters compound there similar to the one in Dhahran, although much smaller, and Trans World Airlines had installed a team to train pilots and mechanics for Saudi Arabia's national airline, which began service in 1947. Dhahran and the other oil towns had been created from scratch by Americans; Jeddah by contrast was a long-established trading entrepôt and transit center for pilgrims from all across the Muslim world, so the American role and presence were considerably smaller. But the driving forces behind the modernization of Saudi Arabia were American, and the historic Red Sea port inevitably felt the impact of American influence. Before the reign of King Abdul Aziz, Jeddah had been the capital of a separate country, the Kingdom of Hijaz, ruled by a rival of the al-Saud clan who had been installed in power by the Ottoman Turks. Because of this history and Jeddah's relative cosmopolitanism, King Abul Aziz and his brothers from the Nejd disliked Jeddah and seldom went there; correspondingly, they were less rigorous in enforcing their standards of behavior in that part of the country.

Laura Brown moved to Jeddah in December 1950 to join her husband, Glen, an American geologist who spent much of his professional life in Saudi Arabia. Glen Brown established an outpost of the U.S. Geological Survey (U.S.G.S.) that is still operating, and his discoveries of minerals and aquifers made him a favorite of King Abdul Aziz. Brown, who is credited by colleagues with finding the water supply that still serves Riyadh, had won so much respect in the Kingdom that he could express his disapproval of what he thought was improper conduct by senior princes. When he learned that Crown Prince Saud was planning to sink four wells for his own use into an aquifer Brown had discovered west of Riyadh, Brown complained to Abdullah Sulaiman that Saud's plan would deprive the public of the water. "The water in Wadi Hanifa should most properly be used for domestic purposes before it is diverted into irrigating gardens," Brown said.[28] Sulaiman, however, lacked the authority and the will to curb the excesses of the senior princes.

The Browns lived in the Bechtel compound in Jeddah, a refuge from the unpleasant environment of the city. "Jedda is spread out along the sea and is filthy," Laura Brown wrote to her parents soon after arriving. "The buildings are stone or brick, crooked, even the new ones sag; lanes between them. We are about a mile away from the sea . . . in the Bechtel compound. I'm perfectly safe here. There's a wall around the compound and within a stone's throw are 90 American men who room two to a room in one-story barracks."

The Browns' living quarters had "all the comforts of home, stove, washing machine, freezer, radio player, upright piano, phonograph, air conditioning." While her husband was out in the field looking for water or useful minerals, she reported, "I am eating my meals sent from the mess hall. Last night I had soup, wonderful filet mignon (cooked like Dad would have liked), butter beans, Irish potatoes that tasted like new, ice cream and cake . . . the King picks up the grocery bill." When they ate at home, she did her grocery shopping at the Bechtel commissary.

In another letter, she recounted a bridge game with two TWA wives and a Bechtel wife. "People are very nice to me and I have something to do all the time," she told her parents. "I practice my music, knit, study Arabic some, and people drop in so much."[29]

Jeddah was still hot and smelly, but at least by 1951 it had a reliable electricity supply and an ice plant. As they had done on a much larger scale at the other end of the country, the Americans had introduced tools, technology, and creature comforts to a corner of Arabia where they were all but unknown before Americans arrived. In Jeddah, however, there was less pressure than in Dhahran to share these modern conveniences with the Saudis in any systematic way. The region's most important economic activity, the annual pilgrimage, was a two-week annual event for which Americans had no responsibility; the rest of the year, the government was mostly content to leave the progress and welfare of Jeddah and the Hijazi population to the natural course of events. No American or other foreign enterprise provided the mass stimulus to development that Aramco provided on the faraway Persian Gulf coast. One result in Jeddah was glaring disparities in wealth among the Saudi population, obvious even to the rawest newcomer.

"It was easy to see that a certain class of people in Arabia had prospered along with the government, but many still lived in abject poverty," observed Lou Searcy Nelson, a woman from Georgia who lived in Jeddah in the early 1950s after marrying a Swedish engineer who worked in a Saudi gold mine. "I was appalled at the pervasive ignorance and illiteracy of the common people."[30] This was fifteen years after the discovery of oil; it helps to explain the State Department's concern about whether the government was spending its money wisely, a concern that would eventually prompt the United States to take a direct hand in running the Kingdom's affairs.

CHAPTER 3

Little America

By the time young Nora Johnson arrived in 1955, more than twenty years into the oil enterprise, Dhahran was no longer a hardship post. It had evolved from a rough-hewn oil camp where workers lived in tents into a thriving American small town, a pastel comfort zone that provided refuge from Arabia's harsh climate and some freedom from its grim social restrictions. It resembled an Arabian Levittown, or the community depicted in the movie *Pleasantville.*

To the Saudis of the Eastern Province, the development of Dhahran and the other villages of the oil settlement was part of their astonishing single-generation crash course in modernization. Although they were excluded from living among the Americans in those days, they could see what the Americans had, and it changed their way of thinking. It expanded their definition of a comfortable life. Saudi men began to want wives who knew how to run a house with a kitchen and indoor plumbing and, as they acquired education themselves, they wanted wives who could read.

The villages of the American community—Dhahran, Abqaiq, Ras Tanura, and later Udhailiyah—were tidy, safe, and well-organized. The schools were thriving and the students who attended them lived in neat modern houses with air conditioning and modern appliances. Dhahran had swimming pools, a golf course of sorts, television, movies, sailboats, baseball diamonds and tennis courts, theatrical groups, cooking groups, and bridge groups. (They were called groups because the Saudis frowned on clubs, which they regarded with suspicion as organizations outside the government's control.)

Members of these groups worked energetically to import culture and ease the community's isolation. Celebrity pianist José Iturbi gave a recital. Arnold Toynbee and Margaret Mead gave lectures. Hal Holbrook brought his *Mark Twain Tonight*. Ken Rosewall and other Australian tennis champions played exhibitions matches and conducted clinics on their way to and from Europe. "We created our own oases," wrote Evadna Cochrane Burba, a high school teacher from Rockford, Illinois, who accompanied her husband to Dhahran in 1948 and stayed eighteen years.[1]

But Dhahran was also the ultimate company town. Nobody was there for any reason other than Aramco. The stimulus offered by competition was absent; social life outside the oil company was virtually nonexistent. As the Aramco librarian Mary Elizabeth Hartzell wrote to her mother in 1955, "There's no getting around the fact that your neighbors in the office are your neighbors at home."[2]

Dhahran has often been described as a unique community, but it was unique only in that it was entirely civilian. Comparable environments can be found on American military bases in foreign countries: Separated by language and culture from the people outside the fence, the Americans do their best to re-create the familiar inside it. The military provides schools, grocery stores, and recreational facilities. Everyone works for the same employer. Some inhabitants thrive in this environment; others chafe at it. Some are fearful or contemptuous of the people outside; others throw themselves into local life with language lessons, volunteer work, cultural expeditions, and experiments with food. Aramco's men were obliged to have some contact with Saudi Arabs because they worked alongside them on the drilling rigs and in the exploration parties. Aramco women could avoid Arabs entirely if they chose, and many of them did so.

Nora Johnson was exactly the sort of person who would find Dhahran sterile and confining. She was a bright-lights-big-city New

Yorker, the daughter of Nunnally Johnson, the renowned theatrical producer. She grew up among writers and artists, nurtured by New York's diversity and irreverence. At the age of twenty-two, fresh out of Smith College, she married an Aramco man and decamped for Dhahran. Here is her description of the community:

> There are, except in rare cases, no grandparents, widows, orphans, or socially maladjusted people. There are no teenage gangs or in-law problems. There are no restaurants, hotels, bars, nightclubs, or department stores. There are no crimes or juries, no package stores, Sunday sabbaths, fireplaces, radiators, or snow, no maids, pediatricians, Jews, haunted houses, or churches, and no dogs, psychiatrists, staircases, train stations, or pine Christmas trees. If these lacks make Dhahran sound like the bare bones of a place, there is, on the other hand, bridge, air-conditioning, buffet suppers, oil, oleander and bougainvillaea, Indian houseboys, sandstorms, mail-order catalogues, airplanes, shipments, Siamese cats, guest houses, and wine made of canned blackberries.[3]

The streets, she observed, were wide and clean, but there was nobody on them except for Indian houseboys on bicycles. Most of the American inhabitants were married couples, usually with children. "The two other kinds of people in Dhahran are the bachelors and the bachelorettes, who live in 'barastis,' portables with four rooms each which look like the beat-up dormitories of a college with no endowments."[4]

Having married too young and moved unquestioningly to the faraway place where her husband worked, Nora Johnson was restless and bored. Until her first child was born, she tried to fill her time by playing bridge, but she wasn't good at it. She was unhappy and her marriage was doomed.

Yet in fairness to her fellow citizens of Aramco country, Johnson recognized and acknowledged that none of this was their fault. They were all friendly. Many were well-educated. The men worked hard, the women made do, and the children thrived. She said she wasn't Carol Kennicott on *Main Street* because "For the most part I liked the people I met." It just wasn't for her. As she noted, "While a good many people in Dhahran find the life there dreary and limited because of its many deficiencies, a good many others find it refreshingly simplified. They find it frees the sprit, rather than cramps it, to make twenty thousand dollars a year and be halfway around the world from their in-laws, to go to Europe annually, to never again shovel a sidewalk or be thrown out of a bar. And gone, too, are the irritations of life in other places, where doctors send enormous bills, where butchers put their fingers on the scales, where desirable women suddenly turn out to have husbands. In Dhahran the chaff simply isn't there, and you always know where you stand."[5]

For most of the Americans, it was a good life in many ways. Although Johnson didn't last long, and some went home almost immediately after arriving, others stayed many years, even decades, and remember their years in Dhahran as the best of their lives, their sentiments about Saudi Arabia and the Saudis correspondingly favorable. Long after they retired and returned to the United States, these Aramco alumni still reminisce fondly about a place that seemed not only comfortable but idyllic. They get together for reunions and celebrate what they built and what they experienced. They call themselves "Aramcons," permanently linked by their unique shared experience.

Eula Matthews, honored by Aramco on her hundreth birthday in 2002, told a company magazine that her years in Dhahran, from 1949 to 1961, were "the happiest time of all my life. Thanks to the oil companies we had well-furnished homes, with the very best air conditioning, free buses to the beach, a large, nice dining room, a well-stocked grocery store nearby, a large well-equipped hospital with the best qualified physicians, and school, library and movies. But the best place of all was the patio around the pool. It had music day and night. How we danced the hours away under the stars and a silvery moon!"[6]

By and large, these former Aramco families represent the largest and most cohesive group of pro-Saudi Americans. They generally share the views of their colleague Paul J. Nance, who lived in Saudi Arabia for more than thirty years and spent his retirement creating a museum of Saudi culture near Kansas City. Nance admired the Saudis as "people who, before the era of oil, survived a hostile environment and abject poverty with faith, endurance and a great depth of spirit . . . people whom I came to respect for their individuality, shrewdness, frequent gentleness, and for their unfailing consideration of others. Honesty was so ingrained in their being that we never locked our doors." In his view, the Saudis epitomized what Americans refer to as "family values": "The Saudis anchor their lives to their families, treasure their children and give respect and dignity to the elderly."[7]

And why shouldn't these Americans look back fondly on their experience in Arabia? The Aramcons, or at least the men, worked at challenging, well-paid jobs in a demanding environment, their families were safe and well cared for, the travel benefits were lavish, the Arabs were generally hospitable, and they could feel good about themselves as they saw the Arabs making progress all around them. Watching the clinics and schools being built, the roads paved, and the water wells dug, the Americans could take comfort in knowing that they were doing good while doing well. In truth, discontent and envy were rising among the Arab workers, but the Americans were slow to perceive it because they had little social interaction with the Saudis. They did not even have Saudi house servants; the "houseboys" and cooks were imported.

Nora Johnson's venomous description of Dhahran was not entirely accurate. There were "socially maladjusted people"; Bill Mulligan, a journalist, writer, and public relations strategist who spent thirty-two years in Aramco's Government Relations Department, described one colleague as "offensively aggressive, self-centered, coldly calculating, unprincipled, and amoral."[8] And there were occasional crimes. Most of these involved the importation and distribution of alcohol, which was permitted until the early 1950s but then banned by King Abdul Aziz shortly before his death.

"Some of those people could really drink," Paul Arnot recalled. "They could get off work at 4:30 or 5:00, whatever time, and they'd be drunk or seem to be drunk by 6:00."[9]

Over time, the Aramco people became quite accomplished at making their own alcohol. The first time I visited the community, in 1977, I was invited to a party at which I was offered a choice of "brown" or "white." I had no idea what the waiter was talking about. It turned out those were the two colors in which one found the home-brewed booze

Party time. Aramcons at an Arab-free cocktail party, ca. 1950.
ARAMCO PHOTO FROM THE WILLIAM E. MULLIGAN COLLECTION, COURTESY GEORGETOWN UNIVERSITY LIBRARY.

known as *sadiki* (my friend). It resembled bourbon or gin in color, if
not in flavor. Most of the time, as long as this beverage was brewed
and consumed inside the Aramco compound, the Saudis tolerated it;
but Aramco people and, later, other Americans frequently found
themselves in trouble with the law when they tried to import the real
thing. The memoirs and oral histories of American diplomats in Saudi
Arabia are replete with tales about trying to get these Americans out
of jail.

In Aramco's copious literature about itself, life in the oil community
is depicted as idyllic:

Americans often say the communities remind them of quiet suburbs in
the U.S. Southwest: trim one- and two-story houses surrounded by well-
watered lawns set off with hedges, trees, and flowers, and curving streets
with cars parked by the curbs, the kind of small town where many peo-

ple bicycle or walk to work and most still go home for lunch. Each community has tennis courts, a swimming pool, bowling alley, baseball diamond, and golf course. Each also has a mail center, barbershop, laundry, snack bar, library—its shelves crammed with the latest books and magazines—and a supermarket stocked with familiar brands. . . . When they are not at work, employees and their families in the four communities keep busy in a seemingly endless variety of pursuits. In Dhahran there exist more than fifty clubs and associations dedicated to sports, hobbies, crafts, and professional interests of all kinds.[10]

In addition to providing creature comforts, vacations, and generous salaries, Aramco sought to engineer an atmosphere of comity by mingling housing for executives with housing for lower-ranking workers and encouraging socializing across status lines. According to Brock Powers, who joined the company in 1947 and retired as president in the 1970s, pioneers such as Tom Barger and Fred Davies built Dhahran with this policy in mind. "They're the ones who agreed they weren't going to build separate executive housing, and they perceived that it would do just what it would have done. As it was, the electrician lived next to the president, and that's the way it worked," Powers said. "It made for good cement, because contrary to the British it wasn't stratified." Aramco's professional class—the geologists, engineers, doctors, lawyers, and Arabic scholars—"socialized across the board" with the artisan class of mechanics, drillers, and electricians.[11]

Baldo Marinovic, a Trieste-born Yugoslav who was a senior financial manager at Aramco for several years, explained the effect of this policy. In similar enterprises around the world, such as the Panama Canal administration and other oil and mining companies, he said, "the social relations are hierarchical. You know, the vice president invites all the other vice presidents for dinner. It's all by layer. In Aramco, this simply did not exist. . . . The golf group, the bridge group, or parents of friends of your children were the focus of social life. And the husband may be a mechanic or he may be a vice president."[12]

The other social leveler was the fact that the great majority of Aramco children attended the same elementary schools, separating only when they left the country for high school (an expense Aramco picked up). All

"Rah-Rah Girls," cheerleaders at a Dhahran sports event, ca. 1947.
PHOTO BY AL MCKEEGAN, COURTESY ARAMCO EXPATS.

the American children were thrown together in the classroom, creating a bond of parental interest that crossed lines of salary and status.

Aramco invested heavily in the schools on the theory that good schools would make employment in Saudi Arabia more alluring for prospective employees. Teachers had to have at least five years' experience to be hired. Most of time this policy paid off; but, as in any small town, a major change in curriculum or educational theory could create turmoil, which is what happened when Owen C. Geer was hired as superintendent in 1969.

Geer was an advocate of an experimental instructional program developed by Westinghouse Corporation known as PLAN, an acronym for Program for Learning in Accordance With Needs. Among other things, this called for abolishing the traditional classroom and creating "learning centers," where more than a hundred youngsters might be thrown together to do pretty much what they wanted. The children were theoretically guided by teachers who responded to their pupils' individual needs, but in reality the children were turned loose to talk or wander off. It was "bedlam," according to an official company history.

Mothers united in protest. The traditionalists denounced the innovators and vice versa. The company decided to create an elected school board. Geer was sent packing. The board abolished PLAN and returned to the traditional system. Two truckloads of PLAN instructional materials were burned in a public ceremony. Papers that did not go into the incinerator were fed to the goats. Order was restored.[13]

Aiding the social cohesion in Dhahran was the fact that most of the Americans who worked for Aramco did so as a career. They were mostly permanent employees, not temporary workers waiting to return to their stateside positions after being assigned by the parent companies to get their Saudi Arabia tickets punched, as was the pattern in other Middle East oil concession companies. They may have started out in quite different corporate cultures at one of the parent companies, but they took on the coloration of Aramco. If they wished to stay in Saudi Arabia and advance with the company, as many did, it was necessary to develop loyalty to Aramco and its way of doing things, and to respect if not admire Saudi customs and culture. The few malcontents and dissenters who slipped through Aramco's rigorous prehiring interview process were sent home.

Not that everybody always agreed about everything, of course. Just as in any small town, there were civic disputes and petty jealousies. The memoirs and letters of Americans who lived there in the 1950s and 1960s even contain the occasional hint of sexual misbehavior. "No two people had the same reaction to that life," Evadna Cochrane Burba wrote. "For some, it was another Peyton Place; others found God there."[14] "There are an awful lot of single men a long way from home, and not nearly enough girls to go around—even if all of us were willing to 'go around'!" Mary Elizabeth Hartzell wrote to her mother.[15]

In replicating as much as they could the life of small-town America in the Eisenhower era, the Americans of Aramco largely replicated its Ozzie and Harriet family structure, which meant that for the most part the men had interesting work, while the role of the women was to care for the men, manage the household, and raise the children. In that sense, life at Aramco was just like life back home; some women accepted it, some wanted more.

"You certainly had women there who were very unhappy," Ellen Speers recalled. "I think one of the problems you ran into is many of the men were in such exciting jobs. Here you were at the cutting edge, it was the biggest thing that was going if you were a geologist or a petroleum engineer, you were dealing with something that was really, really exciting. And they were on a high. And here was the wife at home. You had many marriages splitting up because one was happy and the other was miserable."[16] Ellen Speers, who was a graduate of Oberlin College and held a master's degree from the Fletcher School at Tufts, had been a foreign service officer in the State Department before marrying Pete Speers and moving to Dhahran, where she had to abandon her career. She made a full life for herself for twenty-five years and recalled it fondly, but others were less able to adapt.

One of them was Joy Santoro Wilson, Radcliffe class of 1957, who spent eleven years at Aramco with her husband, Robert, an economist. She was comfortable while her small children were still at home. "My routine was that of a typical mother and housewife, filled with grocery shopping, taking the children for a walk or a swim, and a little housework," she recalled. "For daily diversion from house and children I joined the Women's Group, which sponsored bridge, fashion shows, and teas; and a monthly book group, which was my source of intellectual stimulation." She dabbled at Arabic lessons, played tennis, and swam.

"Arabia for our children was paradise," she recalled. "Apart from travel, life was uneventful but happy with nursery school, 'Sesame Street,' swimming, and birthday parties followed by Little League, Cub Scouts and elementary school. The children tolerated religious education and religious services. The boys learned to fish and were learning to sail and play tennis the summer we left. But best of all, my children say, was the proximity of their friends, who were always ready to join them in play."[17]

When the children were all in school, her outlook changed: "I found myself increasingly restless and frustrated by the limited environment of

Chorus line: Aramco wives at an amateur theatrical production, ca. 1950.

camp life. I calculated how the hours between 8:00 a.m. and 3:00 p.m. could be filled more productively and challengingly than with squash, tennis, trip planning, and studying Arabic. The jobs offered by the company for secretary, errand girl, file clerk, and nurse were not the challenge for which I was looking." She finally insisted on going home, even though her husband and children wanted to stay.

Mary Elizabeth Hartzell's situation was the reverse of Joy Wilson's. As librarian in the Arabic research division, she had a challenging full-time job, and she was unmarried. Yet the letters she wrote to her parents in Seattle from 1952 to 1965 depict a life of relentless banality. She goes on at eye-glazing length about cleaning her linoleum, organizing her flowers, choosing her wardrobe, and deliberating on the best time to wash her hair during sandstorm season.

"My parties last week were lots of fun," she wrote in the summer of 1952. On July 4, she attended a cocktail party at Bill Mulligan's house.

Shirley Mulligan "served delicious shrimp & sauce, & a 'cheese bowl,' an Edam hollowed out about halfway and filled with creamed blue cheese (or gorgonzola?) to be scooped with potatoe [sic] chips," Hartzell reported. She asked her mother for a copy of her gumdrop recipe. Her Sudanese assistant at the library quit. The young women of the sewing circle are making cotton flannel nighties. She had waffles and coffee for breakfast. She shortened that plaid skirt they bought at Richert's: "It looks very pretty over my crinoline." And by the way, "They make the best potatoe [sic] salad in the dining hall—much better than any I ever had in New York."

Because she was unmarried, Hartzell was assigned to group housing with six other "girls." She described them in a letter to her mother on September 5, 1952, that probably could have been written in any female dormitory or sorority house of that era back in the United States:

Doris Nelson. Brown-eyed Swedish American from Chicago, works in the cable room. Good disposition. Fond of music, swimming, bowling.

Irene Hodel—Doris Nelson's roommate, also from Chicago, in the steno pool so far, and very new. Blonde.

Janet Johnstone, from Long Island, stenographer. Fun, but easily irritated at times! Especially on Friday mornings. Brunette and tall.

Phyllis Bontempo, New York. Steno. Very brunette, & slightly chubby. Janet's roommate, even tempered. Dating an engineer from Holland.

Rita Butler. Laboratory technician from California, also Ohio & Spokane. Works in the lab of the Arab hospital. Red curls & nice curves, tall, and lots of fun. Claims she has a temper, but we have yet to see it.

Elinor Adams, petite brunette from Chicago, slight limp from polio. Worked for the Navy as steno on Guam. Swims and dances well.

Solon T. Kimball, a New York anthropologist who visited Dhahran in 1955, reported that there were about three hundred of these single women in the community. (One of them was Florence Chadwick, who

William E. Mulligan, Aramco public relations executive and archivist, 1946–1978.

ARAMCO PHOTO FROM THE WILLIAM E. MULLIGAN COLLECTION, COURTESY GEORGETOWN UNIVERSITY LIBRARY.

later gained fame as the first woman to swim the English Channel both ways.) Some of these young women, Kimball observed, were there for money, some for adventure, some for husbands, and then "There are those who are running away from something." Their sex lives, Kimball reported, "are the subject of a great deal of interest, talk and speculation."[18] There was virtually no possibility that any of these women who were looking for husbands would find them outside the gates among the local population; social contact was minimal, and in any event most of the Arabs had little to offer an American woman. Arab women were completely off limits to foreign men.

The Saudis' reluctance to expose their wives and daughters to contact with outsiders made it difficult even for Aramco's married couples to mingle socially with their Arab hosts. "You could not ask a typical Saudi to bring his wife," Baldo Marinovic recalled. Over time, as Saudi men acquired education and began to marry relatively cosmopolitan women from Egypt and Lebanon, "with that particular group you had a more normal social interchange, but it was purely work-related," he said.[19]

Mary Elizabeth Hartzell and her colleagues were in a turbulent part of the world many thousands of miles from home. They lived and worked in an unfamiliar and exotic setting and they were surrounded by an indigenous community entirely foreign to their experience; yet relatively little of this shows up in Hartzell's letters, or in the accounts of other contemporary Aramco workers. Grant Butler, for example, who was an Aramco public relations representative from 1948 to 1951, wrote in a memoir that one of the first things he saw, on the ride from the airport, was a human hand that had been severed from its owner's arm by local law enforcement authorities as punishment for theft and hung from a pole as an example. "Some time afterward, I witnessed a beheading," he recounted. He says virtually nothing else about these local customs or any others: Life inside the compound, he noted, made it "hard to realize we were actually seven thousand miles from New York."[20]

By Hartzell's accounts, life in Dhahran could have been painted by Norman Rockwell: Her begonias are thriving. One of the schoolteachers showed slides of Okinawa. Esther has laryngitis. The ninth grade play was *Cheaper By the Dozen.* The eggplant casserole turned out well. The Sears catalogue arrived. The commissary has frozen TV dinners. They heard about a coup in Iraq but it didn't affect them. Her houseboy polished the brass without being told. Roast pork, mashed potatoes, and chocolate cake for dinner.

Of course, her parents wanted to know about her life, her health, and her activities; but it is regrettable that Hartzell did not relay more of her observations about the Arab community outside the gates because she could be perceptive. In April 1955, for example, after visiting the Arab health center with a visiting Dutch doctor, she reported that "there were some very small children who had been badly burned. It is a common injury here. Arab toddlers tumble over their own and their mothers' robes and fall into the unguarded cooking fires. The women are often burned, too, as their long gowns catch fire while they bend over their cooking fires."

The most nuanced account of life in this American outpost in the 1950s was provided by Solon Kimball, who was on the faculty of Columbia University Teachers College. In the summer of 1955, he spent a week in Ras Tanura, a week in Abqaiq, and a week in Dhahran.

He reported that Dhahran had about 10,000 residents, the other two towns about 5,000 each. American workers and their dependents totaled 6,400, or a third of the population. Aramco had 20,400 employees, of whom 3,000 were Americans, 13,400 were Saudis, and the rest were from other countries. In addition to the American housing areas, he found barracks of concrete or cement blocks for the non-American foreign workers, who, unlike the Americans, were generally not allowed to bring their families.

"The last residential area," Kimball observed, "is one that was neither planned nor welcomed. To Western eyes it is reminiscent of the Hoovervilles of Depression days. Houses have been constructed of every kind of scrap material with a scattering of more traditional palm-leaf native barastis, and an occasional substantial building of concrete block. These settlements represent the attempt by Arabs to establish a type of community life with which they are familiar. Here the employees, mostly Saudis, may bring their families." They also brought their livestock; Kimball found sheep, goats, donkeys, and camels.

"Both Aramco and the government are disturbed by these settlements," Kimball reported, "and efforts are under way to encourage their replacement by the development of planned Arab-type towns through subsidies and other devices."[21] The residents of these shantytowns, of course, were well aware of the differences between their accommodations and those of the Americans, as were the king and his ministers; Kimball had identified the source of the labor unrest that would plague Aramco for most of two decades.

More than the physical surroundings, however, Kimball was interested in the morale and psychic condition of the Americans who lived and worked in this unique environment. He found "an omnipresent sense of precariousness" arising from the social restrictions imposed by their Arab hosts, including the new ban on alcohol. "These restrictions provoke frequently expressed anxieties that further repressive measures may appear or that certain types of punitive action may be imposed upon individuals, and perhaps on Aramco. . . . The employees look to the high levels of Aramco to provide them protection, although they are also aware that certain breaches of law mean immediate deportation, a fate viewed more favorably than languishing in an Arab jail."[22]

These anxieties were not unique to Aramco's Americans; they were felt at the U.S. consulate as well. "That was one of the things that made life in Saudi Arabia so difficult—you always felt you were violating the law and that on that basis you might be thrown out of the country any day and your career might be ruined as well," said Walter McClelland, who was at the consulate from 1959 to 1962. As an example, he noted that at the time the Saudis prohibited phonograph records and dolls, so importing these quotidian household objects was always risky.[23]

Kimball found that Aramco compensated for the hardships faced by its American workers with a very generous package of pay and benefits; but even so, "Utopia realized is far less attractive than as a hope. When one begins to probe beneath the surface attractions, it is not difficult to discover manifestations of discontent, anxiety and frustration. . . . The outstanding positively affirmative statement one hears is, 'I'm here for the same reason as everyone else—the money.'"

Yet even as Kimball was writing, the world around Aramco was changing and expanding. The very presence of the oil enterprise and the U.S. airfield and consulate, and all those people with money to spend, combined with Aramco's policy of supporting the development of local contractors and suppliers, was transforming al-Khobar and Dammam from fly-specked outposts into modern towns with an international flair. New shops and restaurants opened at last. Entrepreneurs built apartment buildings, where Americans who wanted less Aramco conformity and more contact with local people could live on their own.

Ellen Speers recalled that in the early 1950s, she had to guess what size shoes her children would be wearing in two years because they had to be imported from home in Aramco's periodic shipments. But when she and Pete left in 1977, "there wasn't anything you couldn't get" in al-Khobar.

Evadna Cochrane Burba reported that she purchased new eyeglasses from a German optician working at a spotless new well-stocked pharmacy in town. Food products not available in the Aramco commissaries showed up in local markets. A supermarket with shopping carts opened. English-speaking sales personnel appeared. Burba's book shows a reproduction of an advertisement, in English, for "New Arabian Store" in al-Khobar, the place to go for Merle Norman cosmetics, Clairol products, Parker pens, and Arrow shirts. "With unbelievable speed, al-Khobar leaped from fifteenth-century somnolence into the jet age," she noted.[24] The Westernization—indeed the Americanization—of Saudi Arabia, so improbable when Krug Henry and Bert Miller waded ashore in 1933, was in full flight.

CHAPTER 4

Arabs and Attitudes

PRINCE SAUD IBN ABDUL AZIZ, son of the king and heir apparent, wanted to see the drilling rig operate. It would have been easy to arrange a demonstration, but the foreman known as Ed refused to do it. "To Ed," Tom Barger noted, "the Prince was just another Bedouin bothering him. Saud asked again to see the rig operate, but Ed wouldn't even listen to him, and the Crown Prince of Arabia walked angrily away."

That night in June 1939, all thirty-five barrels of drinking water stored for the drilling crew were emptied. Prince Saud had sent a squad of soldiers to overpower the sole CASOC watchman and seize the contents. "Had Ed been civil," Barger observed, "the Prince's men would have used a few barrels of water at most, and everyone would have been happy. Some Americans here forget whose country this is and that we are only here on the sufferance of Ibn Saud."[1]

Aramco's leaders tried not to forget whose country it was. They quickly absorbed lessons like the one the prince taught Ed, and so did officials of the other American organizations that entered Saudi Arabia in Aramco's wake, such as Bechtel Corporation. The Saudis might be poor and unschooled, but they were proud and sensitive; they would

Crown Prince Saud ibn Abdul Aziz (left) visits the oil camp with his retinue, 1939.
ARAMCO PHOTO FROM THE WILLIAM E. MULLIGAN COLLECTION, COURTESY GEORGETOWN UNIVERSITY LIBRARY.

not be pushed around. By the 1940s, as a matter of policy the Americans were instructing newcomers that they must treat the Saudis with respect and that foreigners could remain in Saudi Arabia only so long as the Saudis accepted their presence. No Saudi worker was to be struck or unexpectedly touched, regardless of the provocation, and local customs were not to be ridiculed: Do not enter mosques or attempt to photograph Saudi women, Americans were told.

At Aramco, fear of losing the concession was the ultimate motivator. Profits depended on good behavior. A handbook distributed to workers at Aramco's Ras Tanura camp included this admonition: "Patience and open-mindedness are necessary virtues in dealing with Arab employees. Aramco is their contact with high-speed American industrial technique. Our own American forefathers would be at a great loss to adjust themselves to the industrial age, and the case is even more pertinent with our Arabian partners. The privileges and remuneration we enjoy here are a result of Arab co-operation."

Cautioning Americans not to judge the Arabs by the "bathtub complex" of hygienic standards or to make racial generalizations about them, the handbook said of the Arab worker that "there is no more reason that he should at this time be able to drill an oil well than there is for you to know how to open a camel's stomach to obtain the water there from, which frequently in the open desert makes the difference between life and death."[2]

Phil McConnell, chronicler of the *The Hundred Men,* said that Aramco foremen who respected the intelligence of the Saudis and helped them learn were promoted; those who did not had short careers. "Those Americans who recognized the potentials of these recruits made progress in training and obtaining work performance," he wrote. "Foremen who concluded that the Saudis were stupid because they were untrained and didn't speak English soon found themselves returning to the States."[3]

At Dhahran Airfield newcomers were warned, "Never ridicule the appearance, customs or religious practices of the people. Theirs is an old culture and U.S. military personnel are guests of their government. . . . Do not expect to impose western military standards or operational improvements overnight. The Arab is not about to discard age-old habit and custom without reason, and is in no hurry. Much can be accomplished by example and by indirection, whereby he comes to consider the idea his own, or is gradually persuaded of its merit."[4] This observation was perceptive. Even today, Americans doing business in the Kingdom say the most effective way to sell an idea to a Saudi associate is to make it appear as if it had originated with the Saudi.

Most Americans in the pioneer years seem to have taken these behavioral exhortations to heart. Some threw themselves into the culture, learned the language, cultivated Arab friends, and developed an appreciation for indigenous art and handicrafts, limited though they were. Nevertheless, the American companies were reflections of the United States, culturally and socially as well as technologically. Many of the construction workers and oil roughnecks grew up in the segregated South; it was an era of Jim Crow policies and ethnic jokes. What they thought in private and what they said to each other did not necessarily square with company policy. The material and educational gap between the Americans and the Arabs was so wide that some conflict was inevitable.

"The intellectuals of Dhahran put up with the town and cherish the Muslim culture and the barren challenge of the land," Nora Johnson found. "The less inspired ones cherish, with equal fervor, the startling efficiency with which the oil company has imported all the comforts and mediocrity of home . . . and they consider the Arabs repulsive."[5]

"Inevitably, throughout the company's history, there were some Americans who had a racist attitude and looked down on the Saudis as inferior or unclean," recalled Pete Speers. "I don't think there were very many of these, and those that there were either left or learned to keep their prejudices to themselves."[6] His wife, Ellen, said, "You just had people like that—the ones who referred to the Saudis as 'ragheads,' and looked down on everything Saudi."[7] Even Wallace Stegner, in his official history of these early years, noted that although Aramco's leaders might promulgate constructive policies, in the field "the contact was man to man, and since each man was the product of a culture profoundly different from that which had formed the other, there were inevitable incidents of misunderstanding, prejudice, conflicting notions of law and justice."[8]

Stegner himself ran afoul of Aramco's corporate sensitivity on this point. Aramco suppressed his manuscript for years because, according to Bill Mulligan, "his glorification of the early American oil men tended to put our Saudi friends in a bad light. As Stegner told the story, when the Americans arrived in Saudi Arabia there was little more than flies, sand, and ignorant Arabs on hand." That might have been true, but Aramco's executives thought it would offend the Saudis to say so. The company's public relations staff eventually sanitized Stegner's manuscript and printed it as a series of articles in the company magazine. The unexpurgated original has never been published. Asked for it many years later by an editor at *Harper's,* Mulligan said he did not have a copy; and even if he did have one, he would not release it because "to some extent the unedited manuscript would do Stegner a disfavor. It would also insult a number of very nice people that Aramco does not wish to insult."[9]

What happened to Stegner's manuscript was not an aberration: The company's fear of offending Arab sensitivities was at the forefront of

West meets East: Aramco board members and executives in suits and ties at a "goat grab" with Saudi hosts, ca. 1950.

ARAMCO PHOTO FROM THE WILLIAM E. MULLIGAN COLLECTION, COURTESY GEORGETOWN UNIVERSITY LIBRARY.

even the most minor decisions, as Nora Johnson discovered when she received an offer to write for an English-language newspaper in Beirut about Arabian culture and the life of the bedouin. The company's public relations officials nixed the project because they thought it might upset some of the Arab workers.

How could it? Johnson argued. The articles would be innocuous and even laudatory accounts of what she observed, and they would be published in English; most of Aramco's Arab employees could not even read Arabic, let alone English newspapers published in another country. "What I had to understand," a public relations man named Vern told her, "was that the Saudis were just poised for criticism. In their secret hearts they felt themselves inferior to us in many ways. But it was absolutely forbidden even to hint at this, much less point it out. Even company literature trod delicately around this point. You never said backward or undeveloped, you said 'adjusting to new influences' or 'on the threshold of a new era.' Best leave the whole subject alone."[10]

Mike Cheney got a quick education on this subject when he became editor of the company newspaper, *The Sun and Flare,* in the 1950s. He said he found the name inappropriate because the paper shed little light and generated no heat: "The first thing any sensible editor avoided was news." The motto seemed to be, "When in doubt, cut it out," lest somebody somewhere have a complaint, he recalled. "As its staff and ambitions increased, so did its restrictions and limitations, so that decreasingly interesting material was presented in an increasingly glossy publication." According to Cheney, *The Sun and Flare* was not even permitted to describe anyone as a "native" of some place or other, because the very word was proscribed.[11]

Cheney arrived in Saudi Arabia in 1948, on the Bechtel payroll but assigned to Aramco projects. He lived in Dhahran, where he met an Aramco veteran who bemoaned the fact that most of his compatriots closed themselves off from the Arabs. "All they see is a bunch of characters with rags on their heads, picking their noses and crapping around in the sand dunes," Cheney's interlocutor said. "They don't see them as tenth-century shepherds who've jumped straight from a donkey onto a Kenworth truck, or kids trying to reconcile the Koran with an Esquire calendar. They don't bother to sympathize with tribal elders faced with working out a whole new social system for a new nation."

Many of his Aramco colleagues, this man told Cheney, were just oil-field roughnecks working for money the same as they would have in Venezuela or Indonesia, unconcerned about the local culture. He gave Cheney sage advice: "This is something you can't see anywhere else in the world—a unique laboratory experiment, a tribal world that's been cut off for all time from outside influences, suddenly thrown open to the modern world. Go meet the people."[12]

In part the attitude Cheney heard about reflected Aramco's evolution from a tent-based field operation where Americans and Arabs lived together in forced intimacy into a giant industry where the Americans were supervisors and executives and the Arabs were hired hands. It part it derived from the growth of Dhahran into a comfortable community whose inhabitants—families now, not bachelors roughing it in the wilderness—

created their own amusements and were isolated from the Arab people around them. "Some of the American women tended to look down their pretty little noses" at the Saudis, one Aramco chronicler recalled.[13]

Even Aramco's critics acknowledge, however, that the company labored mightily to improve the living standards and health of the Arabs, to educate them and to impart the technical skills they would need to advance in their new careers as oil workers. The Arabs learned to operate and repair equipment they had never heard of a few years before. They learned to read, to drive, to use slide rules, to agitate the water in their canisters so that mosquitoes would not settle and breed. Aramco taught them to wear Western-style clothing and boots so they could work safely, their robes no longer prey to fast-moving machinery and their toes no longer exposed. In the books Aramco published about itself, the years after World War II were described as a time of breathtaking progress, when the Arabs were stuffed at breakneck speed with information, technology, nutritious food, and life-saving medicines.

In his memoir of Aramco during World War II, Phil McConnell reflected on these Aramco betterment programs, public health efforts, road construction, and other good works, and asked rhetorically, "Was this attitude of an oil company one of altruism, of seeking to 'do good'—or was it simply good business? It was both. The approach was one of common sense and enlightened self-interest."[14] By comparison with oil companies in other parts of the developing world, Aramco had reason to congratulate itself. The Arabs, fast learners, absorbed and even appreciated the avalanche of progress; but trouble was brewing. So much time and effort did Aramco pour into its efforts to help the Arabs learn and modernize that the company grew complacent about its relations with the Arab staff. It assumed they were happy because Aramco thought it was treating them well. The Arabs wanted something less easy for Aramco to deliver than trucks and generators: They wanted respect.

༄

In *Cities of Salt*, a fictionalized account of the coming of the oil company from the Arab perspective, Abdelrahman Munif describes a society unhinged by American behavior, American machinery, and American women. He writes of the Americans: "These foreigners who strode around and shouted, raising their arms and behaving with unheard-of peculiarity, took no notice of the people around them or their astonishment. They were completely self-absorbed."[15] At the end of the day, the Arab workers "wanted to get to their tents as quickly as possible, to fling themselves on the ground, to flee in deep sleep from the imbecile manners and mocking smiles and sneers that pursued them every moment of the day."[16] Munif's bitter tale dramatizes for effect, but it is drawn from real history. However quickly the Arabs learned to do the amazing new jobs that came with oil, their sensitivity to insult and the cultural agitation that came with modernization produced years of strained relations between Aramco and its local workers. As Michael Cheney recalled, "Touchy Arab pride often aggravated the natural misunderstandings between our disparate groups, and got hundreds of Americans in very hot water through no real fault of their own. It was difficult to predict just what might strike the Saudi as an insult."[17] In retrospect, it should not have been so difficult.

First, the Saudis adjusted slowly and uneasily to the demands of corporate organization and industrial output. McConnell reported optimistically that "the Americans learned that customs observed for a thousand years are not to be altered in a season, and possibly not at all. The Saudis learned that industry, to be effective, depends on organization and moves on schedule."[18] But it was not that simple. For the local staff, wearing unfamiliar clothes was bad enough (work boots issued by the company quickly appeared in resale markets in Bahrain, and the Saudis refused for years to wear helmets); working on a schedule was at first incomprehensible to people whose lives had always been timed by sun and season and the needs of their animals. As late as 1975, Seymour Gray, a doctor from Boston traveling to the Kingdom, met an Aramco veteran who told him, "That was one of our most challenging problems. The Arabs are nomadic by nature and the idea of coming to work every morning at seven o'clock and working five and half or six days a week came as a severe shock. The concept of staying on and working month after month until vacation time seemed utterly absurd to them."[19]

Another difficult concept was that of rank and promotion. "The Saudi Arabs have no experience with the promotion of a man from the ranks to authority over his fellows," Bill Eddy wrote. "A man does not expect to rise out of his class, and when he is promoted out of his class by Aramco, his fellows who think they are as good as he is are outraged."[20] The Saudi man takes orders only from the king, Eddy said, and even the king does not expect subservience.

These attitudes of course presented a conundrum for Aramco, which was proudly promoting Arabs who showed up on time, mastered tools, learned English, and proved themselves reliable. Putting such men in supervisory positions stirred the resentment of the supervised; but Aramco was also criticized by other Arab staff members who learned their lessons and mastered new skills only to find Americans and other foreigners filling the jobs to which they now felt themselves entitled. By 1949, despite all the training programs, about 85 percent of the company's 10,000 Saudi workers were unskilled laborers in the three lowest of Aramco's ten pay grades. Only 80 Saudis were classified as "journeyman" or "skilled craftsman," and although a handful had been promoted to supervisor, "No Saudis supervised American employees."[21] By 1953, when Arab nationalism inspired by the republican revolution in Egypt was stirring antiforeign sentiment throughout the Arab world, Aramco had 13,555 Saudi employees, of whom all but 742 were in the five lowest pay grades.[22]

This was an especially sore point because the terms of the original oil concession specified that the oil company "shall employ Saudi nationals as far as practicable, and in so far as the company can find suitable Saudi employees it will not employ other nationals." Abdullah Sulaiman warned the company that this "was a matter in which the King had a particular interest."[23]

"Saudis were resentful that they weren't given the jobs that they thought they could perform," recalled Frank Jungers, a thirty-year Aramco man who became CEO in 1973. Once trained, they wanted to move up to jobs they had trained for. Jungers said he dealt with this by ordering a 25 percent cut across the board in jobs held by Pakistanis and other foreign contract workers to open those positions for Saudis.[24] Job status, however, was only one of the workers' grievances. They were unhappy about salaries and housing conditions as well, and some of Aramco's best-intentioned efforts to improve the Arabs' lot backfired because the oil men failed to anticipate how the Saudis would respond.

An example was the company's lunch program for the workers. Well-drilling crews in Saudi Arabia required fourteen men, twice the size of a crew in the United States. This was partly because the Saudi workers, all men, were frequently absent because they had family duties that women were not able or not allowed to perform, such as taking a sick child to a doctor in town; but it was also because the workers' poor diets made them scrawny and lethargic. They could not perform as much physical labor as their American counterparts. To invigorate them Aramco, acting as always on its principle of "enlightened self-interest," acceded to a request from the king to provide a subsidized lunch.

"Noonday feeding, what a terrible thing to call it," Pete Speers observed years later, recounting the failure of the lunch program. "A trough for animals, and it was sort of patronizing." The food was nutritious and of good quality, he said, but the cooks used untreated water, heavy with minerals, in preparing it, while food for the Americans was prepared with distilled water. "That was just seen as one more insult, and one day, just like that, nobody showed up," Speers said. "There had been hundreds of employees eating there every day and it stopped, just like that. It was very well organized." According to Speers, the boycott was "a way to show their discontent" over other workplace issues.[25]

The lunch program was "a black mark in our history," Paul Arnot said. The food looked appetizing, he said, but it contained items such as carrots that were unknown to the Arabs at the time, and the company failed to provide eating utensils or trays. The staff's attitude was, "The heck with it. If they don't eat it, so what?"[26]

Another sore point with the indigenous workers was the office where Arab personnel matters, including discipline, were managed. This was a squalid facility known as "Bunkhouse 25," which an internal Aramco paper described as a smelly, chaotic corral where Arab workers from all three facilities—Dhahran, Abqaiq, and Ras Tanura—milled around looking for someone to deal with their situations. "Throngs of sandaled and *thaub'*d Arabs would push through the front door and cruise up and down the long hallway, peering into the eight offices on each side of the hall, searching for some kindly disposed *Amerikani* who might take an interest" in whatever was on their minds, this paper said. Visitors were "assailed by a striking combination of odor and noises that gave the initial impression of a zoo at feeding time. . . . A newly arrived American specialist early in 1945 conceived the idea of placing perfumed camphor tablets about the offices as a counteracting influence. These, however, with the traffic and general racket, created the even more offensive ambiance of the men's room at a railroad station and had to be abandoned."[27]

In addition to the workers seeking job transfers, transportation, and other services, the throng included Arabs from all three sites whose American bosses had sent them to be disciplined. Workers would arrive bearing crude notes—the oil field crews were pipefitters and welders, not poets—of which the Aramco paper gives this example:

Ras Tanura
[no date]

Arab Personnel
Dhahran

This here Abdullah, No. 1312, won't work no more. Give him three days off.

Thanx.
John Riley,
Longshoreman

Since it was almost impossible to reach "Riley" by phone to learn the details, the labor specialist receiving this note would simply sentence Mr. Abdullah to three days off without pay. There was no way Mr. Abdullah could defend himself because his alleged offense was not fully described, and in any event Mr. Abdullah and the personnel officer usually did not speak the same language. Next case.

The entire facility, Aramco's internal report said, epitomized "treating masses of Company employees as impersonal, anonymous, faceless numbers." Resentment eased only in 1956, when the company began requiring field supervisors to issue "warning notices" before suspending workers, and disappeared only in 1958, when Bunkhouse 25 was demolished and replaced by a modern facility. The internal report on Bunkhouse 25 noted that the Arab workers referred to the years before its demolition as Aramco's *Asr al-Jahiliyyah* (the Age of Ignorance before Islam). After Bunkhouse 25, the turnover rate among Arab personnel, which had been as high as 80 percent in the 1940s, stabilized at 10.8 percent.

Throughout the entire period between 1945 and the Arab-Israeli War of 1967, Aramco struggled with an insoluble dilemma: The more the Arabs learned, the more money they earned; and the more their living conditions improved, the more they wanted. The better qualified they became, the less willing they were to live in facilities inferior to those of the Americans. Aramco had no choice but to train and promote them, but doing so created inevitable new tensions.

"With the machine comes the educated machinist," Bill Eddy observed.[28] In Wallace Stegner's words, "Long before anyone knew the phrase, a revolution of rising expectations had begun. Saudi Arabia would never be the same."[29]

The first open breakdown in relations between the Americans and their Arab workers came in 1945, the chaotic year when the war ended and the workforce soared as full production resumed. That summer, Saudi workers walked off the job; they demanded salary increases, better housing than the tents and palm-frond *barastis* assigned to them, and an end to what they perceived as preferential treatment for foreigners. They went back to work when the king sent troops to break up the strike, but they did not emerge entirely empty-handed. The king appointed a committee to investigate their grievances, and the committee validated them on almost every point.[30]

In the aftermath, the company set a minimum wage of 2 riyals a day, gave everyone a 20 percent pay increase, and began constructing masonry dormitories with indoor plumbing and ceiling fans. Welcome as these improvements may have been, they failed to satisfy the local workers because the Arabs could see every day the vast disparities between their lives and the lives of the Americans in their air-conditioned enclave complete with swimming pools. The workers' unhappiness at being separated from their families, who could not live with them in the bachelor quarters provided by Aramco, was compounded by the sight of the American wives and children greeting their men at the end of the day.

೧

At a company retreat at a Pennsylvania resort in 1948, Aramco's Government Relations Department circulated memos that made clear the gravity of the situation. "The company today is faced with a problem of great magnitude and of far reaching importance: It is not in good standing with the Saudi Arab government, nor does it enjoy the confidence which heretofore has characterized its relations," one of these papers said. "The recent visit of the finance minister has made us acutely aware of the lengths to which the Government will go to demonstrate its present displeasure." The paper said that Abdullah Sulaiman and Yusuf Yassin, during a recent visit, "pressed the point that living conditions of the Arab employees must approach that provided for the Americans. . . . They told us we should plan our camp layouts so that eventually senior Arab family housing will merge into the American camp."[31]

The most urgent issue, another paper said, was family housing for the Arab workers. "At present the company provides only bachelor housing. Since most of our operations are presently situated at some distance from the native communities, our employees must live the lives of bachelors at least six days a week. This does not permit them a normal existence, and it is apparent that we must soon come to some decision as to whether we will build family housing or assist the government in establishing modern communities, with all necessary utilities and services, near our operating areas."[32]

This presented Aramco with yet another dilemma. The workers, backed by the king and his senior advisers, were demanding company-supplied family housing near their places of work. The company—already in the health care business, the electricity business, the water business, the transportation business, and the road-building business—did not want to get into the home-building business for an entire new cadre of workers. Aramco's ingenious solution was to establish a company-subsidized home loan program that enabled the workers to build their own houses in the Arab communities nearby. This program had the beneficial side effect of providing a stimulus to Arab home-building contractors throughout the Eastern Province.

The government provided land for homesites. Aramco's loans were free of interest, in keeping with Muslim tradition, and the company forgave 20 percent of the principal. The balance was repaid through payroll deductions. If a worker died before the loan was repaid, the balance was written off.

This clever and generous solution to the worker housing issue was popular and generally successful, but not without its own unforeseen cultural conflicts. A decade after the housing loans started, Aramco asked two of its Arabic-speaking American employees to see how the program was working out. Their reports showed how deep the gap remained between American and Saudi perceptions and values.

In the first, Phebe Marr—who later became one of Washington's best-informed experts on Iraq—talked to the wives of lower- and intermediate-level Arab employees. She interviewed women living in new subsidized houses near the company's work sites and women who remained in their remote home villages; her sample group included Sunni Muslims, the majority sect in Saudi Arabia, and Shi'a Muslims, a large and generally ill-treated minority in the Eastern Province who formed a large part of the Aramco workforce.

"Women are not opposed to living in Company houses as such; in fact, they welcome the greater ease and comfort of the Company house," Marr found. However, "They are emphatically opposed to moving out of their own community—where the pattern of their lives is known and accepted—into the new and unfamiliar environment of the townsites. . . . The interviews revealed several cases of husbands moving out of Company houses in the townsites and back to natural communities to please their wives."

In their new quarters, Marr reported, the women felt isolated because, following local custom, they were generally confined to their residences

Ribbon-cutting ceremony at housing project for Arab workers, early 1950s.
ARAMCO PHOTO FROM THE WILLIAM E. MULLIGAN COLLECTION, COURTESY GEORGETOWN UNIVERSITY LIBRARY.

On a camping trip in the Empty Quarter in the mid-1960s, Kevin Mandaville, son of an Aramco worker, watches a bedouin jester transform a *ghutra*, or Arab headdress, into rabbit ears. Desert campouts were a popular form of recreation among Aramco's American employees.

PHOTO BY SAID AL-GHAMIDI, COURTESY ARAMCO SERVICES CO.

and could not cultivate new neighbors or pursue any activities. "The sole social activity of these women is visiting relatives and friends in the vicinity of their homes or gossiping, often while working. Not one of the women interviewed ever went to the market to do her own shopping. . . . Cut off from family and friends of like religion and background, women are left without any means of contact with the world outside their houses. New neighbors are not a satisfactory substitute in the townsites, because backgrounds are different."[33]

Marr's colleague Malcom Quint found that Aramco workers from the coastal oasis of Qatif were reluctant to relocate at any price because of "the inability of the Qatifi to live outside his culture." However compelling the economics of relocation might be, Quint reported, "The Qatifi does not and cannot turn his back on his cultural environment because he is not prepared to cope with life outside his social group. He can barely conceive of a life lived among strangers, i.e., people not connected to him by ties of blood and marriage."[34]

These difficulties notwithstanding, the program proved generally popular and Aramco has always been proud of it. From its inception in 1951 through 1994, according to Aramco, more than $3.7 billion was lent and more than 36,000 dwellings built or purchased.[35] But its inception came too late to stave off the biggest worker uprising ever faced by the oil company, the strike of 1953.

♫

Michael Cheney, a perceptive and witty chronicler of that event, said it was not surprising that Aramco's leaders were blindsided by the uprising. "Our little band of altruistic executives clinging to their shining doctrine [of enlightened self-interest] amid the Stygian night of Middle Eastern politics suggested a troop of boy scouts set adrift in a brothel," he wrote.[36] Trying to please all their constituencies—the king, the American staff, the Arab workers, and the parent companies—they "seldom pleased anyone." And because the corporate cultures of the four oil companies that then owned Aramco—Standard of California, Texaco, Standard of New Jersey, and Mobil—were so different, Aramco was "the neurotic child of four parents" trying to get decisions approved back home. "The ex-drillers, engineers and geologists who managed the affairs of this dizzy enterprise found they had also to be diplomats, sociologists, economists, agronomists and wet-nurses," as well as teachers. "It is easy to second guess them now in many matters."[37]

The company's executives paid close attention as Iran, across the Gulf, nationalized the Anglo-Iranian Oil Company in 1951 and expelled its foreign workforce, an event that reminded Aramco that its privileged position in Saudi Arabia was not guaranteed. Mostly, however, Aramco functioned in a political cocoon, largely sheltered by Saudi Arabia's isolation and the king's protection from the turbulence of the Middle East. To the extent that the United States and Saudi Arabia differed over Israel, that was mostly a matter for the U.S. Embassy, although Aramco's American workers generally sympathized with the Arab side. In the fall of 1953, the outside world intruded on Aramco's complacent enclave.

Young Saudis whom Aramco had sent to the United States for higher education were beginning to return, bringing dangerous new ideas about equality and nationalism; neither they nor the oil company had a clear idea what new positions in the company these young men might now aspire to. (One of them had fallen in love with an American girl and "had simply come unstuck" when forced to return to Saudi Arabia without her, according to Cheney. He worked through his grief by stirring up unrest among the Arabs.) Aramco's Shi'a workforce, a scorned minority in Saudi Arabia although generally well treated by the oil company, was receptive to the lure of Arab nationalism and the pseudosocialism coming from Egypt. And the Aramco work force by that time included about 1,000 Palestinians, imported to teach the local Arab workers how to read and write. These Palestinians regarded the Saudis as "backward rubes," a company history said, but also as willing listeners to messages of anger over the fate of their refugee compatriots.[38] The workers' grievances over wages and housing provided tinder for these sparks.

In May 1953, workers' representatives from the Aramco centers in Dhahran, Ras Tanura, and Abqaiq began circulating a petition demanding higher wages, better housing, improved transportation, and schools for their children. It was signed by 155 intermediate-level Arab workers. Aramco officials met with seven representatives of the signatories, but terminated the discussions when the seven claimed to be speaking for the entire Saudi Arab work force. The workers retaliated by taking their complaints to newspapers in Bahrain; in one article they accused the company of "abominable hostility to the Saudi people."[39]

In September, the workers' representatives appealed to Crown Prince Saud, who appointed a commission to hear their grievances and the company's side of the story. Nobody came to this table with a winning hand. The workers' representatives and the members of the commission understood perfectly well that the Americans were essential to the oil industry and the development of the Kingdom; Saudi Arabia was in no position to do what Iran had done. Although Prince Saud's representatives were sympathetic to the workers they were rigorously opposed to collective bargaining. And as always, the oil company's executives were torn: They did not wish to offend the Crown Prince or his representatives and they understood that to some extent the workers had a case, but Aramco was also dependent on its American employees; their higher salaries and comfortable living arrangements, which the Arabs regarded as unfair, were required to entice them to work in the Kingdom. If paid and housed as the Arabs were, the Americans certainly would not come to Saudi Arabia. Upgrading the living conditions of the Arabs to match those of the Americans would be prohibitively expensive.

The tension boiled over when twelve representatives of the workers confronted the royal investigating commission and shouted demands. They were promptly arrested, whereupon virtually the entire Arab work force walked off the job. The strike quickly spread to the Dhahran Airfield; a U.S. Air Force bus was stoned and burned. The government sent 2,000 troops, who arrested hundreds of the demonstrators, and ordered the strikers back to work under threat of losing their jobs permanently. A handful of non–Saudi Arab strikers were deported.

After two weeks of tense standoff, the workers returned; it was payday, and time to collect their wages. The government's troops and police withdrew. Strike leaders were exiled to their home villages for ten years. A royal decree formally outlawed strikes. Aramco had made no formal commitments—indeed, it could not, because to do so would have amounted to a recognition of the workers' right to negotiate collectively and to strike—but it did quickly offer a substantial package of benefits. It accelerated the home-ownership program, increased the minimum wage, restored food and clothing subsidies cut off the year before, and began constructing schools for the workers' children. Aramco supplied the buildings, the Ministry of Education supplied the teachers and curriculum.[40]

The company's operations quickly returned to normal, but the political atmosphere had been altered permanently. When the government intervened in the strike and sent troops into Aramco facilities, it effectively established the principle that the Kingdom of Saudi Arabia controlled its oil fields, not some absentee landlord in the United States. As Cheney put it, "The King had to some extent made the oil industry his personal property, as if it wasn't already."[41] Aramco was exposed as an instrument of the crown, not an independent actor. The oil company's enforced passivity in the face of the workers and its reluctant acquiescence in government intervention opened the path for the government takeover the of company twenty years later.

In fairness to Aramco, no chronicle of these events should omit the extensive resources that the oil company committed to training and educating its workers, improving their health, and taking care of their families. The many Arab workers who benefited from these efforts appreciated them, and even today—when the company is state-owned and its chief executive and all but one of its twenty-eight vice presidents are Saudi Arabs—the Americans of the early years are generally remembered respectfully, even affectionately, by their Saudi successors.

The best-known of these successors is Ali Ibrahim al-Naimi, who joined the company in 1947 at the age of twelve and rose to become its chief executive officer; he later became minister of petroleum. (How could he have been hired so young when Saudi law set a minimum age of eighteen for Arab workers? A lack of records, the relatively small size of Saudi adults, and differences in the Muslim calendar made age difficult to determine. Eventually Aramco stopped trying and hired everyone who was "yimkin eighteen," or "maybe eighteen," Frank Jungers said.)[42]

Aramco gave the boy Ali his basic education, taught him English and the rudiments of geology, and sent him first to Beirut for high school and later to Lehigh University, where he received a degree in geology in 1962. A year later, he earned his master's degree at Stanford. As company president in 1984, he traveled to the United States to express his gratitude to Aramco retirees. "Many of us had fathers or older brothers who worked for the company," he recalled.

Through them we learned about a one-room schoolhouse in Dhahran that came to be known as the Jabal School. Many of us enrolled, and it is no exaggeration to say that this experience changed our lives forever. When we went to work for the company, we entered a world that was completely new to the Eastern Province, and to Saudi Arabia. It was a world of vastly different technology, much of it in a strange new language, it was a world of instrumentation, field expeditions, construction crews, roughnecks and accountants, scientific analyses, schedules, deadlines, typewriters and reports—lots of reports! . . . Slowly but surely, all this expertise we encountered began to rub off on us. This transfer of technology—this exchange of know how—occurred all over the Eastern Province between Saudis like me and people like you. You came with much needed expertise, a big-hearted desire to share it and an informality that made getting to know you easy.

He described Aramco as "a beacon in Saudi Arabia, and indeed the Middle East and the world, in terms of the substantive, orderly and lasting transfer of technology it has accomplished."[43]

Saudi Arabia today is full of prominent and rich men who got their start at Aramco and would agree with Ali Naimi's description of it as "big-hearted." They were among the most shocked by the participation of Saudis in the September 11, 2001, terror attacks and the subsequent revelations of Saudi complicity in funding the al-Qaeda terror network. They do not share the malign view of America espoused by the radicals. In the 1950s and 1960s, before nationalization, Arab sentiment about the company was frequently less favorable. Strikes and protests flared up periodically. So intense was the anti-Aramco sentiment that in 1961 Tom Barger, by then Aramco's president, ordered up a set of self-justification papers; the company gave these to Saudi government officials to use in defending themselves against critics of Saudi Arabia's ties to the oil company—including Egypt's charismatic Gamal Abdel Nasser, who was berating the House of Saud as a tool of imperialistic Western interests.

These papers were not intended for publication; they were talking points for Saudi princes and officials to use if needed, without attribution to Aramco. One of the papers rejected Arab demands that Aramco purchase more goods and services from local suppliers, saying these vendors could not meet the company's standards for "dependability of supply and prompt delivery" and had no idea how to process reject claims. Aramco had no intention of advertising for bids, as Arab editorial writers were demanding, because it would be swamped by unqualified bidders.

Another rejected demands for equal pay, but acknowledged that such demands "have a strong nationalistic appeal." The company said it paid workers what was required to obtain the workers it needed, which meant that Americans had to get more. "American employees have the skills and experience the Company needs," the paper said, "but they are more expensive." In fact, Aramco said, that was the reason it was working so hard to train Arabs to replace Americans.

As for promoting Saudis into management, "The Company recognizes that more Saudi Arabs should be in management and now has a specific program for finding and developing potential managers among them. . . . However, to place a Saudi Arab in a management position for which he is not qualified by talent, training and experience is a disservice to the man himself, to Aramco and to Saudi Arabia." Moreover, Aramco said, Saudi Arabs who did become qualified for supervisory and management positions were often recruited away by new enterprises springing up around the country as the oil money flowed in.[44]

Aramco's arguments were correct as far as they went, but agitation was in the air in Saudi Arabia and around the Arab world. The strike of 1953 was followed by another in 1956, to which the authorities responded by jailing the instigators. In the summer of 1964, unhappy employees organized a boycott of some company facilities. Malcolm Quint, the company Arabist who was sent to interview six of them, found a "constant theme that the Company was not concerned with the welfare of its employees. . . . They complained that Mr. Barger is a Jew, in the sense that he is tight-fisted and *bakhil* (a miser). [They complained about] the lack of any future in the Company for the average Saudi employees."[45] In June 1966, electricity outages ignited demonstrations in Dhahran and Ras Tanura. The workers' grievances erupted again on "Rock Wednesday," during the Six-Day War of 1967.

Israel's quick humiliation of Egypt and its Arab allies sent a wave of rage and pain over the Arab world, including Saudi Arabia. This had nothing to do with Aramco's policies, but the oil company was a fat and conspicuously American target. A group of students attempted to block the fueling of an American ship at Ras Tanura. Crowds formed and broke up. Some workers left their jobs. On June 7, a riot erupted as students stormed Dhahran's airfield and attacked the U.S. Consulate. Aramco itself was next.

Brock Powers, as junior man in the Government Relations Department, stayed in the office that day when his colleagues went home for lunch. They did not return, cut off by a mob. "There was a riot, right in our back yard! They were burning cars right outside my window," Powers recalled. He got through by telephone to his wife, Marte, and told her go to the gymnasium, where families were gathering. She packed small bags for herself and one for her son, of a size they could carry "if we had to walk to the airport."

According to Powers, a call to Emir bin Jiluwi brought troops within half an hour. Their commander "fired his pistol in the air half a dozen times, and that was the end of that riot. . . . In all honesty, it was a half-hearted riot. Number one, they didn't know how to riot to start with, because there's so much discipline in Saudi Arabia. Number two, their hearts just weren't in it really, because all they did was knock down a fence and they didn't even know how to do that, really, very well."[46]

Pete Speers concurred that it looked worse than it was, as cars were overturned and the mob marched toward the Americans' residential areas, where the windows of two houses were smashed. "People who

Thomas C. Barger, an early Aramco explorer who became chairman of the board of the oil company.

ARAMCO PHOTO FROM THE WILLIAM E. MULLIGAN COLLECTION, COURTESY GEORGETOWN UNIVERSITY LIBRARY.

saw them coming just stayed in houses, terrified of all this. Actually very little happened" at Aramco, Speers recalled.[47]

At the U.S. Embassy in Jeddah, where a bomb had gone off at the compound's fence, Ambassador Hermann F. Eilts met with Minister of State Omar Saqqaf to request "immediate and adequate protection" for American facilities and American citizens. Eilts told the State Department that "Saqqaf had been deeply disturbed and reiterated his assurance that American citizens were in no danger." Prince Mishal, the governor of Mecca, called on Eilts to tell him that King Faisal and Crown Prince Fahd were deeply disturbed by the events of June 7 and had ordered the ringleaders arrested. Eilts rebuffed a request from Washington to order the evacuation of Americans from the Kingdom.[48]

In public, King Faisal was obliged to join his fellow Arabs in denouncing Israel and its American supporters and in pretending to take action. In a speech at Riyadh's race track, he called his citizens to jihad, and ordered a cutoff of oil shipments to the United States and Britain.[49] Aramco had stopped loading tankers because of the disturbances, so the announced embargo was essentially a hollow gesture. Its real significance lay in the skillful intervention of the oil minister, Ahmed Zaki Yamani, who made it appear that the company was acting under his orders in halting and then resuming shipments. As had happened in 1953, government intervention to stop a riot in Dhahran presaged

Prince Faisal ibn Abdul Aziz welcomed to Dhahran by Aramco executives, late 1940s. Faisal became king in 1964.

ARAMCO PHOTO FROM THE WILLIAM E. MULLIGAN COLLECTION, COURTESY GEORGETOWN UNIVERSITY LIBRARY.

direct government control of the company. As Anthony Cave Brown wrote in his book about Aramco, "Rock Wednesday signified a wake-up call for the Americans who believed that their paternalism would keep the oil fields American forever."[50]

In reality, American control of the oil fields was entering its final decade; the Saudi government nationalized Aramco in the 1970s after extensive negotiations in which the Saudis were as relentless as the Americans were reluctant. By the 1970s, the era of the Middle East oil concession was over: Iraq, Algeria, and Libya had followed Iran's lead and ended foreign control. The flamboyant Ahmed Zaki Yamani was committed to state ownership, but he did not wish the Americans to pull out entirely: Saudi Arabia needed their transportation and distribution networks to market the oil a state-owned company would extract from the wells, and the company still needed American managerial expertise. For that reason, Yamani negotiated patiently, but the outcome was inevitable. Saudi Arabia was going to retake control of its oil fields; it might retain Aramco as operating contractor, but it would not be obliged to do so.

"We all have to be realists," Aramco's chief economist, Thorn Snyder, said in October 1974, when the government had taken a 60 percent "participation" in the company. "The substance at this time is that the Saudi Arabian government effectively dominates this company in any way they choose—any way they choose. They are completely in control" in fact if not yet in law. "They set the production level. They call it giving you 'guidance.'" This "guidance," he said, "comes from a sovereign government."[51]

Yamani finally squeezed out a formal agreement in 1976 under which the Saudi government would acquire all of Aramco's assets and facilities in Saudi Arabia, based on book value. Aramco could continue to market the oil and provide other services to the country. Today, Saudi Arabia is virtually the only oil-producing country in the Middle East or North Africa that retains a cordial relationship with the foreign company that originally developed its oil fields. Now known as Saudi Aramco, the company retains thousands of American employees, some of them second- and even third-generation, and markets much of its oil through major American companies.

As its official history of itself says, "Today, Saudi Aramco continues to have good relations with the former U.S. partners, participating with them in such important activities as technology transfer and training. The former U.S. partners, in turn, retain close marketing ties with the country that has consistently stood, within OPEC, for moderation in price and stability of supply of the crude oil that the energy-hungry world relies on."[52]

The reason for this amicable relationship is that the Saudi people benefited from American development of their oil fields. As difficult as relations may have been at times, the Saudis do not think of themselves as victims of exploitation; they think of themselves as a people who were lucky to have had a wise king who picked the right partner.

Abdullah Jumah
S/S   104063

١٠٤٠٦٣
104063

Current Affairs
News Analyst

Aramco employee ID photo of Abdullah Jumah, a pearl fisherman's son who rose to become chairman of the company.

ARAMCO PHOTO FROM THE WILLIAM E. MULLIGAN COLLECTION, COURTESY GEORGETOWN UNIVERSITY LIBRARY.

"The Saudis felt no inferiority complex. We were not occupied and the Americans were not occupiers," Saudi Aramco chief executive Abdullah Jumah told me. "The oil industry and the connection with the United States have been good for us and we're proud of it."[53] Jumah rose through the Aramco ranks to become chief executive of the world's biggest oil company. His father was a pearl diver.

CHAPTER 5

Funny Money

ON MY DESK IS A SILVER ONE-RIYAL Saudi Arabian coin, about the size of a quarter. It was minted in Philadelphia in 1944, one of 3 million. The coins were loaded aboard a World War II liberty ship, the SS *John Barry,* and dispatched to Ras Tanura, but they did not arrive. The *John Barry* was torpedoed by a German U-boat and went down in the Arabian Sea off the coast of Oman. Fifty years were to pass before any of the cargo was recovered in a daring maritime salvage operation.

The fact that the coins were minted in the United States was a reflection of the economic and fiscal chaos that plagued Saudi Arabia during the war. Disrupted oil shipments, the rising cost of imported food, dwindling revenue from a tax on pilgrims to Mecca, and royal profligacy combined to empty the treasury. There were no Saudi banks, no national currency, and no paper money of any kind. The Netherlands Trading Society, popularly known as the Dutch Bank, had an office in Jeddah that served Muslim pilgrims from the East Indies and handled the government's foreign currency transactions. Individuals haggled with free-lance money changers in the *souk*. The national treasury was a trunk that traveled around with Abdullah Sulaiman, the finance minister. "When the money came in from taxes and so on, it went into the trunk until the king decided to spend it," Tom Barger observed. "When the king gave someone a chit for 100 riyals, Abdullah would redeem the chit. This would go on as long as there was money in the trunk; if the money ran out, Abdullah would make himself scarce."[1]

During the war, the money did run out. The royal treasury could not meet its payroll or pay its debts, and people in the hinterlands were threatened with starvation; the oil company diverted scarce manpower and vehicles to run emergency food convoys. These conditions opened the way for the United States to undertake direct involvement in the operations of the Saudi Arabian government.

At the time the *John Barry* was lost, the unified Kingdom of Saudi Arabia was only twelve years old, and the various types of coins used by its people reflected the fact that full centralization of the state under the rule of the al-Saud was not yet complete. A British proposal to create a national paper currency had been opposed by the Saudi religious hierarchy and rejected by the king. As recounted by the scholar Kiren Aziz Chaudhry in her study of the developing Saudi economy, "Metallic currencies were used throughout Saudi Arabia, but each region particularly valued the preferred currency of its trading partners. In the Hijazi entrepot the British gold sovereign, Indian silver rupee, [Austrian] Maria Theresa thaler, Turkish majidi, and several denominations of Ottoman currency circulated simultaneously. In the Nejd and Asir, the silver Maria Theresa thaler held sway; in al-Hasa, the eastern province's longstanding direct trade with India made the Indian rupee the preferred currency."[2] Aramco's Tom Barger reported that bedouin who sold a sheep to soldiers escorting a drilling team in 1939 wanted to be paid in the Austrian coins known as Maria Theresa thalers, or dollars, rather than in Saudi riyals.[3]

Compounding this chaos, Aramco was required to pay for its oil liftings in gold. Just as SoCal's oil concession agreement was being finalized in 1933, the United States abandoned the gold standard, and Dean Acheson, then undersecretary of the Treasury, denied SoCal's application for a permit to export gold from the United States. As a result, the oil company paid in British gold sovereigns purchased through a bank in London.[4] When the supply of sovereigns was insufficient, CASOC, and then Aramco, paid in dollars at a conversion rate of $12 per sovereign. Meanwhile, CASOC's American workers were paid in dollars, but other employees were paid in Indian rupees and in company chits that could be used for transportation and supplies.

Throughout the 1930s, the Saudi government—such as it was—still depended heavily for revenue on taxes extracted from commerce among the population, but the multiplicity of currencies greatly complicated this process and undercut the authority of the fledgling state. It also made real estate difficult to value. To deal with this problem, King Abdul Aziz in 1936 introduced the silver riyal coin, equal in size and silver content to the Indian rupee. In the penury of the World War II years, however, Saudi Arabia lacked the silver from which the coins were to be made.

James Moose, the U.S. minister in Jeddah, warned Washington in 1943 that "without silver, Ibn Saud could neither finance the approaching pilgrimage nor dispense patronage to the tribes—developments which might adversely affect his personal prestige and control."[5] Fearful that Britain would capitalize on Saudi Arabia's economic distress to rebuild its influence there and entice Saudi Arabia into the Sterling bloc of countries, the State Department lobbied assiduously within the U.S. government for direct economic assistance. And because the U.S. Army Air Corps was about to seek permission for nonstop flights across Saudi territory, the department was also looking for ways to butter up the king to gain his approval.

On February 18, 1943, President Roosevelt approved aid to Saudi Arabia under the wartime Lend-Lease program. "I hereby find that the defense of Saudi Arabia is vital to the defense of the United States," he wrote in his official directive, thus declaring Saudi Arabia eligible for assistance. In October, Washington agreed to lend Saudi Arabia 5,167,000 troy ounces of silver from Treasury Department stocks, to be minted into riyal coins. The silver was to be repaid within five years after the war.[6]

When the loss of the *John Barry* the following August left the Saudi royal treasury virtually empty, Aramco paid the $26,000 freight bill to ship 4 million new riyals to replace the lost cargo. With the coins' arrival, followed by the end of the war, the reopening of shipping lines and a quick increase in oil production, Saudi Arabia's immediate fiscal crisis dissipated. As it gained acceptance nationwide, the silver riyal displaced the other currencies. That did not bring fiscal stability, however, because fluctuations in the world prices of gold and silver made it impossible to determine true values. Moreover, mismanagement of revenue and royal profligacy continued, to Washington's growing alarm, as did the sheer practical difficulty of using coins for all transactions.

"If you wanted to go down and send a cable, for example, you had to carry a large sack of silver riyals because the only currency in the country [by then] was the full-bodied riyal and it was very difficult to conduct large transactions with these vast amounts of small heavy coins," recalled William D. Brewer, who served in the embassy in Jeddah in 1950.[7] *Life* magazine printed a photograph by David Douglas Duncan showing a merchant in al-Khobar counting his take: pile after pile of silver coins. The merchant is seated at a desk, sorting coins into neat stacks. His bare feet rest on four gunny sacks of coins.[8]

"We used to arrange for the government to mint some more silver riyals, and then we would get these crates of newly minted silver riyals stacked up in our cash offices up to the ceiling," recalled Aramco treasurer Baldo Marinovic. "At that point there was no paper currency—I'm talking about the late forties, early fifties. So all the payrolls had to be met in silver riyals. And every time we had a biweekly payroll, we would send a couple of Kenworth trucks filled with silver coins out to the districts. And the men would line up, take the hat off, or the *ghutra,* and scoop up the silver riyals and walk away from the window. It was quite a nightmare, logistically, to haul all the silver riyals in."[9]

All through the late 1940s and the early 1950s, Saudi Arabia's oil revenue kept rising rapidly, but the demand for money outpaced the increase. The king and his advisers were always looking for ways to squeeze more cash out of Aramco. The government's hand was strengthened when J. Paul Getty's Pacific Western Oil Company acquired the rights to produce oil in the neutral zone between Saudi Arabia and Kuwait on far more generous terms than Aramco was paying; this development convinced the king and Abdullah Sulaiman that Aramco could afford to pay more.[10] At the end of 1950, the Saudis bludgeoned the company into accepting a revision of the 1933 concession agreement that would give the Saudis half the profits. This was the so-called "Fifty-Fifty Agreement," modeled on a formula adopted by Venezuela a few years earlier in the first stirrings of producer-country insurgency against the international oil giants. The Saudi Arabian version of this agreement incorporated complicated arrangements in which money Aramco paid to the Saudi government was listed as a "tax" rather than a royalty. This allowed the oil company to reduce its U.S. tax obligation by a corresponding amount; in effect, American taxpayers subsidized the deal. The left-wing journalist Joe Stork, a critic of the oil industry, provided a lucid description of this arrangement:

> The regime was getting 21 cents per barrel royalty, while company income per barrel was over $1.10. The Saudis pushed for a more equitable division of these monopoly profits. The oil companies and their friends at the State and Treasury departments came up with a foolproof scheme to satisfy Saudi court demands without costing the companies anything. The trick was to increase payments to the Saudis at a 50–50 rate, but to call the royalty an income tax. Under the foreign tax credit provisions of the U.S. tax code, these payments could then be deducted from income tax payments here. . . . Thus, Aramco payments to the Saudi throne jumped from $39.2 million in 1949 to $117 million in 1950. Aramco taxes to the U.S. Treasury were reduced by a similar amount, to nearly zero.[11]

Another analyst of the Fifty-Fifty Agreement, Irvine H. Anderson, said it was not true that the Treasury Department committed itself to the tax deduction in advance—the Internal Revenue Service did not officially sign off on it until 1955.[12] The effect, however, was the same: The flow of dollars into the Saudi exchequer became a gusher.

All through this period, concern was deepening at the U.S. Embassy and in Washington about the amounts that were being squandered on royal excesses or lost to graft. The Americans feared that the Saudis' inability to manage their money threatened the stability of the regime. Abdullah Sulaiman, once a brilliant maneuverer, drifted into incompetence under the twin assaults of age and alcohol. In any case, as David Holden wrote, "Because of the exchange rate fluctuations, Abdullah Suleiman could not have budgeted with any accuracy at this time even if he had been capable of it and royal whims had made it possible."[13] The government fell into arrears on its debts to merchants and contractors. A royal decree of February 16, 1948, created a "Department of Accounts," which consisted of three members appointed by the king and stipulated that "No sum whatsoever shall be paid from the State Treasury before it has been approved by the Department of Accounts." There was, however, a huge loophole: an exception for "sums the payment of which may be ordered by His Majesty the King."[14]

J. Rives Childs, the first U.S. ambassador, recalled of this period:

> As my four years in Saudi Arabia neared their end, I became increasingly concerned with the disorder in the finances of the country. Although the income in 1946 from all sources, including pilgrimage and customs duties and oil royalties did not exceed twenty million dollars, it was mounting almost astronomically from increased oil production. Yet these expanding resources continued to be squandered with a prodigality which for the first time was exciting murmurs on the part of the population. Millions were being disbursed for the king's sons and favorites with an appearance of reckless abandon, made possible by the absence of modern accounting procedures, with consequent widespread corruption."[15]

By 1949, Childs believed that popular resentment over royal profligacy was such a threat to the House of Saud that he took it upon himself to approach the king—not as ambassador but "as one of his own people, or as the son he had come to consider me"—to say that the country was no longer a stall in the bazaar but a modern supermarket, and needed some fiscal controls.[16] He got no immediate response, but the issue did not go away.

In a secret 1951 paper laying out U.S. government policy toward Saudi Arabia, the State Department said the Kingdom could properly manage its money "only under the direction of competent foreign advisers, and the Saudi Arabian government should be induced to recruit and place their reliance on such advisers. It is our objective to provide advisers on monetary and fiscal matters under the Point Four program. . . . The financial aspects of our diplomatic activities in Saudi Arabia are at present, and will probably be for some time to come, as important as the political aspects. Meanwhile, the Saudi Arabia government is casting about for every means of keeping its treasury full, short of the obvious one of putting its financial house in order." This document said it would be U.S. policy to "urge and assist" the Kingdom to implement fiscal reforms and begin to use the money for the benefit of the Saudi people and the development of the country, rather than as a royal slush fund. Such a transformation would require the king and princes to adopt "an attitude of responsibility and trusteeship," which they had not previously displayed.[17]

Three months later, on April 30, U.S. Ambassador Raymond Hare informed the State Department that Aramco had agreed to help the king by paying $4 million in advance on taxes due June 15. Even before Aramco's letter of confirmation arrived, the Finance Ministry asked the Dutch Bank, the paying agent, to deliver the money, and the bank forwarded $1 million on the premise that Aramco was good for it. In a separate telegram, Hare said the government's fiscal plight was only to be expected because "for several years, continually mounting income has been dissipated in spectacular fashion with no thought for morrow." The more money was available, the more the House of Saud spent, Hare noted, and Abdullah Sulaiman made the situation worse by acceding to royal demands: "Since MinFin rashly agreed increase payments to Royal Family, when in Riyadh during budget discussions he in no position go to King and ask for retrenchment," Hare cabled. Hare said the government was trying to repair a leaky water tank by pouring more in at the top, "procedure which we believe will continue as long as more water available."[18]

The situation would get worse before it got better, however, because the charismatic and revered King Abdul Aziz died in November 1953, to be succeeded by his far less charismatic, far less revered son, Saud, a dim-witted incompetent derided by Aramcons as "banana nose." "His mental equipment wasn't very good," Parker Hart said of him. "He just never understood anything complex. He oversimplified and made the wrong judgments. . . . Complicated matters annoyed him because he couldn't understand them."[19]

Saud apparently meant well, but that was part of the problem. "What ruined him were his good intentions," according to British author Robert Lacey. He could not say no to anyone—least of all himself, and continued to indulge his insatiable appetites for palaces and women. Like his father, he took boxes of money with him on drives into the desert to hand out to tribes, "but whereas Abdul Aziz would hand his bounty out carefully through the windows of the car, Saud literally scattered his largesse to the winds, sprinkling gold and silver in showers and laughing happily as children dived for treasure in the dust behind his speeding car."[20] When traveling to other countries, he took with him a groom from the royal stables who "gave everybody all the money the king wanted given. On royal air trips he handed out bunches of hundred dollar bills to members of the household as they got off the plane in Europe or elsewhere," Parker Hart recalled.[21] As princes, merchants, relatives, contractors, and servants helped themselves to cash, Saud built ever more lavish palaces for himself, all the while traveling around the country taking young brides. "The King's living arrangements acquired a gargantuan vulgarity," in David Holden's deft words.[22]

Visiting the United States in 1962, Saud had the temerity to ask President John F. Kennedy for economic assistance. He told Kennedy that his country was "in dire need of hospitals, schools, ports, roads and artesian wells, and relies on the United States for economic assistance." It was true that Saudi Arabia was in need of those services, but the president, smarter and better briefed than his visitor, remarked that the World Bank had provided a development plan for Saudi Arabia and was offering technical assistance to implement it. Kennedy "expressed certainty" that, if the king wished to propose specific development initiatives, "U.S. lending institutions would be willing to consider projects which the Saudi Arabia Government might wish to submit on their merits." In other words, project-specific loans, maybe; cash grants, no. Then, further demonstrating his inability to grasp the situation, the king told the president that it would be necessary to reduce the U.S. military team that was training the Saudi armed forces from two hundred men to eighty to save money. Kennedy said eighty was not enough, at least two hundred were needed—and he reminded the king that the United States paid most of the costs anyway.[23]

So outrageous were the excesses of Saud and some princes that even Aramco, which hardly ever challenged the government, felt obliged to step in. When the Suez crisis of 1956 compounded the fiscal squeeze caused by royal profligacy, chairman Fred Davies limited allowances to the king in an attempt to cut palace spending. One result was that some princes, angered by cuts in their allowances, aligned themselves with Crown Prince Faisal in his power struggle with the king.[24]

That power struggle dominated Saudi domestic affairs throughout Saud's reign. Faisal, who was as austere and disciplined as Saud was self-indulgent and reckless, believed that Saud was not only incapable of managing the country's affairs but completely over his head in dealing with such external challenges as the rise of Arab nationalism and the emergence of Egypt's Nasser as hero of the Arab masses. Saud's extravagance made him and the entire House of Saud convenient targets for the fiery, antimonarchical Nasser.

Supported by a group of like-minded princes, Faisal forced Saud to designate him prime minister, with executive powers, in 1958. Saud resumed control in 1960, but the kingdom's deteriorating fiscal condition and his own deteriorating physical condition obliged him to accept Faisal's return the following year. This contest ended only with Saud's abdication and exile in 1964. When Faisal first became prime minister, Ambassador Hart said, he "found a situation in which sixty percent of all the oil company income was being spent on the royal family for whatever they wanted, and for the hangers-on, who were innumerable."[25] The Treasury contained only 317 riyals, about $100.[26] Needing more than 25 million riyals to meet an upcoming payroll, Faisal sought a bridge loan from Salim bin Mahfouz, one of the country's most prominent financiers, who turned him down. Faisal was furious with Mahfouz and cancelled government dealings with him, but the encounter was therapeutic; the prime minister understood the need for urgent action. He banned the import of private automobiles, restricted the export of capital, cut the generous subsidies Saud had been giving favored Arab rulers, and capped royal spending at 18 percent of national income—still a high figure, but now a firm ceiling difficult for individual princes to evade. "King Saud could go on throwing gold sovereigns from his car windows if he wanted to," Robert Lacey wrote, "but this bounty must come out of his own allowance, and when it was finished there would be no more."[27]

The good news in this morass of extravagance and bad management was that King Abdul Aziz, in the last years of his reign, had accepted a State Department offer of help, which he and Abdullah Sulaiman recognized they needed. In January 1951, the United States and Saudi Arabia signed an agreement under President Truman's program of technical assistance to developing countries known as Point Four. That summer, Washington sent out a fiscal expert named Arthur N. Young to help the Saudis create a money management system and a central bank.

Arthur Young was born in Los Angeles in 1890. He graduated from Occidental College, of which his father had been a founder, earned a doctorate in economics from Princeton, and also held a law degree. His specialty was international finance: Before Saudi Arabia he had been an economic officer in the State Department, tax adviser to the governments of Mexico and Argentina, and financial adviser to the nationalist government of Chiang Kai-shek in China; indeed, Young was actually a member of the Chinese delegation to the 1944 Bretton Woods conference, the assembly that created the structures of the modern international financial system.

Young said his friends at the State Department "knew that I had handled problems of silver and gold in connection with the reform of the Chinese currency, so they felt that perhaps I was the logical person to head this mission to Saudi Arabia." The Saudis "were ready to take advice," he wrote years later in a memoir about his Saudi service. "It was my good fortune to be called upon for this work."[28]

The temperature was 113 degrees when Young and his wife arrived in Jeddah in July 1951. At the time, Jeddah "was considered one of the least desirable posts in the foreign service," Young noted, but they escaped the heat and the primitive local conditions by establishing residence in an air conditioned prefabricated house in the same Bechtel compound where Laura Brown was so comfortable. Young worked from home. Abdullah Sulaiman provided a car and driver, and a Lebanese interpreter whose wife gave Arabic lessons to Mrs. Young.

Arthur Young admired Sulaiman as a skillful politician who had the king's confidence and had succeeded in persuading all the tribes to accept the riyal as the national currency. Still, "He knew that his technical understanding of currency and fiscal problems was limited and was ready to accept help," Young wrote. Even had he still been at the top of his powers, Sulaiman would not have been able to handle the amount of work that fell to him in a government that lacked a trained civil service. In addition to his duties as finance minister, he had de facto responsibility for the public health department, education, the post office, the police, and religious endowments.[29]

Sulaiman's willingness to accept help did not mean that Young had an easy time. He carried around a letter of resignation, which became well-worn from the number of times he pulled it out and threatened his Saudi counterparts with it. Faced with this threat, they generally acceded to his views.[30]

Part of the problem was that there were no statistics or financial data. There was a nominal budget, but it was meaningless in an environment in which the king handed out cash at will and fluctuations in the prices of gold and silver disrupted currency values. Currency trading was unregulated, even though 85 percent of state revenue was in dollars or sovereigns. The tariff system was skewed to favor imports of luxury items over essentials. George Bennsky, the U.S. government's regional economic officer, observed that "nobody knew what the balance of payments in Saudi Arabia was. So one time when I was out there I decided that if I talked to enough people I could figure out what Saudi Arabia's balance of payments looked like. So I talked to a lot of people and found out what they thought about the amount of trade and finance and services, et cetera, and calculated a balance of payments."[31] Young also went to the *souk* twice a week, trying to compile a consumer price index.

The task of creating a central bank presented its own difficulties. Saud, still crown prince at the time, demanded assurance that the bank would neither pay nor collect interest, in accordance with Islamic law. Young told him the bank would cover its costs through commissions on currency exchanges, which the bank would regulate as it took over international currency trading. The very word "bank" caused heartburn among the Saudis, who associated it with the collection of interest. For that reason, when the king accepted Young's draft charter and created the central bank by royal decree in 1952, the institution was called the Saudi Arabian Monetary Agency, or SAMA, the name it still bears.

Once the king made up his mind to accept Young's recommendations, the creation of SAMA was virtually instantaneous. Shortly after Young met Abdul Aziz and explained the rationale for the institution, he received a call from the deputy minister of finance, who told him, "The King wants to issue a decree right away. We need to issue a decree to create this institution, right away this afternoon." Young began dictating. "I got in my secretary and wrote a charter of articles for this central bank, or monetary agency," he recalled. "I'd write an article and it would be translated into Arabic. I produced the whole thing by the middle of the afternoon, a complete charter for the bank, and really a surprise because ordinarily when you set up a central bank you have hearings and expert studies and all that sort of thing, and it takes months or years. Fortunately I had prepared a report in which I explained just what I thought the institution should be and what its powers should be and what it should do and not do." The king approved the draft charter virtually without change, and instructed Young to set up the new institution as soon as possible. The American adviser was authorized to commandeer any building in Jeddah that he found suitable. Young's memoir includes a celebratory photograph of him standing in a garden of sunflowers at his residence in Jeddah, holding up the decree establishing his bank.

SAMA's charter gave it the usual functions of a central bank: issuing and regulating currency, chartering and supervising commercial and private banks, collecting and disbursing government funds, and managing foreign currency and gold reserves. The agency would not lend money to individuals or commercial enterprises, which would be serviced by commercial banks, nor would it issue paper money.

Paper money was the obvious answer to the fluctuations in the value of coins caused by gyrations of the gold and silver markets, but it was an alien concept to the king and his advisers. Baldo Marinovic recalled that when Aramco printed scrip for use in company facilities such as the commissary, it soon began to circulate throughout the Eastern Province, where it was accepted even in the Arab towns, until the government found out and ordered the company to stop printing this paper money.[32]

According to Marinovic, the Saudi government's aversion to paper currency derived from "a religious ruling that you cannot exchange something that is equal for something that's not equal, and obviously paper is not equal to coffee or wheat or beans or anything else. So it had to be silver or gold."[33] David Long ascribed it to "local resistance and concern that it might encourage anti-Islamic banking practices."[34] Arthur Young did not propose that SAMA issue paper currency because he had his own reason to oppose it: He feared that an undisciplined government would print money on demand, igniting ruinous inflation.

SAMA's first director—another American, George Blowers—found a creative way to skirt the ban on paper. In 1953, the last year of Abdul Aziz's reign, SAMA created a scrip for use by pilgrims coming from outside Saudi Arabia to visit Mecca. Pilgrims exchanged their own currencies for these "Hajj receipts," which could then be traded for riyals at one of Saudi Arabia's few banks. Issued in denominations of 5 and 10 riyals, the scrip was not legal tender, but it looked like currency; samples can still be seen in Riyadh's Currency Museum.

The immediate purpose of this scrip was to relieve pilgrims of the burden of carrying sacks of coins with them, but it was also a trial balloon to test public acceptance of paper. "Theoretically it will cease to operate at the end of the pilgrimage," a prescient Mary Elizabeth Hartzell wrote to her mother that summer, "and cannot be spent as money—the scrip could not be used to pay a hotel bill or buy a meal. But we wonder if it may not be the opening wedge" to paper money, as indeed it turned out to be.[35] When a spike in the world price of silver led to the smuggling of silver riyal coins out of the Kingdom and a currency shortage, these "Hajj receipts" gained acceptance as a de facto currency throughout the Kingdom, whether it was pilgrimage season or not. Aramco even used them to pay Arab personnel. They remained in circulation until 1964, after SAMA's charter had been revised to permit the issuance of real paper money.

In SAMA's first decade of operation, true fiscal stability and competent management of the exchequer remained elusive because of King Saud's uncontrolled spending and his feud with Faisal, who sometimes issued contradictory directives. When Faisal finally consolidated his power, however, he found that the institution designed by the Americans provided a firm foundation for his economic and fiscal reforms, including an influx of foreign banks that found the new Saudi regulatory environment reassuring. Among those was Citibank of New York. Citibank no longer operates under its own name in the Kingdom because all banks now are required to be majority Saudi-owned, but it is still an economic power-house there as manager and part owner of Saudi American Bank, one of the Kingdom's largest and most influential commercial banks.

"SAMA over the years has proven to be a fairly effective administra-tor and regulator," said Bob Eichfeld, a Citibanker who served two tours in Saudi Arabia. "In fact I would rate them throughout that re-gion as being the best. SAMA has kept the currency stable, and done a pretty good job of regulating the ten or eleven banks that are there. . . . They've always had strong leaders, and they get a lot of respect, not only from the business community in Saudi Arabia but also from the inter-national regulatory community."[36]

Thanks largely to SAMA, the era of pseudomoney, sacks of silver, and coins from Philadelphia is far in the past. The young Saudis who can been seen transferring money between accounts or checking their portfolios at the high-tech automated teller machines in Riyadh and Jeddah have no memory of fiscal chaos. Saudi Arabia has had a stable currency, a low inflation rate, and generally a sound banking network in good times and bad, for forty years. "Perhaps the ultimate accolade from the banking profession itself," according to Brad Bourland, Saudi American Bank's chief economist, "is that SAMA is the only Middle Eastern central bank that has been invited to join the Basle-based Bank for International Settlements, a sort of central bank of central banks, whose members are mostly OECD countries. SAMA knows its local banks well [and] regulates with a cautious guiding hand that has kept the Saudi banking system well-capitalized, transparent, largely shielded from political pressure, and scandal-free."[37]

Before Arthur Young went to Saudi Arabia, the American organiza-tions that most influenced the country's development were Aramco, Bechtel, and the U.S. Air Force, which was operating a strategic base at Dhahran and training Saudi pilots. Young's work opened a new period in which multiple agencies of the U.S. government, along with other corporations and nonprofit institutions, would increasingly become in-volved in building the modern Saudi Arabia.

CHAPTER 6

The Little Screen

GREAT AFFAIRS OF STATE WERE on the agenda when Crown Prince Faisal traveled to the United States in the fall of 1962 to attend the United Nations General Assembly session and meet with President Kennedy.

On September 26, a military coup overthrew the monarchy in Yemen, Saudi Arabia's neighbor to the south. The revolutionaries declared Yemen a republic and aligned the country with Saudi Arabia's most feared rival, the fiery nationalist President Nasser of Egypt, who promptly sent troops to Yemen to support the new regime. Kennedy viewed Nasser as an important figure and sought good relations with him; Faisal saw him as a stalking horse for communism who was stirring up trouble throughout the Arab world, and he hoped to convince the president of that. Kennedy had little use for the profligate, inept King Saud, but he developed a respect for Faisal, in whom he saw the promise of reform and progress.

Parker Hart, ambassador to Saudi Arabia at the time of that 1962 meeting, depicted Kennedy's conversation with Faisal as a blunt encounter between two shrewd, hard-headed men who sized each other up and decided they could do business: "Faisal got what he wanted from Kennedy, which was a reaffirmation of the vital interest and concern that the United States had in the independence and territorial integrity of Saudi Arabia. On the other side of the coin, without making it a condition but clearly implying the two matters were interrelated, Kennedy got something from Faisal which was very important. That was a program of reforms in the government of his country which were badly needed and, in particular, the abolition of slavery."[1]

Kennedy emerges from the diplomatic record as one of the few important Americans in government or business to put serious pressure on Saudi Arabia's leaders to modernize and liberalize their society. On November 2, Kennedy followed up on his conversation with Faisal with a letter: "Under your firm and wise leadership, I am confident Saudi Arabia will move ahead successfully on the path of modernization and reform which you so clearly desire. In pursuing this course you may be assured of full United States support for the maintenance of Saudi Arabia's integrity."[2]

Less than a week later, Kennedy's secretary of state, Dean Rusk, sent Faisal a strong reminder that the president had meant what he said about reform. Rusk instructed Ambassador Hart to deliver Kennedy's November 2 letter personally and to make some additional points: "We wish Faysal fully understand our commitment to royal family as such contingent upon progress and reform in Saudi Arabia," he said in the peculiar stilted language of the diplomatic cable, "and does not connote preservation Saudi royal family at all costs. US pleased at evidence of serious intent carry out reforms."[3]

Kennedy and Faisal met at a moment of turmoil inside the Saudi monarchy as the rivalry between Faisal and King Saud approached its dénouement. A year later, on November 3, 1964, Faisal and his fellow princes, in collective recognition that the bumbling, corrupt Saud was not capable of managing the impending confrontation with Egypt, forced him to abdicate and leave the Kingdom. Faisal became king. Three days later, he announced a domestic reform program that included the abolition of slavery, just as he had told Kennedy he would.

As momentous as these events appeared when they occurred, another outcome of the Kennedy-Faisal conversation that drew little notice at the time has probably had a greater long-term impact on the evolution of the Kingdom. The United States led Saudi Arabia into the age of television.

Kennedy, the first American politician to grasp fully the power of television as a tool of mass communication, said to Faisal, "How about TV, this is the thing of the present, everyone has TV sets. Do you think we can help you with a TV station or chain of stations so you can talk directly to the people, so they can see you?" To which Faisal responded, "What would a blind person want more than a pair of eyes?" "I will talk to my people," Kennedy said, "and I promise you that we will do our best and it will be done."[4]

The television commitment was not Kennedy's idea—his advisers had inserted it into his talking points for the meeting—and the president evidently forgot about it after his talk with Faisal. The prince, who envisioned television as a medium of mass education and wanted his people to have something to do at night besides listen to anti-Saudi propaganda on Nasser's Voice of the Arabs radio, did not forget about it.

The following March, Kennedy sent diplomatic troubleshooter Ellsworth Bunker to Egypt and Saudia Arabia to try to broker a settlement between Riyadh and Cairo, which by then were fighting a proxy war in Yemen. At the conclusion of Bunker's meeting with Faisal, which Ambassador Hart attended, "Faisal suddenly asked for U.S. assistance in establishing television in Saudi Arabia. He wanted a television station in Riyadh and for the Western Province, and he wanted to avoid importunities and arguments from Saudi business rivals by being able to say, 'the American government is building this facility,'" Hart recalled in his book about the bilateral relationship.[5]

In his oral recollections, Hart gave a slightly different version, in which Bunker does not appear. Hart said he and the king were having a wide-ranging meeting at the palace one evening when the conversation turned to economic development. "I mentioned television. Faisal said, 'I would like very much to get assistance from your government in building for me a television station. I would like to be able to say to all the eager merchants and businessmen around here that, if they want to get into this project, they have to see the Americans.'"[6]

Hart's accounts make it sound as if the television project were a new idea, raised for the first time in conversations in Riyadh. According to

Isa K. Sabbagh, the embassy's colorful cultural affairs officer and translator, that was because Hart had not accompanied Faisal to Washington the previous autumn and had never been informed of Kennedy's offer. Sabbagh, however, had been at the Washington meeting, as the president's interpreter. When Faisal asked about the television promise at his meeting with Bunker months later, Hart was caught off guard, Sabbagh recalled. "Poor Pete Hart said, 'I beg your pardon?' Faisal replied, 'When I was in Washington with Kennedy he mentioned that you would be willing to help us with the establishment of a TV chain or station.' Pete Hart said, I think genuinely, 'I will have to look into this, as I don't remember this.' Faisal raised himself and said, 'I am surprised, your excellency, your colleague and my brother Isa was there himself, do you remember?' 'Yes I do,' I said. 'Of course I do.' I suggested in Arabic to Pete Hart that he really look into it and ask Washington for a copy of the memo which I had drafted. Things started moving after that."[7]

On December 9, 1963, seventeen days after Kennedy was assassinated and five weeks after Faisal replaced Saud as king, Ambassador Hart wrote to Omar Saqqaf, the deputy minister of foreign affairs, to confirm details of the U.S. government's commitment to create a government-owned television network for Saudi Arabia.

"The United States Government shall assume responsibility for contracting for the installation of television transmitting facilities, for the training of operating personnel and for the initial operation of the stations. The U.S. Army Corps of Engineers shall carry out these responsibilities on behalf of the United States Government," Hart's letter said. Imported equipment and material were to be exempted from customs duties. The Saudi Arabian government was to make land available for the broadcast stations and of course pay for the whole project.[8]

This agreement began a new phase of relations between Washington and Riyadh in which active-duty U.S. government personnel, military and civilian, took an increasingly broad and direct role in operations of the Saudi Arabian state. The Saudis could, of course, have eliminated the government middleman by seeking bids directly from television companies in the United States, Europe, or Japan; but, as Ambassador Hart's recollections indicate, the king did not want to get involved in haggling over contracts with Saudi businessmen, who would have demanded a piece of the action. Moreover, since they lacked the competence to manage large-scale international contracts, the Saudis felt more comfortable—and less vulnerable to overpricing and exploitation—when dealing with their friends in the U.S. government. To the extent that they could have this role fulfilled by Aramco or Uncle Sam, they preferred to do so. On the American side, such arrangements ensured that a large portion of the Saudis' growing oil revenue would be spent in the United States.

There was a political dimension as well. American officials saw these arrangements as a tool to court favor with the Saudi populace. In an eerie preview of what would happen after September 11, 2001, when the U.S. government turned to television in an effort to reach the Arab masses and overcome anti-American sentiment, the State Department urged quick implementation of the television agreement as a channel for increased communication with the Saudi people. "We should increase information among target groups about the U.S., its institutions and policies through circulation of periodicals and books in both Arabic and English; through lectures and other events; and by placement of selected materials in the Saudi press and on Radio Mecca when possible," a State Department memo said. "The United States should promptly fulfill the commitment made under the recently signed United States-Saudi agreement to supervise installation of two telecasting stations and should provide programming assistance and appropriate television materials to Saudi officials responsible for the stations."[9]

Although they had no stations or programs of their own, the people of Saudi Arabia were not entirely ignorant of television. Aramco Television had been transmitting since September 1957. It was the first Arabic-language station in Saudi Arabia and the second in the Middle East after one in Baghdad. Its signal could be received throughout much of the Eastern Province.

About one-third of the programming was educational, including lessons in arithmetic, English, and the Arabic language. Other instructional broadcasts dealt with science, agriculture, marine life, and traffic safety. These lessons proved extremely popular, especially among women, who had no other access to education. What the Saudis really liked, though, was the entertainment programming. They were soon lapping up such mainstream American fare as *I Love Lucy*, *Father Knows Best*, and *Perry Mason*, all with soundtracks dubbed into Arabic. By 1968, Aramco estimated 380,000 Arabic-speaking viewers tuned in every night.[10] The original English dialogue was transmitted via radio to Americans inside the Aramco compound.

All material to be broadcast was subject to Saudi censorship and purged of scenes or dialogue that might be offensive to local sensibilities. Only male voices were used in the Arabic dubbing until Radio Mecca, the government station, put the first women on the air in 1959. These restraints avoided trouble with the Saudi authorities but didn't enhance the enjoyment of the American audience. "By the time kissing scenes, scanty clothing and alcohol portrayals were excised—along with the advertising content—a program that had run an hour in the United States might be 20 minutes long when we viewed it," one Aramco viewer grumbled.[11]

Joy Wilson recalled that she tried to persuade the television station's managers to show more culturally ambitious fare. "I managed to convince the company TV station to bring us better programs, such as Kenneth Clark's *Civilization* series, *Elizabeth R*, *The Wives of Henry VIII*, and *War and Peace*," she wrote. "Eventually there was such an abundance of such programs that there was a loud outcry from company employees to return to *Star Trek*, *Kojak*, *The Partridge Family*, and sports films."[12]

～

Americans who think the never-ending argument about high-quality television vs. trash television is unique to this country would be enlightened by a paper titled "Aramco Television Programming" that the company's public relations staff prepared in 1962. This was one of the self-justification papers that Tom Barger ordered up for distribution to Saudi government officials to use in defending the oil company. Defending the content of its television broadcasts, Aramco said:

Although over-all response to Aramco Television is overwhelmingly favorable, some critics in the Saudi Arab press, claiming that people in the Eastern Province spend much of their leisure time watching Aramco Television, allege that the programs are a waste of time. They say that the programs lack educational and cultural value, instill violence in children and even adults through crime and cowboy shows, and include harmful propaganda. The only Arabic films broadcast, so the critics say, are "silly" ones rather than serious ones about present day problems.

Were these criticisms justified? Of course not, Aramco said. All programs "comply with the religious, social and cultural traditions of Saudi Arabia." The station's managers "realized it is impossible to please all viewers with all programs, so they presented a wide variety of programs appealing to different age levels and to different members of the family." There were programs for mothers, children, students. Scholarly lectures by Arab intellectuals were presented frequently. It was basic policy to "steer clear of politics," and "no harmful propaganda of any sort has appeared." Much of the material broadcast was purely educational; Aramco offered free textbooks to help viewers master the material.

As for violence, "Some of the cowboy and adventure shows do contain violence. In these shows, violence is an integral part of the triumph of good over evil, as, for example, the fist fight between the cowboy hero and the villain. Studies conducted in the United States point out that young viewers are in no way adversely affected by such violence." Moreover, programs not suitable for children were broadcast late in the evening, after they had gone to bed.[13]

Aramco continued its Arabic-language broadcasting to the Arabs of the Eastern Province until 1970, when the government-owned network created by the Corps of Engineers reached that part of the country.

✍

Once the television agreement between Saudi Arabia and the Corps of Engineers was in place, the Americans moved swiftly. The corps engaged American construction firms to build the studios and transmitters in

Riyadh and Jeddah, RCA Corporation to provide the equipment, and NBC to operate and maintain the stations. These arrangements brought into the Kingdom a new cadre of Americans who were not involved in the oil business or construction. They were the vanguard of what would become a substantial, more or less permanent American presence throughout the Kingdom.

Among them was Doug Boyd, a young Texan who at the time the television project began was one of three English-language announcers on the Saudi Arabian government radio station in Jeddah and had previously taught English at a school in Riyadh. That Jeddah station, the country's first broadcast outlet of any kind outside of Aramco, began service in 1949 with a tiny 3-kilowatt transmitter. Even after the RCA Corporation upgraded it to 50 kilowatts, the transmitter reached only the Hijaz, or western Saudi Arabia, throughout the 1950s.[14]

Doug and Carol Boyd met as graduate students at the University of Texas, where he was studying for an MBA and she was working toward a master's degree in French.

When a professor asked him whether he would like to go to Saudi Arabia to teach, Boyd recalled, "I said no. I had been married two weeks, I had a red MGB, I was a rock-and-roll disc jockey, and I was doing my MBA. Life couldn't be any better. I went home and told my wife and she said, 'Why don't we go?' She had studied in France. I had never been outside the United States."[15] Ten days later, they were in Riyadh. It was November 1963, just about a year after Faisal's meeting with Kennedy in Washington.

The reason for haste was that Saudi Arabia suddenly faced a critical shortage of English teachers. Most of the English instructors had been Egyptians; when Nasser supported the coup in Yemen and began his propaganda assault against Saudi Arabia, the Egyptians were expelled. Adventurous young Americans such as the Boyds filled the openings.

"From November 1963 to June 1964, that's what I did, I taught English, my sole qualification being the ability to speak the language," Doug Boyd recalled. "We had a wonderful time. We were very young—Carol was twenty, I was twenty-two. You have to remember, Riyadh was a very small place in the 1960s. At Christmas in 1963, we had a party at the house of the Aramco representative and every American that I know of in Riyadh was there and it couldn't have been twenty-five people, including spouses."

Doug Boyd said they were able to save "quite a bit of money because we lived so modestly" in what he called "a graduate student's apartment," with boxes and crates for furniture. Carol Boyd turned out to be a quick study in Arabic. And she wasn't bored because she snagged a clandestine job in the Riyadh office of Getty Oil Co., which operated in the so-called neutral zone between Saudi Arabia and Kuwait.

The Boyds returned to the United States when Doug's teaching assignment ended in the spring of 1964, but they were "kind of smitten by the Middle East and taken by the possibility of going back," he said. It didn't take them long.

At the beginning of 1965, Boyd wrote later, "the Ministry of Information began an English-language [radio] station in Jidda in the hope both of reaching the large foreign community there and of communicating Saudi news, views and other information to diplomatic missions that might not (it thought) have personnel to translate the daily Saudi newspapers from the Arabic." The ministry engaged two Britons and one American, Doug Boyd, to do the broadcasts.[16] Thus he was already in Saudi Arabia when the Corps of Engineers hired him for the television project.

One of his assignments was to manage the NBC contract; another was to train Saudi broadcasters and technical staff. "We sent a lot of students to the United States for short-term courses and some degree programs," he said. The Americans "did not get involved in program content" except to "offer some conceptual ideas and try to make the news better."

On July 17, 1965, Saudi Arabian television went on the air in Jeddah and Riyadh, with two hours of programming beginning after sunset prayer. The content was mostly religious, with Koran readings and lessons, and the news, but it included *Mighty Mouse* cartoons supplied by the Americans. Soon, the stations added American entertainment shows that had already been broadcast elsewhere in the Arab world and thus were already dubbed, such as *The Wackiest Ship in the Army.*

Boyd, who went on to make an academic specialty of studying the Arab media, remembered Saudi television as an "overnight smash success." He recalled "a scene in downtown Jidda during the brief evening transmissions in August 1965: people stood five and six deep on the sidewalks to catch a glance of the television sets in shop windows."[17]

According to Boyd, "Television was the ideal medium for Saudi Arabia. This is a home-centered society, people don't go out, nightclubs don't exist, families don't go out to hotels, there are no movie theaters, and so it was the ideal situation, where you could have something of symbolic modernization that Faisal could bring in, plus you have the ultimate censorship because TV signals don't travel long distances."[18]

In the Saudi Arabian context, King Faisal was a modernizer like his father. An Arab historian described his outlook as a combination of political conservatism and "a vision that Saudi Arabia can import technological expertise and modernize economically while remaining faithful to authentic Islam."[19] The king well understood that the introduction of television would be opposed by the country's conservative religious establishment and others in society. After all, they had opposed the introduction of the telegraph, the radio, and even the automated telephone, which they feared would encourage unmarried men and women to talk to each other undetected.

These critics took literally the Prophet's injunction, "Beware of newly invented matters, for every invented matter is an innovation and every innovation is a going astray and every going astray is in Hellfire."[20] They said television would expose the population to alien ideas, erode Muslim culture and doctrine, and violate Islamic prohibitions against representations of people and animals, which derive from the Prophet's ban on idol worship. The religious leaders also feared that television would undermine their monopoly on the faith.

To circumvent these reactionaries, the crafty Faisal at first proceeded cautiously, even duplicitiously. He insisted that the first broadcasts were not broadcasts, they were only tests to see whether television could be useful to the Kingdom. These "tests" consisted almost entirely of prayer, sermons and theological discussions, demonstrating to the religious elders that television could be useful in spreading the message of Islam.[21]

Even so, the introduction of television did not unfold entirely without incident.

The station manager in Jeddah was Paul S. Watson, who was working for NBC International in Barbados when his supervisor asked him whether he was interested in moving to Saudi Arabia. "I was twenty-five years old, married with two children, and I said sure," he recalled. "We got there before it was a fashionable place to be." He said he and his family never were the targets of the opposition to television that he knew existed in Saudi society, and they enjoyed their life in Jeddah. But he recalled that when a transmitter was being built in Buraida, a citadel of backwardness 175 miles northwest of Riyadh, "They built a 300-foot tower and when they got it up there was a huge rainstorm that flooded the town. Some locals said the tower punched a hole in the sky and all this water came down. The minister of information drove up there and got a meeting of all the elders together and said, 'This is ridiculous. Let me tell you what TV can do for you. This, Mr. Religious Leader, is your medium, you can reach more people than in any mosque, you can reach an entire area.'"[22]

A far more serious incident occurred in September 1965, a few months after broadcasts began. Prince Khalid ibn Musaid, an unstable grandson of King Abdul Aziz, joined forces with a group of extremists who believed modernization and innovation had gone too far. "At Koran readings and praying together," Robert Lacey wrote, "the little group of militants had worked themselves up to a holy fury, and now they planned to throw themselves upon the idolatrous foreign equipment." They attacked the television station and spurned an emissary from the king who carried an invitation to them to discuss their grievances. On orders from the king, the police then stormed the station. When Khalid pulled out a revolver, the officer in charge shot Prince Khalid dead.[23]

That was the end of organized resistance to television, but not the end of the episode. A decade later, Prince Khalid's younger brother assassinated King Faisal.

Today, television is ubiquitous in Saudi Arabia. The government network has been fully operated and maintained by Saudis, without American assistance, since about 1970. Its programs are still conservative and, to a Western viewer, mostly quite dull (except perhaps for professional wrestling, which quickly gained popularity).[24] News broadcasts avoid all controversy. But the people of Saudi Arabia are no longer dependent on the government network; satellite television has opened the world to them.

Satellite is both a positive and a negative development. It has given the people of Saudi Arabia nearly unfettered access to the rest of the world and freed them from dependence on their own restricted media. Through satellite television and the Internet, ideas and information are flowing into the country. But ideas and information can be dangerous, as the Saudis learned when their renegade countryman, Osama bin Laden, appeared on the al-Jazeera satellite channel and imparted his message of hatred. It cannot be assumed that the people of Saudi Arabia will embrace what they learn about the world from satellite television and the Internet. They could just as well decide to tune it out and seek the shelter of reaction and xenophobia against the dangerous minds assaulting them from outside. They may decide that isolation from the world and domestic tranquility are preferable to involvement and upheaval. And to the extent that Arab satellite networks present an inflammatory picture of the struggle between Israel and the Palestinians, the Saudis' growing access to information may be more curse than blessing for Americans.

CHAPTER 7

Come Fly With Me

BORED AND RESTLESS IN A dead-end job at the New York office of Trans World Airlines, Dick Margrave was looking for adventure. He wanted to get out of Dodge, go someplace new and different. It was late 1967 and TWA, which in those days was a powerhouse of international aviation, was expanding its support operations in remote outposts in Africa, Asia, and the Middle East. Flying to these destinations, company officials recognized, required the training of local personnel, construction of facilities, and even direct investment in local carriers—"a private version of the Marshall plan for the development of aviation," as a company history put it.[1]

This global buildup provided the opportunity Margrave was looking for: an assignment as crew scheduler for fast-growing Saudi Arabian Airlines, which TWA was managing. Single and unattached, he had nothing to keep him in New York, so he took off for Jeddah; there, he joined TWA colleagues who were flying the planes, training Saudi flight and ground crews, and managing the airline's front office. The airline of Howard Hughes was converting Saudi Arabia from a one-aircraft aviation backwater into a regional aviation leader complete with international routes, a modern fleet, and lavish airports. No longer a desert hardship post, Saudi Arabia by then had modern facilities and a lively, growing international community; the idea of going there for fun was no longer outlandish.

Margrave's job was to compile and enforce work schedules for pilots and flight attendants. That is a difficult task at any large airline; at Saudia, as the airline was then known, it was especially difficult because the airline had a diverse fleet, including piston-driven aircraft as well as jets, and not all pilots were qualified to fly all planes. Moreover, Margrave recalled, the pilots were about 60 percent Saudi and 40 percent American, some of whom worked well together, some of whom did not. "Some of the American pilots were jealous that the Saudi pilots were as capable as they were," Margrave said. "My impression was that as more Saudi pilots became qualified, there would be fewer jobs for American pilots."[2]

The flight attendants, being female, were all non-Saudis; they came from Lebanon, Egypt, France, and some Asian countries. Not all of them spoke Arabic, but each crew had to include Arabic speakers.

On the other hand, "There was no danger of work stoppages," Margrave said. "People would have been sent home." This being Saudi Arabia, work rules were imposed, not negotiated.

His biggest problem was that most of his crews did not have telephones at home to receive notices about assignments or schedule changes. "We had to have drivers carry hand written messages to individuals," he said.

Margrave stayed in Jeddah more than five years, and he remembered that period as a highlight of his career with TWA. "It turned out to be the best thing I did," he said. "A number of Saudi pilots entertained me in their homes, they sort of adopted me. I liked them; they were well-qualified and showed up on time." With a busy social life and frequent swimming expeditions to the Red Sea beaches popular with Jeddah's expatriate community, it was a pleasant life, and well-paid, too.

"The perks were plentiful. Not only were the homes furnished free, but there were no utility bills and gas was only fifteen cents a gallon. The automobiles were free, too," as one airline chronicler wrote.[3] Hundreds of TWA employees shared this experience over nearly four decades as the American airline built its Saudi Arabian client into the largest carrier in the Middle East.

The public documentary record of TWA's involvement with Saudi Arabia is thin. Nevertheless, enough information is available from TWA personnel who participated in the Saudi Arabia project and from the little that has been written to establish that it was American expertise, American equipment, and American training that enabled the Saudis to move from camel travel to jet travel in virtually no time, and to achieve a prominent position among contemporary airlines.

‿͡ᔆ

Saudi Arabia came late to the aviation age. Before the end of World War II, only a few Saudis had even a glancing acquaintance with aircraft. King Abdul Aziz himself had seen one fly during a visit to Kuwait in 1916.[4] British seaplanes provided some support to the Arabs of Hijaz during their uprising against the Ottoman Turks during World War I. In 1927, British Royal Air Force planes bombed Saudi raiders who attacked a British-built police post deep inside Iraq. Aramco imported a Fairchild 71 monoplane to augment its geological exploration with aerial photography. With his first revenue from the oil concession, the king had acquired a few British fighter planes, along with British crews to fly and maintain them. An Italian warplane, aiming to strike at a refinery in British-controlled Bahrain in 1940, mistakenly bombed Dhahran instead. But the story of civil aviation in Saudi Arabia did not begin until February 14, 1945, at President Roosevelt's famous meeting with the king aboard an American cruiser in the Suez Canal. The president's gift to the king was a DC-3 Dakota, a two-engine, propeller-driven workhorse of the type that was a mainstay of early commercial fleets in the United States.

"A TWA captain, Joe Grant, flew the DC over there," a historian of TWA wrote, "and for the next thirty years Saudi Arabia became a place to live and work for hundreds of TWA people—at one time TWA had more than three hundred maintenance personnel alone assigned to the Saudi Arabia mission, plus two hundred more in sales, pilot training, in-flight service, reservations and passenger handling."[5]

Saudi Arabia's vast size and lack of roads made the need for an airline obvious, but the king wanted it for another reason as well: to expedite pilgrimage travel for Muslims from nearby countries. The Hajj was arduous, and the king—who in those days still collected taxes from each pilgrim—wanted to make it easier for the faithful to reach Mecca. Without airports other than the American facility at Dhahran, and lacking pilots and mechanics, the Kingdom could not create an airline without help.

TWA had its own reasons for wishing to establish a relationship with Saudi Arabia. In 1945, the Civil Aeronautics Board, which then regulated U.S. airlines, granted TWA a certificate to fly extensive international routes, including service to India. The following spring, the American diplomatic legation in Jeddah informed Washington that "the Transcontinental and Western Air Co. (TWA) has indicated its desire to begin air services from Cairo to Bombay via Dhahran beginning on June 17, 1946."[6] A few weeks later, Crown Prince Faisal and a representative of the airline signed an agreement authorizing TWA to carry passengers, freight, and mail from the United States to Dhahran and onward for two years.

The airline wasted no time in commencing service. The Aramco company newspaper *Sun and Flare* reported that "on July 5, 1946, a group of spectators watched curiously as Trans World Airlines inaugural flight from Washington, D.C., landed at Dhahran at 8:36 A.M. The flight, a DC-4, had left Washington July 2 and had taken 41 hours 15 minutes to make the trip," with stops at Gander, Shannon, Paris, Rome, and Cairo.[7] This service put TWA into competition with Aramco, which used its own fleet of passenger planes to transport its American workers to and from New York. Not until 1961 did Aramco give up its international passenger service.

As always, the Saudis wanted something in exchange for granting access, in this case help with developing a Saudi state airline. On September 28, 1946, TWA agreed to create "a government-owned Saudi Arabian Airlines to be managed and operated by TWA for a period of five years. The airline was to provide air transport services within Saudi Arabia and between Saudi Arabia and other countries."[8] That five-year commitment turned out to last more than three decades.

The U.S. government wanted TWA to be successful in this venture for reasons that had little to do with the convenience of Saudi travelers.

As a 1951 State Department document laying out U.S. policy toward the Kingdom put it,

> We support TWA in its management of the Saudi Arabian Airline so long as the relations of this company with Saudi Arabia remain in conformity with US aviation and political policy. We desire to press the negotiation of a civil air agreement and to ease the present restrictive regulations against air traffic in connection with Israel. We also want to negotiate a long term Dhahran Air Base agreement to replace the short term arrangement now existing. We are agreeable to the continuation of American technical and managerial assistance to the Saudi Arabia Airlines. We wish to encourage Saudi Arabia to develop its aviation facilities and to establish an adequate civil aviation department, possibly with some American advisory personnel. We also want to advance a training program for Saudi Arabs in aeronautics.

These aims were to be codified in a bilateral civil aviation agreement negotiated that year.[9]

Developing a domestic air carrier in Saudi Arabia presented unique difficulties even apart from the collective ignorance of machines and technology among the Saudi population.

First, the king, who loved traveling in his gift airplane—fitted with a special throne that rotated so he could always face Mecca—insisted on full control. He had been furious when the original Aramco Fairchild had landed without permission when it arrived in 1934, and he had apparently not forgotten the incident. According to Ambassador J. Rives Childs, "As long as King Ibn Saud lived, not a plane was permitted to take off even on scheduled operation without his express approval."[10] Because the airline initially was part of the Ministry of Defense and Aviation, there was no disputing the king's authority.

Moreover, the king and some of the princes tended to use the planes as their private carriers, just as they had long done with the Aramco fleet. "It was not unusual," Childs noted, "for a commercial flight to be diverted to accommodate some member of the royal family or a minister." Dick Margrave encountered this same phenomenon when he was responsible for the schedules more than twenty years later. "We did sometimes have to juggle schedules for royals who wanted a plane," he said.[11] (Nowadays, the king and senior princes have their own planes, which fly out of separate "Royal Terminals" at the principal airports.)

The Saudi public had to be educated about how to travel on a common carrier. Conditioned to bargain and haggle over every purchase, they did not embrace the concept of fixed ticket prices. During the early years, some passengers attempted to light cooking fires on board to prepare their own food.

The airline was also ill-equipped to communicate with the armies of passengers who poured into the Kingdom's overwhelmed airports as the oil boom developed, or with the staffs of public agencies and other companies providing airport services. As late as 1981, when Phil Holcomb gave up a comfortable job as deputy director of Honolulu's airport to supervise the opening of Jeddah's new terminal, there were "seventeen computer systems to run things, none of them coordinated together—fire alarms, flight information, catering, everybody was selling these guys something, it was unbelievable." Hired by Bechtel, which had a management contract for all the airports, Holcomb and his team found Saudia lacked a coordinated system for organizing flight information and getting it onto departure boards and public address systems.[12]

Another problem TWA faced was that nobody in the Kingdom knew what time it was, or rather there were multiple times. According to a Ford Foundation study, the people of Arabia traditionally set clocks to 12:00 each evening at sunset, but of course in a country as big as Saudi Arabia the sun set at different times in different cities. There was no standardized time system for the government. The study also found that, at the airline, "timetables are based on GMT [Greenwhich Mean Time, the worldwide standard] but reservations clerks quote aircraft departures in sun time. Employees arrive at work according to sun time, but leave work according to airline [GMT] time." This problem plagued the airline until 1964, when the Kingdom adopted a solution proposed by Ford Foundation consultants: The Council of Ministers promulgated a decree setting GMT + 3 as the official time throughout the Kingdom and ordering radio stations to announce the time every half hour.[13]

The Ford study remarked that "Time is a major economic asset." That concept would have been utterly foreign to the bedouin, but TWA succeeded in implanting among its Saudi employees the under-standing that time discipline is essential to running an airline. Of course, the airline tried to accommodate its workers' desire to stop work in response to the muezzin's call to prayer—except when they were air-borne—but for the most part religion did not interfere with running the airline, former TWA employees said.

Larry Hecker, a native of City Island in the Bronx who was Saudia's chief pilot in the 1970s, said he could recall only one incident in which the demands of religion disrupted airline operations. A Saudi pilot brought a full plane in for a landing at Jeddah shortly before sunset, when the holy month of Ramadan would begin. The airport was crowded and no debarkation gates were available, but the pilot was de-termined to arrive at his home before darkness fell. "So this guy gets out of his seat, goes to the door, pops the emergency chute. He slides down with his suitcase, strides off across the tarmac, leaves all his passengers and flight crew on board," Hecker recalled.

This presented a real dilemma: "If you don't show him there's a higher authority in the airline he has to answer to, you have a discipline problem. If you come down on him very hard, you're penalizing him for practicing his religion." Hecker wanted to bust the man back to co-pilot, but his Saudi colleagues talked him out of it; he settled for a two-week suspension.[14]

Years after the Ford study, TWA's schedule discipline was held up as a model for the country by Khaled Al Maeena, editor-in-chief of the English-language *Arab News,* who feared it would erode as Saudis with more casual attitudes increasingly took over management of the airline.

"Let me conclude by telling you about Saudia in the 1970s when TWA's influence was strong," he wrote in a 2002 column. "All heads of departments were in by 7:59 A.M. In fact, it was a shame for anyone, Saudis or others, to arrive at their office after 8:00 A.M. . . . The Saudia staff of that era came early, not out of fear but because they had bosses who were there with them all the time. In those days Saudia employees took pride in their work. I hate to consider what the situation at the airline is now."[15]

As the airline grew, TWA became a major presence in Jeddah. It developed a housing compound for the American staff and a school for their children, which evolved into the principal international school for the entire Western community; some TWA wives found work there. Eventually TWA acquired its own office building near Jeddah's old airport, a high-rise structure in green glass known as the "Jolly Green Giant." As the airline quickly expanded its fleet and its route system, TWA personnel performed more duties. Five four-engine DC-4s were acquired in 1952, and two years later the airline purchased ten Convair 340s, which, it says, were its first pressurized aircraft. In 1961, Saudia became the first Middle Eastern airline to operate passenger jets. It expanded its routes as fast as aircraft and trained crews became available.

At first, almost all the pilots were Americans, but the Saudi presence in the cockpit expanded as TWA selected some bright high school graduates for pilot training in the United States. Other Saudi pilots were trained by the Royal Saudi Air Force, which itself was trained by Americans.

"Most of the early pilots were trained by the Saudi air force on single engine planes," said Hecker, a TWA veteran who became Saudia's chief pilot in the 1970s. "They made the transition to the DC-3 and the DC-4. These kids had no education at all—the vice president of flight operations literally was leading a camel around by the nose before he started. He was almost illiterate, but he had a certain innate feeling for an airplane. He understood technology and he could assimilate information very quickly."[16]

Behind that first group, Hecker said, came a second wave who were high school graduates. This was the cohort TWA sent to the United States to learn to fly jets, beginning with the Boeing 737.

Hecker said he found "enormous strife" among the airline's three groups of pilots—the Saudis, the TWA team, and a roster of Americans hired on contract from here and there—but he added, "We tried to make it as seamless as possible. We tried to make the Saudi operation the same as or better than any of the competitors. And we succeeded."

Hecker was working as a TWA flight manager at New York's John F. Kennedy Airport in 1974 when he was asked to go to Saudi Arabia and help the Saudis with the crucial transition to the wide-bodied jets that would "bring them into today's world of aviation."

"How much time do I have to make up my mind?" he asked the manager who offered him the assignment. "He said, 'Right now,' and I said 'I really should call my wife and discuss it with her.' He said, 'You have time for one phone call,'" Hecker recalled.

"So I called Claire and told her. Her dad was a World War I professional military man, she's hardened and adventuresome, so I said [to my supervisor], 'OK, we'll go, with one proviso: We go over and take a look.' But we both knew we were committed to go over. I couldn't turn it down."

As chief pilot, Hecker was Number Two in the TWA hierarchy in Jeddah; he reported to another American who was director of flight operations. "My boss brought his wife over," Hecker recalled, "and his wife was a typical American gal, she didn't like it, it was too hot and on and on, he lasted ten months. So when he left, he said, 'Well, you're going to become the big boss now,' so I moved up a notch and became the head of all flight operations, scheduling, training, everything."

In that ten-month period, Hecker said, he identified a "really capable" Saudi pilot, whom he installed to replace himself as chief pilot upon his promotion. "Politically it was great," Hecker said. "That was a terrific thing in the eyes of the Saudis: TWA identified one of us and put him in as chief pilot." That was Captain Ahmed Mattar, who later became director general of the airline and ran it for fifteen years.

Hecker's biggest task was to shepherd the airline through its acquisition of the Lockheed L-1011, its first wide-body jets, and then the Boeing 747, which is still the mainstay of Saudia's international fleet. But first he had to get rid of the pilots who were alcoholics.

"Some of those American crews had fallen into decay," he said. "They were alcoholics and made *sadiki*. The Saudis knew who was making *sadiki*, they knew who was buying 100-pound bags of sugar," Hecker said. "As long as you don't sell it to Saudis, that's fine. But there were some guys who really got themselves in trouble."

Slim Morgan, a TWA maintenance supervisor who was in Jeddah for ten years, recalled that in addition to making alcohol, some TWA personnel imported contraband hams, labeled "reindeer," and pork sausages concealed inside turkeys. "Our wives would even wrap sliced bacon in Saran Wrap and hide it in their bras to smuggle through customs," he said. "We called it 'breast of bacon.'"[17]

He, too, recalled that the Saudis were aware the TWA people were brewing bootleg liquor "because we'd go to the market and buy 200 pounds of sugar. But as long as you didn't get greedy and start selling the stuff to cab drivers, they didn't object."

The booze problem was not uncommon among old propeller plane jockeys who found homes at airlines in developing countries; I encountered alcoholic French pilots on Royal Air Lao out of Vientiane, in Indochina. But Hecker said he was not going to put up with it.

He made an example of one of his pilot instructors—"a real Huckleberry Finn type, everybody loved him"—who was caught twice smuggling whiskey into the country. The first time he got off with a reprimand; the second time, Hecker sent him home.

"I was extraordinarily strict with the people I brought over there," he said. "I brought over a ton of pilots, as instructors. I brought six initially, and then the airline was growing so fast we brought in TWA line pilots. They were given an indoctrination before they came over on what life was like in Saudi Arabia. The big thing was, do not bring alcohol in. You can find ways to get it once you're in there, you can make it yourself, but don't sell it to Saudis."

Aside from alcohol, Hecker said, "The wives were the key" to a successful tenure. "The wives have to behave themselves. You live with the culture. Some of the American wives said, 'Why can't I drive?' or 'I was down at the *souk* and this guy came up and smacked me on the bottom with his club.' We'd say all right, you went through indoctrination, what were you told? You're a guest in their country." The women who couldn't handle it were sent home, he said.

Despite these difficulties, Hecker recalled, "for the most part our guys kept their noses clean and made an enormous contribution to the airline. They bonded very well with the Saudis. We griped and grumbled, but they saw a different way of doing things. There was an atmosphere of 'We can get this accomplished,' and they did."

~∽

One pilot on Hecker's team, Bob Trojan, was assigned to make sure that Saudia pilots were capable of flying Boeing 737s on their own. The qualification program was based on TWA's own and used TWA manuals, he said, but required twice as much in-flight checking time.

He said the Saudis chose young men in their mid-teens as potential civilian pilots—based on what he called "political connections"—and sent them to the United Kingdom for initial training. About 10 percent survived that first round, Trojan said, and were then sent to the United States for instrument training. "The Saudi Arabian philosophy was never to start a man in the flight engineer's seat, always in the co-pilot's seat," which meant they would not go into the Saudia cockpit on active duty until they were fully qualified to fly the aircraft. "By the time I got them, they were in their mid-twenties. They were pretty well Westernized, they'd met a lot of girls in England," he said, and they were competent pilots who had completed at least 2,000 hours of flying time.

He was in Saudi Arabia for three years, always on the TWA payroll. All the TWA pilots were there on contracts that allowed them to go home at any time, he said, and many left early because they "found the culture distasteful." He took the other fork in that road: He brought over his wife and son, cultivated Saudi friends, and made a point of seeing the country. On flights heading north from Jeddah, he said, the pilots would sometimes fly low to examine the ruins of the old Hijaz railroad, the Ottoman line connecting Damascus and Medina, which had been destroyed in the Arab uprising led by T. E. Lawrence during World War I. "You can still see the blasted-out cars on the ground," he said.[18]

Today, Saudi Arabian Airlines is an immense full-service carrier offering an extensive network of domestic and international routes that carry about 14 million passengers a year. Aside from the prayer broadcast into the cabin on takeoff and the absence of alcohol from the drinks cart, it's pretty much like any other large international airline;

the safety record is good, ground staffs are competent, and cabin service is adequate. The airline runs its own food service and offers vegetarian meals, salt-free meals, meals for diabetics and ulcer patients, and food services for the blind, with menus and labels in Braille. In 2001, the airline completed a major expansion through the acquisition of twenty-three Boeing 777s, five Boeing 747-400s, and twenty-nine McDonnell Douglas MD-90s, a $7.5-billion package that raised the fleet to a total of 137 aircraft, all American made except for eleven Airbus A-300s. The original DC-3, Roosevelt's gift to the king, remained in service, flying the short Dhahran-Bahrain hop, until 1975.

According to a company statement, "The Airline has reached 99.6 percent Saudization in its sales and ground services staff, followed by 96.4 percent in executive and supervisory posts. More than 81 percent of its engineers and 77 percent of its pilots are Saudis." The airline now runs its own training programs.[19] Its maintenance shop is the only one in the Middle East certified by the U.S. Federal Aviation Administration for "full-scale airframe, engine, avionics, and electronics overhaul and maintenance for all major jet aircraft."[20]

The airline flies to New York, Washington, Johannesburg, Singapore, Jakarta, and Dakar, as well as to a dozen cities in Europe, most Arab capitals, and all principal towns in the Kingdom. It is not profitable because it must operate a subsidized housing compound for the foreign women it still recruits as flight attendants—and will continue to recruit until Saudi women are permitted to take those jobs—and because domestic and pilgrimage fares are kept artificially low by order of the king. Independent of the Ministry of Defense and Aviation since 1963 but still state-owned, the airline is theoretically slated to be privatized. To make money, however, private owners would have to raise domestic and pilgrimage fares dramatically or negotiate a subsidy from the government.

TWA, of course, no longer exists, having filed for bankruptcy and been absorbed by American Airlines, and there is virtually no trace of it in Saudi Arabia. Unlike the American oil companies that were parents to Saudi Aramco and are still featured proudly in official histories, TWA has been expunged from the corporate memory of Saudi Arabian Airlines. The historical chronology on the airline's Web site does not even mention TWA, nor does the carrier's name appear in the airline's official history, written on commission by R.E.G. Davies, an aviation history specialist at Washington's Air and Space Museum, and published in 1995; the book says only that "Training of aircraft specialists could not keep pace with heavy demands, and for many years Saudi Arabian Airlines was assisted by foreign technicians and specialists."[21] When I visited the Jeddah headquarters of Saudi Arabian Airlines in the fall of 2002, staff members told me they could find no records of the airline's association with TWA.

CHAPTER 8

A Ford in Their Past

IN AMERICA, THE WORD "BUREAUCRAT" is a pejorative term, evoking images of unproductive paper-pushers who take the taxpayers' money to throw obstacles in the way of commerce. We Americans have the luxury of maligning bureaucrats with such caricatures because we take them for granted; we expect that public servants will report for work and perform their duties, that the census will be taken, water will flow when we turn on the tap, building permits will be issued, restaurants will be inspected, textbooks will be distributed in schools, streets will be paved, outbreaks of disease will be controlled, airports will be operated safely, cargoes coming into our ports will be inspected and appropriate duties levied. In Saudi Arabia, there were no such expectations as the country entered the modern era. The Kingdom had a desperate need of the people we deride as "bureaucrats": competent, honest civil servants who would conduct the daily business of government. The task of running a complex modern state was not only beyond the Saudis' competence, it was beyond their comprehension.

In the lifetime of King Abdul Aziz, the monarch was the state; the mission of his inner circle of advisers was to impose his will upon the citizenry. The only law was the law of Islam, as interpreted by the extremely conservative and narrow-minded *ulama,* or senior religious authorities. Decrees were issued and government departments were nominally created, but that was not the same as having an organized state apparatus. Rodger Davies, who in 1948 was a junior political officer at the U.S. Embassy in Jeddah, described this phenomenon in a landmark study:

> It would be dangerous to read too much into a compilation of the official decrees bearing on the development of the state. Such a compilation may easily create an impression of an orderly arranged political machinery with precisely defined functions for its component parts. Such a tidy arrangement of governmental organization does not exist in Saudi Arabia; the idea of a devolution of governmental power and administrative functions upon ministers and directors-general with large staffs of administrators and clerks maintaining files and records is foreign to the traditions and historical development of the country. All authority stems from the King and even minor questions are referred to the King and his Council for decision.[1]

This system enabled Abdul Aziz to cement his authority over the country's diverse population of nomads, traders, and fishermen. Absent roads, electricity, schools, hospitals, and telephones, the only truly nationwide functions of the central government were to collect taxes and to maintain an army, both of which further consolidated the power of the House of Saud.

Communication other than face-to-face was virtually nonexistent. Only gradually did Abdul Aziz learn that the people he ruled had expectations, and this was through stories brought back by the agents he dispatched around his huge domain to ensure that the dictates of Islam were enforced. "Handsome men rode patient camels over dangerous deserts to strengthen the enforcement of Islamic law," one American chronicler wrote. "They brought back information about the need for more water, for improved food supply, for better trails for pilgrims from other countries, and for Saudis, for medical services and for trade goods."[2]

Except in the Eastern Province, where he relied on Aramco to deliver education and health care to the local population, the king could not have met these aspirations for public services, even had he been so inclined. The problem was not just a shortage of money; it was a nearly complete lack of the administrative apparatus necessary to plan, build, and maintain public facilities and to operate government agencies that could let contracts, provide public service, and anticipate development needs. Only in 1953, the year of his death, did Abdul Aziz establish ministries of communication, education, and agriculture and water, as well as a Council of Ministers intended to address the growing needs of an increasingly complex society; but as Davies had observed five years before, establishing ministries was not the same thing as establishing functioning public service agencies. In 1963, the Ford Foundation took on this daunting task.

Ford, one of the largest and most ambitious of the charitable foundations established by American business tycoons, was interested in promoting modernization in Third World countries, including the Middle East, and maintained a regional office in Beirut, Lebanon. It first considered working in Saudi Arabia in response to a proposal from Aramco in the early 1950s. Aramco was under pressure to provide schools for Arab children, and, as usual, was reluctant to take on responsibilities unrelated to the oil business. Aramco proposed that Ford develop a demonstration group of schools and train teachers for them; Aramco would pay for it, and would provide an equal amount of money for projects elsewhere in the Middle East.

Saud, then crown prince, vetoed the project because he did not want curricula for Saudi children to be developed by foreigners and non-Muslims.[3] Ford, however, remained interested in working in Saudi Arabia and in 1954 approached Prince Saud again through the intervention of Karl Twitchell. That was the year in which John J. McCloy— former president of the World Bank, former U.S. administrator of postwar Germany, and renowned cold warrior—became president of the Foundation, eager as he was to use its assets to shape the developing world to American interests. During that year, Rowland Egger, the Foundation's regional director, traveled from Beirut to meet Saud, who had become king after the death of his father. In a follow-up letter, he proposed a list of possible Ford projects.[4]

While in Saudi Arabia, Egger met with U.S. Ambassador George Wadsworth, who encouraged Ford to become involved with the Kingdom; but he advised, according to an internal Foundation narrative, that "we ought to be very careful to keep whatever program we eventually decided to cooperate with in Saudi Arabia simple enough to be understood, small enough to be doable within a relatively short period, and obvious enough so that the benefits it conferred could be plainly seen." He pointed out that the Saudis, like other Middle Easterners, "were happy to be in a position to blame their own inadequate performance on others."[5] Ford would have done well to heed Wadsworth's advice.

Ford offered to provide assistance in "six major areas of program activity": economic planning, organization and methods; budgeting, accounting and auditing, personnel administration, public works, and training.[6] But these were concepts beyond the ability of the incompetent Saud to comprehend. So vague was his grasp of what Ford was offering that he thought the Foundation was proposing to take over the operations of Aramco.[7]

Because of Saud's profligacy and incompetence, and his decade-long power struggle with Faisal, nothing came of Ford's interest in Saudi Arabia until the early 1960s. At the time, the country was receiving most of its assistance with governmental operations from the Egyptians, which—as anyone who has experienced the nightmare of the Egyptian bureaucracy could have told the Saudis—was a prescription for disarray. In effect, the country squandered a decade. Fast-growing oil revenue that could have been used for the orderly development of infrastructure and public service was dissipated by Saudi involvement in the civil war in Yemen, royal extravagance, and ill-advised, wasteful projects that soaked up cash to little public benefit. Faisal's desire to balance the budget and impose fiscal discipline could not be reconciled with Saud's desire to rule in the patriarchal, imperious style of his father; Saud was still dispensing largesse to tribes and sheikhs to ensure their loyalty.

Yet in that same period, the first generation of Western-educated young Saudi technocrats was coming of age and beginning to assume positions of responsibility. One of them was Hassan Mishari, deputy minister of finance, who had worked for Aramco and earned an MBA degree from the University of Southern California. On his initiative, the government created an Institute of Public Administration to train civil servants. To run it, he appointed Muhammad Abalkhail, another up-and-comer, later to be finance minister. The government agreed to put up $2 million for this venture. Ford selected a group called the Institute of International Organization to operate it, and agreed to provide a "public administration specialist" as an adviser and contracting officer. The first course convened in August 1962.[8]

Two months later, Faisal returned to de facto control of the government as prime minister.

Unlike Saud, the shrewd and visionary Faisal possessed a keen sense of the country's needs and the government's inadequacy. Where else would he turn for the help he wanted and advisers he trusted but to the United States and American institutions? By 1963, American institutions public and private—Aramco, Bechtel, TWA, the United States Air Force, the Corps of Engineers—had established credibility and good faith in Saudi Arabia. Faisal was smart enough to see that Ford could be useful. When McCloy visited him in March 1963, the king urged the head of the Ford Foundation "to permit the Foundation to assume a central role in assistance to Saudi Arabia. Although the Saudi government had funds to finance a reform program, it lacked the capacity to organize and direct such an effort."[9]

In that critical period of the Cold War, when Saudi Arabia represented a bastion against growing Communist influence in the Middle East, McCloy may have been eager to establish Ford in the Kingdom, but it was not an easy decision for the Foundation precisely because Saudi Arabia—unlike other countries of the developing world—had the money to pay for its own modernization. "Saudi wealth was an issue with the Foundation in the early 1960s, when assistance was first requested," according to a key internal evaluation of Ford's program. "The Foundation's decision to work in Saudi Arabia was delayed for years because of it."[10] This ambivalence is reflected throughout the records of Ford's work in Saudi Arabia; projects were constantly undercut by the Foundation's reluctance to commit its own resources and by a general disdain for Saudi participants in Ford Foundation projects.

On October 15, 1963, the Ford Foundation and Saudi Arabia signed a formal, wide-ranging agreement providing for Ford to help the Saudis establish a functioning government. Ford's role was to provide assistance in "training the personnel needed to properly staff the civil service; improving the organization and procedures of existing governmental agencies; creating certain new agencies and institutions; transferring functions between agencies; and finally helping to develop the government's capacity to plan and implement programs and projects."[11] Under these broad outlines there were specific objectives, such as developing realistic capital and operating budgets, standardizing the accounting of the Kingdom's revenue, standardizing government forms and reports, and implementing a government-wide payroll system.

The king created a "High Committee for Administrative Reform," chaired by his brother Prince Sultan, to work with the Ford consultants. As Ford's consultants were later to realize, "Administrative Reform" was a misnomer. Reform implies that existing institutions are to be improved, but in truth there were no existing institutions. What was needed was "administrative development," virtually from the ground up.[12]

The original "program plan" for Ford's work contained this caution: "The Ford Foundation recognizes that it cannot and should not plan, budget, train personnel, or build institutions and procedures for the Government of Saudi Arabia. The Foundation can only assist the Government to do these things."[13] Yet, as many later documents and self-evaluations in the Ford archives make clear, there was a fundamental misunderstanding between Ford and the Saudis on this point: The Saudis, accustomed to hiring outsiders to do their important work, expected Ford to carry out whatever recommendations it made, but Ford wanted the Saudis to take charge of their own system. It took the members of Ford's team the better part of a decade to recognize that they had wildly overestimated the ability—and the desire—of the Saudis to run a competent government. Ford went through a ten-year reality check that ultimately led the Foundation to reexamine its entire approach to developmental assistance.

On one level, according to Ford analyses, Saudi Arabia ought to have been an ideal laboratory for an experiment in creating a public service system in a virtual vacuum. With each passing day, more young Saudis were being educated. The country had not only money but also a leader who was willing to change what was clearly a dysfunctional system. Faisal, a disciplined and perceptive ruler, had the authority to order implementation of whatever Ford came up with. He detested disorder; he also understood that his country was incapable of deciding how to spend its money effectively, planning and implementing major development projects, or satisfying the growing public appetite for education, health care, agricultural assistance, and transportation. As one perceptive Ford assessment put it: "While large financial resources became available in the 1950s, the Government did not have an organization structure for assuring that funds were used wisely; nor had the culture and harsh conditions prevailing in the country previously prepared its leaders for affluence. They understood and could deal with subsistence. They were not prepared to deal in economic terms with plentiful financial resources."[14]

Not knowing how to allocate resources effectively, the Saudis squandered money on ill-conceived projects that were unrelated to any overall development plan, Ford found. "The new leaders of affluent Saudi Government organizations were totally unprepared to assess the validity of the mass of development proposals which flooded Riyadh and Jeddah after the oil began to flow," according to Ford's assessment. As a result, "They were sold turn-key Texas farms; sophisticated irrigation and drainage schemes; Pittsburgh factories; London and American universities; old Egyptian administration, agriculture, and education; grandiose Greek city plans, and much more. Many of these attempted transplant actions failed to work at all, or at best worked badly. Failure was caused in large measure by a shortage of Saudi manpower qualified to understand, apply or benefit from new technology."[15] The Saudis paid for the construction of impressive buildings, only to discover that "the construction or acquisition of physical facilities does not necessarily imply that important program functions are being performed" inside them.[16]

These were conditions that could be overcome with time, training, and money. More difficult to address, Ford specialists found, were issues of attitude among young Saudis recruited for government service: They cared little about serving the public, were indifferent to caring for public property, and had an exaggerated idea of their own importance. The idea that they would work hard in the interests of people they had never met—that is, most of their fellow citizens—was alien to them. The harsh language on this subject that appears throughout Ford's internal memoranda of that period reflects its specialists' growing frustration.

"There exists in this country a serious personal motivational problem related to undesirable attitudes toward care of public and private property, quality of work, integrity, accepting responsibility, serving the public, working in private industry, accepting change, etc.," one memorandum said. "The foremost problem facing the Kingdom may well be to modify the value system as it relates to achieving appropriate personal enlightenment."[17]

"The average civil servant is poorly educated, incompetent, underemployed, given to corruption and unwilling to perform useful low-status functions," said another.[18]

These perceptions were not unique to Ford's specialists; they were common knowledge. David Holden, a British journalist who knew the country well, wrote that "the majority of largely illiterate Saudis drifting in from the country had neither the qualification nor the inclination to do anything much more than drive taxis and trucks and become tea-makers or doorkeepers, or find employment in other peripheral occupations that did nothing to reduce dependence on expatriates. The disdain for demeaning manual labor on the part of men of desert origins had become more manifest than ever. It seemed almost intensified by the wealth thrust upon the country and the perceptible feeling that Saudi citizens were God's chosen people."[19] And since half the Saudi population—the female half—was excluded from the labor pool, the quest for talented, dedicated workers was, of course, made even more difficult.

Moreover, access to university education was making these problems worse because the Saudis regarded college degrees as status symbols that opened the door to privilege, not as credentials for serious work.

Saudi Arabia was plagued by "the obsession with degrees as symbols of prestige, regardless of their utility, so that many man-years are devoted to the unnecessary and even counter-productive pursuit of degrees, [and by a] tendency to view a degree as a complete substitute for training and experience," one Ford staffer complained.[20]

Whereas many workers were untrained for the tasks assigned to them, Ford discovered, others were "given more training than is necessary or desirable," including an insistence on advanced degrees at the expense of technical competence.[21] The Saudis could not grasp the notion that a proliferation of doctoral degrees should follow basic economic and governmental development, not precede it. (This remains true to a great extent in Saudi Arabia and throughout the Arab world.)

In addition, Ford consultants encountered a widespread aversion among Saudis to the entire concept of planning. To some, it evoked images of central planning as practiced in Communist countries. To others, planning was suspect for religious reasons. Believing as they did that the future was in the hands of God, they did not appreciate the need for rigorous interagency analysis, based on accurate data, of the country's anticipated needs and how to meet them in a coordinated way. Besides, Saudis like to be able to change their minds; it is inconvenient to have commitments in writing, as many a foreign businessman discovered when trying to enforce a contract.

In one memorable episode, government officials asked to approve the construction of a tomato paste factory based their decision on the estimated cost of input and price of output. They omitted such considerations as whether the foreign workers who would be needed could obtain visas, whether Saudi customs officials could arrange for timely entry of tomato seeds and processing machinery, whether the proposed factory could get electric power and sewer service, the availability of reliable telephone service, and the potential cost of taxes, license fees, and import duties.[22] Ford never found a way to overcome this indifference to coordination and detail, which persisted in the Saudi government until the energetic, talented Hisham Nazer became planning chief in the late 1960s.

The difficulties confronting Ford were not all on the Arab side. The foundation made its own mistakes, beginning with the assignment of the wrong personnel. The first director of the advisory team for the

Institute of Public Administration was Colonel A.S.B. Shah, a Pakistani trained at the British military academy, who "gave almost no attention to the IPA program" and lasted less than a year, according to an internal evaluation by Ford. His successor, Roy Colbert, a former training supervisor for the U.S. Post Office Department, "experienced particular difficulty relating to the Saudis" and was "terminated" in the summer of 1964.[23] Overall, the members of the original Ford group were short-time hires with little or no experience in Saudi Arabia.[24] Of ninety-eight specialists hired, four were fired by Ford and six were terminated at the request of the Saudis. "An additional dozen were considered unqualified for employment on the project," a Ford self-analysis reported. "Terminated and incompetent specialists combined account for approximately 30 percent of all persons recruited."[25]

In addition to being of dubious competence, some of the Ford team irritated their hosts by operating all the lights and air conditioners in their villas all the time, living at Saudi government expense in comfort the Saudis could not replicate. This was part of a long-running dispute over the Ford team's living conditions that caused "disruptions in sensitive relationships," Ford later acknowledged.[26]

The foundation struggled against these obstacles for four discouraging years of mounting frustration and limited achievement. The Institute of Public Administration was deemed relatively successful as the annual number of graduates rose from 52 in the first year to more than 1,400 by the end of the 1960s, but Ford's effort to create a national merit-based civil service system went nowhere. When the Saudis created a Central Personnel Bureau, theoretically responsible for recruiting and assigning workers government-wide and setting uniform pay grades, Ford supported it and trained its staff in recruiting techniques. Once trained, however, these workers had nothing to do "because the Bureau did not have legal authority to direct recruitment," Ford learned. Its director, Omar Zeini, lacked the stature to impose his authority on other government agencies, so they continued to hire their workers separately. In Saudi Arabia, a Ford retrospective analysis observed, "the effectiveness of a program seems to depend more upon the power and prestige of the individual heading the program than upon the power and prestige of the position which he occupies."[27] Moreover, the directors of individual government departments had a strong disincentive to cooperating with the Personnel Bureau: They were competing against each other for the Kingdom's scarcest resource, skilled manpower.

In another setback, Ford drafted and submitted to the High Committee a 39-page, 34-article "proposed personnel law for the Kingdom of Saudi Arabia," but it was never promulgated by the government.[28]

Faced with all these difficulties, Ford retrenched at the end of 1967. It reduced the size of its team, gave up on government-wide programs, and, in 1968, adopted a new strategy of working only with ministries and agencies it deemed amenable to progress, which it referred to as "targets of opportunity." These were the ministries of Health, Finance, Education, and Agriculture and Water, Riyadh University, the Central Personnel Bureau, and the Institute of Public Administration. On this new tack, the program began to show results. Some were quite mundane, if necessary, such as the publication of standard specifications for the purchase of office furniture. Others, by Ford's reckoning, were genuine breakthroughs that started Saudi Arabia on a course toward a modern government, beginning with the computerization of personnel records and a system for collecting economic data.

The Saudis, more responsive under Faisal than they had been under Saud, implemented some of Ford's commonsense recommendations, such as transferring responsibility for government-owned experimental farms from the Ministry of Finance to the Ministry of Agriculture.[29] Other Ford recommendations that seemed logical to the Americans, such as the establishment of a department of prisons and corrections and a restructuring of health programs to distinguish the mentally ill from the retarded, were ignored. Why did that happen? "I suspect," Ford staff member Leo C. Pritchard wrote in 1968, "that a great many of the recommendations we have made are somewhat advanced and out-of-step with the government's readiness for them. . . . The Saudis have many problems standing in their way. We cannot always understand them even when we know what they are."[30] The overriding reason was probably, as the American diplomatic analyst David Long noted, that the king, while forward-looking and willing to make changes, "was in no rush to import alien Western political institutions."[31] To the extent that restructuring proposed by foreigners appeared to threaten the Kingdom's fundamental social and religious order, it was unwelcome. That is still true more than three decades later.

ﬡ

Ford's original 1963 agreement with the Kingdom was amended in November 1964 to add that Ford would provide "economic advice to help in the production and implementation of the Economic Plan and Program."[32] In 1967, when at last the king implemented Ford's recommendation to create a Central Planning Organization, its first director, Hisham Nazer, transferred this function from Ford to a new team of advisers from the Stanford Research Institute in California.

Nazer was and is one of the smartest and most successful Saudi technocrats. According to a biographical sketch compiled by Aramco's research department in 1961, he was one of thirteen children. He attended high school at Victoria College in Alexandria, Egypt, an elite school for future stars of the Arab world, where he learned English from British teachers. As a government scholarship student, he earned a bachelor's degree in international relations and a master's degree in political science from the University of California at Los Angeles. "During his sojourn in the United States, he acquired a taste for baseball, movies and other aspects of American culture," the Aramco biographer observed approvingly.[33] (Nazer was minister of planning when I first met him, in 1977. Some years later, as minister of petroleum and minerals, he took me to lunch at a restaurant in Jeddah. To have lunch in a public place in Saudi Arabia with the country's oil minister is to be the target of a hundred curious stares and the subject of a hundred whispers.)

With his appointment as director of the Central Planning Organization in 1967, Nazer inaugurated a cycle of five-year development plans that sought to bring order out of chaos. The first was published in 1970; today, the country is in the middle of the seventh of these plans, which covers the years 2000 to 2004. Over time, these documents have become the principal means by which the Saudi government articulates its development priorities and allocates funds. The first stressed infrastructure development, for example; the second, published at the height of the dizzying oil boom of the 1970s, emphasized social welfare and the development of industry, especially petrochemicals. The seventh, currently in effect, emphasizes diversification and privatization of the economy.

David Long has described these documents as "a combination of wish lists and statements of intent. They are not intended as detailed instructions for budgetary expenditures, nor should they be considered outside the context of the flexible Middle Eastern sense of time. Budget allocations and target dates should be viewed impressionistically rather than literally. The plans, however, are fairly accurate indicators of the direction Saudis believed they should be taking at the time and what lessons they had learned from the previous plan."[34]

One reason to view these plans with some skepticism was that all statistics were suspect, to the extent that there were any statistics. Even census data of dubious accuracy were closely held—so much so that many Americans who lived in Saudi Arabia in the 1970s told me with great assurance that the results of the census taken in 1974 were entirely secret, probably because the government did not want to reveal how few Saudis there actually were. It turned out that this was not true. The Ministry of Finance published the results in an official journal in 1976, and the following year I obtained a copy with little difficulty and wrote an article about it in the *Washington Post*. It showed a total 1974 population of 7,012,642. The suspicious precision of that figure was undermined by the fact that it included resident foreigners without specifying how many there were, which, of course, was a crucial question.[35]

Nevertheless, the creation of the five-year plans represented exactly the sort of interagency long view of the Kingdom's development that Ford's specialists had encouraged. Through the first five of these planning cycles, the Kingdom received advice and technical assistance from economists and administrative specialists dispatched to Saudi Arabia by the Stanford Research Institute—another example of how today's Saudi Arabia was shaped and influenced by Americans.

Stanford Research Institute, now known as SRI International, was a for-profit consulting company created by the trustees of Stanford University. Its board of directors included such prominent figures as A. W. Clausen, president of Bank of America; George Shultz, then president of Bechtel Corporation; and Steve Bechtel himself. It was the Bechtel connection that took SRI to Saudi Arabia, according to Ed Robison, who was a member of the Stanford team for fifteen years.

He said that Nazer, whom he described as "a very nice fellow," learned about SRI from Bechtel. "He came to Stanford one day and wanted to know if we would help them," Robison recalled. "We held his hand all the time" through the development of the first three plans, he said.[36]

The first contract was for "technical assistance to the Central Planning Organization, headed by the young Hisham Nazer. The others were with the Ministry of Planning, headed by a more mature, wiser Hisham Nazer," said William Grindley, another Stanford team member.

Grindley said the team at its largest comprised about twenty-five professionals, mostly "sector specialists" in fields such as transportation and industry. "My own expertise was housing and urban infrastructure," he said. "There was an expert on telecommunications, an expert on highways, an expert on resource development, experts on education and the central banking system. We had no relation to any of the security issues."

The goal, Grindley said, was to "help the Saudis shape allocations at the national level and by province." For each sector, the plans set "a broad framework for priorities," such as which components of a national telecommunications network should be developed first. Most of these decisions were made for technical and economic reasons, but there was also a political component, as would be expected, Grindley said. For example, he said, the third plan allocated disproportionate resources to the restive Shiite communities of the Eastern Province, which the government feared were responding to the lure of the Iranian revolution on the other side of the Gulf.[37]

The amazing amount of cash that flooded into the Kingdom after the oil price surge of the early 1970s can be measured by the raw numbers of the first two five-year plans. The first, prepared in the late 1960s to guide development from 1970 through 1974, anticipated a total development expenditure of $9.2 billion. The second, prepared when the torrent of money was at its strongest, called for spending $142 billion in the same amount of time. (The figure for the third plan was $250 billion, but that proved wholly unrealistic when the bottom fell out of oil prices in the 1980s.)

Ghazi al-Gosaibi, who was minister of industry in the 1970s and returned to the cabinet as minister of water in 2002, offered this assessment of what his country was up against in trying to manage its development in the boom years: "Many economists tell us that we cannot compress the century-long process of development—creation of an infrastructure, manpower training, industrialization—into a few decades. But since no nation with our resources has ever tried to do so, no one really knows if it can be done. We shall try," he told Robert D. Crane of *Fortune* magazine in 1978. Crane was reporting from Saudi Arabia at a time when the planning process was imperceptible amid the construction equipment, but it did exist, setting at least notional priorities based on feasibility studies. "The government commissioned so many [feasibility] studies during the formulation of the first and second plans that Planning Minister Nazer was labeled 'Mr. Feasibility,'" Crane reported. "And the Stanford Research Institute, which played a major role in putting together both plans, got to be known as a feasibility factory."[38]

The rise of Nazer and the commencement of interagency planning marked the beginning of the end of the Ford Foundation's involvement in Saudi Arabia. Despite its own mistakes and the endless frustration of Ford team members over Saudi attitudes, the foundation's work was not without results. The government organization chart of 1972 was quite different from the chart of 1964, the changes mostly based on Ford recommendations. The Central Personnel Bureau and Central Planning Organization had been created, and they would work with the Institute of Public Administration. A "Grievance Board" and a "Disciplinary Board" for public employees had been established. There was at last a Central Purchasing Agency. Whereas the 1964 chart showed all agencies reporting directly to the king, the 1972 version showed that they reported through the Council of Ministers, which had its own technical assistance department. The railroad and the national airline had been spun off from cabinet agencies into quasi-independent corporations.

In addition, the government had at last established a central personnel system based at least theoretically on the merit principle, in which jobs were described and salaries set according to uniform criteria. Ford also claimed credit for "Reorganization of the Ministry of Finance, to give greater emphasis, through the newly created position of Minister of State for Finance, to Government effectiveness and efficiency."[39]

Yet the most important changes may have been attitudinal rather than organizational, according to a retrospective analysis by Conrad C. Stucky, Ford's senior program officer. "Accompanying this institutional development has been the evolution of new attitudes by a significant number of young educated Government employees," he wrote in 1972. "This changing mentality has brought the Saudis into a program which has begun to lead to meaningful cooperative involvements. A foundation has been laid for undertaking much useful work; the language of management and development is being mastered; interest has been generated in about a dozen and a half major Government agencies to find way to improve their operations and therefore to increase the pace of development."[40]

Stucky's paper, prepared for a Ford Foundation regional review conference, recommended the phase-out of the Ford program because, he said, the Saudis were now capable of selecting their own advisers and running many of their own programs. Moreover, as Saudi wealth grew, there was less justification for committing Foundation assets to the Kingdom, especially since Foundation officials were finding Saudi Arabia's new technocrats less than grateful. "Like a man who has just won a large pot at poker, the Saudis feel their current position relative to the less fortunate of the world is really more due to personal virtue than to having been dealt four aces," Ford's Courtney A. Nelson wrote to a colleague after visiting the Kingdom in early 1974.[41]

Ford's last American staff member, Wesley Edwards, left Saudi Arabia in July 1976. The Foundation retained an apartment in Riyadh, to which it moved its files, and kept on payroll a driver, a houseboy, and a part-time secretary. This arrangement ended the following year, according to an internal memo to Ford President McGeorge Bundy, who had been President Kennedy's national security adviser. On January 22, 1977, a representative from the Saudi Ministry of Interior arrived at the apartment and told the secretary that all Ford operations were to be shut down and the apartment closed within a week. Requesting an explanation, the secretary was shown a memo from the deputy prime minister to the minister of finance "charging that the Ford foundation was 'an organization with Zionist aims.'" Ford complied with the shutdown order, but also made inquiries about the origin of this absurd accusation. William Porter, the U.S. ambassador at the time, told Ford he thought it was prompted by "our withdrawal a year ago from a project with the Ministry of Foreign Affairs to assist with the design of a new building and organization of the Ministry's function."[42] The documentary record does not explain why Ford pulled out of the Foreign Ministry project.

This episode ended Ford's project in Saudi Arabia on a sour note, but by that time it hardly mattered because the Saudis had imported a new and much larger American organization to help them operate their government ministries and public agencies: The United States Department of the Treasury.

CHAPTER 9

The American Way

THE ARAB-ISRAELI WAR OF October 1973 ignited a period of extreme turbulence in relations between the United States and Saudi Arabia. The Saudis participated only marginally in combat, but, like all Arabs, they supported Egypt and Syria against Israel and its principal international backer, the United States.

Egyptian troops crossed the Suez Canal and attacked Israeli forces on the Sinai peninsula on October 6. Syria attacked simultaneously on Israel's Eastern Front. The Arab armies struck on October 6 because in 1973 that was Yom Kippur, the Jewish day of atonement, and the Israeli Defense Forces were on a low state of alert; many troops had gone home for the holiest day of the Jewish calendar. With the advantage of surprise, the Egyptians and Syrians scored early gains that caused near panic in Jerusalem and Washington, and inspired elation throughout the Arab world.

Even before the war, global oil prices were rising as demand exceeded supply. Producing countries such as Libya and Kuwait were agitating for new arrangements in the oil market that would let them capture some of the surging profits being reaped by the concessionary companies. With the onset of war, the Arab producers seized the opportunity to deploy what came to be known as the "oil weapon": They raised prices and cut production to squeeze the United States and other supporters of Israel.

On October 14, U.S. military planes carrying emergency war supplies landed in Israel, an action that inflamed Arab sentiment. That same day, price negotiations between oil companies and the Organization of Petroleum Exporting Countries (OPEC) broke down. Theoretically, these negotiations were unrelated to the war, but the war had stiffened the negotiating backbones of the Arab producers. Two days later, Iran and the five Arab Gulf states, including Saudi Arabia, announced a 70 percent increase in the posted price, to $5.11 a barrel. As Daniel Yergin noted in his comprehensive history of the oil industry, that was a crucial moment for the oil-producing countries: Not only did they secure a huge surge in their revenue, but they did it on their own, without the consent of the oil companies. The price increase was imposed, not negotiated. "This is a moment for which I have been waiting a long time," said the Saudi oil minister, Ahmed Zaki Yamani. "The moment has come. We are masters of our own commodity."[1] Yet the drama was only beginning.

On October 17, Arab producers agreed to a 5 percent cut in oil production to tighten economic pressure on Israel's supporters, especially the United States. On October 19, President Richard Nixon asked Congress for a new $2.2 billion package of aid for Israel. King Faisal was furious; he had repeatedly warned the United States that overt intervention on the side of Israel would jeopardize American interests throughout the Arab world. The next day, Saudi Arabia and other Arab producers imposed a total embargo on oil shipments to the United States. The news reached Secretary of State Henry A. Kissinger as he was traveling to Moscow to try to arrange a ceasefire in the war, in which the Soviet Union was backing Egypt and Syria. Momentous as these events of October 20 were, they were overshadowed by a political earthquake that struck Washington that same night—the "Saturday Night Massacre" in which Nixon fired Archibald Cox, the special prosecutor investigating the Watergate scandal. The attorney general, Elliot Richardson, and his deputy, William Ruckelshaus, resigned in protest.

The following day, Yamani summoned Frank Jungers, Aramco's president, to tell him that Aramco, still mostly owned by its four American parent companies, would be required to enforce the embargo on shipments to the United States. Aramco thus became the instrument of a policy intended to undermine the economic security of the country in which its majority owners were based and most of their stockholders lived. The embargo cut off what had been a daily oil shipment of 638,500 barrels.

Jungers was personally sympathetic to the Arab position. Earlier that year, he had undertaken an extensive mission back to the United States to meet with other business executives and seek their support for a campaign to moderate U.S. support for Israel and adopt a more "even handed" policy in the Middle East. His message was not overtly anti-Israel, but it stressed the importance of good relations with the Arabs because of American dependence on their oil. To King Faisal, however, this embargo was not about Jungers or the oil companies, it was about American foreign policy. Oil was the biggest weapon at his command; Frank Jungers's personal views were irrelevant because they had not prevailed in Washington. Faisal did not want a complete break with the United States and signaled that by complying with a request from the Pentagon that he permit petroleum products to continue their flow to the U.S. Navy in the Far East; but, as always, he was torn between his desire for good relations with the United States and his visceral antipathy to Israel.

Aramco complied with the boycott because the alternative was immediate nationalization, Jungers said many years later. "There was no doubt about this. We did it in lieu of being nationalized. We had no choice," he said.[2]

The war ended with a ceasefire in place on October 25. Kissinger then undertook his famous "shuttle diplomacy" mission, many weeks of flying from Jerusalem to Damascus and Cairo to broker military disengagement agreements and postwar United Nations resolutions to set the terms for lasting peace. The oil embargo lasted until March 18, 1974, imposing on Americans a dreary winter of waiting hours in gasoline lines and digging deep into their wallets to pay the ever-rising price of a commodity that consumers previously had taken for granted.

Aramco's board of directors meeting alfresco in 1962, when the company was still American-owned. The oil rig behind them is Dammam Number 7, Saudi Arabia's first productive well, which began the country's oil boom by striking oil in 1938. Fourth from left is Ahmed Zaki Yamani, who had just been named minister of petroleum and who orchestrated the nationalization that ended American control of the company.

PHOTOGRAPHER UNKNOWN. ARAMCO PHOTO FROM THE MULLIGAN ARCHIVES, COURTESY GEORGETOWN UNIVERSITY LIBRARY.

As difficult and dangerous as that period was, these events ultimately had a paradoxically positive impact on relations between the United States and Egypt and Saudi Arabia. Diplomatic relations with Cairo, broken during the 1967 war, were resumed, and the United States began supplying economic assistance to Egypt as President Anwar Sadat—having restored Arab honor shattered in 1967 with the initial successful attacks of 1973—realigned his country away from Moscow and toward Washington. With Saudi Arabia, the United States commenced a new phase of cooperation that was to intertwine the two countries in previously unimaginable ways.

The October war, the oil embargo, and the oil price increases imposed by the newly assertive producer countries had greatly elevated Saudi Arabia's strategic importance to Washington. American officials wanted oil price stability. They wanted Saudi Arabia to spend as much of its rapidly increasing wealth as possible in the United States. And they recognized that Saudi Arabia still lacked the governmental competence it needed to manage its money and develop its infrastructure effectively, despite the Ford Foundation's modest accomplishments of the previous decade.

As soon as the oil embargo ended, the United States government began negotiating a wide-ranging and ambitious technical assistance agreement with the Saudis, along with new military training and equipment accords. The most unorthodox outcome was the creation of the United States–Saudi Arabian Joint Commission on Economic Cooperation, an unprecedented venture that would install American government officials directly into the day-to-day workings of Saudi Arabia's ministries, universities, and economic agencies. As David Holden noted, "It was the most far-reaching agreement of its kind ever concluded by the U.S. with a developing country. It had the potential to entrench the U.S. deeply in the Kingdom, fortifying the concept of mutual interdependence," which was exactly Washington's goal.[3]

Prince Fahd traveled to Washington to finalize the agreement in the first week of June; he was accompanied by an A-list roster of technocratic and military talent, including Yamani, planning director Hisham Nazer, and Muhammad Abalkhail, the number two man in the Finance Ministry and soon to become minister.

The following week, President Nixon, nearing the end of a presidency crippled by Watergate, toured the Middle East in his last diplomatic hurrah. His final stop was in Saudi Arabia, where he received a lavish welcome as the first U.S. president to visit. The complete rupture between Washington and Riyadh that had seemed imminent eight months earlier had been averted and the ill feelings generated by the war and the embargo dissipated. Two months later, Nixon resigned and went home to California in disgrace. His successor, Gerald Ford, committed the U.S. government enthusiastically to the program envisioned in the creation of the Joint Commission.

Aramco's Brock Powers may have been the first American to recognize the tidal wave of cash that was going to wash over Saudi Arabia as global oil demand rose in the 1970s. He was working then in Aramco's New York office as liaison officer to the four parent companies: Exxon, Mobil, Texaco, and Chevron, the former SoCal. One of his jobs was to coordinate their "nominations," proprietary projections of how much oil each was planning to lift in the coming month and the coming year. Because the companies would not tell each other for competitive reasons, Powers was the only one who knew. He had to inform Aramco headquarters so that Aramco would know how much to produce.

"So I'm sitting there one month," he recalled, "and I couldn't believe it. The nominations were right through the roof. They were astronomical, compared to the base we were operating on." He went back to the parent companies to confirm the numbers, then broke the news to Dhahran. To fulfill the "nominations" of the parent companies, Aramco would have to undertake a multi-billion-dollar capital program and hire many more workers. "I laid out what it meant in terms of cost that was going to come about as a result of this, and do you guys really want us to gear up to do this? And they all agreed that we were going to go ahead with it. . . . They were very parsimonious, and they weren't going to build anything we didn't need."[4] What actually happened was beyond his imagination.

It is difficult for anyone who did not experience it first-hand to comprehend the amount of oil money that poured into Saudi Arabia in the 1970s and the spending frenzy that it fueled. The selling price of Saudi crude oil was $1.39 a barrel on January 1, 1970. On January 1, 1974, it was $8.32. On January 1, 1981, it was $32. Since consumers kept buying anyway, state oil revenue rose from $4.34 billion in 1973 to $22.5 billion the next year, kept rising through the entire decade, and peaked at almost $102 billion in 1981. In accordance with the Second Five-Year Plan, the government embarked on a mammoth construction program: roads, schools, hospitals, airports, power plants, military facilities, ports, telephone networks, and brand new cities. Ordinary

Saudis received free education and medical care, and generous subsidies for housing and agriculture. Even so, the government could not spend nearly as much as it was taking in; cash reserves in the tens of billions of dollars piled up in American and European banks.

Months-long backlogs developed in the country's overwhelmed ports. The few international hotels were booked to overcapacity for months at a time. Their smoky lobbies were thronged with foreigners trying to secure contracts from Saudis who routinely broke appointments and ignored schedules. Desperate businessmen paid taxi drivers to drive around with their air conditioners on all night so they could sleep in the back seat. At the Kandara Palace Hotel in Jeddah, which in those days had no telephones in the rooms, only a single unit in the lobby, I watched an American pleading with the beleaguered desk clerk: He had to come back to Saudi Arabia, the American said, and would do so whenever the hotel could guarantee him a room. When would that be? Never, said the desk clerk; there was no date on which the hotel could guarantee that a room would be available.

For those with the luck, stamina, and influence to win a share of the Saudi bonanza, the prize was worth the effort. In 1980 alone, American companies received contracts to build classrooms for the Saudi navy, construct eight buildings for Riyadh University, design the residential areas of the new industrial city of Yanbu, build a headquarters for the National Commercial Bank in Jeddah, construct military housing, build a 318-bed hospital in Taif, construct a factory for binding epoxy to pipes, build and manage an ethylene plant in Yanbu, operate a 500-mile pipeline, train the staff of a lube oil refinery, design and engineer a fertilizer factory in Jubail, operate air traffic control at thirty-one sites, maintain the fleet of F-15 fighter jets that Saudi Arabia's modernizing armed forces had acquired, train fire and emergency crews at fifteen airports, and train Saudi naval crews to operate radar and sonar systems.[5]

It seemed that everything was done on a massive scale. Even Aramco, long established and well capitalized, was caught up in it. The company was assigned by the Ministry of Petroleum to capture and use the natural gas that was a byproduct of oil production, rather than flare it off as waste, which it had been doing for decades. At the time, more than

4 billion cubic feet of gas was being wasted every day and the Petroleum Ministry, reasonably enough, wanted to use that gas as feedstock for petrochemicals. Aramco became, in effect, the general contractor for what company treasurer Baldo Marinovic called "the single largest industrial project in the world ever undertaken."[6] The project was budgeted at $14 billion and was scheduled to take eight years.

To do this job, Aramco needed to import 30,000 workers, Marinovic said. There was no housing for such a group, so Aramco decided to import prefabricated housing units. The workers who came to install the prefabs needed housing of their own, so Aramco ordered "enormous barges from Singapore. Then, on these barges, they installed portable cubicles, dorms, stacked six deep. And we had dining facilities and so on. So these barges would pull up, moor along the shore at a strategic spot, and we had up to 1,000 contractors working and living in each barge. And when the work was finished there, you could tow the barge somewhere else," he recalled.[7]

Even basic public services were undertaken at a scale that would have stunned government officials in the United States or Europe. For a while, school lunches were brought in daily from France by air freight. On one trip to Riyadh, I met a man from Illinois, David Blomberg, who had become the de facto sanitation commissioner of the capital. His company, Waste Management Inc., had been hired by the governor of Riyadh, Prince Salman bin Abdul Aziz, to clean up the streets; the contract was for five years at $50 million a year. Waste Management's assignment was to plan and create a complete city sanitation department, recruit more than 2,000 workers from India to collect trash, build a camp to house them, and provide the trash-collection equipment. In came two hundred bright yellow American trash compactor trucks and 120,000 plastic garbage cans, complete with extra-heavy lids that would not blow off in sandstorms. "No place else in the world would do anything like this," Blomberg told me, "and there is no place else where it would be necessary."[8]

Phil Holcomb, who was hired in the late 1970s to help manage the opening of the new international airport in Jeddah, said he was offered a compensation package that included a car, first class air travel for home

David Blomberg, of Waste Management Inc., displays a sandstorm-proof trashcan lid his company developed for the city of Riyadh cleanup project, 1978.

PHOTO BY THOMAS W. LIPPMAN.

leave, and housing, as well as a salary of $65,000 a year. "I asked for $85,000 and they gave it to me on the spot. In the end, with bonuses and everything, I made a lot more than that," he recalled. "That was the period of wild west spending out there."[9] He had been making $25,000 as assistant general manager of the airport in Honolulu.

Holcomb was hardly alone. Tens of thousands of foreign workers flooded into the country, all looking to make more money than they could at home. This labor army included illiterate Egyptian construction workers—all over rural Egypt, new brick houses with television antennas sprouted during the 1970s, financed by remittances from workers in Saudi Arabia—as well as Palestinian and Pakistani teachers and nurses, cab drivers from Yemen, Bangladeshi street sweepers, American and British doctors, and legions of American engineers.

Many people, including members of the royal family, made spectacular fortunes selling land, importing automobiles and consumer goods, developing hotels and supermarkets and, as everyone knew, collecting "commissions" that were barely sanitized bribes. So brazen was the payoff system that Congress tried to break it up with enactment in 1977 of the Foreign Corrupt Practices Act, which made it illegal to bribe foreign officials to obtain contracts. The law was not specific to Saudi Arabia, but it was the Saudi contracting binge that inspired it.

According to the Department of Commerce, Congress acted after investigations by the Securities and Exchange Commission in the mid-1970s "revealed that over 400 U.S. companies admitted making questionable or illegal payments in excess of $300 million to foreign government officials, politicians, and political parties. The abuses ran the gamut from bribery of high foreign officials in order to secure some type of favorable action by a foreign government to so-called facilitating payments that allegedly were made to ensure that government functionaries discharged certain ministerial or clerical duties."[10] In other words, foreign companies paid Saudi officials to give them contracts, then paid other Saudi officials to issue the permits and customs waivers required to fulfill the contracts. For Americans, the new law made such payments illegal.

European business executives ridiculed this attempt to legislate away the traditional business practices of the Arabian *souk;* and it does seem to have put some American corporations at a disadvantage because many of the princes whom they would have paid to help them secure contracts over foreign competitors were also government officials to whom such payments would have violated U.S. law. There was widespread suspicion in the American business community that the new law was at least partly responsible when American firms were shut out of one of the biggest projects of all, a $3.14-billion contract to install 470,000 telephone lines throughout the Kingdom and to computerize the phone system. That contract went to a consortium consisting of I. M. Ericsson of Sweden, Phillips of the Netherlands, and Bell Canada. The agent for Phillips was Prince Muhammad bin Fahd, son of Prince Fahd, then the powerful crown prince and later king. The agent for Bell Canada was Salem bin Laden, a son of the wily old road builder, a favorite of King Abdul Aziz, who built the bin Laden family business empire from which Osama bin Laden derived his personal wealth.

How the Saudi system worked in practice was explored in riveting detail in a 1982 congressional hearing. The subcommittee on Commerce, Consumer, and Monetary Affairs of the House Government Operations Committee was looking into the activities of Whittaker Corporation, a California conglomerate that was raking in big profits by operating hospitals in Saudi Arabia. The star witness was Joseph Alibrandi, Whittaker's chairman.

Alibrandi was not a doctor. He was an engineer who first went to Saudi Arabia in the 1960s to supervise the installation of the Hawk antiaircraft missile system that Saudi Arabia had purchased from Raytheon Corporation. Raytheon's Saudi Arabian agent at the time was Prince Khaled bin Abdullah, a son of the commander of the National Guard and a nephew of King Abdul Aziz.

Alibrandi spotted a business opportunity in providing health care and hospital services to a country that desperately needed them. American institutions involved in the training of large numbers of Saudis, including Aramco and the U.S. military, had felt the need to provide health care for their Saudi clients, who lacked basic immunizations, suffered from poor diets, and had little access to modern medicine. By the 1970s, the government was investing huge sums in expanding medical care and hospital services to the general population.

Under Alibrandi's leadership, Whittaker put together an unsolicited proposal to operate government-owned hospitals in several Saudi cities. To obtain consideration of this proposal in the overheated atmosphere of the late 1970s, where corporations from all over the world were scrambling for a share of the Saudi pie, Whittaker created a network of partners and board members who had influence in the Kingdom, Alibrandi testified.

First, it created a separate subsidiary for its proposed Saudi Arabian operations and sold 30 percent of the shares to Prince Khaled for $750,000. Then it hired Adnan Khashoggi, the preeminent wheeler-dealer and middle man of that era; Khashoggi's Triad International Corporation was to receive 3.06 percent of the value of any Whittaker contract.

Khashoggi, Alibrandi said, "was invaluable in contacting people, saying, 'Hey, here are a bunch of guys who have a real approach to health care delivery. It is new and different. How about coming down next Tuesday morning and sitting there and listening to it?' We would go and make a presentation."

Whittaker also arranged to purchase its medical supplies exclusively through a firm headed by Shamseddin al-Fassi, an influential businessman whose daughter married one of the king's brothers. He was guaranteed a minimum of $20 million in annual sales and a profit of 10 percent. Whittaker gave a seat on its board of directors to John C. West, who had been U.S. ambassador to the Kingdom during the administration of President Jimmy Carter. And the company's biggest non-American stockholder was none other than Sulaiman Olayan, one of the richest and most respected of the first generation of nonroyal Saudis to become business tycoons.

With all that clout, Whittaker cleaned up. By the time of the 1982 hearing, the company was operating five hospitals and several walk-in clinics; about 4,200 workers treated 19,700 inpatients and 604,000 outpatients annually. These operations accounted for 17 percent of Whittaker's $1.6 billion in annual sales and nearly half its profits. Prince Khaled had collected $33.3 million in profits on his $750,000 investment. Payments to Khashoggi had exceeded $8 million. Because none of Whittaker's Saudi associates held an official government position, payments to them were not prohibited by the Foreign Corrupt Practices Act; and Whittaker, although it had skillfully gamed the system, had not done anything illegal.

Not only had it acted ethically, Alibrandi said, but Whittaker had performed an important service both to Saudi Arabia, which needed the medical care, and to the United States, which benefited by bringing the oil dollars back home. "Our relationship there is no different than our relationship would be in any other country," he said. "Sure there are customs. There are things—there are things that you do and don't do, doing business in Saudi Arabia, that unless you are aware of the customs and so forth, you can insult people, and you don't get many business contracts that way."[11]

At the time, Alibrandi's was the prevailing view: Let the good times roll. The Saudis are getting their schools and hospitals and roads, and Americans are raking it in. Nobody paid much attention to prophetic naysayers in the left-wing press or dim-view academics such as William Quandt. Quandt warned that an anti-American backlash could easily develop: "Whatever credit is won by the regime by improving the prospects of the average Saudi citizen could be eroded by the frustration felt by Saudis as they see the country's wealth wasted on useless projects, as they hear lurid stories of corruption, and as the seamy side of Western culture makes itself felt in the Kingdom. If these negative aspects of development outweigh the positive gains, Saudis could turn much of their resentment against the United States as the source of their unhappiness."[12] Who wanted to hear that?

〜⁀

Into this gold rush environment stepped the U.S.–Saudi Arabian Joint Economic Commission, known as JECOR. Its mission was similar in many ways to that of the Ford Foundation in the previous decade, but JECOR had far greater resources in money and personnel. In addition to training Saudis in how to perform basic government functions, such as collecting customs duties and setting standards for electric appliances, the commission took on specific projects, which Ford had declined to do. These ranged from the creation of an accurate consumer price index to the development of the country's first national park.

JECOR was the opposite of a traditional foreign-aid program: The Saudis were paying for it. The commission operated for more than twenty-five years, spending billions of dollars, with virtually no congressional oversight because Congress was not appropriating the funds. Congress was not even called upon to approve the creation of the commission because it was done by executive agreement, not a formal treaty.

The overall manager of JECOR was the Treasury Department, which handled the money. The Saudis, rolling in cash, would deliver hundreds of millions of dollars to Treasury, which held on to the funds until they were needed to pay vendors or employees. This system ensured that the Saudi money would be recycled back into the American economy, which was one of Treasury's objectives. It also ensured that the commission's managers could undertake whatever projects they and the Saudis agreed were useful without having to justify them to Congress.

The commission's objectives were listed in a joint statement issued in Washington by the American and Saudi officials who signed the agreement creating it: "Its purposes will be to promote programs of industrialization, trade, manpower training, agriculture, and science and technology." On the American side, it would include representatives from the State, Treasury, and Commerce departments; the National Science Foundation; and their subsidiary agencies, such as the Customs Service. On the Saudi side, the participating agencies were the ministries of Foreign Affairs, Finance and National Economy, Commerce, and Industry, and the Central Planning Organization (soon to become Hisham Nazer's Ministry of Planning). Projects and programs would be proposed to the commission by joint "working groups" on manpower and education, technology and research and development, agriculture, and industrialization. The industrialization group would "consider plans for Saudi Arabia's economic development, paying special attention to the use of flared gas for expanding the production of fertilizer," a reference to the Aramco gas-gathering venture.[13]

"In 1974 the Saudis had billions of dollars and high expectations but no real government," said Charles Schotta, who was deputy assistant secretary of the Treasury and U.S. coordinator of the commission. The driving force behind the commission on the Saudi side, Muhammad Abalkhail, "had a clear vision of what he wanted to see, a competent government of people who could interface with the outside world," Schotta recalled. "The Saudis understood that a tree doesn't spring up fully grown the day after you plant the seed. You want to push people forward, but not so fast that you develop a discouraging failure rate. The Saudis understood that they were forcing the pace, and they were going to waste some money, but they didn't want to wait twenty years. They wanted to ramp up."[14]

Schotta and other Americans who participated in JECOR's work described an unprecedented deployment of U.S. government employees directly into Saudi Arabian government agencies, where they worked alongside Saudi counterparts, conversing in English, offering advice, evaluating personnel, selecting Saudi employees for further education and training, and exploring ideas. "The U.S. person in charge of the project, let's say the census, would have an office in the department," Schotta said. "The Americans sat and talked with the people they were working with, in English. . . . There was social interaction, a lot of conversation the Saudis never would have had with embassy people, some 'what if' conversations and trial balloons, or my brother heard about this or that."[15]

Having been established in the mid-1970s, when the oil boom was at its most overheated, JECOR had an extensive roster of projects up and running by the early 1980s, just as a worldwide oil glut was knocking down oil prices to the point that the Saudis had to consider serious retrenchment. By some accounts, Saudi ministries whose budgets were squeezed by the oil revenue shortfalls shifted costs to JECOR accounts, turning the commission into an off-budget purchasing agency.

Although Congress had no jurisdiction over JECOR's activities, a subcommittee of the House Committee on Government Operations did ask the General Accounting Office (GAO) to examine the process by which JECOR contracts were awarded. The GAO compiled a list of JECOR's projects shown in Table 9.1 as they were on September 30, 1983.[16]

Within that list, the Americans seem to have had a widely varying set of responsibilities because the Saudis used them in different ways. One American wound up writing speeches for Muhammad Abalkhail, who became minister of finance not long after JECOR was established. Several were assigned to the National Center for Financial and Economic Information, a sort of private economic "think tank" that provided Abalkhail with information on global trade, tax policy, and whatever else came up. (This group produced papers that Abalkhail used to derail a proposal then being considered by the king to tax expatriate incomes.) Some were solar energy scientists whose mission was to help the Saudis convert some of their endless sunshine into useful electricity. Some were Census Bureau statisticians laboring to help the Saudis establish credible processes for collecting census data in a society where it is considered rude for men to inquire about women. One group of Americans helped the Saudis establish food safety standards; another trained them to use sniffer dogs for customs inspections. The Agriculture Department sent Texans who knew how to raise crops in an arid environment. JECOR advisers helped the Saudis create a national network of vocational training schools.

The Americans also took on responsibility for arranging medical residencies in U.S. hospitals for Saudi doctors.

TABLE 9.1   JECOR projects as of September 30, 1983

Project	Year signed; duration	Purpose	Cost	U.S. Agency	U.S. Staff in Saudi Arabia
Audit Services	1978; indefinite	Accounting standards, training for Saudi General Auditing Bureau	$6,930,000	Treasury Department	10
Desalination Research and Training	1977; indefinite	Train Saudis in water desalination techniques	$35,941,000	Interior Department	3
Highway Administration	1977; 6 years	Upgrade Saudi highways, road maintenance	$15,544,000	Federal Highway Administration	8
Transportation Services	1978; 6 years	Transportation needs assessment and planning	$5,167,000	Transportation Department	6
National Center for Financial and Economic Information	1977; indefinite	Data collection and analysis for Ministry of Finance	$67,079,000	Treasury Department	33
Agriculture Bank	1978; 5 years	Train personnel of Saudi Arabian Agriculture Bank	$11,628,000	Farm Credit Administration	12
Agriculture and Water Development	1975; indefinite	Research and technical assistance in agriculture, water	$113,778,000	Agriculture, Interior Departments	62
Solar Energy	1977; 8 years	Solar energy R & D	$84,736,000	Energy Department	2
Supply Management	1978; indefinite	Develop centrally controlled procurement system	$12,668,000	General Services Administration	14

TABLE 9.1 *(continued)*

Project	Year signed; duration	Purpose	Cost	U.S. Agency	U.S. Staff in Saudi Arabia
Consumer Protection	1977; indefinite	Food safety and inspection; weights and measures	$27,422,000	Treasury Department, Food and Drug Administration	1
Customs Administration	1978; indefinite	Training customs officers and dogs	$95,611,000	Customs Service	12
King Faisal University	1980; indefinite	Develop academic exchange program	$8,208,000	Treasury Department	5
National Center for Science and Technology	1976; indefinite	Develop applied research capabilities	$6,185,000	National Science Foundation	0
Statistics and Data Processing	1975; 10 years	Statistics compilation methods	$36,483,000	Census Bureau	28
Manpower Training and Development	1976; 9 years	Vocational training facilities and curriculum	$121,247,000	Labor Department, General Services Administration	50
National Parks	1977; indefinite	Create Asir National Park	$6,493,000	National Park Service	1
Tax Assistance and Training	1981; 3.5 years	Training tax auditors, computerization	$1,407,000	Internal Revenue Service	3
King Saud University	1982; indefinite	Faculty performance evaluation	$456,000	Treasury Department	2

"Getting graduates of Saudi medical schools into U.S. residencies was hard," Schotta said. JECOR's solution was to sign a contract with Tufts University to set up residency matches for qualified Saudis with eight to ten American institutions, which would agree to accept them on a take-it-or-leave-it basis. "We would say to them, 'Here's one opening in dermatology, and if you don't take that, no slot this year.' It worked very well," Schotta said.[17]

Of all these projects, the only one to which the U.S. government contributed funds was solar energy development, and for that reason it seems to have been the only one in which tensions arose between American and Saudi participants. Holsey G. Handyside, a career diplomat who was the senior U.S. government representative to this project, called it "one of the most difficult diplomatic assignments I ever had."

The problem, he said, lay not in deciding what the objectives were—converting solar energy to electricity for air conditioning, and developing a working solar-powered water desalination plant—but in allocating responsibility. The Saudis wanted to be treated as equals, but the Americans, putting up half the money, felt they lacked the skills and knowledge required for equality.

"What quickly became obvious was that all the Americans who were involved were going to have to face up to squaring a very difficult circle," Handyside said. The Saudis were "clearly little brothers in this research and development effort. . . . The theoretically equal partners were almost the farthest things imaginable from being equal."[18]

Participating Americans who have recorded their recollections of the other projects have described a cooperative atmosphere of shared learning and good intentions on both sides.

The one National Park Service staff member on the GAO's list was Ivan D. Miller, who now manages Buffalo River National Park in Arkansas. In 1981, he was assigned to Saudi Arabia to help the Saudis establish their first national park, in the beautiful, mountainous Asir region in the far southwestern part of the country. In earlier times, many Saudis would not have grasped the concept of a national park because in bedouin tradition all land was everyone's land. In the Asir, Miller said, the Saudis and their American advisers agreed that vil-

lagers living within the boundaries of the park at the time it was created could remain, a principle, he said, that has since been adopted by
the U.S. park system.

Although he was for some time the only National Park Service person in the community, he was far from the only American: He and his
wife lived in Khamis Mushayt, where McDonnell Douglas and the
Corps of Engineers had installed a team to build and manage an air
base for the Saudis. Despite the remoteness of the region, the Millers
found an American housing compound and an international school.

The park covers 1.1 million acres; it includes mountain peaks of 10,000
feet and beaches on the Red Sea. "It's beautiful there," Miller observed.

He said he arranged for his Saudi counterparts to tour American national parks and study their management, visitor accommodations, and
conservation policies. Under his supervision, the Saudis created a visitors' center and installed campgrounds and picnic areas. "The managerial level was very receptive" to his input, he said, and by 1985 the
Saudis had assumed full responsibility for all aspects of the park's operations except maintenance work, which was carried out under contract
by Filipinos.[19] The park is now a centerpiece of Saudi Arabia's incipient
effort to attract tourists.

Brian Hannon, an economist and statistician with a degree from
University of Maryland, spent thirteen years (two tours) in Saudi Arabia
on JECOR projects. Although he was sent to Riyadh by the U.S. Bureau
of the Census, his assignment was not to count people but to help the
Saudis compile an accurate consumer price index. Census had a team of
about twenty-five members, he said, that trained and assisted the Saudis
in the compilation and analysis of basic statistical data, such as the consumer price index and the labor force, and computerized the records.
The client was the Central Bureau of Statistics, which was part of
Abalkhail's Finance Ministry.

Hannon said the Americans adopted the Saudi work week, Saturday
through Wednesday, which meant that, as U.S. government employees,
they were entitled to 5 percent extra pay for working Sundays. They
worked in their Saudi offices, alongside their Saudi counterparts, from
7:30 A.M. to 2:30 P.M., the Saudi government work day, and then went

back to the JECOR office to perform administrative work and translate documents.

Because women were not permitted to work in the ministries when he first arrived, he said, "We didn't have any secretaries in the ministry. This was before PCs and laptops, so if we wanted to write something out we would write it out in longhand and then take it to the JECOR central office, where each of the teams had a secretary or two who would transcribe handwritten notes into typed papers."

This cumbersome arrangement was only one of the difficulties Hannon faced. Another was that the Saudis tended to be secretive, even about basic economic data compiled by the government. They collected information but were reluctant to share it with the people who needed to have it.

"They were not always completely open with the data after it was completed," Hannon recalled. "Sometimes they seemed to hide it away in a closet and only a certain number of people would get access to it. Even with the Consumer Price Index (CPI), which should generally be shared with everyone—sometimes it would be very frustrating, when you had a small production run, maybe only 300 were printed."[20] (This should not have been surprising, given the absence of public participation in Saudi government decisionmaking.) The king, of course, received a copy of his unit's reports, as did the crown prince and some other key officials, but not the public or the news media, and there was no legislature to be kept informed.

The task of setting up systems for compiling and distributing basic statistics may seem mundane, but it was essential to the development of modern government in Saudi Arabia. Except in the oil industry, the Kingdom's published economic and population data have always been suspect. In the late 1970s, Kiren Chaudhry found that "government statistics were literally manufactured in the ministries of Finance and Planning."[21] As recently as 2002, the U.S. Embassy's annual report on the Saudi economy said that "one of the principal challenges for an analyst of the Saudi economy is developing reliable and consistent data. All too often there is little or no data available for key indicators, or if multiple sources exist they are often contradictory."

The Saudis also tend to be sensitive about information that might tarnish their image, as Hannon found out one month when the CPI rose sharply, partly because of a sudden spike in the price of gold.

"I wrote up an analysis and explanation of why prices had changed," Hannon said. "As part of that I mentioned that gold had gone up on the world market." This brought a chewing-out from Abalkhail for Hannon and Ahmed Rashid, the director of the Central Department of Statistics. The minister was concerned that if they drew attention to the importance of gold to Saudi consumers, it would "give the wrong impression" to people outside the Kingdom. Hannon dropped gold from his monthly CPI analyses.[22]

Like the Aramcons of earlier decades, Hannon and his JECOR colleagues learned that working amicably alongside Saudis did not necessarily lead to socializing or close personal relationships outside the office, partly because of the restrictions on Saudi women.

"You were not at all restricted from participating in the culture to the extent that you wanted to," he recalled, "but the culture was very different." The Saudis' idea of a dinner party was an alcohol-free event at which the women dined separately and the conversation was mostly in Arabic, Hannon said. "They're very hospitable, but there's a limited amount of exchange you can have," he said. "I was there for almost a year before I first met a Saudi woman."

‌‌↩

Charles Schotta's reference to "conversations that the Saudis never would have had with embassy people" reflects JECOR's anomalous position in Saudi Arabia. For years it operated almost entirely outside the control of the U.S. Embassy, even though in theory the ambassador is the ultimate boss of all nonmilitary U.S. government personnel stationed in a foreign country. JECOR was based in Riyadh even when the embassy was still in Jeddah, and remained separate after the embassy relocated to the capital.

That might have been the most effective way to get things done, but it naturally rankled the State Department—so much so that Chas

W. Freeman Jr. said he made it his first priority upon becoming ambassador in 1989 to assert some measure of embassy control. He did so by exercising his prerogative to veto a planned visit to the Kingdom by a senior Treasury official. "My first act," Freeman said, "was to try to straighten this out by denying the deputy assistant secretary of the Treasury country clearance, thus establishing who was in charge. It took several months of discussion on the phone, and finally face to face, to establish a pattern by which JECOR, while remaining quite autonomous, not only informed me of what they were doing but actually took guidance."[23]

At that time, Freeman said, "the luster had quite worn off JECOR," and after his maneuver it was revitalized and reorganized. He was not the only American who thought JECOR had somehow lost its way. It was probably inevitable that, as the commission became institutionalized inside the Saudi governmental apparatus, the Saudis would come to think of it as a tool at their disposal rather than as a source of new ideas and skills. With no input from Congress and scant scrutiny in the media, JECOR was insulated from fresh thinking and constructive criticism.

"The Saudis were increasingly frustrated," said Gene W. Heck, who was economic officer at the U.S. Embassy from 1984 to 1987 and still lives in Riyadh. "Treasury wasn't structured to provide what they needed. We were teaching how to do CPR on crash-test dummies, but not how to create meaningful economic development."[24] The GAO, in one of the few reviews of JECOR's work by any agency in Washington, found "general disappointment with the management and passive approach of the Joint Commission office in Saudi Arabia" because of "lack of leadership"—and that was in 1978, long before Freeman tried to wrestle JECOR into submission.[25] Other Americans expressed similar views.

The most detailed criticism of JECOR's activities came from an insider, David K. Harbinson, a Treasury Department "program officer" for JECOR from startup until 1988. Charles Schotta dismisses Harbinson as "a disaffected former employee," but because Harbinson's paper on JECOR was published in the respected *Middle East Journal* and stands as the only extensive published critique, it has acquired a certain credibility.

His basic argument is that members of the JECOR team were followers of the Saudis rather than leaders. In the "hyperventilated" 1970s, according to Harbinson, the commission had no time to deliver long-term technical assistance and the Saudis had no time to absorb it. Instead, JECOR became "another frenzied participant in the building and buying boom that characterized these years. . . . It allowed individual Saudi ministries to set the agenda for the commission's work. For most ministries this involved using commission advisers as a resource in much the same way as they used contractors and third-country nationals." Some JECOR projects assumed responsibility for "such mundane tasks as buying routine ministry supplies and contracting for janitorial services," Harbinson reported, and, over time, "the American staff was increasingly integrated into the ministries' day-to-day activities as statisticians, economists, researchers, and administrators."[26] But was that necessarily bad? It could be argued, as Schotta and others do, that the Saudis were making good use of the Americans' skills, getting necessary tasks performed competently until their own newly trained staffs were capable of taking over. The Saudis may have had complaints, but they reviewed the JECOR agreement every five years for a quarter of a century, learning all the time. By 1996, more than 9,000 Saudi Arabs had been trained under JECOR auspices.

The Joint Commission came to an end in 2000, for reasons that have never been made entirely clear. The Clinton administration and the Saudi Arabian Ministry of Finance let it expire when they did not sign a new five-year extension, and the last $5 million of Saudi money, which the Treasury Department had been holding in escrow to pay holdover claims, was returned to Riyadh in 2002. No official announcement was ever made.

According to Treasury Department officials, who spoke on condition that they not be identified, and other insiders who followed the commission closely, Lawrence Summers, treasury secretary in the last year of the administration of President Bill Clinton, disliked working with Saudi Arabia and disapproved of the entire JECOR program; for their part, the Saudis had reached the point where they no longer felt they needed the kind of assistance JECOR was providing. They wanted to decide how to spend their own money. Trying as always to avoid a public display of displeasure or disagreement with Washington, they proposed that JECOR be restructured to help Saudi Arabia take the steps necessary to join the World Trade Organization. Unable to reach agreement with the Treasury Department on how to do that, they pulled the plug, and the JECOR office in Riyadh was closed. In Charles Schotta's view, that was a sign of mission accomplished: "Our objective was to move the Saudis to the point where they didn't need this service."[27] Today, the Saudi government is relatively competent and efficient, at least by Middle Eastern standards. The things that need to be done mostly get done, and they get done by, or at the direction of, Saudi Arabs.

CHAPTER 10

Down on the Farm

MILDRED LOGAN FEARED THERE would be quite a stir when she first arrived at al-Kharj in 1950. Tall, blonde, unveiled, Texas brash, and toting a one-year-old daughter, she was an exotic apparition to local Arabs, who had never encountered anyone like her.

"What would these Arabs think of me, the first American woman ever to be given permission by His Royal Highness the Crown Prince to live deep in the interior of this vast kingdom?" she wondered as she flew down to al-Kharj, about sixty miles southeast of Riyadh, on an Aramco C-47. "Many of the Arabs at al-Kharj had never seen a white woman, or any other woman, unveiled other than their mothers, sisters, or wives."

At the age of twenty-three, she was heading out into the boondocks to join her husband, Sam, who was managing a 3,000-acre experimental farm. About eight hundred Arabs worked in the fields and tended the animals under the supervision of five Americans; the only women most of the Arabs had ever encountered were those in their immediate families.

Mildred Logan's apprehensions were soon relieved. "First and foremost, I was the boss's wife and just naturally received respect. Not just respect, but real graciousness that overwhelmed me in view of what I had supposed would happen. There were Arabs who stared at me, some who even giggled, and others who acted as though I was nothing out of the ordinary at all."

"They treated me like a man," she recalled. "And they found out right quick that I was anxious to do stuff to help them." And, of course, they all made a fuss over her little girl, Linda.[1]

The Logans found life at al-Kharj a panorama of contrasts almost as sharp as those of Dhahran: between the well-watered crops and the desert that surrounded them; between the Americans' comfortable air-conditioned quarters and the ill-washed poverty of the Arab laborers; between the huge trucks that brought their supplies and the camel-based lives of the local population; between the robust good health of the Americans and the lice-infested, disease-plagued existence of their workers.

The American woman was a college graduate who drove a car from the farm to the market in town, such as it was. The Saudi women, who had no education, "peer around the corners like Hallowe'en characters—just two peepholes for their eyes in the stiff black masks, or veils, if you feel like being romantic. The sun beats down on their black robes as the women go scurrying along with their heavy bundles on top of their heads."

To Mildred Logan, life at the farm was "one chain of fascinating experiences, some amusing, some sad, inspiring, disgusting, admirable, and frightening."

But why were Americans living at al-Kharj in the first place, in the middle of nowhere, hundreds of miles from the oil patch? Today, many Americans are familiar with al-Kharj as the site of Prince Sultan Air Base, where the U.S. Air Force developed a major installation in the 1990s; but half a century ago, it was more remote than the Australian outback, a most unlikely place to find Americans raising chickens and growing melons and tomatoes.

Sam Logan and his colleagues were there because King Abdul Aziz and his influential finance minister, Abdullah Sulaiman, wanted them there. It was central to their vision of the country's development to find water, introduce irrigation, produce more and better food, and entice the bedouin into giving up their harsh nomadic life and taking up farming. Moreover, the fast-growing royal entourage in Riyadh had to be fed, and Sulaiman wanted alternatives to the costly imported food supplied by Aramco.

There had always been agriculture on the Arabian peninsula, mostly around the oases and in the fertile, mountainous southwest; but without irrigation, pumps, fertilizer, tractors, and modern methods of animal husbandry, output was limited and quality, except for dates, was often poor. For help with this, as with so many other things, the king turned to the Americans.

The Saudis knew there were extensive underground reserves of water around al-Kharj. When Aramco's Tom Barger and Dick Bramkamp went there at Sulaiman's request in 1938, they saw water in "great pits with straight walls, 70 to 100 feet in diameter. The clear, blue water was about 20 feet below the surface and deep. The Shaikh [Sulaiman] claims to have lowered a big rock on nearly 700 feet of rope without touching bottom. He wants to irrigate from these pits with pumps. It is quite feasible, as there is much flat bottomland in the valley floor, but the trouble is they have no [electric] power, and the cost of fuel oil will be terrific," Barger observed.[2]

Karl Twitchell, who at the king's request traveled throughout the country in 1942 looking for water and potential agricultural sites, concluded that "all land in the el-Kharj development will produce satisfactory yields of adapted crops." His team recommended experimenting with long-staple cotton, but also identified promising sites for wheat and barley cultivation.[3]

So it wasn't unrealistic to envision large-scale farming in the desert if modern techniques and equipment were applied. Sulaiman had imported farmers from Iraq and Egypt who brought a few pumps and six tractors. But who had the seemingly unlimited supplies of fuel oil, generators, pumps, and pipe that would be needed for a large-scale undertaking? Aramco.

Agriculture was not exactly Aramco's core business, but the oil company was well accustomed to its role as all-purpose contractor and engineer for the Saudi government. Aside from its general desire to curry favor with the king and Sulaiman, Aramco had a good reason to support an agricultural project at al-Karj: Buying food from there would reduce the need for expensive imports. During World War II, when shipping lanes were closed, Aramco's "Hundred Men" marshaled the collective skills from their pre-Arabian lives to grow some vegetables and increase the meat output of local livestock—they even taught the Arabs how to cut the fatty tails off sheep so the animals would store their fat elsewhere on their bodies and thus make better eating—but they did not have the manpower or expertise to take on a project at al-Kharj on the scale envisioned by Sulaiman.[4]

When the experimental farm's Egyptian managers left in 1943, Aramco assumed responsibility for the project because there was no one else to do it. With its access to pumps and equipment, Aramco was able to expand the project and distribute the water to new acreage. Aramco engineers built a 10-mile canal to distribute water pumped up from the aquifer. But the company did not want to manage the project permanently because manpower was short during the war, and al-Kharj was too far from Dhahran, so it appealed to Washington for assistance.

President Roosevelt's Foreign Economic Assistance Administration sent "a remarkable three man demonstration team," David Rogers, Karl Quast, and Rahleigh Sanderson, desert agriculture specialists from Arizona with graduate degrees. "All three were soil scientists, agronomists and horticulturalists," Parker Hart recalled.[5]

"The people who briefed them in Washington had no idea what the conditions were going to be like," Hart said. "They told them to just rent rooms in a hotel and send vouchers," as if they were going to Kenya. "If you had a mud hut to shelter yourself in at al-Kharj, you were doing very well. There was very little there."[6]

Soon to join them was Glen F. Brown, a geologist from New Mexico. He had already explored the country extensively; in 1948 he and Aramco's Bramkamp had published a paper on "ground water in the Nejd, Saudi Arabia," a coffee-stained copy of which is in Brown's collected papers at the Georgetown University Library in Washington. Jane Hart remembered him as "a marvelous little man" who "could have been elected to sainthood" in Saudi Arabia because he had identified a water source for Riyadh.[7] This was the same Glen Brown who would later establish an office of the U.S. Geological Survey (U.S.G.S.) in Jeddah and spend much of his professional life helping the Saudis find water and mineral resources.

Saudi Arabia is the largest country in the world with no river. Rainfall is minimal. Only in the mountainous southwest and around a few large oases is crop cultivation possible without extensive irrigation, and even then the harsh sun, high saline content of soil and groundwater, and prevalence of crop-destroying insects inhibit agriculture. Much of the water supply Saudi Arabia did have was needed for the cities. Part of the task undertaken by the Americans was to find techniques for coping with these difficulties.

The Arizonans and Brown introduced the long-handled shovel to the Nejd, and taught the Arabs to use camel dung as fertilizer.[8] "They subjugated and planted the terrain, brought in the water from the deep pits and grew some very fine vegetables. Then the locusts came and destroyed the whole thing all at once—the hoppers, millions and jillions of them. They had to start all over," Parker Hart recalled. "I used to drive out every two or three weeks with mail to see how they were getting on, and give them a chance to relieve their isolation and blow off steam."[9]

When U.S. government funding for the al-Kharj project ran out in 1946 and the Arizonans departed, Aramco reluctantly resumed management responsibility, installing a man named K. J. Edwards to run it, with the understanding that whoever finally assumed permanent control would retain him as manager. Edwards brought in a new team of American farmers, including Sam Logan. They inherited a productive enterprise.

"For the entire al-Kharj project the list of crops grown reads like a seed catalogue," a visiting scholar from the University of Michigan observed. "Besides dates, wheat, alfalfa, and grain sorghum, the following were seen: barley, oats, maize, tomatoes, watermelons, onion, eggplant, sweet and hot peppers, carrots, parsley, cabbages, cauliflowers, lettuce, daikon cucumbers, pumpkins, squash, turnips, rutabagas, beets, okra, beans, peas, peanuts, lentils, pomegranates, figs, citrons and grapes."[10]

Most of these were foreign to the Arab diet, but Aramco was purchasing most of the output.

Aramco was in fact the lifeline of the farm project. When Pete Speers joined the oil company in 1950, his first assignment was to run the supply line from Dhahran to al-Kharj.

"The people living there, the American employees, had housing there, of course," he recalled, "One of them, the manager, had his wife there, and child [they were the Logans.] But they depended on Dhahran for practically everything. All the car parts, the tires, any kind of maintenance work, and a lot of the food for the Americans came out of the Aramco commissary in Dhahran. Once a week they'd send in a list of what they needed and I had to go collect all that stuff together and load it on four or five trucks with Saudi drivers. . . . It must have been a twenty-four-hour drive, no roads of course."[11]

Aramco benefited from the farm's output, and had little choice but to support the project because Sulaiman wanted it and it was dear to the king's heart—he kept his four hundred horses at al-Kharj. But Aramco was playing a double game with the Saudis: It withheld information about water resources elsewhere in the country because it did not want to be called upon to develop farms around those as well.

On November 18, 1949, Ambassador Rives Childs informed the State Department that he had been told by Brigadier General Richard J. O'Keefe, commander of the Dhahran airfield, that "ARAMCO has very extensive data relating to water resources in this country," which it had shared with O'Keefe "in great confidence." According to the general, "This data has never been disclosed to SAG [the Saudi Arabian government] by ARAMCO owing to the fear that if it were made available ARAMCO would be called upon by the Saudi Arabian government to undertake exploitation of the water which its geologists have determined to be available at certain fixed points." Childs suggested the State Department consult with Aramco "discreetly" about making the information available to the U.S.G.S. team that Glen Brown would set up in Jeddah.[12]

If Childs thought it important for the Saudi Arabian government to have that information, he should have asked Brown for it directly: The abiding commitment of Brown's entire professional life was to compile information about the minerals and aquifers of Saudi Arabia and deliver it to the Saudi government. In the 1950s, Brown and his colleagues found three hundred new wells. "Perhaps the most important contributions were water supplies for Riyadh (when there was almost none), Yanbu al Bahr, Jiddah (Wadi Khulays), Jizan, Al Qunfudhah, and eleven towns or desert watering points," Brown wrote later.[13] Unlike Aramco, Brown and the U.S.G.S. had no hidden agendas.

In a budget memo for the initial U.S.G.S. program, Brown and his boss asked for $15,892 to cover the salaries and expenses of two men for four months. They said the team would look for water sources, dam sites, undiscovered ground water reservoirs, and "any other mineral wealth that might come to light." In support of this request, they noted that "the proposed project can do more than any other type of scientific research at this time to raise the standard of living of the Arabian coolies."[14]

～

Sam Logan, whose boyhood on an isolated ranch in West Texas nurtured him into a quiet, methodical man, despised Edwards, whom he regarded as a self-serving blowhard, so he quit the farm in 1948 and went home to Texas. At the time, Logan was divorced and the father of a child from his previous marriage, but he didn't stay unattached for long. On parent-teacher conference night at the local school he met his daughter's third-grade teacher, the willowy Mildred Montgomery, who was immediately smitten. "He was a very handsome specimen of mankind, I knew he was the one," she said. "I flirted my head off. It took me six weeks to get him to ask for a date."

Their daughter, Linda, was born the following year. Those were hard times in Texas agriculture, Mildred Logan recalled, because of a severe drought. When Edwards was ousted as manager of al-Kharj in 1950, Sam Logan accepted an offer to return as his replacement.

Their home consisted of four air-conditioned rooms in a twenty-room adobe building that housed all the Americans. It had "a nice roomy bathroom," she noted. While Sam managed the farm, Mildred kept busy arranging for supplies and sending requisition lists to Pete Speers, tending to Linda, conducting tours for visitors, and showing Arab children how to play with Linda's toys. She was "the official pants patcher for the American boys," she said, and, like Jane Hart in Hofuf a decade earlier, she introduced the Arab women to Western clothing, including undergarments. She taught one of the Arabs to make pecan pie, which was good except for the time he used red pepper instead of nutmeg.

Once a week, a military plane brought a movie. The Americans and the farm's Italian cook played bridge and canasta. They rode the royal horses, which were stabled nearby. It was not an unpleasant life, except when the harsh realities of Arabia intruded, as they did when the sons of their interpreter died.

The interpreter, Abdul Aziz, was the father of twin boys, a rarity in Arabia. "It is so hard to feed one baby in this arid country, and two is almost impossible," Mildred Logan recalled. "Abdul Aziz was almost pitiful in his plea for me to help him raise his sons so they would be healthy like our Linda." She agreed to help, with the proviso that he do what she told him to do; her instructions called for the infants to be permitted to move freely instead of being immobilized in tightly wrapped garments, as was the local custom.

By the time the twins were three months old, they were "fat and sassy in Linda's Philippine hand-made dresses and diapers. They took a supplementary bottle of Carnation milk to make up for their scant breast feedings. They were as clean and sweet as any babies in the world."

But the boys died, of some unexplained malady, to Mildred's dismay. She blamed the royal Saudi government, which she said was wasting its oil revenue on "palaces, expensive cars and other non-essentials of life" instead of "adequate medical facilities, decent schools or modern sanitation in the villages."

In the spring of 1952, Sam Logan's contract expired and the Logans went home to Texas. Three years later, King Saud asked Sam Logan to return for a second tour as farm manager, as a direct employee of the king.

When they arrived, Mildred Logan recalled, they found that "the farms had fallen into disrepair, our return came as quite a surprise to the Arab managers, and some difficult months followed" before her husband was able to bring in a new team of Americans.

By that time, Aramco had assigned an excitable Swiss cook named José Arnold as chef of the Royal Household, which meant preparing and serving more than a thousand meals a day in five residences for all the princes, wives, children, and royal hangers-on. (In one particularly stressful episode, President Nasser of Egypt and Prime Minister Nehru of India visited the Kingdom simultaneously, and Arnold was responsible for catering the banquets.)

Arnold's memos to Aramco about his needs reflect a perpetual exasperation. His typewriter ribbon had red ink as well as black, and he would type some words in red for emphasis. A typical memo from November 1957 was signed "Your highly insulted, frustrated and discouraged, loyal and devoted HUMBLE servant."

Arnold was under constant pressure from the Saudis to import less food and buy more locally, especially from the al-Kharj farms. As he observed in one of his monthly operations reports, "Our al-Kharj supply of vegetables and meat and butter has been quite erratic and of course not sufficient in quantity. The quality however was quite satisfactory. We receive turkeys, chicken and beef. The poultry is very good and fresh; however the beef appears to be suitable mostly for boiling or stewing."[15]

One reason the poultry was "very good and fresh" was that Sam Logan had brought in an incubator and a scientific feeding program. The Arabs, Mildred Logan observed, were astonished to see "chickens produced by machine," and all the same color.

Bill Eddy, in uncharacteristically condescending tones, added his own anecdote illustrating how the introduction of new machines sometimes flummoxed the Saudis of al-Kharj, who were two decades behind their countrymen up at Dhahran in learning from the Americans. The life of the American farmers, Eddy recounted,

was very austere in the torrid, lonely desert, and they imported a Servel kerosene refrigerator to an area which, of course, had never seen snow or ice. The Arabs installing the Servel asked what was the purpose of the heavy white box. [Dave] Rogers replied, "It makes ice." This fantastic statement caused a stir and a near riot. What is ice? A Syrian was found who swore on the Qur'an that ice exists and he had seen snow himself on Mount Hermon. A spokesman demanded that they be given a demonstration. Rogers replied that it would take some hours but he was ready to oblige. He got down on his knees and struck a match to light the pilot beneath the coils. "Wait a minute," yelled the spokesman. "You are building a fire to make ice?" "Yes," said Rogers, whereupon the Arab worker fled and did not return to work for several days.[16]

According to retrospective notes Mildred Logan sent to Bill Mulligan some years later, when Prince Faisal elbowed Saud aside and took over direction of the Saudi government as prime minister in 1958, he tried to solve the problem of a permanent manager for the farms by forcing this responsibility upon Muhammad bin Laden, a prominent construction contractor (and father of Osama bin Laden): Faisal told bin Laden he would be cut off from further government contracts unless he took on the farm project.

"In six months it became obvious bin Laden had no intention of further developing al-Kharj farms or even keeping them in operation," Mildred Logan wrote to Mulligan. "No seeds, no fertilizer, no dairy or poultry supplements were on order so Sam sent Bin Laden a message which read something like, 'If you are not interested in the successful operation of the Al Kharj farms we think you are wasting your money and our time to keep us on the payroll.' Bin Laden fulfilled our contract requirements and we left Arabia in June, 1959, along with all American personnel."[17]

The departure of the Logans and their little band of Americans put a temporary end to the direct involvement of Americans in Saudi Arabian agricultural production. Aramco, no longer responsible for managing the al-Kharj farms, established a technical assistance fund that provided Saudi farmers with seeds, chemical fertilizers, light equipment, and instruction in their use.

The expansion and modernization of agriculture, difficult as it was in such a hostile landscape, remained a cornerstone of government development policy, for political as well as economic reasons. At the beginning of the 1960s, agriculture and livestock herding accounted for 75 percent of the Saudi labor force, although only 0.34 percent of the land was cultivated, according to U.S. Embassy calculations.[18] By another calculation, "Farmers constituted 12 percent of the total population; breeders and herdsmen, 66 percent."[19]

Harold F. Heady, a professor of range management at the University of California, traveled around Saudi Arabia for six months in 1963 as a consultant to the United Nations Food and Agriculture Organization. He calculated that the country had 1,004,000 camels; 4,158,000 sheep; and 75,000 donkeys, tended by a bedouin population of about 1.12 million, which was declining as industrial development, road construction, and increasingly mechanized agriculture undercut the bedouin way of life.[20] Heady bemoaned this trend, which he said would reduce meat and milk production and thus require additional imports. Government planners recognized that declining rural populations would mean declining agricultural output, but they regarded the bedouins—roaming the land as they always had in search of forage and water for their herds—as part of the country's problem, not part of the solution.

As the population increased, the cost of importing food became an increasing burden on the government budget. The government's ambition was to develop state-sponsored agricultural projects and settle the bedouins on them through economic incentives. Because the bedouin way of life conflicted with the House of Saud's ambition to modernize the country and assert the authority of the central government over the tribes, the government wanted them to become sedentary, but it did not want them to migrate to the cities and create shantytowns, as they were beginning to do.

"The government pushed agriculture to promote self-sufficiency as a hedge against food embargoes, diversify the economy, distribute oil income to Saudis, and stanch the flow of rural Saudis to the cities," according to one critical analysis. The problem was that the policies and techniques adopted by the government to promote these objectives were enormously costly and produced at best mixed results.[21]

A government land-distribution program favored city dwellers who could meet the financial and familial criteria for acquiring acreage, to the general exclusion of traditional farmers. As a result, by 1981, "82 percent of private land was held by 16.2 percent of the landowning population, making Saudi Arabia's one of the most inequitable land tenure systems in the world."[22] These new owners of agricultural land, mostly absentee farmers who hired expatriate labor to work the fields, were flush with government subsidies that allowed them to tap into water resources identified by the U.S. Geological Survey team or provided increasingly through the desalination of seawater.

Large demonstration projects, intended to acquaint the farmers with modern production techniques, exceeded government management capabilities and tended to become boondoggles. Perhaps the best known was the 10,000-acre al-Faysal Settlement Project at Haradh, which was laid out for farms and resettlement villages for a thousand bedouin families, to whom farm plots would be given. The project would provide housing, electricity, and basic health care, none of which the bedouin had in their nomadic state. The idea was that the project would pay for itself through revenue from the sale of its output.

Consultants from the Ford Foundation recommended foreign specialists to be hired by the Haradh project, specified and ordered the equipment, and prepared a budget. Aramco contributed $400,000 to this venture, even though an internal company analysis identified potential problems: If it succeeded, it would attract the farmers' relatives to "parasitic shack villages" to demand a share of the bounty. Islamic inheritance laws would reduce the size of the farm plots with each generation. "The transition to settled life will be particularly difficult for the women of the families, who will be expected to deal with the unfamiliar hygienic and mechanical contrivances of modern town life."[23]

This was one case in which Aramco, however well intentioned, encouraged a wasteful and ill-conceived project because of its reluctance to say no to the government. The Haradh project's outcome was reported in a 1974 memo from one Ford Foundation consultant to another:

You know of the Haradh project, where $20 million was spent irrigating a spot in the desert where an aquifer was found not too far from the surface. This project took six years to complete and was done for the purpose of settling bedouin tribes. At the end of six years no bedouin turned up and the government nervously had to consider how to use the most modern desert irrigation facility in the world. Currently, they are growing alfalfa and raising sheep, running the scheme as a state-owned corporation.[24]

In conjunction with the Haradh farms, the government developed a $6-million agricultural research center, assessed by Ford experts as one of the best-equipped in the world. Unfortunately, no Saudis knew how to use that equipment. "The government, which has just paid $6 million for its construction, has no idea of how to find people to use the laboratory and only the vaguest of ideas about what to use it for. . . . These are classic examples of perceiving the form of Western institutions, but not their content," the Ford consultant wrote.

Such setbacks did not deter the government, which poured billions into the effort to build productive farms and a modern food processing industry. In addition to distributing land and water to farm operators, it provided cheap credit, constructed roads between farms and markets, built silos, handed out free seeds and fertilizers, and paid direct cash subsidies for many crops. It was these subsidies that took Terry and Martha Kirk to al-Kharj in 1982, where their experience would parallel that of the Logans thirty years earlier.

Of course, Saudi Arabia was much less primitive when the Kirks arrived. Riyadh, ninety minutes away on a paved road, was by 1982 a booming modern capital with restaurants and air conditioned shops. Even al-Kharj had a convenience store with a soft-drink cooler and a pay phone. Sanitation conditions were greatly improved. The farm where the Kirks worked was owned by a private Saudi businessman, not the king. But the biggest difference was that their farm produced only wheat, because that was where the real money was to be made.

∽

Terry and Martha Kirk grew up on ranches near Lubbock, in the West Texas panhandle. They met as students at Texas Tech, married young, and stayed on in Lubbock while he studied for his master's degree in crop science. They knew little of the wider world and nothing about Saudi Arabia.

Their lives changed when he spotted an ad in the *Lubbock Avalanche-Journal:* "Farm manager wanted in Saudi Arabia." Up to that point, Martha Kirk recalled, "Terry and I had been living a comfortable life in Lubbock. We lived near our parents and were active in our church. . . . The last thing on our minds during the Thanksgiving holidays of 1981 was uprooting ourselves and moving eight thousand miles, halfway around the globe."[25]

In the spirit of adventure, Terry Kirk answered the ad and a few months later found himself being interviewed by Abdul Latif al-Shaikh, owner of a wheat farm near al-Kharj. "Shaikh Latif," as they called him, said he had come to America because the Saudi Arabian government was pouring so much money into subsidies for wheat—paying up to ten times the world market price—that farm owners "could afford to hire the best farmers in the world, and in their eyes, the best were found in America."

Shaikh Latif hired Terry Kirk, age twenty-five, as assistant manager of his farm and Martha Kirk, twenty-three, to computerize the farm's books. They signed up for two years; they would stay for five.

Like many other Americans who went to Saudi Arabia, the Kirks were absurdly unprepared. "We knew nothing about Islam, not even that the practice of other religious faiths is prohibited," she recalled in her book about the experience. They were inoculated against the wrong diseases. She bought Middle Eastern cookbooks, but wrongly assumed that their descriptions of bedouin diets and culinary practices were out of date. Terry Kirk bought Arabic-language instruction tapes and worked hard at them, only to discover later that the dialect he learned was Egyptian colloquial, incomprehensible to rural Saudis (though he did later become fluent in the Arabic of the Nejd).

Terry Kirk insisted on going out by himself for a three-month trial period to evaluate the living conditions. "If Saudi Arabia was a place where an American woman could not live with comfort and dignity, then I would never go, and he would return to Texas," his wife wrote later. "Little did I suspect at the time how his standards of comfort and dignity might differ from mine."

Their mistakes and misconceptions continued even after Terry decided to stay and summoned his wife to join him. It took her six months to get a visa, and when she did it contained a restriction: She could not work, no matter what their employment agreement said. As her flight approached Dhahran International Airport, she was astonished to see all the female passengers head for the restrooms to don their veils and abayas, as if she did not believe the little she had read about the country. Terry Kirk let her arrive at Dhahran unmet, expecting her to transfer for a continuing flight to Riyadh. Neither of them knew that women in Saudi Arabia are generally prohibited from traveling alone; only a sympathetic policeman, after a heated discussion with his colleague, let her board the Riyadh plane. Nor could she check into a hotel without her husband. She didn't know how to use the Turkish toilets. She had multiple Bibles in her luggage, intended as gifts for Filipino workers on the farm. Her husband was waiting for her at the Riyadh airport's international gates, not realizing that the Dhahran-Riyadh leg of her trip was considered a domestic flight.

This was not an auspicious beginning for a young couple's life in the Arabian outback. Yet by their accounts, the Kirks learned, adjusted, prospered, and developed into perceptive and sympathetic observers of Saudi Arabian life. Over time, they made lifelong Arab friends. Their early isolation was eased when they met John and Patsy Zielske, a couple from Ohio managing another farm only eight miles away. (The Zielskes, who had two teenage daughters, piled rocks in front of the windows of their trailer home because "bedouins and Saudis visiting from the city walked right up to their windows to peer in at the American females.")[26] The Kirks also socialized with Egyptian, Pakistani, and British neighbors living on other farms in the area. They learned how to eat Saudi-style at the communal meals known as "goat grabs." They learned to bargain at the *souk* and to forecast the weather from the changing sky and shifting wind. They learned to appreciate cardamom coffee and camel's milk. They discovered where to get pork and alcohol. She drove the farm's pickup truck, and encountered bedouin women who drove too. As Martha noted, moving now by truck instead of by camel as in generations past, the bedouin needed adult drivers, so their women drove. She discovered that "whereas Americans try not to serve guests the same food the second time they are invited, the Saudis would never think of serving anything other than the traditional fare."

As they integrated themselves into the life of the community and began to socialize with Saudi families, Martha Kirk noticed that the Saudi men stared at her, and then stared some more. At first she was uncomfortable, but "I soon became accustomed to the stares of these men who saw no more than a few different women's faces in their life-times. I think this acceptance of their stares as no more than curiosity helped me to adjust more easily to the country. I knew several women who were never able to adjust to the constant stares, wherever they went. They became hypersensitive to such scrutiny and allowed the staring to make their time in Saudi Arabia uncomfortable."

More than most Americans, Martha Kirk entered the realm of Saudi women. In a bedouin tent, she was invited to try on a brightly colored native dress. "Feeling a little self-conscious because I only had a bra and half-slip on underneath, I pulled off [my] dress. The women cackled and laughed, examining my underclothes. I could understand their amuse-ment; they wore something that looked like a sweat suit for underwear."[27]

The Saudi women could not understand why the Kirks were childless after almost three years of marriage. "When I explained that we had de-layed having children because I had been starting a career, I was met with uncomprehending stares," she recalled. In such encounters, Martha Kirk wrote, she came to think of herself as "an anthropologist who had been catapulted into the past, with limited time to learn as much as pos-sible about a place that had its roots in ancient civilization."

Terry Kirk had his own cross-cultural encounters with the local peo-ple. After harvest, bedouin drove their flocks in from the desert to for-age on the stubble. This was now privately owned land, but the concept of land ownership was still foreign to many bedouin, to whom the desert had always been community property. Their herds trampled the cultivated ground, and their camels damaged the irrigation equipment.

Shaikh Latif's farm was a "pivot farm," in which an irrigation pipe, ro-tating from a central point, spreads water in a circular pattern, producing the green circles that always puzzle first-time travelers to the Kingdom when they see them from the air. When camels were let loose, they broke the sprinkler heads. Terry Kirk's tractor drivers resorted to driving their tractors right into the bedouin tents to force them to move on.

During a trip into al-Kharj, the Kirks discovered a mill that ground wheat into flour. When wheat imported from the United States was ground, the flour was sold to consumers at 3 riyals per kilogram, or 39 cents a pound. When the wheat was of Saudi Arabian origin, the flour was 8 riyals per kilo, or $1.04 per pound. "This only made sense," she observed, "because wheat in America was selling for three dollars a bushel, while the Saudi government was paying their farmers thirty dollars a bushel for wheat."[28]

It made sense for the miller; but it did not make economic sense for the Saudi government, which had allowed the farm subsidy program to balloon out of control, at crippling cost. Shaikh Latif and other large landowners were cleaning up the expense of a government pursuing agricultural self-sufficiency from a barren land.

According to Mansour Aba Hussein, then deputy minister of agriculture and water, the government subsidies available to farmers at that time included 45 percent of the cost of machinery, 50 percent of the price of irrigation pumps, 50 percent of the price of fertilizer, and 30 percent of the cost of poultry breeding equipment. Rice, wheat, and other crops were subsidized through guaranteed prices. Livestock owners received cash payments: 20 riyals per sheep, 60 riyals per camel. In addition, the government paid to purchase dairy cows abroad and airfreight them into the Kingdom, and then provided to dairy farmers a subsidy of 30 percent of the cost of milking machinery.[29]

The ambitious wheat program was the brainchild of the well-intentioned consultants dispatched to the Kingdom by the Ford Foundation in the 1960s. The objective, as defined by Ford, was to demonstrate to farmers that "the use of high yield varieties of wheat seed, suitable amounts of fertilizer, herbicides and water, and the application of modern production techniques and equipment result in substantial increases in yield and quality of wheat, and by implication that this process could be adapted to the production of many other crops." Ford consultants prepared a budget for the program, chose "stiff-strawed high-yielding Mexican type wheat" to be cultivated, and began training Saudis in soil preparation and irrigation techniques.[30] The first plantings went into the ground in 1971.

By the time the wheat farms lured Terry and Martha Kirk to al-Kharj, the program represented the best and the worst of the government's drive to promote agriculture.

It stimulated a spectacular increase in wheat production, from about 3,300 tons in 1978 to more than 3.9 million tons in 1991, by which time Saudi Arabia was the world's sixth-largest exporter of wheat.[31] But it did so at enormous cost, not only in money—by the early 1990s grain subsidies were costing the government nearly $3 billion a year[32]—but also in irreplaceable water. The water pumped from the pits at al-Kharj was "fossil" water—that is, it had been there since some previous geologic age but was not replenished. There was no active spring. Once used, it was gone forever.

Terry Kirk said he did not question whether the wheat program was wasteful or counterproductive. "All they wanted me to do was produce the product, and I did that, abundantly," he said. By the time Terry got to al-Kharj, however, the program was drawing high-level criticism from Washington, in the person of John R. Block, secretary of agriculture in the administration of President Ronald Reagan.

Visiting Saudi Arabia in 1983, Block discerned an opportunity to promote American agricultural exports by inducing the Saudis to cut back on their self-sufficiency campaign. He said he decided during that visit that it was "crazy" for the Saudis to be spending billions to develop agriculture in a hostile environment while the United States was taking fertile land out of production, especially because oil prices, and therefore Saudi state revenue, were then in rapid decline.

In a speech to a U.S.-Saudi business conference, Block said it did not make economic sense for Saudi Arabia to go on "paying farmers $1,000 a ton to grow wheat in the desert while we are lying idle 82 million acres of the best farm land in the world" through his department's payment-in-kind program. The Saudis "have a comparative advantage in the production of oil, and we have a comparative advantage in food," he said, urging the Saudis to give up and buy cheaper American products instead of growing their own at such great cost.

Block said Saudi officials—remembering their country's cutoff of oil shipments to the United States after the 1973 war in the Middle East and the U.S. embargo on grain shipments to the Soviet Union after the 1979 Soviet invasion of Afghanistan—had expressed "concern about the U.S. commitment to be a reliable supplier of farm products." To alleviate that concern, Block, with the president's approval, gave the Saudis a written commitment that the United States would never cut off shipments for political reasons.[33]

Block's proposition made economic sense, but the Saudis did not view agricultural development in purely economic terms. They saw it as a good use of their oil money to encourage the development of the private, non-oil sector of the economy. The farm program did that by giving money to farmers and stimulating the growth of related enterprises such as farm equipment, and the transportation, storage, and processing of food. To the extent that agriculture deterred people from migrating to cities, that was an additional benefit. Another decade would pass before the government undertook to rein in the farm program's abuses and control its cost. The largest subsidy programs were phased out during the 1990s as the country ran up annual budget deficits. The support price for wheat declined from $1,035 per ton in 1981 to $400 in early 2003.[34] Wheat exports have been banned.

Critics of the commitment to agriculture have naturally stressed its negative aspects: Many of the biggest food-sector companies that benefited were owned by members of the royal family or entrepreneurs enjoying royal connections, a situation that was not exactly spreading the wealth to the masses. These patroons tended to import cheap Egyptian and South Asian labor rather than train and pay Saudis. The wheat subsidies were so great that they enticed farmers to give up other crops that consumers needed. This led to ruinous overproduction; in the 1980s, much of the crop was given away to impoverished Muslim countries or left to rot. Excessive irrigation increased the salinity of the soil to the point where it was no longer productive; some of the farms that were created when this water became available have been abandoned.[35] A *New York Times* reporter who flew over Qassim Province early in 2003 saw circular wheat fields strewn across the desert like "forest-green poker chips," but these were outnumbered by "the ghostly silhouettes of fields left to fade back into the sand, places where the kingdom's gamble on agriculture has sucked precious aquifers dry."[36]

On the other hand, the agricultural sector has fulfilled a lot of the ambitions that the Saudis held for it, and they are proud of its development. During a visit to the Kingdom in 1990, when I asked Ministry of Planning officials how the country had benefited from the massive pump-priming of the previous two decades, they produced studies showing that agriculture accounted for 570,000 jobs, against only 47,000 in the production of oil. Today, agriculture is the largest sector of the economy other than petroleum and employs 16 percent of the labor force.[37]

By the mid-1990s, the country was fully self-sufficient in milk production and had achieved 68 percent self-sufficiency in chickens for eating, 85 percent in vegetables, 66 percent in fruit, and 46 percent in red meat. Overall, the agricultural sector has grown at an annual average rate of 8.7 percent since the Ford consultants first proposed the wheat program, and today accounts for almost 10 percent of gross domestic product (GDP).[38]

The country turns out vast tonnages of barley, fish, poultry, alfalfa, and cereal grains. It is the world's largest producer and exporter of dates. The al-Safi farm near al-Kharj is said to be the world's largest integrated dairy farm. Milk production in Saudi Arabia is 1,800 gallons per cow yearly, one of the highest outputs in the world.[39]

At the same time, rapid population growth has increased demand for food faster than the Saudis can stimulate domestic production. The five-year economic development plan for 2000–2004 projects a 3.05 percent annual growth in agricultural output, but the population is increasing by an estimated 3.5 percent a year. As a result, the Kingdom imports $3.2 billion worth of food products annually.[40]

Those numbers add up to big business, as I saw on a tour of an international agricultural trade fair in Riyadh in 2002. This event featured distributors, manufacturers, and purveyors from all over the world displaying their wares to potential Saudi customers, and Saudi food-processing entrepreneurs showing off locally produced products to potential export buyers.

Fair visitors saw giant tractors from England, their tires six feet in diameter; pumps and irrigation equipment from several countries, including Iran; animal health products and vaccines from Australia; Rain Bird sprinkler systems, like the ones found on American golf courses; Brazilian seed spreaders; Honda pumps and generators; poultry-feeding gear from Holland, Taiwan, and Italy; a sheep from Australia with a sign above its pen saying "Guess the Weight. The Prize Is the Sheep"; and a man from Japan hawking a vegetable slicing tool—in Arabic.

Saudi producers displayed peat moss; grouper, sea bass, shrimp and other sea food from the Gulf and the Red Sea; immense watermelons; live chickens and frozen chicken meat; Saudi-made foam food trays; and ostriches bred for meat.

These agricultural enterprises no longer depend on irreplaceable fossil water. With the help of the U.S. Geological Survey, Saudia Arabia has built an extensive network of dams and catch basins to collect what little rainfall there is, and produces more 220 billion gallons of water a year from desalination stations on the coasts;[41] that is more than 70 percent of urban consumption. It is by no means certain, however, that the country can collect or desalinate enough water to serve its fast-growing population, maintain or increase agricultural output, and nurture a lifestyle that now includes swimming pools and car washes, as well as flush toilets.

Terry Kirk, now back in Texas with Martha and raising cotton and three children, said he isn't convinced the commitment to agriculture is sustainable. "In my opinion, it's primarily viable from an animal feed standpoint," he said. "There's a large number of camels and sheep in the small countries around there, like Abu Dhabi, and there's no feed for them. Not for consumer consumption."

CHAPTER 11

Christians and Jews

A YEAR BEFORE THE FIRST OIL concession was granted in 1933, fewer than fifty non-Muslims lived in all of Saudi Arabia, mostly European diplomats in the handful of legations in Jeddah.[1] The Kingdom did not encourage infidels to visit and did not permit infidels other than diplomats to take up residence.

The Christian doctors and nurses from the Reformed Church's mission hospital in Bahrain were welcomed as guests and appreciated as healers, but they were never invited to remain. Their requests for permission to set up a permanent facility were rebuffed.

The people of Saudi Arabia practice a puritanical and xenophobic form of Islam that is disdainful of non-Muslims and even of other Muslims whose religious rituals and interpretations may differ. In Saudi Arabia, adherents of this rigorous Islam are referred to as *muwahhidin,* usually translated as "unitarians," for their absolute insistence on worshipping one God only, to the exclusion of the saints, holy men, and prophets venerated by Muslims elsewhere. This Islam is known to Westerners as Wahhabism after its founder, an eighteenth-century scholar and reformer named Muhammad ibn Abdul Wahhab, who forged a political and religious alliance with the al-Saud family that is still the foundation of power in the Kingdom. The absence of other faiths from Arabia, however, long predated Abdul Wahhab.

The Prophet Muhammad himself, originally on good terms with the Jews of the Hijaz, expunged them after a falling out; two of the three Jewish tribes of Medina were expelled from the city, and the third, which had supported Muhammad's opponents, was put to the sword. To dramatize his separation from Judaism, the prophet changed the day of congregational prayer in his new religion from Saturday to Friday and the direction of prayer from Jerusalem to Mecca.

Christianity never penetrated the Arabian heartland, although before Islam there was a Monophysite community at Najran, in far south-western Saudi Arabia. About the time of Muhammad's birth in AD 570, a Christian general named Abraha invaded from Ethiopia and marched on Mecca, only to be foiled by smallpox, an outcome commemorated in the Koran.[2] In the Islamic era, brief incursions by the Byzantines, Crusaders, and Portuguese were repulsed.

After Abdul Aziz ibn Saud unified the Kingdom and created modern Saudi Arabia in 1932, the exclusion of non-Muslims was, in effect, made law. All citizens of Saudi Arabia must be Muslims. No other religion may be practiced publicly. Symbols of other faiths such as the cross may not be displayed. The law of the state is Islamic law, or *shari'a*. Some customs and restrictions peculiar to Saudi Arabia, such as the exclusion of women from the male workplace, derive more from bedouin tradition than from doctrine, but that is a distinction without a difference; the custodian of tradition is the religious hierarchy.

Outside Saudi Arabia, Islamic communities since the dawn of the faith have tolerated Jews and Christians as "people of the book," monotheists who base their religions, from which Islam itself derives, on a revealed scripture. Although second-class citizens, excluded from many positions and required to pay a special tax, these non-Muslims for the most part lived peaceably alongside their Muslim neighbors and often thrived. Egypt, Syria, and Iraq have substantial Christian populations. Before the creation of Israel, there were large Jewish communities in Iraq, Egypt, Yemen, and Morocco. Saudi Arabia, however, was exclusively Muslim, and wished to remain so.

How, then, to accommodate the church-going Americans of the oil company and of the other enterprises that would follow? As the oil camp evolved into a community, the residents would want religious services.

Here was another example of the shrewdness and flexibility the Americans admired in King Abdul Aziz: He adopted a policy familiar to Americans in another context as "Don't ask, don't tell." The Christians at Aramco could have their services so long as they were not advertised and Saudis did not attend them. Inside their compound, the Christians more or less had freedom of worship. No churches were constructed—services were held in the theater or gymnasium—and clergymen were admitted to the country thinly disguised as "teachers." According to Bill Mulligan, these clerics kept a low profile. They and their flock were instructed not to talk about religion where Muslims could hear them, to keep religious titles and symbols off envelopes sent through the mail, and to be careful about papers they left around or threw away.[3] Within those limits, a lively religious life developed, one not much different from what would be found in any small American city.

An American woman who arrived at Aramco in 1948, Evadna Burba, discovered an adult Bible class on Friday mornings, Protestant services that included traditional hymns, and a chorus that presented oratorios, including Handel's *Messiah*.[4] Members of the chorus came from Aramco and from the other nearby institutions where U.S. citizens were working: the consulate, the airfield, and, beginning in 1964, the College of Petroleum and Minerals, now known as King Fahd University of Petroleum and Minerals. That school, Saudi Arabia's best institution of mining and engineering studies, was created by Americans to train the Arab geologists and petroleum engineers Aramco needed as it matured into a Saudi-operated company. Aramco donated buildings for its first campus.

The driving force behind the creation of the college was Ahmed Zaki Yamani, the colorful and energetic oil minister, who already envisioned a day when Aramco would be owned and operated by Saudis. From the beginning, all instruction was in English. Robert King Hall, a former director of training for Aramco—where he had irritated his colleagues by his insistence on being called "Doctor Hall"—toured the United States to recruit instructors, ensuring that this institution, too, would acquire an American character. The teachers, administrators, and their families joined the ranks of Christians who participated in religious services in the Dhahran area.

Paul J. Nance, a longtime Dhahran resident, wrote that "Christians among the expatriates could worship as they did in their home countries, but privately in homes reserved for that purpose, or in company school and recreational facilities adapted with portable altars. Ministers and priests received their work visas under the job title of 'Special Teachers.' The Saudis had no objection to these practices so long as there was no proselytizing of Muslims and no construction of Churches."[5]

"Of course we had religious services for Christians," said Baldo Marinovic, Aramco's chief financial officer. "We had Catholic priests there, and to solve the problem of the multitude of Protestant denominations, they somehow got lumped into two large groups. There was a high church group—Episcopalians, Anglicans, and so on—and officially the group was a self-directed group, just like the tennis club. It was called the Canterbury Group. Then the Baptists and Methodists and so on, they had a minister, and they were known as the fellowship group. And the Catholics were the R.C. group. . . . Of course the whole thing had to be conducted quietly, *sub rosa*."[6]

These groups may not have advertised themselves, but the people of Aramco country were well aware of them and the religious life of the community expanded as the population grew. Mary Elizabeth Hartzell wrote to her mother in 1964 that the company had "turned over three 8-bedroom dorms to the churches to use as a residence and parish house—Catholic, Protestant interdenominational, and Episcopalian."[7] The Catholic congregation was so large that it was organized like a regular stateside parish. It was named for Our Lady of Fatima, and its church bulletin listed various activities just as it would have done at home. By 1979, the Aramco communities had twenty-four resident Catholic priests who celebrated Mass for 2,000 worshippers weekly and ran First Communion classes and even an Alcoholics Anonymous group.[8]

Christmas was a major event on the Aramco calendar. Residents imported Christmas trees and decorated their houses. The community Christmas pageant evolved into an extravaganza.

"They would put on a Christmas pageant, the whole nativity business, with real camels and Mary on a donkey and so on," Pete Speers recalled. "And then there used to be a Santa Claus who arrived by helicopter and who'd be driven down the main street in an open car, and that helped contribute to the appeal of all the Christmas activities. The [Arab] population would come out and cheer Santa Claus. Most of them didn't know who Santa Claus was or what he was."[9]

In the Christmas pageant, "The Wise Men rode on camels, the shepherds herded real sheep, Mary rode on a donkey," Ellen Speers said. "The pageant was a pantomime, performed to a reading of the biblical story, backed up by a chorus performing appropriate carols."[10]

The religious services may have been semiclandestine, but the Christmas pageant was no secret. The United Nations Relief and Works Agency, a Jerusalem-based organization that provides aid to Palestinian refugees, sold Christmas cards that featured a photo of the Aramco nativity pantomime. The journalist Dorothy Thompson observed the pageant during a visit at Christmastime 1956 and wrote about it a year later in *Ladies Home Journal.* Not only were Saudi Arabs aware of the Christmas pageant, Thompson noted, but some of them participated, as camel drivers. In Dhahran, "every single house is decorated in colored lights," Thompson found.[11]

Still, the question of Christian practice was always sensitive, and restrictions were tightened or relaxed periodically, sometimes in response to a specific complaint, sometimes for no reason known to the Americans.

Rives Childs, the first U.S. ambassador, recalled that in response to a U.S. statement urging the admission of 100,000 Jewish refugees to Palestine, the Saudis banned the below-the-radar services in Dhahran: "Through a tacit understanding these had been permitted under the auspices of Aramco and the Air Force in a private hall but without the display of any religious images. An officer of the embassy who was so rash as to raise the issue with the government during my absence drew in reply a formal note banning even private services. It was only as the result of a pressing appeal on my part to the King that the note was withdrawn." The king accepted Childs's plea that such matters be settled "informally." Don't ask, don't tell.[12]

In 1950, Saudi passport offices were suddenly instructed not to grant any more visas to "missionaries, priests, ministers, clergymen, etc." Aramco's vice president, Floyd W. Ohliger, persuaded the king to allow them to resume visits as "teachers," but in exchange "was personally held responsible to see that no proselytizing of Muslims was carried on and that no outward displays of Christianity were made likely to inflame the Muslim population."[13]

The following year, the State Department reported that

the spiritual needs of the large number of Christians living in the Dhahran area have been taken care of by assembly in private on Aramco premises and on the air base under the auspices of the Air Force chaplain. The regularity of such assembly attracted the attention of local Arabs who entered and witnessed the proceedings. Saudi Arabian officials asked that such services be discontinued and that the chaplain be recalled. The [U.S.] Embassy [in Jeddah] and the [British] Foreign Office, however, never allowed the subject to become a matter of official record because it was recognized that our government could not agree to depriving American citizens of their spiritual requirements, nor could the Saudi Arabian government approve what [Islam] forbids. It was accordingly agreed that Christian services hereafter would be conducted in strictest secrecy behind locked doors and the chaplain would be replaced.[14]

Ambassador Childs's account and the State Department memo reflect a consistent U.S. government policy of accepting Aramco's practice of deferring to the Saudis on religious and cultural issues, apparently with the consent of the American community. Nora Johnson was a lonely voice when she asked in her memoir, "Did anyone, I wonder, ever say, 'We're going to build a church because our religion is as important to us as yours is to you?' Why should they respect us if we didn't respect ourselves?"[15] She apparently didn't ask that question herself until she had left Saudi Arabia.

After Prince Saud succeeded his father as king, he gave permission for Christian clergymen to take up residence at Aramco; under the previous arrangement they had lived across the water in nearby Bahrain.

When in the summer of 1955 an international news agency reported that King Saud had given such permission, the government denied it—but did not revoke the agreement.[16]

As the Western corporate and industrial presence spread to other regions of Saudi Arabia under Saud, and especially under his successor, Faisal, in the 1960s and 1970s, arrangements similar to those at Dhahran enabled Christians to attend semi-clandestine services, even in Riyadh. One diplomat at the Irish Embassy, for example, was a priest who conducted Catholic services. In Jeddah, Raytheon Corporation obtained a residence visa and a work permit as a "personnel counselor" for a Capuchin priest, who conducted services in ambassadorial residences. A 1977 memo by Bill Mulligan describing this arrangement observed that the priest, a Father Bartholemew, "does not celebrate daily Mass for his congregation at his home. He considers that that would attract undesirable attention to him and his house. He tells the children to call him Uncle Bart. Until Fr. Bart arrived in Jeddah, Catholic services were held at the American embassy by visiting priests, usually from Lebanon. Protestant services, long held in the American embassy, had been held for some time in Lockheed compound."[17]

"We had our own little place," said Larry Hecker, who worked for Trans World Airlines in Jeddah in 1970s. "Of course it was prohibited, if you said you were going to have a Christian service on Sunday and it's going to be in this place—well, that just goes a little bit too far. But if they know you're going to have a service they aren't going to say anything as long as you don't beat a brass band, or recruit Saudis."[18]

Lou Noto, who represented Mobil Oil Company in Riyadh in the 1980s and later became Mobil's chief executive officer, said that as "a practicing Catholic, I would go to services at one of the facilities in town set up to do that. I'm sure the Saudis knew those services were going on. They never bothered anybody. At the end of the day I never got upset. Today a lot of people are upset that they can't outwardly manifest this activity. It never dawned on me. I could do it, I went, I went home, I'm sure the Saudis knew I was doing it. They never bothered me."[19]

Frank Jungers, Aramco's CEO in the 1970s, said he tried to resolve this issue once and for all by brokering a diplomatic agreement between

Saudi Arabia and the Vatican. At the suggestion of his friend Monsignor John Nolan, a frequent visitor to Aramco as head of the Middle East Foundation, a Catholic charity, Jungers went to see Ahmad Abdul Wahhab, the chief of royal protocol.

"I suggested that I thought it would be possible to begin a program that might lead to establishment of relations with the Vatican, realizing how sensitive this was," Jungers recalled. "Perhaps the Vatican would respond if we could get the Saudis to respond, maybe we could start a dialogue." Some time afterward, Jungers was informed that the Saudi minister of justice, a man renowned for his piety, was willing to invite a small Vatican delegation to visit the Kingdom as his guests. The delegation consisted of Monsignor Nolan and a Cardinal, described in Jungers's recollections as "very well connected in the hierarchy that dealt with foreign affairs," but not named; they arrived in due course, "complete with cassocks, hats, the whole bit. This was unprecedented in Riyadh."

The visitors were cordially received, according to Jungers—so much so that when Saudi Arabian Airlines lost the Cardinal's suitcase, which contained the liturgical items he would need to celebrate Mass, the king himself intervened and told the airline that the bag "had better be in Riyadh early tomorrow morning. There were no excuses allowed." Sure enough, the luggage was delivered to the Cardinal the next morning.

The Saudis sent a return delegation to Rome, Jungers said, but the assassination of Faisal in 1975 put an end to this initiative. "The whole effort withered," he recalled.[20]

↩

According to several accounts, Saudi as well as American, the Saudi authorities became much more rigid and doctrinaire about restricting Christian worship after the events of 1979, one of the most traumatic years in Saudi Arabian history.

In that year, the Iranian revolution brought to power across the Gulf an aggressive, theocratic Shi'a Muslim regime that targeted the Saudis as tools of the "Great Satan," the United States. The split in Islam between the majority Sunni Muslims and the minority Shi'a developed in the first century after the founding of the faith and had to do with the succession to the Prophet's worldly authority over the Muslim community; it remains the deepest division among the believers. The events in Shi'a Iran inspired deep anxiety among the Wahhabi Sunnis of Saudi Arabia because Saudi Arabia has a substantial and restive Shi'a community in the Eastern Province, many of whom had been employed by Aramco. (The Saudis were not reassured to see their friends the Americans, longtime supporters of the Shah of Iran, stand aside as he was overthrown.) Also in 1979, the peace treaty between Egypt and Israel split the Arab world and forced the Saudis, for political reasons, to align themselves uncomfortably with Iraq and other radical regimes against Egypt. In November, a band of armed extremists seized the Great Mosque in Mecca and held out for two weeks against government efforts to retake control—an event that shocked the Muslim world and challenged the House of Saud's legitimacy as protector of Islam's holiest site. (Sixty-three of the insurgents were publicly beheaded after the siege ended.) And then at the end of December, Soviet troops invaded Afghanistan, reinforcing Communist rule over a Muslim country and threatening regional stability.

In response to this dismaying sequence of events, and in particular the mosque takeover, the House of Saud—under pressure to reinforce its religious credentials—in the 1980s encouraged the most conservative religious and social elements in Saudi society to strengthen their influence over social practice, education, and the behavior of the country's residents, foreigners as well as Saudis.

Writing presciently in 1980, the American scholar James P. Piscatori said that one consequence of 1979's turbulence and the mosque takeover could be a challenge to the legitimacy of the House of Saud—not from the left, by that time mostly a spent force in the Arab world, but from the right. It would take the form of "the rise of militant fundamentalist Muslims, who, like the *ikhwan* of an earlier period [King Abdul Aziz's fanatical tribal warriors], will strike at fiendish innovations and their perfidious agents—in this case, the Al Saud. . . . The problems of corruption and concentrated wealth seem particularly galling in light of the Sauds' pretensions to wear orthodoxy's mantle."[21]

In the words of Richard Murphy, who arrived in the Kingdom as U.S. ambassador in 1981, "The mosque thing was such a shock, the royal family decided then and there that no one would outflank them on the right."[22]

"The Saudi government became quite concerned about being out-maneuvered by the Iranians," Baldo Marinovic said. "You know, it's a little bit like in the old days, when the communists were more afraid of the Trotskyists on the left than anybody on the right . . . [The Saudis] were terrified that somebody was going to be a better Muslim than they were."[23]

Part of the ruling family's response was to crack down on social behavior, among foreigners as well as Saudis. Murphy and others said the reaction was not instantaneous but evolved over several years. "In my time my wife never covered [her hair] when she went out, but then it got much more conservative," Murphy said. "Five years after my tenure, I went back and I was surprised to see the women of the consulate had to cover, which they didn't before." Tolerance for offenses such as mixed-sex parties and the possession of alcohol diminished rapidly.

The other part of the royal response was to co-opt the religious extremists by giving additional power to the most conservative elements within the ruling establishment. The mosque uprising "led the government to give more power to Saudi Islamists and to emphasize its commitment to Islamic education and the enforcement of strict Wahhabi social practices," one recent study said. "The government did not change the Saudi curriculum and teaching practices to make them more Islamic and conservative, but it did fail to continue to modernize them."[24]

Some Americans believe that unleashing the religious absolutists and the behavior police known as *mutawa'in* was also a deliberate move by Fahd ibn Abdul Aziz, crown prince in 1979 and clearly destined to be king before long, to clean up his own reputation before assuming the throne. Widely known in his youth as a playboy and wastrel, Fahd needed to burnish his religious credentials before succeeding the ailing Khalid, as he did in 1982.

The expanding power of the religious authorities under Fahd coincided with a severe economic crisis as the world price of oil crashed in the 1980s. To the Arab scholar Madawi al-Rasheed, it was "no surprise" that young Saudi men who had not cashed in on the boom of the 1970s and young women who found their hopes for greater freedom dashed "responded favorably to Islamic preachers calling for a denunciation of the West, [and of] materialism, corruption and consumerism. Non-government religious organizations started to proliferate in the late 1980s. A strong Islamic rhetoric promoting a return to Islamic authenticity attracted people who had grown frustrated with a truncated modernization, inequality, corruption of the government and close ties with the West, which began to be increasingly defined as the source of social and economic evils."[25]

To the expatriate community, including the Americans, one painful consequence of this trend among the Saudis was the increasing scrutiny of, and strictures on, their religious practices.

Bill Mulligan's papers contain a 1983 memo from a Christian clergyman who had formerly ministered to the Aramco flock complaining that "ever since the 1979 Iranian crisis, civilized life in Saudi Arabia that was gradually attained up to that point has been regressing. Human rights and conventional civilized practices are now taking a back seat to a snow-balling, over-zealous Muslim religious and national movement that affects everyone's daily life. Hit broadest by this movement are (1) Christian church gatherings; (2) women; (3) Westernized Muslims; and (4) Westerners and Filipinos in general," who, this memo said, were living under a "reign of fear." The memo detailed a crackdown on Christians:

"Crucifixes, holy water and church bulletins are no longer permitted at R.C. masses.

"Ten fellowship members were recently deported for conducting religious services in private homes in Riyadh.

"To keep a low Christian profile, church services in the theatre will soon cease. Protestants are now holding their services in the Dhahran Hills Elementary School."

In addition, the writer complained, the Ramadan fasting rules were being enforced upon non-Muslims. Even at Dhahran International Airport, eating and drinking were prohibited from dawn to dusk.[26]

At least two of the priests of the Capuchin order who staffed Aramco's Our Lady of Fatima parish were expelled in the 1980s. One of them, known as Father Paschal, was celebrating Mass for a group of Filipinos when the Saudis broke it up, arrested him, confiscated all his religious materials, searched his home, locked him up for twenty-four days, and then expelled him from Saudi Arabia. In a letter to parishioners afterward, he reported that he was not ill-treated and that the incident had its humorous aspects: "It took some time to convince those who were searching my house that a red plastic vaporizer was just that and not something sacred."[27]

This thrust-and-parry game continues in the new century. According to the State Department's International Religious Freedom Report for 2002, "The Government recognizes the right of private worship by non-Muslims; however, it does not always respect the right in practice. . . . Non-Muslim worshippers risk arrest, imprisonment, lashing, deportation, and sometimes torture for engaging in overt religious activity."[28]

༄

Most of the Americans I interviewed for this book said that they and their friends had been able to cobble together some sort of arrangement for religious observance while living in Saudi Arabia if they wished to do so. They understood the rules and were willing to live by them. Kevin Taecker, a banker and economic analyst who lived in Riyadh for several years, said he and his family, who are Methodists, were part of a group that held services in the compound of the U.S. military advisers to the Saudi Arabian National Guard—until al-Qaeda terrorists bombed the advisers' headquarters in 1995, killing five Americans. He said that Crown Prince Abdullah "is truly a pious man, and respects the religions of others. Even under circumstances where that congregation was found out, he protected them, right up until the bombing, which basically put that compound out of business. Osama bin Laden blew up my congregation."[29] These pious Americans, however, were all Christians. Another religious group has had a far more difficult relationship with the Kingdom: Jews. For decades they were not permitted to enter Saudi Arabia at all.

There were no Jews at Aramco, no Jews at Bechtel, and no Jews among the U.S. military personnel in Saudi Arabia. The Kingdom refused to grant visitors' visas to Jewish members of Congress. For some years, Jews were not even permitted to land at Dhahran airport in transit to somewhere else. In documents granting American organizations the right to operate in Saudi Arabia, the Saudis inserted a standard clause saying personnel to be assigned "may not include anyone whose presence is considered undesirable" by the government, which meant Jews.

This exclusion policy long predated the issue of Israel and Palestine. King Abdul Aziz himself, rejecting a request from President Roosevelt that he meet with Zionist leader Chaim Weizmann, said that "the Jews are a peculiar case and the President must know about the enmity which is between us in earlier and in recent times. This enmity is well known and mentioned in our holy book."[30] Indeed, the Koran classifies Jews and pagans together as enemies of Islam: "You will find the Jews and idolaters most excessive in hatred of those who believe."[31]

With that outlook, the creation of Israel exacerbated the Saudis' aversion to Jews. King Abdul Aziz "is suspicious of all Jews and he hates Zionists and their doctrine," the State Department reported in 1951. "He is strongly opposed to Israel. . . . He fears the Jewish state as a bridgehead into the Near East of communist ideas and influence."[32] Until the 1950s, Americans in Saudi Arabia and the U.S. government refrained from challenging or questioning the Saudis on this subject because they had more important interests: retaining the oil concession, maintaining rights to the Dhahran air base, and moderating Saudi anger over the creation of Israel. The State Department argued that the Saudi government was doing its best to modify odious policies in the face of "fanatical religious opposition," and that "it behooves us, therefore, to applaud what Saudi Arabia has done and is doing, and not criticize it for what it has not yet been able to do."[33] Then agitation by Jewish groups back home and some prominent members of Congress, Jewish and otherwise, obliged the State Department to raise the issue with the Saudis.

In May 1952, the State Department's Bureau of Near East Affairs sent an internal memorandum to the department's congressional liaison team. It said that Senator Herbert Lehman and Representatives Jacob Javits and Emmanuel Celler, all Jews from New York, had been inquiring on behalf of constituents about Saudi Arabia's boycott of products and services from Jewish-owned firms. "Efforts by the Department and the Embassy in Jidda have recently been successful in causing the Saudi Arabian government to discontinue this discriminatory practice," and the three members should be so informed, the memo said.[34]

Not so fast. In November, the Saudis refused to allow a plane carrying an American delegation to a social welfare conference in India to refuel at Dhahran because the group included Jews and the plane had stopped in Tel Aviv. David K. E. Bruce, the acting secretary of state, cabled Ambassador Hare in Jeddah to complain, noting that the State Department had a "strong interest" in the India event.

Writing in the truncated language used for cable communication because fees were charged by the word, Bruce said, "During past year Emb and Dept have made attempts soften SAG [Saudi Arabian Government] attitude discrimination toward Amer Jews. . . . However there is evidence hardening rather than softening SAG attitude. . . . Dept had hoped persuade SAG its attitude doing SA far more harm than good before it became public knowledge in US that SAG discriminating between Amer citizens. Dept seriously concerned this whole matter may break in US press soon with serious harm to SA reputation and deterioration US-SA relations." That is, the State Department was concerned not about discrimination against Jews in itself but about the possibility that it would become public knowledge and damage U.S.-Saudi relations.[35]

Bruce "suggested" to Hare that he approach the Saudis to make certain points:

1. Religious discrimination between US citizens particularly abhorrent Americans. 2. Many Amer citizens who are Jewish are not only not Zionists, some vigorously anti-Zionist. . . . 3. Inevitably, continuance SAG attitude will undermine friendly relations US. Impossible for USG indefinitely to regard its own officials as belonging to two classes, one of which is regarded by SA as "undesirable" in total disregard ideology or feelings toward Arabs and based on false assumption religious affiliation

in itself creates attitude of enmity toward Arabs or Islam. 4. Dept is not in position to explain or defend SAG intransigence these matters to US public or even to other government agencies.

Hare responded that the Saudis were quite well aware of Washington's views but felt strongly about this subject and would react negatively if pressed. "Saudi attitude is not only result Pal[estine] troubles but goes back to time Prophet Mohammed," he cabled. "Attitude of Saudis re Jews is paralleled by practically identical policy toward Communists, both being regarded as potentially dangerous from standpoint security." (The king had been alarmed by the migration of Soviet Jews to Israel. Because they came from the Soviet Union, he regarded them as a Communist dagger aimed at the heart of the Middle East.) Hare assured the State Department that "there is no discrimination here against American Jews as such. Saudi restrictive measures apply to all Jews regardless of nationality."[36]

In accordance with Saudi wishes, the U.S. Air Force refrained from sending Jews to Dhahran Airfield. When the agreement allowing U.S. use of the base came up for renewal in 1956, Senator Lehman introduced a resolution objecting to this exclusion. The State Department naturally opposed the resolution; in a letter to the Foreign Relations Committee it argued that "it is fundamental that sovereign states have the right to control the internal order of their affairs in such a manner as they deem to be in their best interests." It said the department did not "condone" discrimination, but added that "in making assignments, however, the Department must take cognizance of local attitudes and traditions which might be likely to make an individual subject to embarrassment or place him in jeopardy." In other words, it excluded Jews from assignment to an important country for their own good.[37]

At a hearing on the Lehman resolution on July 20, liberals such as Wayne Morse of Oregon and Hubert Humphrey of Minnesota railed against the agreement and against the Air Force.

"I think the issue becomes very simple," Morse said. "You either recognize our citizens, free of this kind of discrimination, or we pull out." If the United States defied the Saudis and acted in accordance with its own principles, Morse said, the Saudis would be forced to accept it because they had no other place to go in their quest for security and protection. Would they turn to the Soviets? Of course not, Morse said.

"I'm for pulling out if they want this kind of agreement," said Humphrey, who objected to the designation of some Americans as "second class citizens."

"Why do we want these bases?" Lehman asked. "Why do we want this oil? Is it not because we want to protect and defend our American way of life? And how can that way of life be protected and safeguarded if we barter away our rights and freedoms for an airstrip?"

Brigadier General C. J. Hauck Jr., representing the Defense Department, said the senators were wasting their time. "It would be futile for us to submit lists of names of persons of Jewish faith to the Saudi Arabian Government when we have been informed that they would not be accepted."[38] Several more years would pass before the Air Force changed its policy.

In the same year as those Senate hearings, the American Jewish Congress began legal proceedings against Aramco under New York state law prohibiting discrimination in employment. The case grew out of a "help wanted" ad in New York newspapers seeking welders for work overseas. When applicants were asked about their religion, the AJC filed a complaint with the New York State Commission Against Discrimination, or SCAD. A SCAD investigator reported that "the welders were being recruited by a sub-contractor of the Arabian American Oil Company for work on a pipe line in one of the Arab countries, and that a visa from the Arab country was a prerequisite for employment. The investigating commissioner was informed by the Arabian American Oil Company that the Arabian government does not issue visas to persons of the Jewish faith. The company advised that it had an agreement with the Arabian government to screen all prospective employees for work in Arabia before they applied for visas, for the purpose of excluding persons of the Jewish faith to whom visas will not be granted."[39]

After consulting the State Department, which objected to proceedings that would "adversely affect" Aramco's relationship with Saudi Arabia, the SCAD investigator ruled that, because of Saudi policy, not being Jewish was a "bona fide occupational qualification," and there-fore Aramco was not legally liable.[40] The investigator, Elmer A. Carter, found that the real purpose of the AJC complaint was to force Aramco out of Saudi Arabia.[41]

The American Jewish Congress challenged that finding in a lawsuit against SCAD. A trial court upheld SCAD's dismissal of the AJC com-plaint, but that ruling was reversed by the New York Court of Appeals, which ordered SCAD in 1961 to rule in favor of the AJC. The com-pany did subsequently hire a few Jews, although as Phil Baum, the AJC's lawyer in the case remarked years later, "There weren't that many Jews lining up for jobs in Saudi Arabia anyway."[42]

∽

President John F. Kennedy, more willing than most Americans to con-front the Saudis about their retrograde attitudes, raised the treatment of American Jews, and specifically of Jewish members of Congress, when he met with King Saud on February 13, 1962. At the time, a Jewish congressman from New York, Seymour Halpern, was making an issue of the Saudis' refusal to grant him a visa.

Apologizing for bringing up an "irritant," the president complained about "the inability of American citizens of Jewish faith to transit Dhahran airport and the refusal of the Saudi Government to issue visas to American Congressmen of the Jewish faith." The king replied that the restriction applied only to "Zionists," and said that many non-Zionist American Jews had been allowed into his country.

According to the official State Department account of this conversa-tion, "The President commented that Congressmen of the Jewish faith, whether or not they are Zionists, are Americans who have pledged alle-giance to the United States. The Saudi refusal to allow them to enter Saudi Arabia is grist for the propaganda mill and hurts the Saudi cause. The President surmised that some who claim a desire to visit Saudi Ara-bia would probably not go once they were issued visas."[43]

This was a demonstration of Kennedy's brilliance at public relations. He was telling the king, in effect, "Your majesty, these guys don't really want to visit your country. They're just making an issue of it to embarrass you and the Arabs. Pull the plug: Give Halpern a visa to shut him up, and you won't even have to receive him in your country."

The ever-obtuse Saud did not get the message. He "promised that he would give the matter consideration upon his return to Saudi Arabia."[44] A few months later, Harold Saunders, a senior official in the State Department's Near East Bureau, informed McGeorge Bundy, Kennedy's national security adviser, that Ambassador Hart "has not had a chance to take up with [the King] the matter of visas for American Jewish travelers to Saudi Arabia, and Saud has offered nothing. In the current climate, it doesn't look as if we can hope for much progress for the present."[45]

Saunders's informal note to Bundy alerted the White House that the State Department would not be providing good news on this subject to the president, who had instructed the department to follow up on his conversation with Saud. Where was that follow-up, Bundy wanted to know? The department's response, in a paper sent to Bundy on June 30, 1962, said that Saud's failing health and the press of events had prevented Ambassador Hart from meeting with him to raise the subject. In any case, the State Department said, "We are convinced that successful amelioration of Saudi Arabia's exclusionist policy can only come about through quiet and persuasive diplomacy and that attempts at undue pressure on our part might well inhibit prospects for making progress in this matter and even jeopardize our relations with a country whose interests and orientation coincide in many respects with our own." As for Halpern, "We have informed the Congressman of our continuing efforts and have expressed the view that, while we are vexed by the Saudi inaction, little would be gained, and perhaps much lost, by public recrimination."[46]

This was classic State Department oatmeal: Don't make an issue out of this, even though it's contrary to American principles, because the host country might be offended. The department would have been more comfortable if the issue had just gone away, but it would not. It arose the following spring at a critical moment in the military deployment known as "Operation Hard Surface."

The United States offered to send eight fighter jets to Saudi Arabia as part of the intricate diplomacy involving the civil war in Yemen, which was a proxy contest between Saudi Arabia and Nasser's Egypt. American pilots and crews would operate the planes.

According to Ambassador Hart, "On the very threshold of the departure for the Kingdom of the promised air unit from its base in Tampa, Florida, Emmanuel Celler, a Jewish congressman from Brooklyn, was alerted by American Jewish organizations that here was an opportunity to ensure that non-discrimination would be put into effect. He demanded and received from the Department of Defense assurance that there would be no discrimination and he announced to the press that he had been also assured that there would be Jews in Hard Surface."[47]

The Saudis, who wanted the planes, would have looked the other way if there were Jews among the Air Force personnel—Don't ask, don't tell—but Celler's public announcement forced them to dig in.

"I was summoned on an emergency basis by Faisal," Hart recalled, "who informed me of this challenge to Saudi authority, and was told in oblique Arabic that 'if the vessel is to contain the wrong materials it may be best not to have the vessel delivered at all.' I sensed that while Faisal was incensed at this invasion of Saudi prerogatives by the Department of Defense, his rather elaborate metaphor meant that he wanted us to find a way out."[48]

The departure of the planes was delayed while Hart discussed the issue with deputy foreign minister Omar Saqqaf. Having made their point, the Saudis allowed the issue to blow over after a few days and the planes took off.

"Subsequently, I asked the commander whether there were in fact Jews in his personnel," Hart said. "Implying that records did not show religious affiliation, he said that he thought there might be one. All of the unit was allowed in by blanket visa without designation of individual particulars."

This issue continued to plague relations between the United States and Saudi Arabia for many years, especially because in that era Saudi Arabia still adhered rigidly to the Arab boycott of Israel. The Saudis refused to do business with or import products from any U.S. company that operated in Israel or was reported by the Arab League's boycott office in Damascus to be aiding the Israeli economy in any way. At one time or another Coca-Cola, Ford, Xerox, Monsanto, RCA, and even Topps Chewing Gum were blacklisted, along with many other companies. This issue was especially complicated by Saudi insistence on clauses in contracts requiring the exclusion of subcontractors who were on the boycott list.

The boycott restrictions and the ban on Jews were constant irritants as economic ties between the United States and Saudi Arabia ballooned during the great oil boom of the 1970s. As American firms arrived on the scene seeking to cash in, more and more of them ran into the anti-Jewish restrictions that limited their ability to make money; those who chose to comply with the Saudi rules exposed themselves to discrimination claims at home. In turn, more members of Congress felt compelled to raise the issue.

Faisal ibn Abdul Aziz, king from 1964 to 1975, was second to none in his aversion to Jews and Israel. "As time went on," Aramco's Frank Jungers recalled, "the king became more and more disenchanted with American foreign policy, the blind backing of Israel at every turn. This became almost an obsession with him. I would get lectures from him on why we had to change this and how short-sighted it was and how the Americans were driving the Arab world away from the West. . . . He talked to everybody at every opportunity on this subject, and he was very irritated about it"—to the point that he put his country's entire relationship with the United States in jeopardy with the oil embargo after the 1973 Middle East war.[49]

Hume Horan, an Arabic-speaking American diplomat who knew Faisal during that period, said the king was a firm believer in the "Protocols of the Elders of Zion," a notorious forged document from Czarist Russia about a supposed Jewish plot to control the world. Faisal was generally "wise, balanced, and prudent" in conversations with foreign dignitaries, Horan said. "But then at the end of every meeting, very often he would turn to his chief of protocol and say, 'Have they got the book?' And Ahmed Abdul Wahhab, in so far as the chief of protocol could, would sort of roll his eyes and say, 'Not yet.' And Faisal would jab a bony finger at him and say, 'Make sure he gets the book,' and the book was the 'Protocols of the Elders of Zion,' of which there was a bookcase full just outside the reception room."[50]

Still, Horan and other Americans said that Faisal was a flexible and self-confident ruler, secure in his Muslim credentials and the approbation of his countrymen; and because he also understood that a growing bilateral relationship with the United States required some adjustment to attitudes about Jews in the Kingdom, he adopted a "somewhat less narrow and bigoted approach," Horan said. The State Department, under pressure from Congress, posted its first Jewish diplomats to the country in this period—according to Horan, one Jewish foreign service officer assigned to the consulate in Dhahran gained entry when the Saudis listed his religion as "monotheist"—and the ban on Jewish members of Congress was abandoned. Several Jews worked for the bilateral Joint Economic Commission, established after President Nixon's visit to Riyadh in 1974.

If it is possible to pinpoint a moment when Saudi Arabia's resistance to Jewish visitors began to break down, it was probably the arrival of Henry A. Kissinger as the first Jewish secretary of state. The Saudis admitted him, the members of his staff who traveled with him, and the reporters riding in the back of his plane, some of whom were also Jewish. It was early in 1974, before Nixon's visit, a dicey moment in relations between Washington and Riyadh because the oil embargo was still in place and Americans were suffering in gasoline lines.

In his memoirs, Kissinger recalled that Faisal received him with all the ceremony appropriate for a visiting secretary of state. The welcome included a dinner at Faisal's palace, during which the king unloaded his standard speech about how Jews and Communists were working together to destroy civilization.

"Oblivious to my ancestry—or deliberately putting me into a special category—Faisal insisted that an end had to be put once and for all to the dual conspiracy of Jews and communists," Kissinger wrote. "When Faisal went on to argue that the Jewish-Communist conspiracy was now trying to take over the American government, I decided the time had come to change the subject."[51]

By his account, Kissinger was intrigued rather than offended. He concluded that Faisal was brilliant, and that his public statements about the supposed link between communism and Zionism made a certain canny sense: The fear of being encircled and threatened by communism strengthened his case for U.S. protection, and his remarks about Jews shored up his position among Arab radicals. "Faisal deserved his reputation for rectitude," Kissinger wrote. "He was as honorable as he was subtle."[52]

Many years would pass before Faisal's willingness to be flexible when necessary would translate into a routine acceptance of Jewish visitors by the Saudi bureaucracy; Faisal's fundamental beliefs did not change, only his tactics. At the time of his death, the general ban on Jews was still in place, a chronic irritant to relations with the United States.

In 1975, for example, when the Saudi government asked the Ford Foundation for additional help in training a civil service, a foundation consultant wrote, "This raises tough decisions. A Saudi Arabian ban of those of the Jewish faith poses the gravest issues. After much reflection I am inclined to believe that it should not *ipso facto* invalidate somewhat expanded work in Saudi Arabia; but it should require us to estimate not only its cost to what the Foundation stands for against the benefit it might confer but the minimum conditions under which, if asked, we would be prepared to act."[53] Amid accusations of harboring Zionist sentiments, Ford withdrew from Saudi Arabia not long afterward.

In February 1975, Representative Henry Waxman of California became one of the first Jews in Congress to visit the Kingdom. Upon his return, he reported that at first a visa was denied; he obtained entry permission only after State Department intervention. Waxman said he raised the subject at a meeting with Faisal: "The King's responses were curt and forthright. He made it clear that he made no distinction between the State of Israel and Jewish citizens of whatever other nationality. . . . The King told me he regarded all Jews as friends of Israel and therefore enemies of Saudi Arabia. King Faisal said that Jews, regardless of nationality, had no business in Saudi Arabia as visitors."[54]

By the time I first visited the Kingdom, in 1977, Faisal was dead, and his successor, Khaled, had opened the door to Jews a bit wider. The bookshelf containing the "Protocols" was gone from the royal reception rooms. When Saudi Arabia allowed American journalists to enter, Jews were among them.[55] U.S. government agencies and contractors—prodded by President Gerald Ford, who imposed tough rules prohibiting compliance with the Arab boycott—assigned a limited number of Jewish personnel to Saudi Arabia. The General Accounting Office (GAO), in a 1984 report on activities of the U.S.–Saudi Arabian Joint Economic Commission (JECOR), found that this was not an issue in JECOR contracts. "We did not find instances of discrimination against Jewish U.S. citizens," the GAO said. "U.S. officials that we contacted stated that they had not been instructed that Jewish employees would not be allowed in Saudi Arabia. Jewish employees of U.S. contractors and agencies have worked in-country on Joint Commission projects. We did not find that the Saudis make a special effort to determine whether a U.S. citizen is Jewish."[56]

Part of the reason for this transformation may have been that President Ford, cracking down on compliance with the boycott, had made an example of Bechtel. In January 1976, Ford's attorney general, Edward Levi, sued Bechtel Corporation over the boycott despite the objections of Kissinger, who feared political repercussions among the Arabs, and of Treasury Secretary William Simon, who wanted to ensure that the Saudis continued to spend and invest their oil earnings in the United States. Bechtel did not deny that it had complied with the boycott, but argued that U.S. antitrust law, the basis of the suit, did not apply overseas. Facing mounting sentiment against the boycott in Congress and wishing to avoid prolonged litigation that might embarrass Arab clients, Bechtel—without admitting that it had done anything wrong—accepted a consent decree that was upheld by the U.S. Supreme Court in 1981.[57]

So eager were American businesses to get in on the Saudi Arabian bonanza that they sometimes imposed on themselves discriminatory hiring and selection processes that went beyond what the Saudis demanded. Hume Horan recalled an executive from a major corporation who arrived in Saudi Arabia bearing a letter assuring the Saudis there were no Jews among the company's executives, a condition the Saudis did not impose. Perhaps the most celebrated example of this phenomenon involved the medical school of Baylor University in Texas.

In 1977, Baylor entered into an arrangement with King Faisal Specialist Hospital in Riyadh. That-up-to-date facility treats not only members of the royal family but also Saudis from the nonroyal populace who are afflicted with rare, difficult, or medically interesting disorders. Baylor doctors would go for three months at a time, sharing their medical knowledge and techniques with their Saudi counterparts and taking the opportunity to study diseases now rare in the United States, such as rheumatic fever. These well-paid, challenging assignments were widely popular with Baylor's doctors—except Jews, whom the hospital excluded from the program.

In 1982, two Jewish anesthesiologists sued, claiming unlawful discrimination on religious grounds. A federal court ruled in their favor and ordered that each should receive back pay equivalent to what he would have earned "based upon the number of rotations in which he could have participated."

Baylor appealed. In 1986, the United States Court of Appeals for the Fifth Circuit upheld the original verdict. Not only did Baylor discriminate, the court found, but it did so on its own initiative—not at the request of the Saudis. Baylor had told the two doctors they could not participate because, as Jews, they could not obtain Saudi visas; but the appellate court found that "there is no evidence in the record that that statement represented the actual position of the Saudi government with regard to the participation of Jews in the program. In addition, there is no evidence that Baylor even attempted to ascertain the official position of the Saudi government on this issue."

The court noted that an important witness for Baylor, the renowned heart surgeon Michael DeBakey, undermined the hospital's case by testifying that he had been able to get visas for Jewish doctors "to see special patients I wanted them to see. And we had no difficulty getting visas for them."[58]

Congress eventually made it illegal for American corporations to comply with the Arab boycott in any way. Although cases still arise occasionally—enforcement actions are listed on the Web site of the U.S. Department of Commerce—the issue receded in significance in the 1990s, partly because the Saudi government was no longer handing out the blockbuster contracts of the boom days. In 1994, when it appeared that peace between Israel and the Palestinians would be achieved under the Oslo agreement, Saudi Arabia and the sheikhdoms of the Gulf Cooperation Council announced that their secondary boycott of Israel no longer served any purpose and called for a review of all boycott provisions.[59] The primary boycott is nominally still in effect.

More significant was an initiative by Crown Prince Abdullah after Operation Desert Storm to reach out directly to American Jews. He assigned Adel al-Jubeir, an urbane young diplomat from a prominent Saudi family, to engineer a new era in this relationship. Al-Jubeir, now familiar to Americans as television's talking head of Saudi Arabian foreign policy, succeeded so well that he won the informal title of "ambassador to the Jews."

As a junior political officer in the Saudi Arabian embassy in Washington in the 1980s trying to win congressional assent to Saudi arms purchases, al-Jubeir said, he found that Jewish members of Congress such as Representative Mel Levine of California and Senator Rudy Boschwitz of Minnesota were reasonable people who would at least listen to what he had to say. "I realized that if I could tone down the opposition by 20 percent, that's 20 percent you didn't have before," he said. "I said, 'Let's talk to the opposition.' There was a big debate in the [Saudi] embassy over this, but in a couple of years, we turned it around in Congress. You could cut deals, if you could tone down the opposition. Then I figured, why not talk to the American Jewish community? Our message was, We were only asking for what your government told us to ask for" in seeking to purchase U.S. weapons systems.[60]

In 1989, al-Jubeir arranged for the ambassador, Prince Bandar bin Sultan, to meet a group of Jewish leaders privately in New York. "The idea was, let's have a conversation. Let's clear up areas of misunderstanding, we have more in common with each other than not: We want to contain radicalism and spread peace," al-Jubeir said. The big breakthrough was a 1992 visit to the Kingdom by a seven-man delegation representing the American Jewish Congress—the same group that had sued Aramco four decades earlier. The highest-ranking official to receive them was Prince Saud al-Faisal, the foreign minister, who told them that Saudi Arabia had accepted Israel's right to exist when the Arab League endorsed a Saudi plan for Middle East peace in 1982.[61] A larger delegation of American Jews from the Anti-Defamation League was invited in 1995—an even bigger step for the Saudis, al-Jubeir said, because the American Jewish Congress visitors were "peaceniks" but the ADL espoused a tougher line.

"The Saudis are pragmatic," said Abraham Foxman, the ADL's national director, now a veteran of multiple visits to Saudi Arabia. "They will make the compromises they need to make for their survival. When it's pragmatic to reach out to the Jews, they will."

Foxman said that in preparation for that 1995 trip, the ADL delegates insisted on "doing this publicly, not sneaking in." They would write "Jewish" in answer to questions about their religion, they would not sanitize their passports to conceal previous travel to Israel, and they would issue a news release afterward. The Saudis accepted their terms.

While they were in Saudi Arabia, Israeli Prime Minister Yitzhak Rabin was assassinated.

"I watched it on TV in my hotel room in Riyadh," Foxman said. The ADL visitors asked the Saudis for a statement of condolence to carry with them to Rabin's funeral, and the Saudis complied: "But only after we asked. It wasn't volunteered," Foxman said.[62]

On that first visit, the ADL delegation also got no higher in the Saudi hierarchy than the foreign minister. Invited to return, the members said they would do so only if they could have an audience with Crown Prince Abdullah, Foxman said. The Saudis assented, and the ADL party returned to a hospitable welcome from Abdullah, who invited them to his desert retreat and an Arab-style feast.

Al-Jubeir said news of these trips sparked some outcry in other Arab countries, where critics depicted the Saudis as, in effect, soft on Israel, but not in his. "These trips generated no controversy or opposition inside the country," said al-Jubeir. "In the rest of the Arab world, yes, but not in Saudi Arabia."

Many American Jews are now veteran visitors to Saudi Arabia. In December 2002, the official Saudi Arabian news agency announced that Senator Joseph Lieberman was a guest in Riyadh. He was received by King Fahd and had lunch with Abdullah. Lieberman is an Orthodox Jew. Saudi newspapers carried straightforward reports of his visit. The taboo has been broken.

CHAPTER 12

Go Directly to Jail

OF ALL THE AIRLINE PASSENGERS who have ever been bumped from an overbooked flight, it's probably safe to say that few have suffered more as a result than James E. Smrkovski. On August 22, 1985, he went to the airport in Jeddah with his wife and daughter in expectation of flying to the United States for a holiday. Unable to secure seats, they returned home. Two security officers from Saudi Arabian airlines, Smrkovski's employer, were waiting for him. Although it was nearly midnight, they insisted that he accompany them for questioning.

Thus began a fifteen-month nightmare in which Smrkovski, a linguist and English training specialist who grew up in Iowa and Minnesota, was interrogated, tortured, held in solitary confinement, shackled, beaten, and occasionally starved. At one point he was so thirsty he licked up his own sweat. His jailers pulled out six of his toenails with pliers.

Smrkovski was not a neophyte in Saudi Arabia. Having worked for Aramco on a previous tour, he had spent thirteen years in the country; he knew the rules. His big mistake seems to have been that he enjoyed practicing his German with an Austrian resident of Jeddah who was involved in liquor smuggling; the Saudis accused Smrkovski of being part of the ring. They also accused him of being part of a criminal "mafia." It appears the Saudis had some justification for their suspicions: Smrkovski told a State Department consular officer who visited him in prison that a liquor-smuggling ring of Europeans in Jeddah had threatened his life and the lives of his parents back in the United States because he owed them $70,000 "for the shipment of alcohol. He sold a large quantity of alcohol over a period of approximately 14 months to pay the debt."[1]

After some weeks in a tiny underground cell, Smrkovski began scribbling notes about his experience and smuggled them out in a letter to his brother, Lonnie. Here is his description of his captivity: "A glimpse into hell: Solitary confinement. Intense heat, filthy room, 9 x 12, no furniture, no toilet, no sink, no fan, no air conditioning—only 1 blanket and 2 pillows, both filthy with blood and stench of sweat. Bright light on 24 hours a day. Guarded by military special forces. Taken to toilet three times a day for 1 minute. Filthy with excrement on floor." A few days later, he wrote this: "No sleep 4 days and 4 nights, body covered with bruises and rash, filthy, could barely walk. Asked for doctor. Denied. More questions, accused of having 2 passports and spying for Iran. Denied. Beatings and electric shocks. Denial. Next day planned suicide with plastic bag."

Over the next year, Smrkovski was moved from prison to prison. Sometimes conditions improved and food was adequate; at other times he was cast back into his dungeon and the abuse resumed. When representatives of the U.S. Embassy visited, he was warned by the Saudis not to complain about his treatment lest it get worse. Bobby Watson, a consular officer who saw him in prison four weeks after his arrest, said, "It soon became obvious to me that Mr. Smrkovski had been through a traumatic experience: his hands were shaking, he was very excited, his voice cracked as he spoke, and he wept sporadically throughout the interview." When he was finally released, his wife, Rattana, said, "I hardly recognized him. His hair was cut very short and his skin was extremely pale. He had lost about thirty pounds and looked very gaunt." He was then forty-seven years old.

According to Rattana, her husband still suffered seizures and blackouts seven years later as a result of abuse by the Saudis. "He has been unable to work, and the mental stress which still plagues him continues to affect our relationship. My husband is often short tempered with me and the children. . . . My husband's ordeal has changed our lives. Although he is trying to overcome the effects of his imprisonment, he will never be the same again."

Smrkovski's case attracted considerable attention in Washington, along with that of another imprisoned American, Scott J. Nelson, because the men were represented by Leonard Garment, who had been President Nixon's White House counsel and was one of the most influential lawyers in the capital. Their cases came to him because of his political connections and his strong record as an opponent of torture as U.S. representative to the United Nations Human Rights Commission. Garment arranged for congressional hearings, and he took Nelson's case all the way to the U.S. Supreme Court.

Nelson, once a NASCAR race car designer, worked for Bechtel Corporation as an electrical and safety engineer. In September 1983, when he was twenty-nine years old, Bechtel sent him to Riyadh for two months to work on the construction of King Khaled International Airport. Nelson liked it there, and so upon his return to the United States he answered a newspaper advertisement seeking a "monitoring systems engineer" at King Faisal Specialist Hospital and Research Center in Riyadh, the most modern and best-equipped hospital in the Kingdom. The recruiting agent was Hospital Corporation of America (HCA), which is incorporated in the Cayman Islands; HCA flew Nelson from his home in Miami to Nashville, Tennessee, for interviews and tests. In his eagerness to get the job, Nelson made a serious mistake that would come back to haunt him: He claimed to have an engineering degree from the Massachusetts Institute of Technology, which was not true. He presented a phony diploma to support this claim. In December 1983, he was hired.

Spurious credentials notwithstanding, Nelson appears to have been good at his job. The legal record contains several favorable performance appraisals and letters of commendation, including one from his immediate superior praising his "devotion, professionalism and concern," and his willingness to take on duties beyond those in his job description.

All went well until Nelson discovered that lines carrying the hospital's supply of oxygen and nitrous oxide had been improperly connected to grease valves, an error that presented a serious fire hazard. When superiors brushed off his recommendation that these connections be replaced, he began badgering them, always an unproductive tactic with the Saudis. In one meeting with a Saudi doctor, Nelson said in an internal memo, "He came right out and told me to forget about the problem and he did not want to hear any more about it. . . . I do not understand this. This is a problem that *must* be corrected."

The more he pressed his case, the more the Saudis resented it. A memo from Riad H. Kayyali, director of engineering, complained about the "abrasive and unprofessional manner with which Mr. Nelson responds to requests or suggestions from his colleagues. This kind of behavior is most undesirable and objectionable from any professional regardless how competent that individual is. It actually tends to tarnish the good work he performs."

This back-and-forth continued for some months, during which time the Saudis, apparently looking for some way to punish Nelson for his uncooperative attitude, asked Hospital Corporation of America to recheck his credentials. When MIT said it could not confirm that Nelson had a degree, Nelson was arrested. His experience in Saudi custody was similar to Smrkovski's.

Guards kicked him, beat him with a rod, and forced him to do knee bends with a rod strapped to his legs until he could no longer walk. They lashed the bottoms of his bare feet with a bamboo cane. Then they threw him into solitary confinement. What happened next was recounted by one of his lawyers: "The dimensions of the cell were approximately 10 feet in length by 8 feet in width. It contained neither bed nor bedding, so Mr. Nelson had to sleep on the filthy cell floor. The cell was infested with rats and swarms of insects. The only windows were boarded over. A light bulb hung from the ceiling and was kept on at all times. As he was given no access to a lavatory, Mr. Nelson was forced to urinate and defecate in the cell. The stench became suffocating. During the time Mr. Nelson was detained in this cell, he was given no food or drink at all. Nor was he permitted to receive any visitors." After four days, he was forced to sign a statement in Arabic, which he did not understand; only then was he given anything to drink, a Pepsi.

Nelson then spent more than a month in Malaz prison in unspeakable conditions. He was held in a crowded cell where rats crawled over the inmates as they slept on the floor. Food was dumped in a tray devoid of utensils, so the prisoners had to fight each other for it. He was released after Senator Edward M. Kennedy of Massachusetts appealed to Prince Salman, the governor of Riyadh. Adding insult to injury, the Saudis then asked Nelson to return to his job, saying they did not want him to leave the Kingdom harboring hard feelings. He declined.

"To this day," his wife, Vivian, testified in 1991, "my husband continues to suffer greatly from the beatings and torture he suffered in Saudi Arabia. He cannot work, and the mental stress which still plagues him continues to affect our relationship. We quarrel frequently, causing us at one point to take our son Mathew to live with my sister and her family in Virginia. He is no longer as comforting as he once was, and our sexual life has been severely limited. . . . His back and knee injuries make it impossible for him to climb stairs without risk of falling down, which he has done on several occasions. We are no longer able to go bowling or dancing together."

Nelson tried to sue the Saudis for compensation for his injuries. U.S. law generally prohibits individuals from suing foreign governments, but provides an exception for "commercial activity" carried on by a foreign government in the United States. Nelson's lawyers, including Garment, said the recruitment of Americans in the United States represented such activity. The U.S. Supreme Court rejected the claim in 1993.[2]

"When I left for Saudi Arabia, I was in perfect health, I had a substantial savings account and was capable of supporting my family," Nelson told a congressional committee. "I left Saudi Arabia physically beaten and psychologically broken. I have depleted my savings as a result of my medical expenses and am in debt and unable to work."[3] Nelson did eventually recover enough to resume working. In March 2003, I found him in Kiev, Ukraine, working for a contractor cleaning up the remnants of the nuclear weapons Ukraine had when it was part of the Soviet Union. "You never get fully recovered, either physically or mentally," he said. Neither he nor Smrkovski ever received compensation from the Saudis.

Their attorney Garment, a skillful and well-connected player in the Washington game, later came within a whisker of persuading Congress to amend the Foreign Sovereign Immunities Act to permit Americans who have been tortured overseas to sue foreign governments for damages. In the end, Congress permitted such suits only against countries listed by the State Department as sponsors of terrorism, such as Iran. Saudi Arabia, of course, is not on that list. (Garment blamed the State Department for the watering down of the legislation. He said it has "an institutional urge to maintain stable relations with its foreign 'client' states, including unappetizing ones, not infrequently at the expense of Americans at odds with these governments.")[4] While Congress was considering the issue, the Saudi Arabian Embassy in Washington issued this statement: "The Kingdom totally rejects the allegations of mistreatment and torture."[5] The legal record, however, contains ample testimony from doctors in the United States that Nelson was indeed tortured extensively. His knees required surgical repair.

The Smrkovski and Nelson cases were extreme, but it was hardly unprecedented for Americans to run afoul of the Saudi law enforcement system. The State Department reported to Congress that in 1985, the year after Nelson's ordeal, twenty-three Americans were in Saudi custody as the year began, fifty-nine were arrested during that year, and sixty-one were released during that year, leaving twenty-one in custody at the end of December. "The Saudis are jealous of their reputation for having a well-ordered society and they will not allow foreigners to put it at risk," the department observed. It warned Americans that some common pharmaceutical products, even those available without prescription, were banned in Saudi Arabia: "Americans in Saudi Arabia have received prison sentences of up to two and one-half months and 70 lashes for possession of Captagon," a diet pill.[6]

Americans have been getting arrested in Saudi Arabia since the early days of the Aramco oil camp, where the roughnecks would misbehave after consuming too much alcohol. Most of these were minor cases in which Aramco officials or U.S. Embassy consular officers could talk the Saudis into turning the prisoners loose and letting them leave the country. Some cases arose from traffic accidents, in which Americans and other foreigners could be locked up while a financial settlement was negotiated with a victim's family. Others involved business disputes, in which Saudis had Americans arrested for the alleged nonpayment of debts or nonperformance on a contract.

Of all the Americans who lived and worked in the Kingdom in the twentieth century, the percentage of those who got into trouble with the law was minuscule, but when it did happen it was always troublesome for the U.S. Embassy and the State Department, for two reasons: The diplomats did not wish to offend their Saudi hosts, and there was not much they could do for the jailed Americans anyway. Saudi Arabia was not a colony; the Americans could not order the Saudis to set anyone free. U.S. diplomatic missions in Saudi Arabia stressed this point, as in the warning titled "Information on Arrest and Imprisonment in Saudi Arabia" distributed by the consulate in Dhahran: "In spite of what you have heard to the contrary, neither the United States Government nor its representative, the American Consul, can get you out of prison. While in this country, an American is subject to the same laws as a Saudi citizen. An American passport does not entitle the bearer to any special privileges." The advice offered to Americans in this document was entirely contrary to American legal tradition: "Confession and repentance are viewed favorably by judges since they are acting on the basis of a religious and moral, and not merely secular, religious system."[7]

Moreover, when Americans found themselves in trouble over business disputes, American diplomats often sympathized with the Saudis' fear that unscrupulous foreigners were cheating them. "Some of the Americans deserved what they got," said Hume Horan, one of the State Department's most experienced Saudi Arabia hands. "For the Saudis it was a kind of protective reaction, a necessary one, when you saw all the crooks and fourflushers from around the world that wanted to descend on these simple bedouin sheikhs and take advantage of their money."[8] Similarly, Chas W. Freeman Jr., U.S. ambassador from 1989 to 1992, observed that during the oil boom of the 1970s, the Saudis had "signed contracts with great haste with a large number of companies. In some cases, frankly, they were badly gouged by the foreign partner. The Saudis at that time were inexperienced. This gave rise to both a large number of commercial disputes about contract fulfillment and a rising suspicion on the part of the Saudis that led them sometimes to refuse payment on contracts when in fact the American partner had delivered what was contracted."[9]

Protective as it was of the overall U.S.–Saudi Arabia relationship, the State Department generally declined to intervene in business disputes until all legal remedies and appeals had been exhausted in Saudi Arabia, a policy to which many American businesspeople objected because Saudi Arabia's legal system always favored the Saudi party and the country lacked an impartial dispute resolution mechanism. In addition, Americans who left the Kingdom before disputes were resolved or money owed to them was paid were often reluctant to return for fear of arrest.

In 1992, Lawrence Eagleburger, then acting secretary of state, wrote to Senator Daniel Patrick Moynihan of New York that "allegations by Americans, including Scott Nelson, that they were tortured or otherwise abused by Saudi Arabia are causing very serious damage to our bilateral relations. Because this is a matter of such serious import, I can assure you unequivocally that we will convey to King Fahd the [Foreign Relations] committee's concern over this particular case and others and our own strong view that the Saudi Government should resolve these cases."[10] Nevertheless, when Nelson's case reached the Supreme Court, the State Department sided with the Saudis; it argued that the overall bilateral relationship would be jeopardized if Nelson prevailed, and that such an outcome would expose U.S. citizens and companies to retaliation by Saudi Arabia. Moreover, after the Supreme Court ruling, when lawyers for Nelson and Smrkovski petitioned the State Department to make formal representations on behalf of the two seeking compensation from the Saudi government, the department declined, on the grounds that they had not exhausted the remedies available to them in Saudi Arabian courts—a position that infuriated the lawyers, because it would have required the two men to return to Saudi Arabia and the legal system that had caused their pain.

Americans discovered that to prosper in Saudi Arabia, it was necessary to understand the Saudi business climate and recognize that the Saudis have an attitude about contracts and business commitments that is different from that of Westerners. A deal is not necessarily a deal. Saudis who have connections with the royal family will use them to business advantage. Personal relationships are essential. Haste is discouraged. Payments and favors that would be regarded as corrupt in the United States are an accepted part of doing business in the Kingdom. The business environment is unique.

"The first rule is that all government and private business practices are highly personalized and conducted on the basis of mutual trust," wrote David Long, who spent years in Saudi Arabia. "Without that trust, a contracting firm is likely to encounter all sorts of petty irritants undermining the profitability of the contract. Second, the party expressing the greater desire to conclude a contract is inevitably at a disadvantage, an expression of an age-old Middle Eastern principle of supply and demand. Third, and perhaps most important, *caveat emptor* is the governing principle of business negotiations. For goods and services one charges what the market will bear, and let the buyer beware. . . . Finally it is not necessarily morally reprehensible to accept payment for services rendered that would be considered a conflict of interest or even graft in the West."[11] "Generally," Long observed, "it is the unwitting Western businessman most disadvantaged by these practices who cries corruption."[12]

Gene Lindsey, who managed a consulting firm in Saudi Arabia in the 1980s and evidently did not enjoy the experience, put it this way: "Many Saudis are deal-making opportunists who will invest anything to make large, quick profits with minimal effort, and get rid of their business at the first sign of a declining market."[13] He noted that Saudis have little respect for the private business conversation; they open closed doors, walk in, and expect conversations to continue. Friends and relatives join the conversations. "It is not uncommon," Lindsey wrote, "for families and friends to enter and participate in the meeting as Saudi executives sit and finger their beads or pick their toes."[14]

Compounding the peculiarity of business practices are Saudi rules requiring most foreign workers to surrender their passports to their Saudi employers or business partners. This gives the Saudis maximum leverage in negotiations and disputes because the Americans or other foreigners cannot just pack up and leave.

The Saudis' casual attitude toward contractual obligations and their tendency to interpret all agreements in the way most favorable to themselves reaches even to the biggest projects and the highest levels, as J. Winston Porter discovered.

Porter, a chemical engineer who was international vice president for Bechtel, took on a mission in the 1970s that was central to Saudi Arabia's economic future: developing a master plan for Jubail, a giant industrial and port city and petrochemical center that the Saudis had decided to build on the Gulf coast. Porter said this project was the brainchild of his boss, Steve Bechtel.

"The king [Faisal] and Mr. Bechtel were talking one day," Porter recalled, "and Steve told the king, 'You really ought to figure out a way to quit flaring all this gas,'" a reference to the vast quantities of natural gas that came up from oil wells along with the crude. The Saudis, who had no use for the gas, simply burned it. "'You could make petrochemicals, you could desalt seawater, you could make power and all kinds of other good stuff,'" Steve Bechtel argued to the king, according to Porter. "And the king basically said, 'Can you help us?' And he said sure. Steve was a real visionary." Thus began one of the most ambitious industrial projects of modern times: capturing the flared gas and using it to power petrochemical industries in two cities, Jubail on the Persian Gulf coast and Yanbu on the Red Sea, that would be built virtually from scratch. The task of capturing the gas and making it available for industrial use was assigned to Aramco; Bechtel's job was to design and build Jubail.

This was a pet project of Hisham Nazer, the American-educated technocrat who was then minister of planning and later minister of petroleum. In 1975, he persuaded the king to expedite the plan by breaking it out of regular government structures and creating a separate Royal Commission for Jubail and Yanbu, a somewhat smaller project on the Red Sea. As minister of planning, Nazer had a seat on the commission's board. His deputy, the competent but brusque Fayez Badr, a technocrat who drove a gold Mercedes and a hard bargain, was Porter's principal contact on the Jubail project. (I met Badr a year or so later, when his demanding style had brought him a Herculean assignment: cleaning up the port of Jeddah, which had been overwhelmed by the flood of imports as the country's riches grew. It was not uncommon for ships to ride at anchor for three months waiting to unload, incurring huge demurrage charges. Perishables were offloaded by helicopter. Badr brought order out of the chaos in a year.)

"I had two roles," Porter said. "One was to get the master plan done satisfactorily. The other was to collect our money. Our contract said the Saudis would open an irrevocable letter of credit at Citibank in New York for $11 million and we at Bechtel would draw that down, so many dollars a month." For some months at the beginning of this project, however, there was no visible work product. The contract called for a "Criteria and Strategy Document," Porter said, "but the Saudis wanted to know, 'What the heck is a Criteria and Strategy Document?' So the first time I went in with a big invoice, I had these invoices for $1 million and $2 million, they said, 'Well, we're not going to pay you anything till you do some work.' I said, 'Read your contract.' They read it and said, 'That's not fair.' Dr. Badr looked at the contract and made the point again, 'It's not fair.' Then he kind of got this big smirk on his face and said, 'Why don't you send me down to the religious courts?'" Once the Saudis could see tangible results of the planning process, with maps showing locations and architects' concept drawings, they paid promptly, Porter said. The literal wording of the contract did not determine the course of action.

Porter was working on the Jubail plan at the absolute height of the spending frenzy of the mid-1970s, when the Saudis literally had so much money they did not know what to do with it. The government was overwhelmed by its own ambition and the sheer volume of development projects. "I would be waiting to see Hisham Nazer in his outer office and here would come the prime minister of France or the head of Mitsubishi," Porter recalled. "It wasn't a bunch of junior engineers from somewhere. And the way the meeting system works over there, it's not all that crisp anyway. So every time I went to see Dr. Badr or anyone else over there, I would have my stuff with me just in case I bumped into

Hisham Nazer in the hallway. He would say, 'Oh, Dr. Porter, you got a minute?' And I better be ready, because that was my meeting for two months."[15]

Porter, however, was in a considerably stronger position than Americans such as Smrkovski and Nelson. He represented Bechtel, which, after Aramco, was the most respected and influential American institution in the country; furthermore, the government was fully committed to the project he was working on. (The Royal Commission says it has spent $20 billion, and private investors $42 billion, in converting two nondescript coastal villages into modern industrial centers with a combined population in 2003 of 157,000.) And Porter was dealing with competent, high-level people who had decisionmaking power and deep pockets. None of those positives applied to John McDonald.

McDonald was in the prefabricated housing business, for which Saudi Arabia was the promised land in the 1970s as a huge wave of immigrant labor poured into the country. The Saudis often required foreign contractors such as Korean road building firms to provide bachelor living camps for their immigrant workers, as David Blomberg and Waste Management Inc. did for the Indian laborers they hired to collect Riyadh's trash. The workers were not permitted to bring their families because the Saudis did not want them to settle permanently in the Kingdom.

McDonald was an experienced international traveler and businessman, but in Saudi Arabia he turned out to be just the sort of "unwitting Western businessman" David Long said was most likely to run afoul of Saudi business practices. His company, Heritage Building Systems International, had a contract with a Saudi partner to construct prefabricated concrete housing for the Jubail project. Heritage was to ship steel for the casting forms to the Eastern Province and assemble them to cast the concrete; his partners were to prepare and provide an assembly site in Jubail.

At the time there was no international hotel in the Jubail area, so McDonald lived in the modest home of one of his Saudi partners; he had one fluorescent tube for light, no running water, no telephone, and the occasional rat for company at night. If there was romance in the desert environment, McDonald didn't find it; he hated the place. He was afflicted by boredom, poor food, bad drivers (and their reluctance to turn on the air conditioning), and flies. His attitude was reflected in his term for the deal that went sour: He called it a "sheikh down."

"I was going to become an independent construction man on projects in the Middle East," McDonald recounted. "What I became was meat for a new breed of opportunists who had grown up as the dollars began to flow in from oil sales to the West. Called 'five percenters,' they five-percent you to death. Always presenting themselves as a prince or a king's relative, these sand sharks hang out in the lobbies of the finest hotels, which pass, in Mideastern countries, as business areas. They are armed with contracts, deals, contacts, and a solid-gold, gold-gilt carrot to dangle before anyone dumb enough to look. I was dumb enough."[16] McDonald seems to have been surprised to encounter this "five percent" phenomenon, as if he had never heard of Calouste Gulbenkian, the legendary petroleum wheeler-dealer of the late nineteenth and early twentieth centuries, who was known throughout the oil industry as "Mr. Five Percent." The rake-off was hardly a new development in the Middle Eastern business bazaar.

By McDonald's sometimes lurid account, the Saudis did not uphold their end of the contract. Obliged by its terms to find and prepare a site, they demanded instead that he do it, and turned to extortion when he refused. The wording of the contract was not even an inconvenience for them; they just waved it away. "How childish, Mr. John, for a man in your position to keep referring to an agreement," one said. In the view of another, the contract was irrelevant because McDonald should have known the Saudis lacked the technical competence to fulfill their part of it.

Depressed by his isolation and his surroundings, he could have given up and left, but he still hoped to salvage some profit from the deal. "I had no appointments, nowhere I had to be, was alone in a strange country spending money at a horrendous rate every day. I longed to be home with Pat and my family, but I couldn't leave," he recalled.[17]

He should have cut his losses and departed. As the dispute turned nasty, the Saudis persuaded the local police to confiscate McDonald's passport and so prevent him from leaving the country. He was able to replace the passport at the U.S. Consulate in Dhahran, but could not get an exit visa because his new passport did not have a valid entry stamp and his partners refused to provide one.

The Saudi lawyer McDonald consulted gave him three options: Go to a Saudi court, where as a non-Muslim foreigner he would surely lose and the decision would be final; go to a business arbitration panel established by the government to deal with such disputes, where he might win but the ruling would not be enforceable; or petition the king. While he was thinking it over, his partners surprised him by deciding on their own to take the case to an arbitrator through a process created by the Chamber of Commerce and Industry.

The arbitrator, a distinguished, unflappable Egyptian, ruled for McDonald, whereupon his partners had him thrown in jail, the first of four such detentions over the next several months. (Some American lawyers with experience in Saudi Arabia are skeptical about this claim in McDonald's narrative. They say Saudi Arabia's internal arbitration system is well developed and that the Saudis have a good record of implementing arbiters' decisions.) McDonald was locked up in "the worst pigsty of a cell you can imagine. There were ten men in the room, which smelled of old shit, unwashed feet and bad cases of ringworm. Flies everywhere, intense heat, and as for the toilet. . . . "[18]

McDonald suddenly learned the hard way the truth of those warnings from the embassy about its limited ability to help Americans in jail. A consular officer visited, but was unable to do much more than inquire after his health and relay messages. "I learned then that no matter how strong the desire of the consulate official to set you free, or how much he might wish to protect a fellow American, there is little or nothing he can do," McDonald wrote.[19]

A prominent Saudi friend arranged for his release after a few days, but the basic problem remained. He could not pursue his business, he had no leverage over his Saudi partners, and he could not leave the country, at least not legally. If he tried to drive over the causeway to Bahrain, he would have the same exit visa problem as at the airport. If he sneaked across the desert to Jordan or Qatar, he risked being caught and thrown into prison for years. A clandestine escape by boat? Equally risky. But after so many months he had reached the point where he "would rather be dead than stay here another day." He devised a desperate scheme.

With the help of a Saudi-hating American friend, McDonald had himself sealed into a packing crate, with a couple of jars of water and a supply of Pampers for toilet needs. The friend arranged for the crate to be shipped to Amsterdam as cargo on a Dutch airliner, making sure the crate was loaded in a pressurized cargo hold so McDonald would not suffocate or freeze. After several hours of lying in the baking sun at Dhahran airport, the crate was picked up by a forklift and stowed aboard. Six hours later, at Schipol Airport in Holland, McDonald opened the crate from the inside and walked away. This daring escapade became the subject of a television movie.

The ordeals of McDonald, Nelson, and Smrkovski attracted attention because they were as unusual as they were dreadful. The vast majority of Americans who have done business in Saudi Arabia have done so without being tortured or incarcerated; many of them made a good deal of money, and many of them cherish the experience of having lived in Saudi Arabia. The records of congressional hearings on this subject are replete with testimonials from American corporate executives who say that their firms have prospered in Saudi Arabia and their employees have been well treated. Still, as the three cases demonstrated, the legal systems and business cultures of the two countries are so different that the potential for misunderstanding and mischief is always present.

The differences are specific and general, legal and attitudinal. Saudis, as David Long noted, prefer to do business on a personal level with people they trust. These ties are more important than mere documents. Their legal system is based on Islamic law and gives preference to Muslims; proceedings are in Arabic and there are no juries. Schedules are notional. Rules require that foreign investors and marketers of imported products work with Saudi partners and agents. Until August 2001, all bids for government service contracts were required to be submitted through Saudi agents, who were entitled to collect up to 5 percent of the contract value. The result of those rules was "to insert Saudi middlemen into all economic transactions," as Kiren Chaudry wrote.[20] Bankruptcy and insurance laws are vague or nonexistent, and dispute resolution procedures are murky.

As Chas Freeman put it, "I spent a great deal of time trying to get the Royal Saudi government to push the process of dispute settlement. When the disputes involved a member of the royal family, particularly a senior member of the royal family, they were particularly difficult." He said that "generally speaking, Saudi Arabia, like most societies other than the United States, abhors the idea of litigation. The dispute settlement process can work, but Americans find it arcane, and it may not yield the results the Americans would expect from another legal system."[21]

In Congress, which is far less tolerant of the idiosyncrasies of the Saudi system than the State Department, business deals in which the Saudis fail to meet their contractual obligations to Americans or fail to pay what they owe have been a longstanding irritant. In Freeman's view, this is because "elements of the American Jewish community were always looking for ways to embarrass the Saudis and complicate relations with Saudi Arabia. So they would provide informal counsel and support of the efforts of disgruntled Americans to press their case in Congress. Some of these became quite *causes célèbres*."[22]

The Saudi government's attempt to discipline its spending after the binge of the 1970s created a new set of problems for some American businessmen. The finance ministry began to refuse payment on government contracts that it had not approved in advance. As a result, contractors experienced long delays in getting paid, and some were not paid at all. Congress enacted legislation requiring the State and Commerce departments to seek settlements and considered measures to link a satisfactory Saudi response to continued arms sales. At the time, in the early 1990s, the annual volume of bilateral trade was about $13 billion, and the United States was the largest foreign investor in Saudi Arabia; there was powerful support for Saudi Arabia in the U.S. business community.

Representative Lee Hamilton of Indiana, then chairman of the House Foreign Affairs Committee, opened a 1992 hearing on the subject of *Problems Confronting U.S. Businesspersons in Saudi Arabia* by complaining that nothing had happened to resolve some longstanding commercial disputes since a previous hearing five years earlier. "Despite the extensive commercial relations we have with Saudi Arabia and the close bilateral ties we have developed, many American companies have suffered and continue to suffer because of inaction, delay, and the absence of an effective dispute resolution mechanism," he said.[23]

Senator John Glenn of Ohio, the former astronaut, appeared at that hearing on behalf of a company in his state, Bucheit International, an engineering firm in Youngstown. According to Glenn, Bucheit had a contract with Prince Mishal bin Abdul Aziz, a son of the founding king, to build a shopping center in Riyadh. The work was completed in 1984, but a dispute arose over who was responsible for paying cost overruns. "Rather than work the matter out with Bucheit or submit the issue to arbitration, as was called for in the contract," Glenn said, "Prince Mishal held fifteen Bucheit employees hostage, refusing to allow them to leave Saudi Arabia in an attempt to force Bucheit to accede to his demands." The "hostages" were released when Bucheit posted a $1.3 million letter of credit.

Glenn said Prince Mishal "fraudulently" posted the letter of credit to his own account and steadfastly refused to negotiate a settlement or go to arbitration. "There seems to be no way to legally compel him to address Bucheit's claims," Glenn said. "No Saudi attorney will touch a case involving such a high-ranking member of the royal family. There is no Saudi court, tribunal, or other decision-making body where Bucheit can go to get his case heard." Representative James Traficant, who represented Bucheit's Youngstown district, denounced Mishal as a "crooked, dishonest thief," and expostulated, in his usual colorful style, that it was "intolerable," a year after U.S. troops fought to defend the Kingdom in Operation Desert Storm, "that the Saudi Arabian government cannot help us to obtain justice after what the United States sacrificed to protect it." (This was a decade before Traficant went to prison himself.)

A witness from the Commerce Department, Karl S. Reiner, told the committee that the department had been frustrated by its inability to bring the Saudis to the table in the Bucheit case. "We simply could not bring the matter to a conclusion," he said. "We have had to tell Mr.

Bucheit that a settlement is not feasible and advise him to seek remedy in the courts." That prompted this exchange with Representative Benjamin Gilman of New York:

GILMAN: You heard the testimony today that there is no remedy in United States courts?
REINER: That is correct.
GILMAN: So you are sending him back to the Saudi authorities?
REINER: We may have to, yes.

The contretemps with Prince Mishal bankrupted the Bucheit firm.

Reiner gave the committee a list of major cases in which a U.S. company had been unable to gain satisfaction from the Saudis. In one of them, First Chicago Bank filed a case with the Saudi grievance board against the Ministry of Industry and Electricity. In 1990, it actually won a $6.9 million judgment from this Saudi tribunal, but the ministry refused to pay. In another, the Plaza Hotel in New York was trying to collect from Prince Abdullah bin Jiluwi, who had declined to pay the cost of a business meeting in 1988 for the novel reason that "the meeting was unsuccessful." The Saudi Embassy in Washington eventually paid the bill, but the Plaza was seeking reimbursement for $225,000 in legal fees.

Overall, Reiner said, the Commerce Department was tracking "eighteen major cases, involving fourteen American companies, with claims of approximately $500 million. Many go back eight to ten years."

David Mack, a career specialist in Arab affairs, was the State Department's representative at that hearing. "The vast majority of the commercial contracts, some 40,000 a year that are entered into, are completed to the mutual satisfaction and profit of both U.S. companies and Saudi companies," he said. Mack said he doubted that there was any country where one could not find some procedures that Americans would regard as "atrocious," but "the problem in Saudi Arabia has been that the disputes which have developed, although not necessarily a very large number, have proven very difficult to resolve. That is a problem which is related primarily to a decision of Saudi Arabia to reserve dispute resolution to its own courts. It is not a decision with which we agree, but it is a decision that stems from some unfavorable experience that they had in the early years of economic development when disputes were usually submitted, with their willingness, to foreign courts. They felt from that experience that they were disadvantaged."

Over time, Americans doing business in Saudi Arabia came to recognize that they needed legal assistance to navigate the maze of rules, permits, and required documents—especially because all legal documents and court papers in the Kingdom must be in Arabic. Precision in translation is essential. Several prominent American law firms have offices in Saudi Arabia, usually in partnership with Saudi lawyers.

Today the gold rush atmosphere has subsided and experiences like those of Bucheit and McDonald are rare. Many Saudis are experienced international businessmen who understand the rules of global trade and recognize that their country must accommodate them. Businesses are well established. The legal system has evolved. In August 2001, the Saudis announced the repeal of the rule requiring foreign contractors to have a Saudi agent. The State Department's annual report on the Saudi economy says that Saudi Arabia has updated its tax and investment codes. The Saudi Arabian General Investment Authority was established to encourage foreign investment and streamline procedures. The Council of Ministers issued a new penal code prohibiting the coercion and abuse of prisoners and limiting pretrial detention to five days. Saudi Arabia is now a party to the New York Convention on Foreign Arbitral Awards, which generally requires Saudi Arabia to honor an arbitration award issued in another country. Saudi Arabia also ratified an international Convention on the Settlement of Investment Disputes Between States and Nationals of Other States. In short, the "survival of the fittest" era is in the past, but legal requirements and court procedures still differ greatly from those in the West, and there is always an element of uncertainty. As late as 1997, the U.S. Embassy was advising Americans that Saudi courts "do not generally recognize the concepts of limited liability, escrow or the time value of money. Many businessmen prefer to resolve private commercial disputes either through non-binding chamber of commerce arbitration or ministry of commerce tribunals."[24]

As always, the Saudis embrace change only slowly and incrementally. According to the State Department's annual review of the Saudi Arabian economy for 2002, the Foreign Direct Investment law enacted in April 2002 was "a good first step, but needs to be accompanied by other measures if significant investment is to flow into the non-energy sectors of the Saudi economy. Specifically, the government must take steps to ensure that there is a transparent, comprehensive legal framework in place for resolving commercial disputes. Prospective foreign investors want convenient access to multiple entry-exit visas without the need for a Saudi sponsor," as well as improved protection for intellectual property.

CHAPTER 13

The Cultural Divide

TRAVELING AROUND SAUDI ARABIA in the spring of 1977, at the peak of the oil boom, I dropped by a new teachers' college in Abha, the principal city of the Asir, a beautiful region of mountains and lush farms in the far southwestern corner of the Kingdom. In a basement room, the students and teachers had created a little museum to preserve the crafts and artifacts of their fast-disappearing traditional life. They had collected curved daggers, camel saddles, ropes of woven leather, bedouin jewelry, and samples of regional clothing.

A few years before, all these items had been in common use. By 1977 they were becoming relics, supplanted in daily life by pickup trucks, computers, power tools, and transistor radios. The Saudis are not sentimental about objects. They tend to use things until they wear out, then discard them. Brass pots, woven rugs, and goatskin water bags, however handsomely crafted, were seldom preserved for their own sake; the bedouin limited their possessions to what they could carry with them. In Abha, the organized display that attracted most public attention was not the modest collection of artifacts at the teachers' college but the pile of wrecked cars set up by the local authorities on a downtown square as a warning to careless drivers. For a systematic effort to preserve the country's traditional crafts, the men to see were not Saudi Arabs at all, but expatriates like John Topham and Paul J. Nance. These two Americans devoted a large part of their lives to the collection and preservation of irreplaceable objects about which the Saudis were mostly indifferent.

Topham was a construction manager from upstate New York who arrived in Saudi Arabia in 1977 as a consultant to Aramco. He spoke no Arabic and had no background in Arabian artwork or artifacts. He did carry with him a curiosity about the world that he had indulged through the extensive study of old maps and the reading of travel literature, including the books of H. St. John B. Philby, the legendary British Arabist who had been the closest Western adviser to King Abdul Aziz.

"I also had an interest in crafts, especially weavings, since one of my artist daughters makes wonderful tapestries," Topham wrote. "Over the years, I had built a small collection of rugs. I developed a special interest in nomad weavings and owned some good kilims and Navajos—flat-weave rugs that have practical value in everyday use."

On his first visit to the *souk* in Dammam, he came across bedouin women selling striped woven rugs. He bought some as colorful coverings for the dull linoleum floor of his house, not as artworks, but he was caught up in the romance of the native market. For the rest of his time in Saudi Arabia, he roamed the *souks* of Hofuf, Riyadh, and other towns, and bought whatever caught his fancy. "I maneuvered the work situation so I could live in different parts of Arabia" to learn and acquire more, he said.[1]

I learned only a few polite greetings in Arabic and some essential descriptive words, but negotiating and buying were not difficult. English is widely taught in Arabia, and I often had eight- or ten-year-old children translating for me, or an adult with English would appoint himself negotiator, graciously looking after my own interests as well as the seller's. Sometimes, when no interpreter could be found, the sellers—usually old ladies—would negotiate by folding my fingers down one by one, each finger representing 100 riyals—then $31 or $32. When they approached my maximum price, I would resist the pressure to fold the next finger down, and often we settled at a half or quarter finger. I bargained less and less as I acquired some feeling for prices and more knowledge of what good quality was. The item was either worth the asking price to me or it wasn't.

Sometimes he probably overpaid, he wrote, but "some of my best things cost the least. I paid only about 700 riyals ($220) for a very old *mubarrid,* a wooden container used to cool coffee beans between roasting and grinding. It is now my favorite item in the entire collection."

Items made of wood were especially rare because trees are scarce in Saudi Arabia and the objects of daily life for which wood had been used, such as trays and boxes, were by then available in plastic.

A person whose interest in Saudi crafts was only casual would never have discovered that coffee cooler; finding such rarities was time-consuming. Topham, however, was a man on a mission, prepared to commit the time to find good pieces. He and a friend were on a five-day exploration tour of southwestern Saudi Arabia when they stopped at a roadside vendor's stand on the road to Najran. "An Arab who came by invited us to follow him to his house where there might be things of interest. This was many miles across rough country," Topham recalled. Making the trek, Topham and his companion found ample reward: the *mubarrid,* "several good pieces of jewelry," and a tasty lunch.

The *mubarrid,* the vintage firearms that Topham also acquired, and a collection of bracelets from Najran were antiques, but the artifacts of cloth and leather were mostly of recent creation. Rugs, blankets, garments, camel tack, and coffee-bean bags, however colorful, were made to be used hard daily by poor people, not admired, and as a result they did not last long. Many of Topham's prize pieces were new when he acquired them.

"Although pride in traditional values persisted," Topham wrote, "identification of the older material objects associated with them was no longer considered important" as the people of Saudi Arabia acquired modern gadgets. "It was difficult to find people—even older people—who had an interest in or knowledge of any objects beyond those with which they themselves had been familiar since childhood." The sight of camels carrying water bags made from inner tubes prompted this sad observation: "Little work in any craft today is as well done as that of even ten years ago."[2] Silversmiths have all but disappeared, and most of the gold jewelry so popular in Saudi Arabia is now made in Italy, Topham found.

Topham became an Arabian pack rat: He roamed the *souks* from the Persian Gulf to the Red Sea and filled his hotel rooms with the treasures he found. He spent countless hours sipping tea with merchants and vendors, questioning them about the origins of their wares, and looking for rare textiles. He bought rugs, garments, baskets, swords, camel feed bags, incense burners, decorative weavings from tents, coffee bags, and even one of those wooden pulleys from the wells of Riyadh that Frances Bolton and other early travelers had heard squeaking decades before.

"But accumulating objects was not my primary goal," he wrote. "I wanted to learn regional and tribal identifications of the patterns, symbols and colors in the weavings and other craft items I was buying, to be able to associate certain objects with certain places and, ultimately, with the people—their skilled hands and designing instincts—who made them." In the absence of documentation, it was difficult to associate individual objects with the artisans who produced them or to establish links between certain patterns and fabrics with the tribes of which they were characteristic. Topham showed the Saudis photographs of his collection when he traveled so that he could build a data bank and track the origins of some pieces.

In 1990, the University of Rochester's Memorial Art Gallery assembled a landmark show, "Traditional Crafts of Saudi Arabia," based on the Topham collection. The show toured museums around the United States, offering many viewers their first look at the cultural creativity of a people whom most Americans knew only through cliché images and stereotypes. A book based on the collection, which Topham cowrote with Aramco's Bill Mulligan and with Anthony Landreau, a rug and weaving specialist and former executive director of the Textile Museum in Washington, is probably the best source of readily available information on the vanishing crafts of Arabia. The Topham collection has since been purchased by Princess Haifa, wife of Bandar bin Sultan, Saudi Arabia's ambassador to the United States. She plans to return it to Saudi Arabia before 2010 and use the material to teach young Saudis about the vanished ways of their grandparents. The princess is in the vanguard of a group of educated Saudi Arabian women who are beginning to organize a campaign to preserve clothing and other objects of the past and understand how they were worn or used.

John Topham was of course not the only American who developed an interest in Saudi Arabia's bedouin culture. For Paul Nance, it was a five-decade avocation. Nance worked for Aramco in Dhahran from 1952 to 1983 and bought into the entire package. He was a true believer in the Aramco way of life, in the oil company as the great engineer of progress in a poor country, and in the Saudi Arabs as friends and colleagues.

"These are people who, before the era of oil, survived a hostile environment and abject poverty with faith, endurance and a great deal of spirit," Nance wrote. "Oil wealth posed its own harsh challenges, but my family and I saw the successful struggle of a people intent on leapfrogging the industrial revolution in a single generation while trying to preserve their religion, language, dress, crafts and customs."[3] It was disingenuous to laud the Saudis as preservationists; John Topham embarked on his buying spree partly because he found the Saudis were not in fact interested in preserving their traditional crafts, which were dying out, but Nance's admiration for the Saudis was so uncritical that he apparently failed to notice this unfortunate trend. Nance seems to have approved of everything he encountered in Saudi Arabia, even the criminal justice system. "We left our doors unlocked, spoke freely with strangers, and moved about as foreigners without fear," he recalled. "Our children needed no admonitions about the potential evils in the streets beyond their homes. Drugs were not a problem. Saudi justice was swift and often harsh by our standards, reminiscent of the Old Testament's 'eye for an eye.' But the crime rate was negligible."[4] Paul and Colleen Nance acquired their own substantial collection of jewelry, artifacts, and garments, including a bedouin tent with all its furnishings.

They supplemented this material with books about the Arab world and Islam and with paintings of life in Saudi Arabia by many artists—including Saudis, who normally refrain from representational art because of Wahhabi Islam's strictures against depictions of humans and animals. After he retired from Aramco, this material was put on display at an idiosyncratic museum that he created in Lone Jack, Missouri, not far from Kansas City. Nance made it his mission in retirement to inform Americans about the culture he and Colleen had so appreciated.

"It is the purpose of the Nance Museum," its mission statement said, "to collect, preserve and share with the broadest possible American audience the art and artifacts of Saudi Arabia and other Middle East and Muslim countries and tell the story of the Arab, Islam and oil." Nance organized traveling exhibits and field trips for schoolchildren. He and the museum's small staff enacted Arabian rituals such as the coffee ceremony, and opened a library. They put up their bedouin tent and arranged domestic artifacts as an Arab family would. They dressed mannequins in the styles of Saudi Arabia's various tribes and regions, and adorned them with Arab jewelry.

"Most of our vistors' questions are about Arab women," Nance observed in his self-published book about his museum. "We demonstrate the three parts to veiling, and student visitors are invited to try on some of the costumes. This symbolic adoption of another culture is entered into enthusiastically with much picture-taking to record the event. We inform our visitors about the practices that set apart most Saudi women from their sisters in other countries."[5]

Not content to wait for visitors to come to his rural outpost, Nance promoted his project tirelessly: He solicited alliances with better-established museums, took parts of the collection on the road, and collaborated with Saudi Aramco and the Saudi Arabian Embassy in Washington to promote a favorable image of Saudi Arabia. He ran his museum until illness and failing eyesight slowed him down. In 2002, he donated the collection to Central Missouri State University, which bills it as "the largest collection of Saudi Arabian artifacts on continuous display in the United States."

In their enthusiasm for Saudi crafts, John Topham and Paul Nance were not typical of the Americans who have lived and worked in Saudi Arabia over the past seventy years, but in truth no one was typical. Aside from being U.S. citizens and speaking English, the hundreds of thousands of Americans who have lived in the Kingdom since the first geologists arrived were more different than they were alike, and their experiences varied with occupation, location, and motivation. As might be expected, those who liked their work, had a sense of adventure, reached out to the Saudis, and accommodated themselves to the peculiarities of the culture generally fared the best, even under difficult circumstances. In Dhahran, Americans lived and still live pretty much as they would have lived in any small American city. In Riyadh and Jeddah, the hardships of Ambassador Rives Childs's day eased as consumer goods and creature comforts became readily available in the 1960s; but elsewhere around the country, Americans sometimes lived in isolation and relative privation. Some thrived on it; some were defeated by it. Probably the majority of Americans, whether civilian or military, were like Barney Jones, a construction project safety manager, who worked in Saudi Arabia for Bechtel for six years. "As long as you behaved yourself and obeyed the rules, you had no difficulty," he said. To him, Saudi Arabia was just another hot place to work, the same as Algeria or India except that there was no beer, he said. He never even went to Jeddah.[6] He represented a large component of the Americans in the Kingdom: They went to Saudi Arabia on contract for a fixed period, did their work, and then went home without strong feelings one way or another. Some Americans went to Saudi Arabia just for the money, but many contributed to the social and physical development of the country.

There were as many stories as there were individuals.

I found Bob Gooch, for example, working happily among the dunes of the "Empty Quarter," the ocean of sand the size of Texas in southeastern Saudi Arabia that must be one of the most desolate places on Earth. The temperature was 118 degrees. There was not a shrub or

Golf in the desert, outside Dhahran. A rubber mat holds the tee; the green is oiled sand.
Photo by Wendy Cocker.

Cultural inroads: Roadside refreshment stand, eastern Saudi Arabia, late 1990s.
Photo by Wendy Cocker.

blade of grass in sight. The nearest human beings other than the seventy men on his oil-drilling crew were four hours away. Gooch, a jovial Oklahoman who called himself "a farmer at heart," was content. "A lot of 'em who come out here, they take one look and they turn around and go back, but it's a good job," he told me. "I used to be a bureaucrat, working in an office, but I kind of like it out here. I like the work and I like the people."[7]

Linda Porter, the wife of Bechtel's Winston Porter, lived in a completely different environment. She was a pathologist in a Saudi government hospital in Dammam in the 1960s, where she worked for Egyptian doctors. "I had just graduated from Berkeley, from the school of public health and microbiology, with all these highfalutin' technology ideas and concepts, and I got plopped down in Dammam, which was very primitive," she recalled. Burn patients were treated with iodine. The medical staff left for the day at three o'clock, regardless of what was happening. "People came to the hospital with the idea that they were going to die," she said. "The hospital was a place of last resort." And yet she found the work "fascinating from a purely scientific standpoint" because she saw afflictions not commonly encountered back home, such as blood diseases and parasites, and her response to the backwardness was admiration rather than condemnation: "They were taking gigantic leaps in progress and that's very difficult to do when you don't have an infrastructure and you don't have a trained society and you have to import all the workers." Some years later, she returned to Saudi Arabia in another capacity altogether: "Bechtel wife, which meant I had to do the social part of it and I also had to hold the hands of the wives who were not familiar with the culture."[8]

Elizabeth Brown was a girl of eight or nine when her parents took her to Jeddah. Her father was Glen Brown, the geologist who established the U.S. Geological Survey program in Saudi Arabia. "I had the best childhood on Earth," she recalled. "I had a wonderful time." The Browns lived in Jeddah, where camel caravans passed by their house. Her amusement was riding the bin Laden family horses. After their initial stay in Bechtel housing, she recalled, the Browns avoided the compounds that real estate entrepreneurs were building for expatriates who wanted to sequester themselves from the realities of Saudi Arabia life, like the Americans at Aramco. "The Americans wanted compounds because they wanted to replicate American life, they couldn't handle no driving and no drinking. But compounds not only keep things out, they keep you in," said Brown, now a pediatrician in Cincinnati. "Some Americans never got invited to Saudis' homes because they didn't interact."[9]

American military personnel, contractors, oil workers, teachers, bankers, and diplomats encountered Saudi Arabia and its people at different levels and with different expectations. Brief examinations of a few of these lives demonstrate the wide range of the American encounter with an utterly different culture.

Michael M. Ameen Jr. was born in Massachusetts to Arab immigrant parents and grew up familiar with the Arabic language. After college and service in the Marine Corps in World War II, he was briefly an FBI agent. He was tracking a criminal ring that stole cars and shipped them to Kuwait and Saudi Arabia when he met the Saudi Arabian ambassador, who introduced him to Aramco officials. From that point on, Mike Ameen was an oil guy.[10]

An unsigned typescript in the Bill Mulligan Papers says of Ameen, "He was a diplomat, a master of bunkum, hokum and flattery. He was a smooth talking man who could minimize the sound of a negative. . . . Among a brotherhood of exotic men, he was, however, peerless. He combined the Arab qualities of generosity and hospitality with American heartiness and vigor. His home in Riyadh was for years an Arab-American club to which attractive people of both cultures were drawn irresistibly. His wife Pat, a former Aramco secretary, was the perfect hostess—warm, competent, a true helpmate, a model of taste and propriety. Mike had drive, energy, self-confidence and obviously enjoyed his work."[11] The American newspaper correspondents who soaked up Mike Ameen's encyclopedic knowledge of the oil business in the 1970s would have been surprised to hear him described as "a master of bunkum."

Ameen was one of the first Americans to take up residence in Riyadh, which until the early 1950s was closed to foreigners except by royal invitation. Before the death of King Abdul Aziz, Ameen recalled, "whenever we went there we used to have to wear Arab clothes." As King Saud consolidated government operations in the capital, Aramco decided to open a representational office there, to which Ameen was assigned in 1958. Riyadh was still quite undeveloped—electricity was only then replacing kerosene lamps in most of the city—and there was still a strong element in the population that opposed all foreign presence in Saudi Arabia. If Americans were going to live and do business in the capital, it was essential for Ameen and his colleagues to ingratiate themselves with the city's population.

Ameen said the company's instinct was to create a closed compound for its four-man Riyadh team, but he argued successfully against it. "Let's live in the natural town, I said." At first the four men, all bachelors, lived in a small apartment. "The water was okay, we had filters," Ameen recalled, "but there was a terrible mosquito problem because the whole town was a septic tank. If we needed medical attention we were rushed to Dhahran. We could order from the commissary by company plane. Then people started making money and building better buildings," including spacious villas.

"I rented four beautiful houses from the deputy minister of defense's brother. We lived in those houses, socialized with Saudis, hobnobbed with Saudis; that's where we made our best friends to this day," Ameen said. When his wife and others joined the men in Riyadh, the group "made arrangements with [Prince] Faisal. We never had to veil our women, just make sure their sleeves went to the elbows and dresses below the knees. They never had to cover their hair. We had no trouble. We hobnobbed with the Saudis, we dealt with them. It worked out better without a compound."[12] (Ameen and his colleagues may have congratulated themselves for mixing with the local people, but their access to the Aramco supply line still gave them a position of privilege. "To the rest of us who depended entirely on the local economy," wrote Frances Meade, the longtime director of Riyadh's international school, "they were clearly living at the top of the Riyadh heap, but we regarded them more with admiration than envy.")[13]

In regular contact with Abdullah Sulaiman and other Saudi officials, Ameen came to think of them as shrewd negotiators who often took advantage of the Americans.

"The Saudis were smarter than us," he recalled. "Take a look at the Tapline agreement, what we had to give and agree to, build a road, provide water and medical treatment for travelers. You talk about the barefoot boy, we were the barefoot boy."

Aramco personnel records in the Mulligan Papers indicate that Ameen could be pushy and difficult to manage, and he was counseled about his excessive use of profanity. But he was also gregarious and charming, and had an affinity for the Saudis that made him an effective representative of the company and of the oil industry. Saudi officials and businessmen who worked with Ameen still talk of him affectionately. In retirement, Ameen was still making the American case vociferously when I last talked to him. "When we were hired, we were told that we were going to train ourselves out of a job, and look who's running Aramco today. TWA did a good job, too. The Americans did a fantastic job," he said. "We did a lot for those people."

꿈

Richard E. Undeland had no background in Arab affairs or the Middle East. He grew up in Omaha, the son of a real estate appraiser, majored in English at Harvard and earned an MBA at Stanford. But he was bored with business and finance, and when a Stanford professor with connections in the Arab world offered him a chance to study in Egypt, Undeland accepted with alacrity. He never went back to the world of business.

He became a career Arab-world specialist in the United States Information Agency (USIA), a unit of the U.S. Foreign Service created during the Cold War to promote U.S. ideals and the U.S. image abroad. USIA sent him to Riyadh in 1983, twenty-five years after Mike Ameen. By that time, it was a sprawling modern city; all the big infrastructure projects ordered during the 1970s oil boom were coming on line and there was no longer any physical hardship or shortage of consumer goods. Undeland found a different set of problems.

His assignment was public affairs officer. The PAO, as this officer is called in every embassy, is responsible for cultural affairs, student exchange programs, the American library, and media relations. As Undeland discovered, running such an operation in a society that was generally hostile to external ideas and prohibited public performances presented a unique challenge, especially during his tenure when religious reaction to the events of 1979 was running high.

"The longer I was in Saudi Arabia, the more I came to respect all that the Saudis had already accomplished and had underway," he recalled. "If there was ever a society that could have come unstuck and disintegrated, it should have been that one. At the same time, Saudi ways, all too often mixed with Saudi hypocrisy, vastly complicated what we wanted to achieve and the tools we would have liked to use."[14]

Cultural programming, for example, was restricted by the prohibition against mixing men and women in public. "For a time it looked like we at last might find a chink in this wall at the prestigious Faisal Institute with an Islamic lecture given by Esin Atil of the Smithsonian, [a woman who was] one of the world's foremost scholars in the field," Undeland recalled, "but at the last minute it was canceled as being too radical or revolutionary a departure to have a woman lecturing to men."

The absence of concert halls and theaters made it almost impossible to import American musical groups, as the U.S. Information Agency routinely did in other countries. "We did put on a couple of concerts," Undeland said, "but in homes, with nothing more than word of mouth publicity and for an audience that was no more than five percent Saudi."

As it did in many countries, the U.S. Information Agency operated libraries in Riyadh and Jeddah that were open to the public. Undeland discovered that hardly any Saudi Arabs visited them. "Reading books for pleasure or other personal satisfaction, at least those in a foreign language, was just not part of the Saudi scene," he said. "I don't say this to be critical, but only to state a reality." He closed the libraries, except for the reference sections.

Undeland said he found respite from the frustrations of his job by spending weekends on Saudi-owned farms outside the capital. He and his wife, Joan,

> got in with a group of highly Westernized Saudis, who had spent long periods in the States and in Europe, who when on their farms cast aside the Saudi world. Jeans and shirts largely replaced the *thobe*, the *ghutra* was put aside, easy relations between men and women emerged, even in one case dancing together by teenage sons and daughters. Of course, they were always on the lookout for an approaching vehicle—the clouds of dust they raised made them easy to see—and for a quick change back into Saudi clothes and ways. The kids were bilingual in English, often speaking a heavily accented dialect learned from the Bangladeshi or Filipino nannies and other English-speaking servants. These were tiring weekends, because they stayed up all night and the Johnnie Walker Black flowed freely.

Undeland developed a deep ambivalence about Saudi Arabia. He was contemptuous of what he called the "hypocrisy" of this clandestine life, yet he admired the Saudis' accomplishments.

"I could have accepted the rigors and fanaticism dictated by honest, sincere observance of the Wahhabi strictures," he said, "but virtually every rule and restriction there was flouted with the connivance of the highly placed, even members of the royal family. There was virtually no sin or vice that could not be satisfied. . . . There was no problem with buying alcohol if you had the $150 for a bottle of whiskey. The same was true with drugs, and women, and others to satisfy sexual pleasures. It seemed the only sin was getting caught."

The tensions inherent in living outside the rules, whether in the gated compounds of the Americans or on the farms of their Saudi friends, were exacerbated by "the widespread contempt existing on both sides," in Undeland's recollection. "The vast majority of foreigners were there for one thing, to make as much money as fast as possible and get out of what they mostly looked on as 'that miserable place.' The Saudis were no fools and saw this clearly, and they responded with, 'We've got the foreigners here to do what we want them to do, but we know they have no real concern or regard for us. So we accept and get along with them, but we'll throw them out just as soon as we no longer need them.'"

And yet Undeland said he recognized that "there was much that was right, admirable, promising" in Saudi Arabia. "The Saudis deserve much credit for what they've done with their country. All of a sudden, technology and unbelievable sums of money engulfed this society. It didn't disintegrate but adapted, finding its path with increasing assurance, and it did so in an amazingly short period of time."

~

American doctors generally refrain from discussing their patients in public, at least by name, but no such compunction inhibited Seymour Gray. He wrote a book about his experience as a physician in Saudi Arabia, complete with names of—and gossip about—some of the Saudis he treated.

By his account, his interest in Saudi Arabia began in 1959, when he was practicing medicine in Boston and was called to examine Princess Iffat, wife of Faisal, then crown prince and later king. He found her "an attractive, articulate and powerful woman," and noted her commitment to the education of women. "As we discussed her medical problems, she chain-smoked long black Turkish cigarettes. When I asked how many she smoked in a day, she replied, squinting to keep the smoke out of her eyes, 'Three packs, more or less.' I knew it would be useless to ask her to stop smoking."[15]

Three years later, he examined King Saud and was "appalled to discover that his majesty was riddled with disease. All of his ailments were chronic, and most of them were irreversible." The king suffered from trachoma, diabetes, and cirrhosis of the liver, Gray observed.

Intrigued by his encounter with the king and by a visit to the royal entourage's Boston hotel, where he found "the atmosphere of a bordello" as princes and hangers-on boozed it up with call girls, Gray set out to learn about Saudi Arabia and the Arabs. He read books by Philby, Bernard Lewis, Wilfred Thesiger, and other scholars and explorers. He sought out Harvard Arabists and Saudi students in the Boston area.

Then in 1975 he accepted an offer to go to Riyadh and join the medical staff of the new King Faisal Specialist Hospital (the same institution where Scott Nelson ran afoul of the administration).

The hospital, Riyadh's newest and finest, was an eye-opener for Gray. Lavishly equipped, the hospital incorporated all the latest medical technology. The facilities "were easily the best I had ever encountered," Gray recalled, including a nuclear accelerator for cancer radiation treatments, a brain scanner, and "a total body scanner so recently developed that it had not yet reached the city of Boston."[16] The irony of this was that there were hardly any Saudi doctors; the Kingdom's first medical school class was still in training. Only foreign doctors were trained to use the new hospital's advanced equipment; there were doctors from twenty-three countries, but no Saudis. (Living in Cairo at the time, I heard about this often from frustrated Egyptian doctors. The Egyptians griped that the Saudis had no doctors but the best equipment while they, the Egyptians, accomplished physicians trained in Europe and the United States, were stuck with antiquated equipment in shabby old hospitals.)

On Gray's first morning of work, he was summoned to treat Prince Yusuf al-Saud, a first cousin and falcon-hunting companion of King Khaled. The prince was bleeding internally. This was not just a medical case, Gray was informed by the medical director, Dr. Hugh Compton, it was a political case as well. The king and other senior royals, Compton said, were accustomed to flying to London for major medical care. They were skeptical that any hospital in the Kingdom could provide the same level of treatment. Moreover, the capital's extremely conservative religious leaders and old-guard princes were suspicious of the entire operation as a foreign institution managed by infidels with alien ideas. To overcome all this resistance, the hospital staff had to cure Prince Yusuf. If the prince recovers, Gray was told, the hospital will have royal support and will prosper. If not, don't bother to unpack.

When the king and Crown Prince Fahd came to visit Prince Yusuf, Gray was asked to brief them on the prince's condition. He was astonished that they had neither security cover nor bodyguards as they rode on an elevator with him, "a total stranger who had been in Saudi Arabia less than twenty four hours and could have easily concealed a small weapon in his coat pocket." Gray was "impressed by their certitude and quiet grace. They had what can only be called a regal bearing, a quality that is as palpable in a person as it is difficult to define. The princes seemed to float on the balls of their feet."[17]

In conversations with Prince Yusuf over several days, Gray discovered that the prince was entirely ignorant of the outside world. He had never heard of Harvard, and advanced degrees from American universities meant nothing to him. Yusuf was content with his world—Islam, bedouin tradition, several wives, camel races, and about $60 million a year, tax free, as his share of the oil money. He treated Gray like hired help. "I was frustrated by his patronizing attitude," Gray recalled, until he found a way to overcome it. He showed the prince a photograph of his big rambling house near Boston on a leafy acre of ground. The prince was impressed that the doctor would leave that house and his family behind to come help Saudi Arabia.[18]

Prince Yusuf recovered, so Gray unpacked and stayed. After a few months, his wife, Ruth, joined him. Without a job and prohibited from driving, she spent much of her time with other foreign women, shopping and gossiping, driven around Riyadh by hired drivers. "When Ruth had been in Saudi Arabia for several months and her days had settled into a comfortable routine," Gray noted, "we realized that she was living a life very similar to that of a Saudi woman, almost a mirror image, except for the absence of the veil. . . . For the most part we spent long hours leading separate lives."

Gray's entrée into the clandestine, alcohol-fueled social life of upper-class Saudis was made possible by a peculiar relationship he developed with a nineteen-year-old princess named Sultana. This young woman's father was a senior prince from a powerful family; her mother was American. Sultana was born in California and lived there as a young girl. She returned to Saudi Arabia with her parents and stayed when her mother bailed out and went home, as many American women married to Saudi men eventually did. She was admitted to Gray's hospital suffering from dysentery.

Gray found her a somewhat blurry window into the Saudi mind. As a child of privilege, she had no complaints of hardship. By her account, she was comfortable knowing that the life ahead of her was that of a Saudi woman, with all its restrictions, not the life of liberty she had known in California. She said this was her free choice. And yet she complained all the time.

"It is difficult to be a Saudi Arabian right now," she told him. "We are not exactly sure who we are. Everyone is cracking up! It is a sort of schizophrenia. Men and women are coming into the country with new ideas—the airplane, radio, televisions. These things may represent progress to you, but they are ruining our society. You see, now that we are threatened by outside ideas, the Wahhabis are stricter than ever. Veils are supposed to be thicker and sleeves longer."[19] This agitation contrasted starkly with the serene self-confidence Gray had observed in the king, Crown Prince Fahd, and Prince Yusuf. They were of an earlier generation.

In his book, Gray recounts eye-opening experiences that only increased his curiosity about Saudi Arabia. He went to the camel races. He watched the pornographic movie *Deep Throat* at a boozy late-night party celebrating the birth of a son to a young prince. He witnessed a beheading. On a desert picnic, he encountered bedouin who had never before met a foreigner; they lectured him about the curative powers of camel urine. He examined a female patient who was willing to disrobe in front of him but only if she kept her veil on so he would not know who she was. He examined upper-class Saudi women who concocted illnesses to gain admission to the hospital so that they could talk to a sympathetic listener about their unhappy sex lives. The Saudis, he concluded, "have a voracious appetite for sex."[20]

At the end of his tour, Gray seems to have emerged with the same sense of ambivalence as Richard Undeland. Repelled by the Saudi Arabian form of government, limitations on political liberty, and restrictions on women, he also admired the total dedication to Islam, the lack of crime, family loyalty, and laws that emphasize the welfare of society. "In your country," a young Saudi doctor told him "you protect the rights of the individual at the expense of society." In Saudi Arabia, Seymour Gray concluded, it is the other way around.[21]

The first time Andrea Rugh organized a tea party for Saudi women, she invited fifteen guests and spent days preparing the food. Only one woman showed up. The others stayed away, this solitary guest explained, because they did not know who else would be there; there might be men, or women of inferior status.

When Saudi guests did come to the Rughs' home, she learned to offer them prepared drinks from a tray, not to ask individuals what they wanted, because each guest would ask for something different and she had to run back and forth to the kitchen filling orders. A woman who frequently visited the neighbor next door would enter her house uninvited and use the sewing machine. Socializing with Saudis was difficult because they lived by a different body clock—the women slept till midday, then stayed up most of the night. With small children in school, Andrea Rugh could not do that.

"I learned everything the hard way in Saudi Arabia," Andrea Rugh said.[22]

Andrea and Bill Rugh were pioneers of a sort, like Mike Ameen. Bill Rugh opened the first official U.S. government civilian office in Riyadh in 1966, years before the embassy moved up to the royal capital from Jeddah. At the time, there were only about seventy-five American residents in all of Riyadh, including the Aramco and Ford Foundation teams and a small contingent of U.S. military trainers assigned to the Ministry of Defense.

"The Saudis didn't allow any embassies in Riyadh and we wanted to have a presence there," said Bill Rugh, a career Arabic specialist in the United States Information Agency who later became ambassador to the United Arab Emirates. "So what I did was open an English language center that said Ministry of Education on the door. The Ministry of Education gave us a building and administrative support and sort of legal cover. We staffed it and ran it. We taught English, mostly to government officials."[23]

Hermann F. Eilts, the U.S. ambassador in Jeddah at the time, "found it a very useful source of information about what was going on in Riyadh," Rugh said. "Because we were teachers, we had a lot of cachet and lot of access. The students would invite you to their homes, confide in you and talk to you. For a diplomat, that was good cover."

Although his assignment was English language instruction, Rugh did import some lecturers and authors to talk to Saudi audiences, who in Riyadh were much more isolated from the world than their fellow citizens in Dhahran and Jeddah. Some were so cut off from the world that they refused to believe that Neil Armstrong had landed on the Moon. Others believed it but denounced it as a blasphemous violation of God's arrangement of the universe.

After the first U.S. landing on the Moon, Rugh recalled, "We brought in a lecturer to talk about the Moon landing and we had a sample Moon rock that we put on display." The lecturer was actually a Saudi Arab who had earned a doctorate at a university in the United States, but that did not enhance the credibility or acceptability of the Moon landing tale among the Riyadh audience, Rugh said.

"After the lecture, one of these graybeards got up and said, 'I don't believe a word of it, it's not true, the Americans are lying, they didn't go to the Moon. Because we know when we watch the Moon that during the month it gradually shrinks and disappears, so how could they have been on the Moon when it disappears?'"

There ensued what Rugh described as "an interesting dialogue." He said the Saudis argued that "these Americans are bragging about something that didn't happen, and if it did happen it shouldn't have because it's a violation of what God would have wanted." Only after Ambassador Eilts showed the Moon rock to King Faisal personally and received his approval to display it did opposition to the display die down. Here was yet another small American contribution to the collective opening of the Saudi Arab mind.

By the time the Rughs arrived in Riyadh, the international community had grown large enough to need a school. The only international schools in the country were the Parents Cooperative School in Jeddah, run by TWA, the Aramco schools, and the school at the U.S. consulate in Dhahran. In 1965, Genevra Abou Seoud, an American woman married to a Palestinian working in Riyadh, created the Riyadh International Community School in a small villa in a nondescript residential neighborhood. It had "an enrollment of thirty-three children of a dozen different nationalities and the atmosphere of an old-fashioned one room school house," recalled Fran Meade, an American who taught fourth and fifth grades and later became principal. "We had desks and chairs and a limited number of textbooks and that was about it."[24]

The Rughs enrolled their three boys in this school, but their education was disrupted when the Saudi government suddenly shut it down because girls were attending classes with boys and because some of the students were Muslims from Pakistan. It was not permitted for Muslims to be educated by non-Muslims, the authorities said. Without the sponsorship of TWA, Aramco, or the U.S. consulate, the Riyadh school was unprotected and vulnerable.

Ambassador Eilts said the Americans had assumed that King Faisal understood that if expatriates were to live in Riyadh they would have to have a school for their children. "When I went to see King Faisal about this, I found that instead of accepting the point of view that the school was necessary, as far as he was concerned the school authorities had done something that was contrary to Islamic precepts and he was not at all disposed to allow it to reopen. Here was a case in which on a practical issue an Islamic value system and an American value system were in a state of conflict."[25]

Eilts said it took five months of negotiation to obtain permission for the school to reopen, under new rules: separate classes for boys and girls, and no Muslim students. "Some poor Pakistani kids who didn't speak any Arabic had to go into the local schools," Bill Rugh said.

Once reopened, the school grew and prospered as Riyadh's foreign community grew, to the point where prominent Saudis and diplomats from Muslim countries wanted to send their children there. Daryle Russ, superintendent from 1982 to 1993, told me that at the start of his tenure, the Ministry of Education notified the school that it could accept selected Muslim students. "We assumed," he said, "that this meant Muslim students whose parents were diplomats or senior company/organization officials." By the time he left in 1993, he said, the Muslim student enrollment was 36 percent.

Boys and girls were again being taught in the same classrooms, Russ said. From time to time, the Ministry of Education would complain. The school always responded the same way: "I always told the Ministry, 'We clearly understood that boys and girls are separated in the local schools. If the Ministry wanted to apply the same procedure to our school we would certainly take the directive under advisement and wait for the US Embassy to offer counsel on the appropriate response.'" The ministry would retreat for some months, then the little drama would be replayed.

All textbooks had to be approved by the Ministry of Education, which deleted all references to Israel, but otherwise the government did not interfere with the school's curriculum, Russ said.[26]

Knowing of my interest in the lives of Americans in Saudi Arabia, a friend at Saudi Aramco suggested I get in touch with Sally Alturki. She is an American woman married to a Saudi Arab man. They are among the most prominent and successful couples in the Eastern Province of Saudi Arabia.

I have never met them, but I had heard quite a bit about them. Khalid Alturki was a generous contributor to Paul Nance's museum. The "Islamic Fountain" in the museum's garden was dedicated to him, and photographs of Khalid, Sally, and their children appear in Nance's book.

When Aramco decided in the 1980s to build a private school for Saudi students, known as Doha School, Aramco education director Edwin Read selected an organization known as Dhahran Ahliyya (Private) Schools to operate it.

"These schools had been set up by a prominent Saudi businessman, Khalid Alturki, and his wife, Sally, as nonprofit, Arabic schools with separate sections for boys and girls," according to an official Aramco history. "Sally Alturki's first school was opened in small, renovated houses at the outskirts of al-Khobar in 1977. 'I visited her school,' Read recalled, 'and I could see she was very capable. She had some other teachers she had selected rather carefully. Later on, I traveled all over Saudi Arabia, all the way to the west coast and even to Dubai, interviewing people who run schools for Arab children. After carefully and honestly looking for a better team to run the Doha School, I still came back to Khalid and Sally Alturki.'"[27]

The recollections of American diplomats who have served in Saudi Arabia are replete with tales of unhappy marriages between American women and Saudi Arab men. "As you would expect," said Chas W. Freeman Jr., who became ambassador in 1989, "many of these marriages took place while people were studying in the United States. The women were young and inexperienced, and had no real idea what they were getting into in marrying someone of a different culture. Some of the marriages were very strong and good, but many of them were not, and they would fall apart under the impact of culture shock and the difficulty of American women adjusting to sexual apartheid and other aspects of Saudi society."[28] When these marriages broke up, Freeman and others recalled, the American women naturally wanted to take their children with them when they left Saudi Arabia, but their husbands usually would not permit it, even if the children were U.S. citizens. "I had a great number of occasions, on weekends and nights and during the day, to meet with and try to help distraught American women, and also, of course, occasions where the women would take the children out of the Kingdom without the permission of the husband or father. [This was] a constant source of distress for me and the consular section," Freeman said.

Clearly Sally Alturki was not in this category, so I sent her an e-mail message asking her to tell me about herself and her life. In response, she described herself as "the wife of a Saudi, a descendant of the Daughters of the American Revolution, and also a very happy and fulfilled woman, personally, socially, and professionally." Reluctant to share personal details with a stranger who wanted to write about her, she sent instead a document that has since circulated widely around the Internet message groups of Americans interested in Saudi Arabia. Titled "Being a Woman in Saudi Arabia," it takes the form of a letter from Sally Alturki to friends, describing her life and work. At the time, in 2002, she had been living in Saudi Arabia for thirty-two years.

She is the head of the girls' division of the private school she founded with her husband. The school has more than 1,700 students, including 800 girls, from pre-kindergarten through high school. "In addition," she wrote, "I am co-director of a publishing company for books in Arabic to train educators and a center for offering training and consulting to other schools that are also trying to develop and modernize. I am also a founding member of a center for preparation of early childhood teachers. We prepare the teachers, develop and publish teaching materials and send consultants out to offer training at other pre-schools all over Saudi Arabia."

She also described a wide range of philanthropic and community service activities, such as membership in a group trying to establish a support center for needy women, including women whose husbands are in jail.

The education of females, once controversial in Saudi Arabia, has been a fact of life since the reign of King Faisal. In her "Dear Friends" letter, Sally Alturki argues that women are now making progress in many fields of social and commercial activity, even under the restrictions that Chas Freeman described as "sexual apartheid."

"Saudi girls are going to school and to universities, and getting jobs in many places as teachers, doctors, nurses, social workers, etc. They are also writing in newspapers, managing their own businesses, controlling their own money, forming committees, and working to improve life generally and particularly for women and children," she wrote. "Many more women are opening their own businesses these days and there are now branches of the Chamber of Commerce specifically to respond to the needs of women in the three main cities."

Change comes incrementally and sometimes imperceptibly to Saudi Arabia, she wrote, but it does come. "Saudi Arabia has a lot to work on but it cannot be compared at all to Afghanistan under the Taliban." After watching these changes for more than three decades, she said, "I don't think I could possibly be happier than I have been throughout this time. I feel completely fulfilled as a woman, as a professional, as a member of society, and as a person who is contributing to the development of that society. My relations with my husband, my extended Saudi family and with so many Saudi friends are warm and deep; I do truly love and feel loved and accepted by so many people that I have come to know over these thirty-two years."

The Alturkis' marriage may have been a great success, but as Ambassador Freeman observed, many unions between Saudi men and American women were not.

Susan Becker, a clinical psychologist and family therapist, had a unique perspective on the failures. From 1984 to 1992, she was the co-ordinator of mental health services at the U.S. Embassy in Riyadh. Her résumé gives this summary of her duties:

> Provided mental health counseling services to adolescents, couples, children, families, and groups of Americans and others of diverse nationalities. Treated a wide range of clinical disorders including depression, anxiety disorders, adjustment disorders, substance abuse, and interpersonal problems. Provided child and/or family therapy for school referrals with behavioral disorders including ADD [attention deficit disorder]. Provided psychological consultation to community physicians in addition to planning and conducting workshops on stress management, assertiveness training, cultural adjustment issues and anxiety disorders during the Gulf War for the expatriate community.

This was not the same happy American community depicted in Aramco's upbeat literature. Susan Becker found that life in Saudi Arabia exposed marital fissures that might have been papered over at home, and that cross-cultural marriages presented unique and sometimes insuperable challenges.

"The dependency of women changed the balance of many of the marital relationships," she told me. "The fact that women were not permitted to drive placed the husbands in the role of drivers, and married couples were constantly together." Strong marriages thrived in this enforced togetherness, she found, but struggling marriages tended to unravel.

Living by Saudi Arabian rules "created stress for those couples requiring individual space, and small issues became exacerbated in this setting."[29] In an account of her observations published in a professional journal, Dr. Becker wrote that "for unassertive women with few economic resources, or for those with uncooperative husbands, life in Saudi Arabia can be overwhelmingly difficult and depressing. Many American male workers return to the United States because of their wives' profound unhappiness in Saudi Arabia. . . . The rules of Saudi life create a power structure in the marital relationship in which the woman asks, and the husband decides."[30]

American women who were single faced a separate set of difficulties that tended to drive them into emotional and physical relationships with bachelor men to whom they were not truly committed, Dr. Becker found. "They had to live in housing reserved exclusively for females, were not permitted to have male visitors in their apartments, and were not to be seen with men in public." Thus the desire for male companionship often led them to spend nights in the apartments of men, whether or not they wanted such intimacy.[31]

As for the marriages between Saudi men and American women, she said, some "do work out well but it involved a lot of adaptation by the women. These couples typically met in the States when the man was a student but when they went back to Saudi Arabia the husband changed and the Saudi extended family took control. Since the women do not have their own families to stand up for them, they are at a disadvantage."[32]

Divorce among such couples often caused emotional upheaval in both spouses, Dr. Becker told me, especially when the husband did not want the breakup. In Saudi Arabia, "the children belong to the father," she said, and there was little the U.S. Embassy could do to help American women forced to leave their children behind if they wished to depart the Kingdom. "The Embassy," Dr. Becker said, "did not want to become involved in domestic situations that could affect business and political relationships."[33]

Susan Becker and her husband, a physician, stayed in Saudi Arabia fifteen years and enjoyed it. She said that Riyadh "was a wonderful place to raise children, something like a small town where everyone knew you and there was a real sense of community. . . . However, with the smallness of the community and living with the same people you worked with was confining and a problem in itself for many of the people I treated. In that environment, problems would be suppressed because jobs might be affected." She would have had no difficulty diagnosing Nora Johnson's unhappiness as a young Aramco wife a generation earlier. As much as Americans have contributed to the development of Saudi Arabia since the discovery of oil, many of them paid a high personal price for it.

CHAPTER 14

From Swords to Missiles

Ambassador J. Rives Childs was working late in his office in Jeddah. It was 11:00 P.M. on December 4, 1947, when he dispatched an urgent, top-secret cable to the State Department reporting on a conversation he had just had with King Abdul Aziz.

The king said he knew Childs was "a sincere friend of the Arabs" and therefore he would speak to him frankly. He said the decision by the United States government to support an independent Jewish state in partitioned Palestine was "most distasteful for the Arab world," but he would not belabor it; that was in the past. The king said his position as an Arab leader required him to oppose the U.S. position on this point, but he did not want a rupture in relations over it. On other issues, he said, his views and those of the United States were in harmony.

What, then, did the king want? "His majesty wished to know how and in what manner he might rely on the United States," Childs reported. More specifically, he wanted to know whether the United States would send troops to protect the Trans-Arabian Pipeline if the upcoming partition of Palestine led to some kind of uprising along the Kingdom's borders with Iraq and Jordan. A few months earlier, the king had asked the United States for a formal military alliance and mutual defense agreement. This was before the creation of the North Atlantic Treaty Organization (NATO), and the United States had no mutually binding defense commitment with any country, let alone an underpopulated desert outpost on the Arabian Peninsula. Washington refused to negotiate a defense agreement, offering instead a general treaty of friendship. This left the king with no clear understanding of how Washington would react to a military threat to Saudi Arabia, which was what he was now asking Childs. He knew Childs could not answer these questions himself; he wanted Childs to go to Washington and ask his bosses.[1]

Ever since Abdul Aziz's famous seaborne meeting with Franklin D. Roosevelt in 1945, every Saudi king has put such questions one way or another to every American president. No matter how many times the Americans have assured Saudi Arabia that they would protect the oil fields and ensure Saudi Arabia's independence and territorial integrity, the Saudis have never been totally satisfied with American pledges nor entirely comfortable with their dependence on the United States.

At times they have doubted the Americans' sincerity or the extent of their commitment: Did Washington really mean it, or would other policy imperatives—such as defending Israel, or courting the Shah of Iran, or trying to keep Nasser's Egypt out of the Soviet orbit—usurp the Kingdom's primacy? The more difficult conundrum for the Saudi kings has been that they depend for their security on a country widely reviled in the Arab world as Israel's protector and armorer. The embrace of the United States is awkward for the Saudis. It is the cornerstone of their security, but it has made them vulnerable to attack from Arab nationalists who brand the House of Saud a tool of imperialists and from domestic Islamists who brand it a tool of infidels. That is why the Saudi rulers have often resorted to equivocation or crude subterfuge in their public statements, as they did in the U.S. war against Iraq in early 2003: The Saudis announced that they would not permit the Americans to conduct military operations against Iraq from inside Saudi Arabia, thus maintaining the façade of Arab solidarity; but then they did quietly permit it, thus maintaining their close military ties to the United States. This same balance of incompatible sensitivities has surfaced again and again as the United States has sought Saudi cooperation in tracking down and apprehending suspected terrorists. The Saudis want to be on good terms with Washington, but they are protective of their sovereign prerogatives and do not wish to be seen as doing America's bidding.

Nor has the discomfort been all on the Saudi side. The United States for more than half a century has been the protector of a government whose every policy and practice is antithetical to American ideals of liberty, equality, and religious freedom. Deference to Saudi sensitivity about sovereignty and cultural independence has produced tolerance for repugnant aspects of Saudi life, and even respect for them. Individual Saudis and Americans have forged deep bonds of esteem and affection, but the bilateral relationship between the countries has often required leaders on both sides to hold their noses. They have stayed together because they need each other. For reasons that had more to do with Cold War strategy and economic necessity than shared ideals, the United States has aided Saudi Arabia's development, shielded the Kingdom from its enemies, and trained and equipped its armed forces. In the 1930s and during World War II, the Saudi Arabian military consisted of small bands of illiterate, camel-riding desert warriors armed with swords and single-shot rifles. The United States Army and Air Force have been to the Saudi military what Aramco was to the Saudi oil industry.

A week after Ambassador Childs's cable, he received instructions from Acting Secretary of State Robert Lovett. In a cable, Lovett said Childs should tell the king that "US appreciated spirit of friendship shown by King and his Govt at this difficult time, agrees that our relations are of closest and that, apart from Palestine, there are no points of difference between two countries whose interests are complementary." The United States was not prepared to send troops to defend Tapline or secure the northern borders, but Childs should stress to Abdul Aziz that "the inability on the part of US to provide him with military aid requested should not in any way be taken as indication of any lessening of friendship on part of US toward Saudi Arabia." Support for Saudi Arabia's "territorial integrity and political independence" was a basic American policy, Lovett wrote. "If Saudi Arabia should therefore be attacked by another power or be under threat of attack the US through medium of UN would take energetic measures to ward off such aggression."[2]

Was that a commitment to defend Saudi Arabia or not? The words "through medium of UN" were an immense loophole that the Saudis could readily discern. This was 1947; the United Nations was just getting started, and one of its first major actions would be to partition Palestine and create Israel, over Arab objections. What was its value in Saudi Arabia's security calculus?

In a commentary on this bilateral exchange, a State Department historian observed that the king "could not conceal his disappointment" with the American response. He said he intended to establish a modern, mechanized military force that would be deployed only to defend vital installations such as the oilfields and the Dhahran air base, which the Americans had completed the year before, and indicated that he would ask the United States for help with the training and the construction of bases for this new army.[3]

Despite the king's fury with President Harry Truman over U.S. support for the creation of Israel and the immediate U.S. recognition of the Jewish state upon its independence in 1948, the years of Truman's presidency proved to be a seminal time in defining and cementing the bilateral security relationship between the United States and Saudi Arabia. The king perceived that the United States now had economic and strategic interests to protect in Saudi Arabia, which increased his leverage in extracting help from Washington. With the onset of the Cold War, the United States increasingly recognized the value of a rigidly anti-Communist ally that was also strategically located and rich in an essential commodity. For the Saudis, paranoia about the spread of communism and an awareness of their own vulnerability left them little choice but to seek security in the protection of the only great power capable of providing it.

In many ways, their fears were justified. Saudi Arabia's vast oil reserves, small population, and weak armed forces made it a tempting target for larger, more powerful neighbors. Its greatest economic assets, the oil installations and the port of Jeddah, were exposed on thinly defended coasts. Despite the country's vast territory, its armed forces could not retreat into the interior to thwart an enemy invasion, as the Russians had done against Napoleon and Hitler, because most of the land was uninhabitable; cut off from the coasts, the country's security forces—such as they were—would lose access to food and water. It made sense, indeed it was imperative, to try to develop a military force that would be capable of securing vital ports and facilities, at least until help could be summoned.

Before and after his conversation with Ambassador Childs, the king made several requests for help with building up Saudi Arabia's defense capability. Some State Department officials were receptive but nothing came of it, partly because of the first Israel-Arab war in 1948 and partly because Congress in 1949 excluded Middle Eastern countries from participating in American military assistance programs.

The outbreak of the Korean War stimulated Washington to expand its efforts to reinforce anti-Communist governments everywhere, including the Middle East. The prohibition against military aid to the region was removed in 1950, and in the fall of that year Truman formally notified the Pentagon that military assistance to Saudi Arabia was "essential" to American national security. "In making this determination," his notice said, "I find that (1) the strategic location of Saudi Arabia makes it of direct importance to the defense of the Near East area, (2) the assistance to be furnished is of critical importance to the defense of free nations, and (3) the immediately increased ability of Saudi Arabia to defend itself is important to the preservation of the peace and security of the Near East area, and to the security of the United States."[4]

When a genuine threat to Saudi Arabia's security developed in the early 1960s, in the form of a contest with Egypt's Nasser over Yemen, Washington was prepared to intervene militarily if necessary to protect the Kingdom and secure the oil fields. At the height of that conflict, when dissident Saudi officers defected to Cairo and Egyptian warplanes actually bombed a few Saudi towns, the State Department circulated a memorandum to other agencies detailing the threat to Saudi Arabia and the Kingdom's inability to defend itself. "A contingency plan is now in the final stages of development," that memo said, "which sets the course of U.S. action in the event of an attempt to overthrow, or the actual overthrow, of the Saudi government. . . . It defines the U.S. intent to prevent military intervention by outside parties either to support any of the conflicting groups in Saudi Arabia or to seize Saudi territory."

The United States would send its own troops if needed "to prevent the imminent entrance of foreign forces or to safeguard American lives."[5]

~~

With Truman's declaration of Saudi Arabia's strategic importance, the Kingdom became eligible for American military training and was allowed to purchase U.S. military equipment. Training the Saudi Arabian armed forces would become a cornerstone of the bilateral relationship for the next fifty years. Like the early training programs of Aramco and the work of the Joint Economic Commission, the military mission would not only involve Americans in day-to-day, hands-on contact with thousands of Saudi Arabs but also forge lasting relationships and expedite Saudi Arabia's conversion from impoverished backwater to modern state. On June 18, 1951, Saudi Arabia agreed to a five-year extension of the agreement allowing the United States to use the Dhahran Airfield. In exchange, the United States agreed to create a standing organization known as the U.S. Military Training Mission (USMTM), to help the Saudis with an ambitious program of military modernization and training.

As USMTM described itself, its assignment was "to provide a small, modern well balanced Saudi Arabian Army, Navy and Air Force designed to maintain the internal stability of the Kingdom and capable of defense against local aggression." Thus the "internal stability" of Saudi Arabia, which meant preservation of the House of Saud, became part of the military mission of the United States.

The United States team also undertook "to train Saudi Arabian nationals, to organize the technical operations of the airport, to provide necessary construction which would become the property of the Saudi Arabian government; to furnish weather service, radio communications, and within its capabilities, rescue and operations services for civilian aircraft using the air field." The agreement specifically provided against "any infringement upon or detraction from the absolute sovereignty of the Saudi Arabian government over the air field." The bilateral agreement committed the United States to provide Army, Navy and Air Force personnel to train Saudis, and to select promising Saudis for training in the United States. Saudi Arabia agreed to pay for the entire program, including housing, vehicles, and interpreters.[6]

～

As negotiations over the military training agreement neared their conclusion, the State Department, anticipating an expanded relationship, undertook a comprehensive review of U.S. policy toward Saudi Arabia. In less than a decade, oil and world events had transformed Saudi Arabia from a foreign policy footnote into an important item on Washington's security policy agenda. American corporate involvement in the Kingdom was multiplying geometrically, oil production was rising, the air force was operating a strategically important base, and the Kingdom was a redoubt of stability and anticommunism in a chronically turbulent part of the world. The king, having rejected a security alliance with Britain, had cast his lot with the United States and wanted security commitments in return.

On February 5, 1951, the State Department transmitted to all posts a "Comprehensive Statement of United States Policy" toward Saudi Arabia. This was a classified paper, not intended to be shared with the public or with the Saudis; it was to be used by American diplomats as guidance for local decisions and for their discussions with Saudi and other Arab leaders. It represented a definitive statement of American policy on, and aspirations for, the Kingdom and the House of Saud. Although it was written more than fifty years ago, in another geopolitical era, most of this paper articulates policies still in place today—a remarkable consistency in policy that has survived multiple wars and upheavals in the Middle East, to say nothing of multiple changes of administration in Washington. It merits quoting at length because it reflects the scope of the U.S. commitment to Saudi Arabia and a sober recognition of the less-appealing aspects of Saudi life and custom:

> The United States desires to maintain close and friendly relations with the Government of Saudi Arabia. It is to our interest that a strong government control Saudi Arabia and toward this end we look with favor

upon [Abdul Aziz] Ibn Saud's regime, hope for a peaceful succession by the Crown Prince when the time comes, and support the independence and territorial integrity of Saudi Arabia. We favor the development of education and political consciousness among the people of Saudi Arabia and a greater feeling of social responsibility on the part of the ruling class. We want to see sound development of the oil industry in Saudi Arabia and on a competitive basis in so far as new concession areas are concerned. It is a major objective that Saudi Arabia's economic possibilities be developed to provide more services and diversify national income, since it is a primitive country which needs development in every kind of public enterprise to raise the standard of living, stabilize the economy, and promote trade and diversification of domestic industry. It is also our purpose to assure for ourselves and our friends and allies the strategic advantages of Saudi Arabia's geographical position, petroleum resources, and the continued general antipathy of the Saudi Arabs for communism.

While United States policy has been the target of adverse criticism and bitterness in some countries of the Near East, Saudi Arabia has remained firm in its friendship for the United States. It has served as our spokesman and interpreter to less friendly Arab states, and has, through the prestige and conservative nature of its King, exerted a stabilizing influence on the Near East generally. In order that we might retain Saudi Arabia's friendship and support it is to our interest to (a) continue our fight against communist infiltration in the Near East and promote the stability of the area; (b) advance the security of Saudi Arabia by the sale of defense materials, training of Saudi Arabian defense forces; and by assurances on appropriate occasions of American interest in Saudi Arabia's independence and territorial integrity; (c) demonstrate our support of and confidence in King Ibn Saud and Crown Prince Saud upon his succession; (d) assist in the orderly development of the economy and public welfare of Saudi Arabia; (e) give friendly counsel to all parties to a dispute involving Saudi Arabia and encourage prompt solution of the controversy; (f) observe the utmost respect for Saudi Arabia's sovereignty, sanctity of the holy places, and local customs; (g) encourage improved fiscal management and monetary stabilization; (h) assist sound American enterprise interested in engaging in desirable business or commercial development in the country; and (i) foster philanthropic, but non-religious, enterprise of public interest. In all our efforts to carry out our policies in Saudi Arabia, we should take care to serve as guide or partner and avoid giving the impression of wishing to dominate the country.

United States policy on economic development assistance to Saudi Arabia is aimed at raising living standards in order to foster political and economic stability. This is especially important in Saudi Arabia since the increasing volume of oil being taken out of the country by American companies leads the people to expect that they will derive direct economic benefits. Sharing of such benefits should be more extensive in order to avoid future possibilities of unrest. We should continue to urge and assist Saudi Arabia to carry out the reforms necessary to permit the effective utilization and distribution of the government's income from oil royalties. This income constitutes the bulk of the national income of Saudi Arabia, and the Saudi Arabian government should be encouraged to view it as available for the improvement of the economic life of the whole population and to develop an attitude of responsibility and trusteeship toward its utilization.

As a result of our policy toward Palestine, Saudi Arabian friendship for the United States cooled considerably, particularly because Prince Faisal, the Saudi Arabian foreign minister, took our policy as a personal rebuff. Even during this period, however, King Ibn Saud maintained a balanced viewpoint and constantly exerted a restraining influence upon Arab extremists. Now that the Palestine problem has entered a less acute phase, our relations with Saudi Arabia are improving. If we continue to take a firm position regarding the frontiers of Israel and the Arab refugees, if we stand firmly against Soviet expansion, and *if we do not attempt to upset the basic religious patterns of life in Saudi Arabia by too rapid an introduction of Western ways,* our relations with Saudi Arabia will become increasingly cordial.

Saudi Arabia has a long way to go to meet the social standards and responsibilities of other nations, but it is trying very hard to improve itself and it has done well, considering that its sustained efforts have been only a post-war development. It has also had [a] serious internal obstacle in the fanatical religious opposition to change and the growth of Western influences. It behooves us, therefore, to applaud what Saudi Arabia has done and is doing, and not criticize it for what it has not yet been able to do.

It has become increasingly evident during the swift expansion of the American political, economic, and strategic relations with Saudi Arabia that for our objectives to be adequately realized, both we and the Saudi Arabs must achieve genuine understanding of each other. To this end it is our policy to give the greatest encouragement and aid to American public and private efforts which are being devoted to the leveling of linguistic and cultural barriers. It remains obvious, however, that the Saudi Arabs themselves have the greater obstacles to overcome, for they must reach an understanding of the whole pattern of Western economic, political, legal and cultural life, which is infinitely more complex than their own. Only when the Saudi Government officials with whom we deal are equipped intelligently to cope with such problems as modern finance can our two countries work intelligently together.[7]

Here was the answer to those Americans who questioned a U.S. policy of friendship and support for a regime that tolerated slavery, suppressed dissent and unorthodox thought, kept its women veiled and sequestered, condoned polygamy, excluded non-Muslims, and concentrated all political and economic power in the hands of a privileged few: It was in the interests of the United States to do so. Whether that answer represented hard-headed realism or corrupting cynicism was open to debate in 1951 and remains so today. It was a policy of enlightened self-interest, just like Aramco's.

Many of the declassified State Department documents from that year, 1951, concern the extensive negotiations over the renewal of the U.S. right to use the air base at Dhahran. The king and his advisers used the negotiations to extract American commitments to provide money, weapons, and military training. They drove a very hard bargain, and it is clear from the comments of American negotiators that the Saudis could not be pushed around. At one point, the Saudis produced a U.S. government press release from 1948 announcing an agreement with Portugal for U.S. use of a base in the Azores. The Saudis said it looked as if Portugal got better terms than were being offered to them. The Saudi negotiators rejected an American request for a twenty-five-year agreement because, they said, any such deal would look as if they were doing American bidding, just as Iraq was doing British bidding. They objected to a U.S. request for a "no transfer" provision that would bar the transfer of American-supplied military equipment to a third country. Storage of American military equipment at the base could continue, but only if the uniformed guards were Saudi Arabs lest it appear that the Saudis had relinquished any element of sovereignty. The chief Saudi negotiator, Yusuf Yassin, argued that "his people were ignorant and [he] did not want give them reason turn against either himself or Americans," Ambassador Raymond Hare cabled to Washington. "Tactics of Saudi negotiators have given new meaning to frustration," Hare complained.[8]

An extension agreement was finally signed on June 18. It renewed the U.S. base rights for five years and included an option on both sides to renew for five more after that. The Saudis would receive military training and, when they had pilots who could fly them, twenty warplanes. American civilian personnel would be exempted from Saudi customs duties and taxes. They could have what Ambassador Hare called "their own social life provided that they should respect the local customs and laws observed in Saudi Arabia." The U.S. Joint Chiefs of Staff had already completed an evaluation of Saudi defense needs and capabilities that called for the creation of an army of about 18,000 men, along with a small air force and navy. The United States would train these military units.

Announcing the agreement in a news release on July 23, the State Department said it was concluded "following the designation of Saudi Arabia as eligible for cash reimbursable military assistance under Public Law 329, as amended. This act provides such assistance as may be extended [to] any nation whose ability to defend itself or to participate in the defense of the area of which it is a part is important to the security of the United States. Saudi Arabia is the first Arab country so designated."[9]

Fred H. Awalt, director of the State Department's Office of Arabian Peninsula Affairs, prepared a briefing paper on Saudi Arabia for a military delegation that was about to go there to plan the training program. "It is suggested," this paper said, "that the group should be admonished against being discouraged or depressed by what they see in Saudi Arabia. The wealth of the country and the benefits of western contacts have failed as yet to touch the lives of most of the population in any fundamental way. Saudi Arabia is still a primitive country served by a very harsh Providence. Illiteracy is the rule rather than the exception. Malnutrition and disease sap the strength and ambition of most of the people."[10] These were the same realities that Aramco had faced in training the first Arab oil workers fifteen years earlier. The raw material of the Saudi armed forces was indeed very raw.

The king and his advisers were familiar with the American military's immense capacity for instruction because an initial small quasi-military training program was already operating at the time of the king's meeting with Ambassador Childs in 1947. The U.S. Air Force, operating the air base at Dhahran under the 1945 agreement, was training thirty-one Saudi Arabs in airfield operations, maintenance, air traffic control, and weather observation.

An U.S. Air Force news release about this program quoted Lieutenant Colonel Dale S. Seeds of Seattle, a bomber pilot running the training program, as saying the young trainees were "like dry sponges. They soak up everything. They have an amazing fundamental thirst for knowledge and are intensely eager to learn. To them aviation is something strange and wonderful, and every one of these kids wants to be an aircraft mechanic as well as an airport manager. Besides learning how to run an airfield, they are absorbing international aviation techniques and it's a safe bet that the Arabs needed to run the Arabian airports of the future will be picked from among these boys."[11]

Officially, this was not military training, which before Truman's finding of 1950 would have been prohibited. The tasks for which the Saudis were being trained, such as weather forecasting, were nominally civilian, and the trainees were not members of a military unit. Their training, however, was military in style, and included reveille, marching drill, and lights out at taps. The students ate in the dining hall and learned to play basketball. Like their countrymen next door at Aramco, they were becoming Americanized, at least externally.

Young Saudi Arab men who were recruited into the fledgling armed forces were like their counterparts at Aramco and Bechtel in that they started from scratch. Americans who joined the U.S. military in the mid-twentieth century grew up tinkering with automobiles and radios, knew how to use tools, and studied physics in high school; their Saudi counterparts needed to acquire all these basic skills in addition to military tactics and discipline. Some of them were familiar with firearms, but most of them were illiterate and knew nothing of telephones, electricity, military field sanitation, radar, vehicle maintenance, or marching in formation. They were unaccustomed to taking orders from strangers, as everyone in a disciplined army must do.

"While an American soldier recognizes the chain of command and knows how to deal with authority, most Arabs have learned to live in a society in which directives from authority should never be taken at face value," one experienced American military adviser observed.[12]

A U.S. officer would say to a Saudi commander, "You know, the generator is sitting out there in the sun, it might not work when you need it," an American who served in Dhahran recalled. He would suggest the Saudis put it under shelter, or cover it. 'And the guy would tell his secretary to make a note of it. The same thing would happen again a few weeks later. And the American would say, 'I know that two weeks after I leave here, he'll fix it.'"[13] This was the same lesson Aramco officials had learned: The best way to persuade the Saudis to do something was to make it appear to be their idea or done on their initiative.

"The complete lack of industrial, technical, or administrative background among the people created a tremendous problem for both the Army and Air Force sections, and particularly for the latter," the training mission said about its work.[14]

By the end of the 1950s, USMTM had units in Riyadh, al-Kharj, Taif, and Jeddah as well as in Dhahran. The Dhahran headquarters had become a "Little America," like the Aramco village, and provided movies, tennis courts, a bowling alley, an American Express office, telephone lines to the United States, and, of course, air conditioning. Life was less comfortable at the other outposts. At al-Kharj and Taif, the units were completely dependent on flights from Dhahran for food, mail, and movies. No alcohol was permitted at any of these installations.

Personnel assigned to USMTM served a one-year "unaccompanied tour," which meant they went to Saudi Arabia without their wives and children, lived separately from the Arab troops, stayed a year, and then went home. This arrangement limited opportunities to develop the closer, longer-lasting relationships that developed at the oil company between some of its successful Arab employees and Americans who stayed on for years, even decades, of daily contact. In the package of agreements that deepened and intensified relations between the United States government and Saudi Arabia after the end of the Arab oil embargo in 1974, the Americans took on another military commitment that would involve them more intimately and on a more personal level with Saudi Arabs. This was the program to train the National Guard.

~/⌐

The National Guard is a separate organization from the regular Army, Navy, and Air Force. The Army, Navy, and Air Force, which are under the control of the Ministry of Defense and Aviation, are conventional armed forces primarily responsible for protecting the Kingdom against attack from other countries. The National Guard is an internal paramilitary security force, created in 1956 and commanded since 1962 by Prince Abdullah ibn Abdul Aziz, a son of the founding king. Abdullah is a half-brother of King Fahd and his designated successor. The guard is a tribal organization, keeper of the bedouin tradition; it is often described as the successor to the "White Army," a royal guard of tribal warriors that included remnants of the zealously Muslim irregular force that helped Abdul Aziz unify the country, then was crushed when it challenged the king's power.

John Yeosock, who as a brigadier general in the U.S. Army was the senior U.S. adviser to the National Guard in the early 1980s, described it as "the glue that holds this otherwise loosely confederated collection of tribes together. This is where the tribes came together under Abdul Aziz, this was the organizational construct that gave legitimacy to the government."[15]

Until the 1973 Middle East war, the National Guard was trained primarily by the British. The postwar agreements between Washington and Riyadh included the transfer of this responsibility to the United States, through the office of the Program Manager-Saudi Arabian National Guard, or OPM-SANG, a unit of the U.S. Army Materiel Command. OPM-SANG's commanding officer is a U.S. Army brigadier general. Most of the actual training, however, is conducted by nominally civilian personnel—mostly former military—employed by a contractor. Since January 7, 1975, that contractor has been Vinnell Corporation, which is now a subsidiary of the giant defense contracting conglomerate Northrop Grumman Corporation.

The original Vinnell contract, a three-year, $76.9-million agreement calling for the company to supply from seven hundred to eight hundred trainers, stirred some antipathy in Congress. It was the first agreement under which operational training of a foreign military force would be provided by a private contractor instead of U.S. military personnel. It called for the training of entire units rather than individuals. It did not provide for the delivery of weapons or hardware, unlike more conventional programs in which foreign forces are trained in the use of newly acquired weapons. Some members of Congress suspected that the Defense Department wanted a civilian contractor to do the work so that the Pentagon would not be responsible for enforcing discrimination against Jews and women.

At a hearing of the House International Relations Subcommittee on International Political and Military Affairs on March 20, 1975, senior officials of the Defense and State departments acknowledged that the Vinnell arrangement was unusual, but said it made sense in the unique context of Saudi Arabia. It was not a conventional military assistance program funded by U.S. taxpayers; the Saudis were paying for it, and only a qualified civilian contractor could supply enough personnel to meet their needs. As for discrimination, Benjamin Forman, assistant general counsel of the Defense Department, said the contract between the Saudis and Vinnell had been amended to remove four clauses the Saudis wanted that might have been objectionable to Americans. These would have prohibited women at all work sites, required participants to have military-style short haircuts, excluded anyone who was a citizen of a country not recognized by Saudi Arabia, and required that contractor personnel "have no history of personal contact or interest in unrecognized countries," namely, Israel.

For almost thirty years since that original contract, OPM-SANG and Vinnell have been deeply immersed in the operations of the National Guard, shepherding its development from an irregular force into a modern light infantry organization that is widely regarded as superior in discipline and capability to the regular Saudi Arabian armed forces. There has been surprisingly little debate about this arrangement in Washington, considering the National Guard's role as domestic enforcer for a regime often criticized as autocratic and corrupt. Trained by the United States, the National Guard is the most efficient weapon in the House of Saud's arsenal.

"They are very loyal, responsive, tough fighters. When you see them, it's time to go back inside," said Brigadier General Martin Dempsey, commander of OPM-SANG when I visited the organization in 2002. He said the National Guard has "accepted and embraced U.S. Army training methodology: a training calendar, the standards, key missions and battle tasks, individual marksmanship training, and now they do physical training. That's what we do all day."[16] Vinnell trainers camp out with National Guard troops on their training exercises, and some of them stay in Saudi Arabia for years, nurturing the kind of personal contacts that Aramco developed in the early years of exploration.

Here is OPM-SANG's description of itself and its mission:

Through OPM-SANG, the United States provides technical and contract supervisory assistance to this force through functions such as organization, training, equipment procurement, construction, maintenance, supply, administration, and medical programs. OPM-SANG personnel are directly involved with all aspects of SANG's force expan-

American military trainers on field exercise with Saudi National Guardsmen, 2002.
DEPARTMENT OF DEFENSE PHOTO.

sion and in helping develop a total army. . . . The Program Manager exercises principal authority over the planning, direction, execution, and control of the modernization effort, which covers all elements, missions, functions and requirements of the SANG. He facilitates increased SANG participation in all aspects of the Program, whose goal is SANG's eventual capability to unilaterally initiate and sustain modern organizations and systems.[17]

"They want an army to emulate and it's us," Dempsey said. "They want to continue to modernize. It's not just that Arabs like toys, modernization is a thought process. They want us to teach them institutional systems, military education, an institutionalized approach to ammunition management."[18]

With about 70,000 full-time troops and another 25,000 irregular reservists, the National Guard has primary responsibility for defending critical installations, including the oil fields and the sacred sites of

Mecca and Medina. Although the National Guard's mission is not spelled out anywhere, its assignment in the past has been to maintain internal stability, which has meant suppressing occasional uprisings by the restive Shiites of eastern Saudi Arabia and other malcontents, and maintaining order during the annual pilgrimage to Mecca. As it has acquired modern equipment, the National Guard has become more like a conventional military force, and it was used as an auxiliary to the regular Army during Operation Desert Storm in 1991. The role and capabilities of the reservists are less clear. "Cynics would say they are 25,000 people being paid by Abdullah for their loyalty," Dempsey remarked.

With about 12,000 applicants a year, the National Guard can afford to be selective in recruiting, and it accepts only high school graduates. That is a long leap from what the first OPM-SANG commander found when he arrived in April 1975.

"We had to start from scratch, really, when you talk about modern operations," said General Richard Lawrence (now retired). "They had some basic native instincts in terms of how to move in the desert and how to operate in that climate, a lot of basic skills they had, but they weren't able to put them together in terms of advanced individual or unit training, especially at a higher level. And there were a lot of leadership problems."

Some of his recruits were illiterate, Lawrence recalled, and few had been educated beyond the fourth grade. "Those in the battalions around the major cities had a little education, some could even drive a car and operate in an urban environment. But the ones levied out of the desert didn't know much of anything except how to drive a camel, milk a goat, and put up a tent."

The troops' unfamiliarity with military organization and modern weaponry was nearly total. "One of the first things we had to do was get them organized into formations we could train at the basic unit level," Lawrence said. This was harder than it sounds because the Saudi Arabs "don't take well to regimentation and hierarchy," Lawrence observed— that is, they don't take orders from men whom they regard as peers, just as Aramco's workers would not in earlier decades. "Then we had to give basic training on how to operate new equipment, light armored vehicles, crew-served weapons that they had never dealt with. . . . They had to deal with maintenance of electrical systems, so we had to train them in how to read. We were dealing with a limited set of capabilities," Lawrence said.[19]

Lawrence, who learned Arabic, made it a practice to visit the troops in the morning and sit with them as they ate breakfast. He did not like what he saw. "Each squad had a communal tray, to bring stuff back to the tent and squat to eat together. They would clean the tray by wiping it off with sand. I got concerned about health and decided we would have mess halls. We spent a lot of money, brought in mess equipment from the States, stainless steel trays. We lined 'em all up the first day for the mess hall and they refused to go in. They said those trays are for hospitals, we won't eat off them." The Americans had to create an example by persuading first the Saudi officers, then the senior enlisted personnel, to eat in the dining halls. Then the troops followed.

The troops also balked at being inoculated against the many diseases that plagued the Arab population. "I'll never forget the first inoculations, for several different diseases," Lawrence said. "We got them lined up and ready to go, they were all pretty brave till we got started, then they broke and ran, it was a stampede." He said the first few men jumped and winced as the needle entered their arms, "so the rest of them lost their courage and away they went."

John Yeosock, who became OPM-SANG project manager in 1981, said that even then some recruits did not know how to read or how to lace up a pair of boots. Yet when he returned to Saudi Arabia as ground forces commander in Operation Desert Storm in 1991, he found the National Guard to be "the most professional and disciplined" of all the Middle Eastern armed forces with which he was familiar.

He described the National Guard as an extension of the family-centered bedouin ethos personified by its commander, Abdullah. If family obligations require a National Guard member to leave his unit and go home, Yeosock said, "the tribe will send a replacement." During his tenure as senior adviser, he said, Abdullah was committed to providing the National Guard with its own comprehensive health care system, including a nationwide network of hospitals to provide care not only to active-duty members but to their families and extended families, which as Aramco had discovered could be very extended indeed. Such was Abdullah's confidence in the integrity of OPM-SANG, Yeosock said, that he entrusted the Americans to select a contractor for this ambitious undertaking. By taking himself out of the selection process, Abdullah insulated himself from the corruption and political maneuvering that characterized the bidding on major Saudi government projects and big-ticket weapons purchases in the 1970s. With the Americans conducting the bidding, Hospital Corporation of America won the contract.

One of the most senior and longest-serving Vinnell managers said he was constantly reminded that he and his colleagues could not take for granted that the Saudis would grasp concepts or understand machines that seem second nature to Americans. Indifferent to maintenance, the Saudis neglected to rotate their truck tires, which would then shred when hauling full loads in the desert heat. Moving into new houses that had been constructed for them and furnished with modern appliances, some of the Saudis put glasses and plates in the clothes washing machine instead of the dishwasher. (Peter Wilson and Douglas Graham, journalists who lived in Saudi Arabia for several years, described videos created to teach the National Guardsmen and their families how to live in modern houses: "The films describe how to use toilets, washing machines, lights and refrigerators. The videos also discourage cooking on the floors of the houses and encourage the use of stoves.")[20] The Saudis stored trucks with the batteries still in them, thus ensuring that the vehicles would not start when needed. When the Americans imported human dummies to use in training medics, Saudi customs officials held them up because the torsos were female. And, of course, the Saudis rejected the field rations known as Meals Ready to Eat (MREs), because some of them contained pork products. "We contracted with a firm in Texas to make *halal* MREs," this adviser recalled with amusement. (*Halal* is essentially the Muslim equivalent of Kosher.)[21]

He learned, he said, that "You have to keep reinventing the wheel" and "You don't eat an elephant in one bite." On the other hand, "They did not treat us like hired help. They invited us into their homes. They were gracious, honest, and frank. If they didn't like something we were doing, they would tell us and we would tell them. We had a damn good relationship, and I have a lot of respect and admiration and affection for them. I watched the guard go from a rudimentary force to something pretty damn good."

Nowadays the orientation packet for newcomers to the OPM-SANG team includes an article by a previous commander, General William H. Riley Jr., with tips about how to get along with the Saudis and persuade them to do things the right way without appearing overbearing or inflexible. Its title is "Leading From Behind."

Riley begins by recounting a field training exercise near Nahran that involved deploying almost 10,000 troops across the desert in what he calls "extreme trafficability conditions." Riley was equipped with every modern navigational device; the Saudi general with whom he was riding across the barren terrain had no such gear. Yet the Saudi officer insisted on taking the directional lead, ignoring Riley's protests that he was off course. "As I juggled odometer readings with azimuths and map location, and as I updated LORAN location with compass readings and distances, the atmosphere in my vehicle was punctuated with harsh words that should not be translated into Arabic," Riley recounts. "My interpreter/driver was harangued by my constant irritation over having to set course corrections and give position updates while bouncing over sand dunes at a high rate of speed and trying to keep all the equipment in the vehicle from becoming deadly missiles."

There is of course no suspense about the outcome of this tale: To Riley's amazement, the Saudi officer's navigation was accurate because he knew the desert. "From childhood he had traveled with camel caravans all over the Kingdom and was an experienced trade-route traveler and guide even as a young adult. He had joined the Frontier Forces and amassed some 25 years of service in traveling over all desert routes in the Kingdom. Whereas I was tied to navigation gear when confronted with the lack of terrain features in the desert, he was guided by the sun, dune directions, previous vehicle tracks in the desert, and other factors unknown to me at the time. In short, I soon realized that in spite of my advantage in technological equipment, my counterpart was truly an expert in desert travel, and rather than being the leader, I had much to learn in the role of being led."

Like so many Americans before him, Riley discovered that the secret of success with the Saudis is accommodation. The American way is "too aggressive and pushy" for them, he wrote. In the Arab perspective, "We are overly concerned with time to produce results. We are ever-present with our checklists, our milestone schedules, our stochastic decision trees and our pert charts. . . . We are irreverent, aggressive workaholics who press for results at any cost." General George C. Patton, he observed, "would be a miserable failure in developing rapport and achieving success with the Saudis" because of his abrasive style.[22]

In navigating the desert with his Saudi counterpart, Riley was like Tom Barger and the early Aramco geologists traveling with Khamis ibn Rimthan in a previous generation. They learned that the Saudi Arabs, although limited in technology and book learning, were nevertheless smart and skillful in their own environment. Success in a joint Arab-American enterprise, whether finding oil or building an army, depended on flexibility, and on respect for the Arab way of doing things.

There is never an end-point to military training. In 2003, Vinnell still had about 1,400 employees stationed with the National Guard all over Saudi Arabia, its nine-figure annual contract channeling oil money back into the United States. The guard, now an up-to-date, mobile light infantry force of three mechanized brigades and six infantry brigades, has its own communications, engineering, artillery, logistics, and military police units. It has a fleet of high-speed, desert-capable wheeled armored vehicles, some of them fitted with antitank weapons, as well as conventional towed artillery systems and some helicopters. It gives the House of Saud a sharp sword that can be wielded quickly against any domestic challenge. Police functions, such as hunting suspected terrorists, are the responsibility of the Ministry of Interior, but overt troublemaking by a group, such as work stoppages or Iranian-inspired demonstrations during the pilgrimage, can expect to attract the intimidating attention of the National Guard without delay.

The evolution of the U.S.–Saudi Arabian military and security relationship in the decades since the 1951 agreement has been well chronicled. In addition to training and facilities, the Saudis wanted the most advanced weapons, including aircraft. From a strategy viewpoint, it made sense for the Saudi armed forces to purchase the most sophisticated weapons systems available. With abundant cash and scant manpower, the Saudis could not muster enough troops to withstand an assault by any of their much larger neighbors; they relied on superiority in weaponry, which they purchased in abundance, mostly from the United States but also from Britain and other countries.

As Parker Hart was preparing to leave Saudi Arabia at the conclusion of his tour as ambassador in 1965, he had one final conversation with King Faisal. "Faisal showed his gratitude for US assistance over the years not by words of thanks but by asking me to request that the US government assume the position of national manager of Saudi development contracts," Hart recalled. "The United States would thus stand between him and all prospective contractors for military construction, studying and evaluating all major proposals and supervising their execution."[23] The United States agreed to this request. Under an agreement signed shortly afterward and extended several times, the U.S. Army Corps of Engineers was designated the purchasing agent and project manager for Saudi Arabia's major military construction projects. By the time the Saudi military buildup was nearing its peak in the late 1970s, the corps had $12.2 billion worth of projects in the pipeline, including huge "military cities" near the borders with Iraq and Yemen, two naval bases, a headquarters for the National Guard, and the King Abdul Aziz Military Academy.

At a 1979 congressional hearing on these projects, Brigadier General James N. Ellis, chief of the corps' Middle East Division, described the division's work in Saudi Arabia as "an exciting program, which has grown at the initiative of the Saudi Arabian government, as part of their mushrooming nation-building effort, although actually ours is only one part of that effort. . . . The Saudis clearly have a vision of nationhood and the capital to follow that vision," he said. He projected that the corps would eventually manage $21 billion worth of construction projects for the Saudi military.

Skeptical members of the House Foreign Affairs Committee asked whether the facilities were too big and too lavish, and whether the corps ever tried to talk the Saudis out of them. Occasionally, Ellis said, but not often.[24]

The same could have been said of the Saudis' weapons purchases. Equating strategy with acquisition, they wanted the biggest and best and most advanced of everything, and suppliers—including many of America's biggest defense contractors—were happy to sell it. Unhappily for the Saudis, their ability to buy equipment usually outran their competence to operate and maintain it.

Occasionally the Pentagon would seek to persuade the Saudis to purchase a less capable or less sophisticated weapon or airplane that was more suitable for them. When the Saudis sought to acquire the Lockheed F-104 fighter, for example, the Pentagon balked. Even the Germans could not handle the F-104, so many of which crashed in Europe that it was known as "The Widowmaker." Washington finally dispatched the famous test pilot Chuck Yeager to persuade the Saudis that the less sophisticated F-5 was a better fit for them.

The White House position on the sale, stated in a June 16, 1965, memo from Robert W. Komer of the National Security Council to President Lyndon Johnson, was expressed this way: "Our goal is to keep our oil-rich Saudi friends happy and insure that if they finally do buy anything we get the sale." The F-5 would represent no threat to Israel, Komer noted, because "Saudi Arabia is too far away and too incompetent."[25]

Lockheed was represented in the negotiations by Adnan Khashoggi, the preeminent Saudi middle man and commission king. Khashoggi also represented Raytheon Corporation, maker of the Hawk missile, which the Saudis also wanted. In the end, he brokered a complicated deal in which the Saudi Air Force bought British Lightning jets instead of the F-104, Lockheed got a consolation prize in the form of a large order for its C-130 Hercules cargo plane along with its TriStar jets for the civilian airline, and Raytheon delivered the Hawks. Robert Lacey calculated Khashoggi's commissions at $136 million for the Hawk sale, and $400,000 per plane for the C-130s.[26]

Ambassador Hume Horan recalled "the constant, constant and hopeless tug of war" with the Saudis over their desire to purchase weapons that were beyond their ability to use. "They desired end items that were very sophisticated and looked great on the mantelpiece, but they never had the manpower to operate or maintain it. They didn't even have high school graduates that could change the tires on these things," he said.[27]

For years, the only real brake on Saudi Arabian purchases of American weapons was the opposition of Israel and its friends in Congress. They blocked or delayed some proposed sales, or approved the deals on condition that weapons be delivered in lower-end versions lacking equipment that could present a threat to Israel. Even so, by the time the Saudis curtailed major military purchases when they ran short of cash in the 1990s, they had bought $93.8 billion worth of weapons and military facilities from the United States. The acquisitions included F-15S advanced fighter aircraft, M-1 A2 Abrams tanks (the same main battle tank used by U.S. forces), Bradley armored vehicles, and the Patriot missile defense system.[28]

The $93.8-billion figure is impressive, but it did not convey as much combat capability as it might seem because most of the money was not spent on actual weapons. Only 21 percent of all purchases from the United States from 1950 to 1997 were for "lethal equipment," according to an analysis by the Congressional Research Service of the Library of Congress. "The largest portion (32%) went for support services (repair, rehabilitation, supply operations, and training.) Another major component of the Saudi program has been construction of military bases and facilities, accounting for 19%." Another 10.4 percent went for spare parts.[29]

Thus the Saudis had top-quality airfields, barracks, naval bases, and military hospitals, but these could not be fired at an enemy. They had some competent military manpower, including excellent pilots, but not enough. And they had fancy weaponry but weak maintenance and logistical systems. As a result, for all that money, they were not prepared to defend themselves when the test came, in the summer of 1990.

CHAPTER 15

Desert Storms

The very presence of United States military personnel in Saudi Arabia, even though unarmed, has long disturbed Saudi and Arab nationalists. The Saudis have been keenly conscious of their vulnerability to Arab nationalist attacks for being host to foreign military forces.

—State Department internal memorandum, 1961

IRAQ'S INVASION OF KUWAIT in August 1990 hit Saudi Arabia like an electric shock. It was bad enough that Iraq had violated all traditions of Islam with an unprovoked attack on Muslim neighbors, and all conventions of Arab solidarity with its announced annexation of a member state of the Arab League. Worse for the Saudis was the fear that they were next.

So flustered were the princes of the House of Saud that at first they could not even agree on what to say about the takeover of the friendly emirate over the border. At the height of summer's heat, many senior princes were out of the country and out of touch with each other. The Saudi media did not even report that the invasion had happened, although everyone in Saudi Arabia knew about it because the BBC and other Arabic-language international radios reported it; and Kuwaiti refugees, including the ruler, were streaming into the country.

Kuwait had historic ties to Saudi Arabia and was a fellow member of the Gulf Cooperation Council, a political and economic grouping of the Arab emirates along the Persian Gulf, but there was little the

Kingdom could do to save its tiny neighbor from Iraq. The Iraqi occupation was a fait accompli. The real issue was whether Iraq intended
to send troops into Saudi Arabia, and if so, how to prevent such an in-
cursion. There was no doubt of Saudi Arabia's vulnerability; Iraq had
a heavily armed, battle-tested army of 1.2 million men, more troops
than Saudi Arabia had total men of military age.

In Washington, Saudi Arabia had not been much on the policy-
makers' radar screens during the years before the invasion. The burning
issue in the Persian Gulf region in the 1980s was the war between Iran
and Iraq; with oil prices relatively low and Saudi internal politics stable,
the Kingdom was not a major concern.

When the shrewd and perceptive Chas W. Freeman Jr. was appointed
U.S. ambassador in 1989, he found that Saudi Arabia "was not on the
policy map in Washington. The relationship was fraying . . . Saudi Arabia was a place that no one thought of except when they needed some
cash to do something and thought they could shake down the Saudis
for that purpose."[1] Indeed, the Saudis had provided a good bit of cash
to support the CIA's effort to arm the guerrillas fighting Soviet troops
occupying Afghanistan and to fund the Contra rebels in Nicaragua.
The bilateral relationship had suffered a breach in 1988, when the
United States discovered that the Saudis had secretly acquired nuclear-
capable medium-range ballistic missiles from China; but in general
Saudi Arabia was such a dependable ally that Washington took it for
granted. Iraq's invasion of Kuwait changed that overnight.

Fearing a disruption of oil supplies and the loss of its strategic partner, the United States promptly offered to send troops to protect the
Kingdom. "We are prepared to deploy these forces to defend the Kingdom of Saudi Arabia," Defense Secretary Dick Cheney told King Fahd
at a fateful meeting in Riyadh on August 6. "If you ask us we will come.
We will seek no permanent bases. And when you ask us to go home, we
will leave." General H. Norman Schwarzkopf showed the Saudis pho-
tos of Iraqi troops and tanks at the border.

Some of the king's most senior brothers and advisers wanted to wait
before taking the politically neuralgic step of inviting foreign troops. In
true Saudi fashion, they would have preferred to negotiate an agree-

ment with Iraq, or to let the Arab League sort it out, or to buy protection with cash. Normally a cautious leader who sought consensus, Fahd responded with uncharacteristic decisiveness and swiftness. He overrode his brothers' objections after a brief argument and told Cheney and Schwarzkopf, "OK."[2]

"The king did not require persuasion and proved to be exceptionally decisive," recalled Freeman, who was in that meeting. "He later said to me that this was in fact the only time in his many decades of public life that he ever made a decision on his own, without waiting for consensus."[3]

His simple response set in motion events that are still reverberating. The deployment of U.S. troops ensured the security of Saudi Arabia and of the Persian Gulf's shipping lanes, and early the following year Saudi Arabia would be the launching pad for the liberation of Kuwait. What few seem to have foreseen was that the deployment would also become the biggest grievance of a growing cadre of angry Muslim extremists who would target not only the Americans but also the Saudi leaders who had invited them into the country.

It is still not clear whether Saddam Hussein, the ruler of Iraq, truly planned to attack Saudi Arabia. Ambassador Freeman said there was a "substantial risk" of such a move. By August 4, he said, two divisions of the Republican Guard, Iraq's best troops, were poised on the Saudi-Kuwaiti border "in a classic resupply-prior-to-advance mode." Freeman said that Iraq planned to "dismember" Saudi Arabia, rather than take the entire country, by seizing control of the oil installations along the Persian Gulf coast, adjacent to Kuwait.[4] Others believe that after grabbing Kuwait, Saddam Hussein would have been able to coerce the frightened Saudis into accepting his demands concerning OPEC's oil price policy and would not have invaded.

In historical perspective it probably does not matter which is correct; once Fahd said "OK" and the deployment of Americans began, the Iraqi military threat to Saudi Arabia was moot. With their survival no longer in jeopardy, the overriding issue confronting Fahd and his brothers was managing the domestic political consequences of a massive deployment of foreign troops on the holy soil of Islam.

By 1990, the people of Saudi Arabia were well accustomed to the presence of foreign civilians; they generally tolerated it so long as the foreigners accommodated themselves to Saudi religious beliefs and social customs, and Americans who lived in the country had learned to do so. The sudden arrival of up to half a million armed young infidels, many of them women and almost all of them ignorant of Saudi Arabia, was another matter.

The deployment polarized Saudi opinion. The social and religious conservatives, as well as the xenophobic radicals, opposed it as a desecration of the holy soil of Islam and a menace to Saudi culture. The liberals and modernizers welcomed it as an opportunity to force air and light into the country's stunted intellectual life. They wanted more fraternization with foreign troops, not less.

There was not much the Americans could do about the furious criticism leveled at the House of Saud by Saudi and other Arab critics, who asked why the Kingdom could not defend itself after spending uncounted billions on sophisticated military equipment. This question became a whip that was used to flog the regime by conservative theologians, among them the fiery dissident Safar al-Hawali, who said the United States was a greater menace to Saudi Arabia than was Iraq.

It was a fair question, but it was not asked to elicit information or inspire reasoned debate. The critics raised it to embarrass the king and incite hostility to foreigners. They charged that the United States was sending its armed forces not to protect Saudi Arabia but to dominate it, and depicted the decision to call on the Americans as further evidence that the House of Saud was a willing tool of Western cultural imperialism. To them the American deployment was a humiliation made necessary by incompetence and corruption in the government. They predicted that American troops would stay on after completing their mission, which turned out to be partly correct.

These criticisms could not be silenced because they were often uttered in the form of sermons by religious leaders, which circulated on cassettes; nor could they be refuted entirely, because they were at least partly valid. With this passionate opposition in the air, the Americans understood that it was essential to manage the behavior of the international troops in ways that would minimize incitement of the local population and avoid playing into the hands of the radicals. The troops' mere presence would be controversial enough; it was important that they not make things worse by public acts that would offend the Saudi people.

If the Americans did not know this instinctively, the Saudis made sure they understood it. "To my consternation," Schwarzkopf recalled in his memoir, "their most pressing concern was neither the threat from Saddam nor the enormous joint military enterprise on which we were embarked. What loomed largest for them was the cultural crisis triggered by this sudden flood of Americans into their kingdom."[5]

So sensitive was this subject that the king and senior princes sought approval or at least acceptance of the foreign troop deployment from the *ulama,* the most senior scholars and jurists of the religious establishment. After extensive consultation with his colleagues, the grand mufti, Sheikh Abdul Aziz bin Baz, reluctantly issued a *fatwa,* or religious decree, giving tepid endorsement: "Even though the Americans are, in the conservative religious view, equivalent to non-believers as they are not Muslims, they deserve support because they are here to defend Islam." The price of this *fatwa* was a promise from the king that the foreign troops would respect Muslim customs and traditions and would leave immediately when the threat had passed.[6] Islam, however, is a creed that stresses the individual's responsibility to God rather than the authority of a human hierarchy. The most committed opponents of the foreign troop deployment were not obliged to heed bin Baz's views and were not persuaded by the *fatwa.*

⌇

Four men were primarily responsible for ensuring that the troops behaved appropriately: Schwarzkopf, Ambassador Freeman, Ambassador Gordon S. Brown, who was Schwarzkopf's State Department advisor, and the overall Saudi commander, Major General Khaled bin Sultan, son of the defense minister. Looking back afterward, the three Americans said they took the initiative to recognize the importance of the behavior issue and address it up front. The Saudi commander said it was he who laid down the law.

By Brown's account, Freeman reinforced the Saudis' concerns about the troops' behavior, and suggested some rules that would minimize cultural friction. Schwarzkopf did not resist. As Brown told it,

> The Command's response to Chas Freeman was, "Tell us what we need to avoid, what we need to do and we'll do it, because the most important thing is to make this work with the Saudis." His people were furious with him. General Order One said, No booze, no this, no that, and all the other things that were no-nos. Can you imagine the military saying, "We're going to live by Muslim rules while we're here in Saudi Arabia"? But it was very important in setting the tone. It was important that the Saudis be protected, and that we had to be almost leaning over backwards in order to avoid incidents. There was a lot of resentment in the military. But Schwarzkopf took it, and he said it was more important that we deal with the Saudis on a constructive basis than we have perpetual little picky fights with them.[7]

The Americans set rules for the troops: No alcohol. No sexy magazines. No female entertainers. Every U.S. soldier was to receive basic instruction in Islam and Arab civilization. Female soldiers were to perform all required duties, including driving, but could not appear in a public place in T-shirts, regardless of the temperature. The women must wear hats. Christian and Jewish religious ceremonies were to be conducted where Saudis would not see them. Chaplains, listed as "morale officers," were to remove their religious insignia when off base.

Because of these limitations on religious display, some news media reported that the troops were being deprived of religious services. These reports still irritate Freeman. "One of the more absurd moments of the whole thing was sitting there while the U.S. press was hammering away at us for failing to provide for the religious needs of our troops when in fact they were fully provided for but we couldn't refute [the media criticism] without violating our understandings with the Saudis," Freeman recalled. "There were more chaplains in this war than in any previous war, and they included Jews and Buddhists."[8]

In General Khaled's account, it was the Saudis who pressed the behavior issue: "As guardians of Islam's holy places, we had to be ultra careful that our Western allies did not cause offense to Muslim opinion, whether at home or abroad. Nothing that clashed with our Muslim customs, national traditions, religious practices and beliefs could be tolerated. To ensure this was an important part of my brief. I hope that history will record that, by insisting on certain rules of behavior from our powerful American ally, I helped preserve the honor and integrity of the Saudi armed forces, and indeed of the Kingdom. At no time were the Saudis treated as the Vietnamese had been treated during the Vietnam conflict, as second-class citizens in their own country."[9] The reference to Vietnam was a cheap shot, probably reflecting the tensions inherent in an overlapping command structure in which American officers were required to show their Saudi counterparts a deference the Saudis had not earned.

With the behavioral code in place, the Americans agreed to a suggestion by Prince Sultan, the defense minister, that the *mutawa'in* inspect the troops. "What they discovered, of course, was a God-fearing, alcohol-free, extremely courteous, disciplined, respectful U.S. Army," Freeman said.[10]

Still, there was palpable culture shock in the general Saudi population. Even an outsider such as myself could sense it. At an early stage of the U.S. troop buildup, I was at a *souk* when a Jeep drove up and two female soldiers disembarked. They were in combat fatigue uniforms, and wearing sidearms. Their faces, of course, were uncovered. A silence fell over the market stalls. For several minutes the only Arab body parts that moved were eyes. The women were not accosted or rebuffed in any way, but there was still a clear sense that they did not belong there.

General Khaled said he understood that women were an integral part of the U.S. Army and could not be excluded from the Saudi deployment, nor, once in Saudi Arabia, prevented from driving. As for Schwarzkopf, the American commander said he kept reminding himself that "I had a lot of guys who could do the military planning, but I was the only one who could assure the Saudis that the Dallas cowgirls were not going to come over and corrupt the kingdom."[11] To make sure that all was well, the American commander and his Saudi counterpart met each night at ten o'clock at the Defense Ministry, where Schwarzkopf learned to wait patiently for Khaled to come to the point.

What neither the American commanders nor the Saudi leadership grasped was that the extremist opponents who would later turn to terrorism could not be appeased by respectful behavior among the American troops. To them, the presence of American military personnel in Saudi Arabia was itself a blasphemous provocation; the comportment of individuals was irrelevant. At the time, this fanatical element of the Saudi population was little known and barely visible; the country's leaders focused on the sensibilities of the mainstream public. Even there, as the Americans discovered, the sensitivity level was very high.

Despite the coordination and the nightly discussions at the Defense Ministry, "We still had lots of picky fights with them," Ambassador Brown said. "Every time a GI pissed on a wall for the first three weeks, we'd get a phone call from the Ministry of Defense saying, 'Your guy, or your woman, has desecrated the holy land!'"[12] (It's doubtful that any of the American women "pissed on a wall." Brown was including them out of political correctness.)

In one of their nightly meetings, Khaled complained to Schwarzkopf that some T-shirts the troops were wearing were "very offensive to us." He handed his American counterpart a bag of samples and demanded that the troops be prohibited from wearing them.

"I thought 'Uh-oh,' because I knew the things some T-shirts in the States had printed on them," Schwarzkopf recalled. "I was imagining obscene mottoes, jokes about getting drunk and pictures of marijuana plants." But the shirts contained no vulgar language or provocative images; they depicted camels, palm trees, and a tank in the desert. Schwarzkopf asked Khaled what was offensive about them.

"We don't like the image of a tank in our desert."

"But there are tanks all over your desert!"

"Yes," Khaled acknowledged, "but we don't want this advertised to our people."[13]

On another occasion, Khaled complained about Christmas carols that were being broadcast over the Americans' radio station. The solution: instrumentals only, no lyrics.[14]

At least the T-shirts and Christmas carols actually existed. According to Schwarzkopf, he was also called upon to placate the Saudis about reports that stirred up public opinion but turned out not to be true. One concerned a Jewish chaplain who supposedly said he would blow the traditional ram's horn in observance of Rash Hashanah—in Saudi Arabia. Another, which Schwarzkopf attributed to Iraqi disinformation, said that U.S. troops had gone to Mecca, which is off limits to non-Muslims, and had drunk beer at the Kaaba, Islam's holiest shrine.[15]

Potentially more serious, according to Freeman and Schwarzkopf, was an episode in which American civilians living in Dhahran put on a show for the troops. It included dance performances by what Freeman called "various young ladies from the American school." Someone decided to invite CNN to televise it, which Freeman called "an incredible lapse of judgment."[16]

Khaled summoned Schwarzkopf to an immediate meeting. "You've got dancing girls entertaining your troops in Dhahran! It's on CNN!" he complained. Schwarzkopf, who had not authorized female entertainers, could not figure out what Khaled was talking about. There were no dancing girls, he said.

"Well, these pictures are being shown, and you must order them taken off the TV!" the Saudi general demanded.

"I was about to launch into a lecture about freedom of the press," Schwarzkopf recalled, "when the telephone rang. Khaled answered, listened for a minute, and turned pale. 'That was His Majesty—they're showing it again.'"

Schwarzkopf ordered his public affairs staff to bring him a tape of the offending footage. "The clip had been shot so that you could only see the dancers' legs, but they were clearly women and were obviously doing bumps and grinds. Right in front of the camera were American soldiers—from the 82nd Airborne, naturally—hollering, waving their arms and going bananas. The tape was as bad as it could possibly be. And CNN was regularly beaming it all over the world."

Two additional performances scheduled for the following day were cancelled. Schwarzkopf laid down the law to his officers, calling them "dumb bastards" for accepting Aramco's invitation to the show and allowing the TV cameras in. No more "girlie shows," he told them. Saudi customs must be respected. Americans don't have "constitutional rights" in Saudi Arabia.[17]

The buildup of American and allied troops that continued through the autumn of 1990 inspired one important public challenge to Saudi authority, but it did not come from any of the foreign soldiers. On November 6, forty-five women from Riyadh's educated elite drove through the center of the city in broad daylight in a convoy of fourteen automobiles, accompanied by men who supported their demand for the right to drive. Some of the women removed their veils. Worse yet, from the viewpoint of the authorities, they alerted a *New York Times* reporter, who wrote an extensive story about the "drive-in," turning it into an international *cause célébre*. The women apparently thought that the presence in Saudi Arabia of half a million American and other foreign troops—including Jeep-driving women—and hundreds of foreign journalists had created a liberalized climate in which they could assert their rights with a bold gesture. They were wrong. In fact, the opposite was true: Because they had invited infidel troops into the country, the Saudi leaders had to reinforce their conservative Islamic credentials by enforcing religious and social orthodoxy.

The response of the Saudi authorities was severe. The women were arrested and publicly reviled by the *mutawa'in;* they were released only under guarantees from their husbands or male guardians. Those who had jobs lost them, as did many of their husbands. The women and their husbands were prohibited from traveling abroad.

If nothing else, the women's timing was terrible. Several prominent Saudis have told me that King Fahd at the time was nearing a decision to permit women to drive but was forced to back off by the furious public reaction to the women's demonstration. The foreign military and journalistic presence only heightened sensitivities and reinforced the House of Saud's determination to maintain the social status quo. The women failed to account for two realities of Saudi political life that resident Americans had long since grasped: First, the House of Saud's highest priority was to protect itself and enhance its own credentials, not to make courageous gestures in support of individual rights; and second, when challenged publicly, the rulers always said no. Persuasion and cajolery could bring results, but confrontation could not.

In Chas Freeman's analysis, the women's protest came at an especially awkward time because the country was already "full of stories and speculations on the disgusting behavior on the part of Christians in particular, and Jews to a lesser extent. There was a great deal of tension, and the king was trying to hold the majority of the country, which was religiously conservative, behind his policy. In those circumstances, to face a social protest from the left, as it were, was a prescription for disaster for the cause these women espoused."[18]

Like the U.S. troop presence itself, the women's demonstration became a permanent count in the religious conservatives' indictment of all things American. As Mamoun Fandy of Georgetown University wrote in his study of Saudi political dissent, "To the Islamists, these acts epitomized the secular conspiracy. According to the Islamists, these liberals, almost all of them American-educated Saudis, were emboldened by the presence of the U.S. troops and wanted to further their own interests and undermine the foundation of the society. Supposedly the women wanted to turn Saudi Arabia into America and wanted women to have complete freedom, in defiance of local custom and law. To the Islamists, these women were infidels who deserved to be killed. In their leaflets attacking the female drivers, the Islamists accused the women of being 'communist whores.' The leaflets listed the names of the women, their telephone numbers, their husbands' names, and their professions, and urged the Saudi public to take action."[19]

That the American military commanders had nothing to do with the "drive-in" and did not know of it in advance was immaterial to the religious and social reactionaries, who, for lack of a better word, are often referred to as "fundamentalists." To them, the episode was proof of the corrupting influence of American culture and ideas. It confirmed their belief that contact with the West, and particularly with Americans, was by definition inimical to Arab and Muslim values. What they had tolerated inside the Aramco community and in the Westerners' walled housing compounds they would not tolerate on the streets of Riyadh. In their minds the rulers of Saudi Arabia, having invited the Americans to their country, were part of the problem, no matter how much they proclaimed their fealty to Islam. To the Islamist opposition, these were the same rulers who had squandered billions on war toys, enriching themselves and their cronies in the process, and now that they were going to war they were doing so in alliance with infidels against brother Muslims instead of against the Zionists. Thus the seeds of terrorism, planted earlier in Palestine, began to germinate in Saudi Arabia.

مرو

Operation Desert Storm, the military's name for the campaign to drive the Iraqis out of Kuwait, was quick and efficient. After a month of relentless air strikes, Iraq's forces put up little resistance as the United States and its allies charged across the border from Saudi Arabia. Ground combat lasted only four days. President Bush ordered a cease-fire at midnight on February 27, 1991. Kuwait's ruling family was restored to power, and peace of a sort returned to the Persian Gulf. For the House of Saud and its American friends, however, a time of trouble was only beginning. Over the first few years of the 1990s, an improbable confluence of domestic and international developments would disrupt the Kingdom's internal harmony, throw up new challenges to the al-Sauds' legitimacy, and inspire the campaign of terrorism against the United States that continues today.

First, not all American or other foreign troops left after the war. Although ejected from Kuwait, Saddam Hussein retained power in Iraq. To protect the Kurdish people of northern Iraq and the restive Shiite Muslims of southern Iraq from Saddam Hussein's brutality, the United Nations Security Council created two large zones in Iraq where the Iraqi armed forces were prohibited from conducting air operations. To enforce the southern "no-fly zone," American, British, and French air combat units remained in Saudi Arabia and used Saudi air fields as their base of operations. Thus, although the foreign military presence dwindled to a tiny fraction of what it had been during Desert Storm, it did not disappear. To the House of Saud's Islamist critics, the diminished numbers were essentially irrelevant; with the king's assent, infidel troops remained in the birthplace of Islam.

Second, the cost of the war undermined the king's ability to buy off his critics and to appease the populace with government largesse. By most accounts, the war cost the Saudi treasury $55 billion and threw the country into a permanent budget deficit. The Saudi Arabian Monetary Agency's current account balance was negative by about $27 billion in 1991 and another $34 billion over the next two years.[20] Combined with a fast-growing population, a sharp postwar decline in oil prices, and a deep drop in the value of the dollar on world markets, which undercut the Kingdom's purchasing power, the cost of the war forced SAMA to borrow heavily just to meet the Kingdom's existing obligations; new social service initiatives were cut short.

According to Freeman, the State Department insisted that he dun the Saudis for payment of the costs of the war; the department brushed aside his argument that the demands outstripped the Saudis' resources and that payment could lead to domestic instability: "We had to bankrupt the country in order to save it," he said of Washington's position. The result, he added, "was to take Saudi Arabia from zero national debt to a national debt equivalent to 55 percent of GNP, overnight. . . . The general view of the American role in the war has shifted from affection, admiration, and gratitude to resentment of financial exactions." The State Department took the reasonable position that the immense personal fortunes of the king and the senior princes should be taken into account when calculating their country's resources; Freeman said this became a "huge irritant" in his dealings with the Saudi leadership.[21] The United States, he said, "actually made money from the war."[22]

The war also unleashed domestic political challenges to the House of Saud. Americans became the lightning rod for a clamor for reform that had not been heard in the boom years when everyone was getting rich. "Rather than strengthening state-society relations, the Gulf War exposed the fragile foundation of this relationship," as the historian Madawi al-Rasheed put it. "During the war the government failed to rally the population behind its policies. When the battle for the liberation of Kuwait was over, the Saudi government had to deal with a deep rift that now began to separate it from its own constituency."[23] The House of Saud seemed to be trapped between forces on the right demanding a purge of Western influence and a return to religious purity, and dissidents on the left seeking greater openness, more personal freedom, and more citizen participation in government decisionmaking. None of the agitators was demanding a fundamental change in the Saudi system that would put an end to the rule of the al-Saud; they wanted social and regulatory changes within the system they had. The difficulty the Saudi princes faced, and still face, lay in trying to reconcile the aspirations of the modernizers with the demands of the reactionaries.

ムっ

In the decades since J. Rives Childs took up residence in Jeddah as the first American ambassador to Saudi Arabia, the post has generally been filled by one of two types of appointee: career diplomats who specialized in the Arab world, such as Parker Hart, Hermann F. Eilts, Richard Murphy, and Hume Horan; and prominent Southern politicians who lacked expertise in Arab affairs but functioned as personal representatives of the president who appointed them. In this category were John West, a former governor of South Carolina appointed by Jimmy Carter, and Ray Mabus, a former governor of Mississippi, and Wyche Fowler, a former senator from Georgia, appointed by Bill Clinton. Charles Freeman, known to everyone as Chas, fit into neither category.

Freeman went to Harvard Law School, but was bored by it. His real interest was China. Entering the Foreign Service directly from law school at the age of twenty-two, he asked for a posting anywhere on the periphery of China except India. (At that time, the United States had no diplomatic representation in China itself.) Despite his request, his first posting abroad was to Madras, India, but he persisted with his study of Mandarin anyway; eventually, he became so fluent that he served as President Nixon's interpreter during his door-opening trip to China in 1972. Freeman also learned Spanish in Mexico, and spoke Portuguese as well. Before becoming ambassador to Saudi Arabia, he held several prominent positions in the State Department, including deputy chief of mission at the embassy in Thailand and principal deputy assistant secretary of state for African affairs. He had no interest in the Middle East, which he saw as a political minefield because of congressional interest and Washington lobbying pressure. In fact, he said of his surprise appointment to Riyadh, "One of my proudest achievements to that date had been to avoid the Middle East."

A gifted linguist, he soon learned enough Arabic to read complicated documents and understand the conversations around him. His background gave him the experience and sense of proportion required to interpret Saudi Arabian society and affairs; it also gave him the detachment needed to appreciate the Saudis without becoming an apologist for them. Harboring no romantic illusions about Arabia, he has a flair for describing Saudi Arabia and the Saudis with pithy observations: "The difference between Moscow and Riyadh was that Moscow was a third world city inhabited by first world people, and Riyadh was the opposite." "Saudi history teaches that the more upright you are, the more oil comes out of the ground." "I often thought the Kingdom's slogan should be 'Progress Without Change' because that seemed to be the objective."

Freeman often said that being U.S. ambassador in Saudi Arabia was like being the mayor of an American town of 30,000 to 40,000 inhabitants. His responsibilities included their safety and well-being, their business interests, their health, and their interaction with the Saudi government. A good bit of his time was occupied by divorce and child-custody cases involving American women who had married Saudi men and wished they hadn't. Busy as he was with his American constituency, however, he made it a point to engage in unscripted political and intellectual discussions with Saudis of different points of view, from the most outspoken Westernized modernizers to the most dedicated conservatives. He would invite them to his residence for free-flowing conversations.

He came away convinced that the religious zealots were more dedicated than the liberals, more confident of their cause and more willing to take risks. They had the courage of their convictions.[24]

And what were those convictions? What did they want, besides the departure of foreign troops? In the succinct words of the Arab American scholar Fouad Ajami,

> the elements of the new utopia were easy to discern. The Shi'a minority in the Eastern Province would be decimated and the Saudi liberals molded on the campuses of California and Texas would be swept aside in a zealous, frenzied campaign. Traffic with the infidels would be brought to an end, and those dreaded satellite dishes bringing the West's cultural "pollution" would be taken down. But for this to pass, the roots of the American presence in Arabia would have to be extirpated—and the Americans driven from the country.[25]

Unlike the Taliban militia who later imposed absolute theocratic rule in Afghanistan, the Islamists of Saudi Arabia were not ignorant primitives, Freeman said. They were well-traveled and educated; many had studied in the United States. They would gather in his Riyadh residence for discussions of human rights and democracy and offer persuasive arguments that went contrary to American views. "They were very familiar with conditions in the United States and were really sometimes, I found, quite contemptuous of the American lack of recognition of the religious roots of American secular values," Freeman recalled. In colloquies with the ambassador, they would argue that Thomas Jefferson's thinking was rooted in Deism, and that the Bill of Rights derived from European religious tradition, even if presented in secular form. They quoted John Locke. They said it was futile to discuss these issues with Americans because Americans were ignorant of their own intellectual history and religious heritage.

From Saudi liberals and modernizers, Freeman said, he heard frequent requests that he make representations to the senior princes "on behalf of this or that liberal cause that they espoused." That is, they wanted the American ambassador to deliver messages that they lacked the courage to deliver themselves. "I basically concluded," Freeman recalled, "that Saudi liberals, unlike Saudi conservatives, were born without spines. Saudi conservatives, many of them very well educated, including in the West, very articulate and well versed in the Koran . . . had no hesitation about standing up in the mosque and railing against what they perceived to be libertine behavior on the part of this or that person in Saudi society. The liberals tended to be doing something else during the Friday mosque ceremony and, if they were there, lacked the strength of religious education and conviction necessary to join the debate on their own behalf." Thus they left the field of political debate in the hands of the religious militants.[26]

I got a taste of this one evening in November 1990, when foreign troops were pouring into the Kingdom in preparation for Operation Desert Storm. Six professors from the College of Petroleum and Minerals in Dhahran invited me to join them for dinner and political discussion. All were holders of advanced degrees from American universities, at ease in conversation with foreigners, and financially well off.

They all agreed that the Saudi political system needed to be opened up to allow greater citizen participation. They wanted a forum set up in which there would take place a serious discussion of the role of women; women must be allowed to participate in this forum, they said. In the country's other universities, it was necessary to rein in the fundamentalists. And Saudis should have more contact with the foreign troops, not less, to come into contact with new ideas. This was all well and good to American ears, but these gentlemen were not about to jeopardize their positions by saying such things publicly or engaging in overt acts to put their views into practice. Unlike the fiery Islamists, they would not risk going to jail.

Into this new, unsettled atmosphere after Desert Storm there entered a new cadre of battle-hardened Islamic zealots who had fought in Afghanistan against the occupying Soviet forces. These were the "Afghan Arabs," young men from Saudi Arabia, Egypt, Algeria, and other Arab countries who had voluntarily gone to Afghanistan to join forces with the indigenous *mujahiddeen,* or "holy warriors," as they are often called. The ignominious Soviet withdrawal in 1989 apparently convinced these Afghan Arabs that they represented the victorious sword of Islam in a global battle against infidels; with God on their side, they would smite the unbelievers, no matter how well armed the unbelievers were. Having overcome the Soviets, they were looking for a new target. Among the Saudis who returned from the Afghan campaign infused with militant zeal was Osama bin Laden, whose father had amassed a fortune as a construction contractor in the service of the Saudi kings. The family was well known to Americans in the Kingdom, but the dark determination of this prodigal son was not yet widely recognized.

Shortly after the Iraqi invasion of Kuwait, bin Laden approached Crown Prince Abdullah with an offer to raise and lead an all-Muslim army to defend the Kingdom. That way, he told Abdullah, it would not be necessary to invite infidel troops into the sacred land of Islam. He said he could muster 100,000 *mujahiddeen,* all combat-experienced from Afghanistan. Abdullah did not take him seriously and rebuffed his offer, thereby stoking bin Laden's anger against the House of Saud and his paranoia about foreign troops.[27]

Osama bin Laden was soon dispatched to exile in Sudan and some of the most vociferous Islamist critics of the House of Saud were locked up. Nevertheless, a strong tide of religious and social conservatism was running in Saudi Arabia and could not be ignored. In the Saudi system, the king rules by consensus, which means accommodation rather than confrontation whenever possible. For religious zealots, appeasement might be a more accurate word than accommodation.

The king's government sought to reinforce its credentials as the upholder of Islam. Abroad, it poured money into Muslim charities and religious foundations, often with little scrutiny of these organizations' true purposes. At home, it increased the enforcement of religious and social strictures in Saudi life, giving the conservative religious leaders more influence over school curricula and textbooks and increasing the authority of the *mutawa'in*. These vigilantes were allowed to raid private parties, abuse women who failed to meet their standards of dress, and beat their unfortunate detainees with impunity.

King Fahd also sought to placate the opposition at both ends of the spectrum and, by decree, to shore up the legitimacy of the House of Saud. On March 1, 1992, he promulgated a new "Basic Law of Government" that attempted to offer something to everybody without fundamentally altering the system. It was the first comprehensive statement of government policy and practice since the basic law implemented by Faisal thirty years before.

Fahd's "Basic Law" reasserted that Saudi Arabia was an Islamic state, and that its constitution consisted of the Koran and the compiled words and deeds of the Prophet Muhammad known as the *sunnah*. The public holidays were religious holidays; the law was Islamic law; the flag was to be green, the color of the Prophet's cloak, and on it were to be inscribed the words, "There is only one God and Muhammad Is His Prophet." Under the terms of this decree, "The family is the kernel of Saudi society, and its members shall be brought up on the basis of the Islamic faith, and loyalty and obedience to God, His Messenger, and to guardians" of the faith. The purpose of education was defined as "instilling the Islamic faith in the younger generation."[28] What could be more Islamic than that?

The "Basic Law" also held that Saudi Arabia was to remain a monarchy, the ruler would be a descendant of Abdul Aziz, and "citizens are to pay allegiance to the King in accordance with the holy Koran and the tradition of the Prophet, in submission and obedience, in times of ease and difficulty, fortune and adversity." That was not exactly the clarion call to reform that the liberals wanted, but the king did announce an important political innovation. In a separate decree, he ordered the creation of a "Consultative Council," its 60 members appointed by the king, who would review policies, propose new laws and regulations, organize topical committees, and nominate members to sit in on government policymaking meetings. Later expanded to 120 members, this council remains the sole authorized channel by which nonroyal citizens who do not hold government positions have any formal influence on decisionmaking.

In retrospect, it is clear that no decree issued by King Fahd would have placated Osama bin Laden or the terrorist legions he was beginning to organize. If the House of Saud was an agent of Western influence and a tool of the corrupters, it made no difference whether or not the Consultative Council had real power. Even if bin Laden and the Afghan Arabs had not existed, however, the Kingdom would have been headed for troubled times in the 1990s because of its sluggish economy. The universities were turning out fast-growing crowds of young people whose technical and professional competence could not match their sense of entitlement. The get-rich-quick era that had propelled their parents into the middle and upper classes was over, yet as prisoners of an education system that stifled innovation and creative thinking, they were ill prepared to thrive in a competitive marketplace; and, in any event, they were largely averse to hard work.

In countries where political discourse is restricted by the government, which means most of the Arab world, Islam has often been a conduit for the expression of dissent. Expressed as "Islam requires" rather than "We demand," troublesome ideas are difficult to suppress. Part of the appeal of militant Islam to disenfranchised and unemployed young Saudis was that it rationalized, even sanctified, poverty. In the perceptive words of Eleanor Doumato of Brown University, the strict interpretation of Islam known as Wahhabism "made deprivation tolerable for the newly urbanized by turning home confinement into religious virtue. The same can be said for those who are too poor to afford fashionable clothes, CDs, or home video equipment. Wahhabism disapproves of all these, and if crushing boredom is one's lot, one can take refuge in the knowledge that religious virtue is on one's side."[29]

For much of the decade after Desert Storm, these political currents had little direct impact on the American community, although some Americans chafed under the tighter social strictures. In April 1994, the U.S. Embassy distributed a "Code of Conduct" for Americans warning that the *mutawa'in* "have harassed, accosted or arrested foreigners, including US citizens, for improper dress or other infractions." This advisory said the *mutawa'in* had become so zealous in enforcing their standards of dress for women that most foreign women had taken to wearing the *abaya* and covering their heads. Some restaurants had stopped serving women altogether, the advisory said, and it warned that couples could be asked to present proof of marriage. "Women who are arrested for socializing with a man who is not a relative may be charged with prostitution," it said.[30]

Two years later, the embassy distributed a separate advisory on what to do if accosted by members of the Organization for the Promotion of Virtue and Prevention of Vice, as the *mutawa'in* are officially known. "Your primary objective should be to end the encounter as quickly and as reasonably as possible," it said. "Any objections to the encounter itself are best channelled in writing, as soon after the incident as possible. There is little to be gained in debating *mutawa'in* on the fine points of Islam; you will not change their beliefs, but you do run the risk of being temporarily detained at *mutawa'in* or police headquarters." For women, this advisory noted, the biggest issue was that of attire. Because Saudi Arabia has no official dress code for foreign women, it was difficult to challenge an assertion by the *mutawa'in* that a woman was improperly dressed; the vigilantes made their own rules.[31] Brian Hannon of the Joint Economic Commission, who was living in Riyadh with his wife in the early 1990s, said the American community asked the king and his advisers to specify the approved standards of dress, but these were always expressed in generalities, such as "dress modestly." Officially, there was no requirement that foreign women cover their hair, but "that message never got down to the religious authorities," he said.[32]

Real estate entrepreneurs developed a thriving business in the construction of walled, gated communities known as "compounds," where foreigners lived out of sight, and mostly out of reach, of the *mutawa'in*. Inside the walls, they could play tennis in shorts, swim together, and drink alcohol with little fear of a police raid, much as the people of Aramco had for decades. (*Riyadh Today*, a guidebook published by the Riyadh Chamber of Commerce and Industry in 2002, listed thirty-two of these compounds, not counting the residences in the capital's diplomatic quarter.)

The threat of harassment by the *mutawa'in*, however annoying, did not disrupt the vast web of commerce that tied the two countries together, which expanded through the 1990s. The Saudis gave American firms huge contracts to supply planes for the national airline, upgrade the country's telecommunications network, and build petrochemical plants, in addition to the contracts arranged by the Joint Economic Commission and the Defense Ministry. By 1999, bilateral trade was nearly in balance as the United States exported $8 billion in manufactured products to Saudi Arabia and imported $8.2 billion worth of oil.[33]

The Five Year Plan that was in effect at the time of Desert Storm projected that 433,900 young Saudis would enter the labor force during that period, but only 213,500 jobs would be created—and the latter figure included low-level jobs such as slaughtering chickens and cleaning hotel rooms, work that no Saudi Arab would do. As this unemployment problem grew, the Saudis increased pressure on American and other foreign companies to hire more Saudi workers. This campaign had limited results because the foreign companies, motivated by profit, wanted efficient, reliable workers at the lowest possible salaries; those criteria tended to exclude Saudis, many of whom were reluctant to start at the bottom or work for market wages. They had university degrees but little sense of productivity or workplace discipline, just as the Ford Foundation's consultants had observed in the 1960s.

"The only organizations with notable success in training Saudis to replace westerners are Aramco, which has spent fifty years and hundreds of millions of dollars in the effort, and [the airline] Saudia, which has been working at it for thirty-five years," the American business consultant Gene Lindsey wrote, "and they both are still heavily involved in training Saudis. It is a slow process."[34]

Not even Bechtel had solved this "Saudization" conundrum, according to Terry Valenzano, the company's principal vice president for Saudi Arabia and the Near East in the late 1990s. Internally, he said, Bechtel managers had to be convinced that prospective Saudi employees would actually do the work assigned to them and that the country's protective labor law, "although difficult, can be worked with." Externally, Bechtel faced competition for the relatively few good Saudi prospects from Aramco and the new petrochemical industries. It was also difficult, he said, "to hire Saudis that are mobile (like our industry) and willing to relocate, and most of all, [to] convince a young Saudi that the construction business is not cyclical."[35]

Mobil Oil Co., which in addition to being an Aramco partner had an independent presence in Saudi Arabia as a builder and operator of refineries, won authorization from the Ministry of Industry to construct and manage a petrochemical plant only on condition that it train Saudis to fill 60 percent of the management positions within five years.

"We took that seriously," said Lou Noto, president of Mobil's Saudi Arabia operations and later CEO of the company. "And to get these kids right, it wasn't just a question of teaching them how to turn a wrench, or management training. In many respects it was taking somebody from literally the back sands, with no work ethic at all, no idea what this was all about, [and telling them] 'You have to get up at six in the morning to get to the plant six days a week.' That's not the most obvious thing for a Saudi to do." The prospective employee had to be made to understand, Noto said, that "he's not going to be a managing director from the first day."

In many ways, Mobil was facing the same problem of Saudi manpower that Aramco had faced in its first decades. For the young Arabs, it was not just a matter of training, it required an entire cultural reconstruction to transform them into legitimate contenders for management positions in an American industrial enterprise.

Mobil's solution, Noto said, was to take over what he called "a defrocked seminary" in Beaumont, Texas, and send young trainees there for a total-immersion course in American life and American business culture. According to the voluble Noto—who talks fast but thinks even faster, so that his ideas sometimes outrun his syntax—these Saudis

were kids, many of them were young, the first time out of the country in many cases. In order to give us peace of mind that their health and safety were protected, substances, alcohol, women and what have you, we put them in the seminary in Beaumont and ran classroom courses and shoveled them over to two plants. Many of those kids started from scratch. Some of them dropped out, but many of them made it. We didn't reinvent the wheel, we took them out, they had to get hands-on

training in the plants, we took them to plants that were close in concept
to what was going to be built at Yanbu [on the Red Sea coast], and we
brought 'em over and we educated them. We built a tremendous relationship with a lot of young people. A lot of our people to this day have
tremendous affection for these Saudis—to watch a kid come from nothing and be a manager of a big facility is a real turn-on. If you don't get
a kick out of that you shouldn't be in this business.[36]

The training program Noto described was yet another example of an
American enterprise that adopted the original Aramco principle of "enlightened self-interest." Mobil was in Saudi Arabia to make money. The
surest way to do that was to be on good terms with the Saudi government and people, which meant investing in the country's physical and
human infrastructure.

All the work done by Aramco, TWA, the Ford Foundation, JECOR,
the farmers at al-Kharj, Mobil, OPM-SANG, and the other American
institutions that had worked in Saudi Arabia since the first oil men
landed contributed to the betterment of the country. By the mid-1990s,
the people of Saudi Arabia were incomparably more affluent, better educated, and healthier than they had been before the Americans arrived.
But Desert Storm had unleashed forces who were less than grateful. The
Saudi government tried to rein in the Islamist movement by jailing some
of the most outspoken critics and forcing others into exile; but invisible
conspirators were at work, united in the belief that all the material
progress of six decades was outweighed by the religious desecration and
cultural pollution that they attributed to the influence of the West, in
particular of the United States.

On November 13, 1995, a bomb exploded at the Riyadh office of
the National Guard training team. Five Americans died. The Saudis
excluded U.S. authorities from their investigation and treated the attack as an isolated event to be handled internally. The following April,
four men confessed to the crime on Saudi television; they were beheaded without having been interviewed by American law enforcement officials. Two months after that, on June 25, a truck bomb
exploded outside a U.S. Air Force housing block in Dhahran known

as Khobar Towers. Nineteen Americans died. This time the Saudis allowed FBI investigators to visit the scene and collect evidence, but they denied the FBI access to suspects who were in their custody. According to Louis J. Freeh, who was FBI director at the time, this was standard Saudi practice—they had never allowed foreigners to interrogate Saudi criminal suspects inside Saudi territory—but it prevented the United States from obtaining the information needed to indict individuals. In a newspaper op-ed column that blasted the Clinton administration's "inaction," Freeh said he sought the intervention of the first President Bush, who is influential among Saudi Arabia's leaders as the man who protected them and saved Kuwait. "Mr. Bush personally asked the Saudis to let the FBI do one-on-one interviews of the detained Khobar bombers. The Saudis immediately acceded," Freeh wrote. "This was the investigative breakthrough for which we had been waiting for several years."[37]

Any doubt that a new and dangerous era had begun for U.S. citizens in Saudi Arabia ended on February 25, 1997, when the embassy in Riyadh and the consulates in Jeddah and Dhahran issued a "warden message," or safety alert, to the American community:

> The embassy notes with deep concern a recent interview aired on London television on February 20 with a well-known terrorist, Usama Bin Ladin, in which he not only threatened again the US military in Saudi Arabia but also called for the expulsion of American civilians. At the same time, the Embassy continues to receive reports indicating possible surveillance or probes of US military and government facilities suggesting that planning for terrorist action against US interests in Saudi Arabia continues unabated. This current period is considered particularly dangerous, since at least one public threat declared that attacks would occur in the Kingdom should certain detained individuals not be released prior to the end of Ramadan.

The advisory urged Americans to "exercise extreme caution in matters concerning personal security. Americans should maintain a low profile, reduce travel within the Kingdom, vary travel routes and times for all required travel, and treat any mail from unfamiliar sources with suspicion."[38]

For sixty years, one of the great attractions of life in Saudi Arabia for Americans had been the total absence of violent crime and a comforting assurance of safety for their families. That era was over.

CHAPTER 16

After September 11

My DINNER COMPANION WAS an amiable, well-spoken Saudi Aramco executive, fluent in English and comfortable with Americans, among whom he had worked most of his professional life. We were in an elegant seafood restaurant in al-Khobar that featured plump fish from the Gulf waiting to be grilled at the diner's selection. In the beachfront park across the road, Saudi families strolled and played in the last light of day.

It was a congenial and peaceful setting, and yet something was wrong. My companion was agitated, and angry at the United States and at Americans who, he said, were being unfair to Saudi Arabia. The American media were slandering Islam, he said, and the United States government was alienating its best friends in the Arab world by its actions. It was October 2002, thirteen months after the terrorist attacks that destroyed New York's World Trade Center and blew a lethal hole in the Pentagon. Deep fissures had appeared in the façade of amity between the United States and Saudi Arabia.

The fact that fifteen of the nineteen September 11 hijackers were Saudis by birth and took their orders from the renegade Saudi Osama bin Laden enraged Americans and shredded the protective cocoon that American business interests and diplomats had built around Saudi

Arabia for decades. All the least palatable aspects of Saudi society—the tolerance for and even encouragement of extremism, the repressive political system, the anti-intellectualism of its schools, the corruption—were suddenly on glaring display. After years of looking the other way, Americans subjected Saudi Arabia to intense scrutiny, and they did not like much of what they saw. On America's radio talk shows and in much of the American media, it was open season on the Kingdom. Some of the most venomous commentary emanated from critics of Saudi Arabia who had never been there and had never experienced Saudi hospitality, but no matter; the Kingdom's friends in the United States were overwhelmed by public outrage. It seemed that everyone with access to the Internet was suddenly aware that Saudi Arabia's schoolbooks were replete with lessons in hatred, that its mosques resonated with fiery sermons calling for jihad against Jews and other infidels, and that the government in the past had done little to counter this inflammatory rhetoric.

"The United States seeks to build a coalition against terror with the kingdom, long a Western business and military ally, and yet the country has revealed itself as the source of the very ideology confronting America in the battle against terrorism," said a front-page story in the *New York Times,* succinctly summarizing the situation.[1]

The events of September 11 and the American response to them shocked the Saudis, too, for different reasons.

Many Saudis, including radical preachers and otherwise sensible newspaper columnists, simply refused to believe that Osama bin Laden and his al-Qaeda network were responsible for the attacks. Good Muslims would not do such a thing, some Saudis said. A lone Arab hiding in a cave in Afghanistan could not possibly have orchestrated such a strike against all-powerful America, others argued. And who benefited from an act of mass murder that drove a wedge between Saudi Arabia and the United States? The Jews, some Saudis said. Therefore Zionists must have been behind it—the evidence being the report that Jews employed at the World Trade Center were warned in advance and stayed home on the fateful day. This preposterous tale gained instant and widespread credence in Saudi Arabia and elsewhere in the Arab world.

Even Prince Nayef, Saudi Arabia's chief law enforcement officer, sub-scribed to the theory of Zionist responsibility, his position reported in a newspaper interview posted on the royal family's Web site.[2]

The degree of Saudi denial, and the willingness of many Saudis to spread and believe the most absurd theories about the terror attacks, presented a whole new perspective on the Kingdom's perpetual tug-of-war between modernism and medievalism, between progress and reaction.

In some ways, Saudi Arabia today functions at the highest levels of modernity and technical sophistication. As I was traveling around the country in the fall of 2002, conjoined twins from Malaysia were sent to Saudi Arabia for surgery to separate them. The successful operation was performed by Saudi doctors, of which there were none before the 1970s. A bank began offering a new service on its automated teller ma-chines: payment of traffic fines. A newspaper presented detailed in-structions to computer geeks about how to download the Linux operating system. New Internet providers went on line. Design work began on a new Ralph Lauren fashion store. This was the "Riyadh is just like Phoenix" phenomenon, as many American residents have de-scribed it.

Intellectually and politically, however, large contingents of the Saudi population live in a netherworld of xenophobia and conspiracy theo-ries. Fearful that their culture and religious purity are being eroded by materialism and Western ideas, these Saudis are often unable to distin-guish fact from fiction, especially about the United States and about Jews, and are susceptible to the reactionary ravings of isolationist, anti-American firebrands in the mosques.

Among this element of the Saudi population, the American response to the September 11 attacks confirmed their most negative feelings about the United States. When Washington imposed visa restrictions on Saudi travelers, froze the assets of various Islamic charities, and in-carcerated hundreds of Muslim men—all while supporting Israel in its efforts to suppress the Palestinian uprising with bloody attacks that Saudis watched every night on television—it provided an opening for the most anti-American elements among Saudis to say, in effect, "We

Strained relations after September 11, reflected in a political cartoon of January 30, 2002.
By Nick Anderson, © 2002, The Washington Post Writers Group. Reprinted with permission.

told you so" to their pro-Western compatriots. All these years you tried to emulate them, the critics said of the Americanized Saudis. You sent your children to their universities, put your money in their banks, bought franchises in their fast food restaurants. And what do we see now? The Americans turn against you and against Islam the minute something goes wrong. They care only for themselves.

"Since World War II, America has not been a democratic republic; it has become a military empire after the Roman model," thundered the prominent preacher Sheikh Safar al-Hawali.

It is even more abhorrent because its administration is ruled by the pressure groups that are the most dangerous to the human race—the companies that create destruction and sell arms. Therefore, the American way can be discerned and defined in one word: war. America unhesitatingly enters into war anywhere in the world, unless it assesses that the benefit of such a war will not satisfy its insatiable appetite. Then it calls for the kind of peace that will permit American companies to sign profitable contracts, with the aim of usurping resources under the slogan of cooperation in development. Thus we notice that America is always seeking an enemy, and if it does not find one it creates one and inflates it, using its terrible media to persuade its people's conscience that the war it has declared is necessary and for a just cause.

With the disappearance of communism, he argued, that enemy was Islam.[3]

"There are dozens, even millions, who lift up their eyes to Osama bin Laden as a savior," Dr. Muhammad al-Khasif told the popular al-Jazeera satellite television network. "If Che Guevara was a model for the fighters in the world and a beautiful symbol of the struggle against American imperialism in South America, then Osama bin Laden is the same symbol for the Muslims."[4]

Who were the Americans to criticize Saudi Arabia's human rights record or its Islamic justice system? a newspaper columnist demanded. What about human rights for the Palestinians? "Americans have played a shameful and conspiratorial role whose main objective for more than fifty years has been to provide political, financial and military cover enabling the Jews to maintain a brutal occupation of Palestinian land. All American presidents, as well as its extreme right politicians who are financed by the Zionists, are party to this," she wrote. "Where was [a critic of Saudi human rights policies] when the Palestinians were butchered and their homes demolished in Jenin refugee camp in front of the television cameras? Where was she when five million Palestinians were forcibly driven out of their land, 260,000 killed, and 350,000 maimed? Where was she when people were buried alive every day under the rubble of their homes? When women gave birth at military checkpoints and then watched their babies die while Israeli soldiers looked on indifferently? Where was the woman who claims to defend women's rights when Palestinian women trying to visit their imprisoned husbands were stripped naked by Israeli soldiers who subjected them to humiliating searches?" And what about America's treatment of Muslims in Afghanistan and Somalia, this columnist wanted to know. She referred to the incarceration of

Muslim men at Guantanamo Bay, Cuba, as "America's shame," and declared that Muslims in America, like all nonwhite Americans, are at best second-class citizens.[5]

These were not ravings from the lunatic fringe. The columnist's comments reflect the thinking of many Saudis and other Arabs. In the atmosphere after September 11, when Saudis were hearing denunciations of their country and their religion from Americans every day, this sort of overheated prose stoked resentment of America and American citizens even among elements of the Saudi population where it has not been visible. In Riyadh, for example, mothers of upper-class children in some of the city's best schools organized a boycott of McDonald's and Starbucks to protest American support for Israel in its conflict with the Palestinians, even though the people most hurt by the boycott were Saudi Arabs who owned the franchises of these establishments.

The Saudis seemed unable to comprehend the ferocity of American outrage over what had happened on September 11. Everywhere I went I met Saudis who complained that the United States was overreacting, throwing out the good with the bad, alienating its best friends in Saudi Arabia, inflicting suffering on Afghan civilians in its indiscriminate attacks aimed at al-Qaeda, providing ammunition to the extremists at the expense of the moderates. Add to that the American support of Israel's suppression of the Palestinians and the suffering inflicted on Iraqi children by U.S. insistence on maintaining an international economic boycott and the result was a wave of anti-American sentiment. Of course, the terrorist attacks were deplorable, the Saudis would say, but those fifteen hijackers were not representative of Saudi society— they were brainwashed by bin Laden's people, and anyway, they lived in Germany. Why are you blaming all Saudis? You Americans are at least as much responsible for this as we are, they would argue, because it was the United States that financed and equipped the jihad in Afghanistan, where bin Laden and his team got their start.

For months American diplomats, journalists, and congressional delegations who visited the Kingdom brought back reports of similar conversations. We all heard over and over again from Saudis who had invested their economic and personal lives in the United States and now felt betrayed and exposed.

Saudis seemed especially rankled by their sudden difficulty in obtaining visas for travel to the United States. Before September 11, Saudis could obtain visas virtually on demand; now they faced waits of many weeks. I encountered several Saudis whose children had been unable to resume their education in the United States because they had not been able to secure renewals of their visas. Other Saudis who could get visas said they were afraid to use them; visiting the United States now could be an unpleasant and risky experience because of the new security procedures. Some said they feared harassment; others said they feared arrest.

Douglas Jehl of the *New York Times* interviewed a student named Sahim al-Shaalan, who interrupted his education in the United States because of the hostility he felt after September 11 and was debating whether to return. "We like Americans, we love Americans, we want to be like Americans," the student said. "But after what happened, we don't want to be there, because of the way they treat us, the government and the people."[6] I met a prominent American-educated Saudi doctor whose American life insurance company canceled policies on his children when they returned to Saudi Arabia from their schools in the United States; he was as furious as he was baffled.

Saudi Aramco, which every year selects about three hundred of the country's best and brightest high school students and sends them to college in the United States, diverted all those chosen in 2002 to other countries because they could not obtain American visas. This was not good for either Saudi Arabia or the United States, said Yusof Rafie, the oil company's senior vice president for industrial relations. "These are the future leaders of our country," he told me. "I don't want to lose the American heritage. I want a Western mentality, with freedom of thinking and flexibility. I want open thinking and an open corporate culture." Not even Britain could match the United States on that score, he said. Rafie said he was personally distressed by the visa cutoff because "Houston is like home to me. I want to retire in San Francisco. I sent my oldest son to Tulane. I believe in it."[7]

"We refuse to see U.S.-Saudi relations take such a turn that an entire people are blamed for a crime committed by a few," Ali al-Mousa wrote in an open letter to U.S. ambassador Robert Jordan published by the newspaper *al-Watan:*

> Mr. Ambassador, over the past decades more than two million Saudis have visited your country and around a million studied at your colleges. . . . All of them according to your testimony have been good ambassadors for their country, religion and nation. Why, then, put them on the spot and refuse even to look at their applications, thus making them the victims of stalling and procrastination? Last summer nearly 150,000 Saudi tourists entered your country and spent $600 million in your hotels and shops, more than the amount spent by any other group of tourists visiting your country. They came back with a clean record without arousing the slightest suspicion. . . . Mr. Ambassador, thousands of our people have invested heavily in educating their children in your country. Some of these students were halfway to graduation; others were just a few months away. Today, many of them find themselves standing in long queues outside your office hoping to return to their colleges but without receiving an answer. By so doing you are putting your country in the list of losers and jeopardizing historic relations that are nearing the breaking point. All this by generalizing things and leveling accusations at the innocent.[8]

I was taken aback by a conversation with Jamal Abahussein, chairman of the Almarfa Medical Group. This prominent businessman represented exactly the kind of Saudi Arab that Americans had cultivated and nurtured for decades: Born in Dhahran, he grew up in a pro-American environment, complete with hamburgers. He was educated in Ohio and California. And yet he said he had canceled all his contracts with American medical equipment suppliers and shifted his business to Germany. He had even traded in his American car for a German model.

For him, the response to September 11 was a secondary issue. The principal cause of his anger was the conflict between Israel and the Palestinians. He predicted that Israel will eventually carry out a policy of "transfer" and expel the Palestinians from the West Bank and Gaza, and that the United States will let Israel get away with it. "I have been radicalized," he said.[9]

"Angry, hurt, bewildered—those are the right words," said Usamah al-Kurdi, a prominent member of the Consultative Assembly. "People are asking, What is it we are not doing that we should be doing, there must be something wrong." He said that many Westernized Saudis felt "betrayed and disappointed," but there was a larger group in provincial cities whose attitude was, "Who cares?" In such cities as Tabuk, Buraida, and Khamis Mushayt, he said, ordinary Saudis reckoned that a breach with the United States would have no negative impact on their lives and might even be beneficial. "Every day they see on TV what's happening to Palestinian women and children, and they don't see the work of the suicide bombers [attacking Israel]. And they associate this with the United States."[10]

In this general atmosphere of disgruntlement, it seemed that everyone I met had some particular bone to pick with the United States, above and beyond their resentment over the response to September 11 and U.S. support for Israel.

One prominent Saudi scholar invited me to his home, served me tea and cookies and, in a gesture of hospitality, invited his daughters to join our conversation. His complaint was that the U.S. Department of Health and Human Services had just announced a $500,000 grant under President Bush's "faith-based initiative" to a group called Operation Blessing. The founder of Operation Blessing was the evangelist Pat Robertson, a serial reviler of Islam and of the Prophet Muhammad, whom Robertson denounced as "an absolute wild-eyed fanatic . . . a robber and a brigand." My host could not understand why the U.S. government would support the activities of such a person.

Several Saudis voiced outrage over a briefing given to the Pentagon's Defense Advisory Board by a mysterious policy analyst named Laurent Murawiec. He told the group that Saudi Arabia was the "kernel of evil" in the Arab world and that its government supported and financed terrorism. If it continued to do so, Murawiec said, the United States should invade Saudi Arabia and seize the oil fields. Because the briefing was conducted under the auspices of the Rand Corporation, a respected think tank, and because the Defense Advisory Board was headed by the prominent Republican security strategist Richard Perle, many Saudis took his presentation to be a statement of American policy, even though it was repudiated by Defense Secretary Donald Rumsfeld.[11] A commentary in the Saudi newspaper *Okaz* said that news of the briefing revealed "the domination of the U.S. administration by hard-line Jewish thinking" and showed hostility to the Kingdom prevalent in American think tanks, "which are backed by the Jewish lobby."[12]

Another irritant cited by several prominent Saudis was a mass lawsuit against the Kingdom and some of the most senior princes seeking $116 trillion in damages on behalf of the September 11 victims and their families. Seventeen American law firms joined forces to file this case in United States District Court in Washington. The named defendants included Prince Sultan, the defense minister and second in line to the throne; his brother Prince Salman, the governor of Riyadh; and nearly two hundred other Saudi Arabian individuals and institutions.

They were described in the complaint as "those who promoted, financed, sponsored, or otherwise materially supported the acts of barbarism and terror inflicted on September 11, 2001." Whatever the legal and factual merits of this case, the Saudis who complained to me about it simply could not understand how such a lawsuit could be allowed to proceed in the U.S. federal court system. It was a massive insult to Saudi Arabia by its very nature, they said.[13]

At the time I was traveling around Saudi Arabia, the United States was beginning serious preparations for war against Iraq. To many Saudis, this was another source of anxiety about their relationship with the United States, not because they supported Saddam Hussein but because of what they feared would follow the war. In their scenario, the United States would make a liberated Iraq the new foundation of its Middle East oil interests, to the detriment of Saudi Arabia. This was absurd, for many reasons, but many Saudis believed it. They had all read news stories about how American oil companies were looking for new frontiers, in Russia or off the coast of Africa or wherever, the Saudis said. Iraq would be easier than Russia. It made sense to them.

These were uncomfortable conversations for me. One reason was that I agreed with some of the Saudi complaints. I thought Israel's tactics in its conflict with Palestinian militants were at best counterproductive, and I did not attempt to justify them. Giving U.S. taxpayers' money to a Pat Robertson organization was an insult to all Muslims; and a crackpot like Murawiec—a former disciple of Lyndon Larouche, the tax-dodging king of conspiracy theorists—should not have been invited to brief at the Pentagon. The larger reason for my discomfort was my sense that many Saudis I talked to seemed to be using these complaints about the United States to avoid coming to grips with the critical problems in their own society. If they could believe that Osama bin Laden and the fifteen Saudi hijackers were as much an aberration in Saudi Arabia as the Oklahoma City bomber Timothy McVeigh was in the United States—as many Saudis told me—they could avoid confronting the unpleasant realities that were all too visible to Americans.

In spite of all these rationalizations and denials, however, the events of September 11 and their aftermath did bring about a period of uncharacteristic introspection and self-criticism in Saudi Arabia, and a recognition that some serious reforms were necessary. Lively and quite public discussions broke out about what children are taught in Saudi schools, about the role of Saudi-based Islamic charities in funding terrorism, about the need for economic restructuring to reduce unemployment among young people, and about the fundamental question of whether true Islam requires hostility to non-Muslims. Saudis began to acknowledge the consequences of all the concessions to religious extremists that had been made in previous years.

"Though few would publicly admit it," the newspaper columnist Sulaiman al-Hattlan wrote, "Saudis have become hostages of the backward agenda of a small minority of bin Laden supporters who in effect have hijacked our society. . . . Because of the dominance of Wahhabism, Saudi society has been exposed to only one school of thought, one that teaches hatred of Jews, Christians and certain Muslims, like Shiites and liberal and moderate Sunnis. But we Saudis must acknowledge that our real enemy is religious fanaticism. We have to stop talking about the need for reform and actually start it, particularly in education."[14]

Sulaiman al-Hattlan was among the guests at a luncheon I attended in the Riyadh home of Prince Abdullah bin Faisal bin Turki, the amiable governor of the Saudi Arabian General Investment Authority, a government agency that encourages and expedites foreign investment in the Kingdom. The prince argued that September 11 had had a positive effect on Saudi Arabia because "it woke everyone up." No longer, he said, could rich Saudis contribute funds without restriction to organizations linked to terrorism. The government, he said, recognized that Saudi Arabian money, some of it laundered through legitimate business and charities, was sustaining al-Qaeda and other extremist groups, and it was cracking down. His two dozen Saudi guests agreed, but they mostly wanted to talk about how their government's response to terrorism was being received in the United States. How could they make Americans understand, they wanted to know, that most citizens of Saudi Arabia are not bomb-building fanatics? They agreed that the answer did not lie in the expensive, multi-page advertisements promoting the Kingdom that had appeared in the *New York Times* and the *Economist,* but where did it lie? As always, there was no simple answer. Believing as they do in the virtue and righteousness of their society, Saudis find it difficult to understand that Americans do not regard it as admirable even in the best of times. Public relations cannot fix that.

I heard the same question from Said al-Suraihi and Dr. Abdulaziz Alsebail, two prominent newspaper editors who asked me to meet with them in Riyadh. What could they do, they wondered, to narrow the breach between Saudi Arabia and the United States that had developed since September 11? How could they counter the negative images of Saudi Arabia and Islam that Americans were seeing? They agreed that there is a need for a credible, authoritative voice of mainstream Islam in the United States that could speak on behalf of the faith—perhaps a serious Islamic university, a Muslim Notre Dame, whose rector would be a scholar of unquestionable nonviolent probity. Yet they acknowledged that the real problem lies not in the United States but in their own country. So closed-minded are the religious zealots in Saudi Arabia, they said, that they spurn even Muslims from other societies, such as

Morocco and Indonesia, however devout they may be, because their practice of the faith is different from Wahhabism.

Usamah al-Kurdi argued that Saudi Arabia is modernizing at an accelerating pace, but that Americans fail to recognize the trend because they focus on the wrong issues, such as the veiled women and their being prohibited from driving. The veil is an honored Saudi tradition, not a political statement, he said, and women are not eager to drive on the Kingdom's chaotic roads.

He said the Consultative Assembly, of which he is a member, has become the vanguard of a Saudi form of democracy, in which the process of conveying the public's views to the king has become formalized and cannot be shrugged off. New government organizations such as a Supreme Economic Council are streamlining the economy and targeting unemployment, he said. Major segments of the economy, including air transport, mining, power generation, and even higher education, are being opened to private competition. New finance and tax laws are in preparation.

"We deserve some credit," he said. "Look at what other countries have done with their oil money, such as Angola and Iraq. We spent it on roads, schools, and hospitals." Now, he said, institutional modernization will follow economic development.[15]

He may be right, but change comes slowly to Saudi Arabia, even when it is most urgent. Swift and sweeping reform is not the Saudi style. Fresh thinking can be found in many sectors of the Saudi government and business establishment—one of the most intriguing innovations is an apparently serious program to develop a tourist industry, headed by Prince Sultan bin Salman, a grandson of King Abdul Aziz—but no fundamental revision of the basic political and religious system is likely in the near future. Many of the changes unfolding in the Kingdom are driven by economic imperatives, such as reducing unemployment, rather than by any commitment to freedom of expression and political pluralism. The threat of terrorism had a chilling impact on the Saudi Arabian economy and investment climate. Market capitalization in the Saudi stock market, which had been growing rapidly, dropped by about 10 percent in the two months after the attacks. Intervention by the Saudi Arabian Monetary Agency (SAMA) was required to maintain the riyal's fixed exchange rate against the dollar. Bin Laden "scored a direct hit on the Saudi economy and its leaders," according to Kevin Taecker, a veteran analyst of the Saudi financial markets.[16]

Rewriting investment laws to increase transparency in the markets and closing certain lines of business to foreigners in an effort to create more jobs for Saudis are not the same as a serious reevaluation of the country's political and religious dynamic. The House of Saud is still the government and Islam is still the *raison d'être* of the state; the royal family's partnership with the Wahhabi religious establishment is the cornerstone of its legitimacy. Whatever changes occur will be at the margins of that reality, which Crown Prince Abdullah has shown no inclination to alter; even if he were so inclined, his freedom of action remains limited so long as he is not king. What will happen after King Fahd and his two designated successors, Abdullah and Sultan, have passed from the scene is anyone's guess.

As the U.S.-led investigation of the September 11 attacks and interrogations of suspected terrorists captured in Afghanistan and elsewhere made clear the extent to which cash from Saudi Arabia was financing terrorism, the Saudis announced a crackdown. The years of willful negligence in which the Saudi authorities chose not to confront religious institutions that were preaching hatred and organizations that were financing violence were declared over. The government put in place new regulations on banks, charities, and money changers aimed at cutting off the flow of money to terrorist groups, froze assets of some individuals and institutions, and created a Financial Intelligence Unit to monitor contributions to charities, although American experts disagreed on the efficacy and completeness of these measures.[17] Hundreds of the most radical preachers were removed from their positions.

Yet as usual in Saudi Arabia, the sincerity of the Kingdom's commitment to crack down on terrorists, their religious mentors, and their financiers was tempered by equivocation; some respected analysts in the United States said the Saudi government's antiterrorism rhetoric was simply not backed up by action. After Adel al-Jubeir (the former "Ambassador to the Jews") told journalists in Washington that some of the

radical imams were fired because they "preached hatred and intoler-
ance," the deputy minister of religious affairs, Tawfeeq al-Sudairi, denied it, saying it was entirely an administrative decision. Al-Jubeir
himself refused to repudiate Hamas, the organization behind the suicide bombings in Israel, because Saudi government aid to Palestinians,
including the families of suicide bombers, was justified by conditions in
the occupied territories: "We give money to Palestinian families in
need," he said. "Are some of those families, families who have had a suicide bomber? Yes. But do we give the money because their son or
daughter was a suicide bomber? No. Is that money an incentive for
them to commit acts of terrorism? No."[18]

This kind of rhetorical maneuvering is probably inevitable, given the
political situation in Saudi Arabia. Having built the state and its own
power on an alliance with a narrow-minded, xenophobic strain of
Islam, the House of Saud cannot simply repudiate it without undermining itself. As Gregory J. H. Dowling, a former Aramco official,
pointed out in a perceptive analysis of the terrorist threat inside the
Kingdom, "There is nothing to suggest that the terrorists themselves are
anything but a marginal element in Saudi society. . . . The recourse to
terrorism is, arguably, evidence of a failure by the militants to mobilize
the broader society to accept their political objectives. It is, therefore,
essential that the government's response be both determined and subtle, attuned to the need to distinguish between those who are opposed
to aspects of Saudi society yet seek a peaceful resolution, on one hand,
and those who reject outright contemporary Saudi society with violence
as the only recourse, on the other."[19]

The government's efforts to cut off funding to terrorist groups and
tone down anti-Western rhetoric had little immediate effect on most
Americans living and working in the Kingdom; for them, life went on
pretty much as before, at least until the spring of 2003. Some American companies took the names off their doors and tightened security.
Some Americans felt discomfort as a chill fell over their relations with
Saudi friends. Most American civilians, however, seem to have felt little threat to their own safety; after all, the only previous terrorist attacks against American installations in the Kingdom had been aimed

at military targets, in keeping with al-Qaeda's commitment to force foreign troops out of the country.

"There were some changes, but probably a lot less than people would imagine," said Hans Sheline, who at the time of the attacks was president of Arabian Chevron, the Saudi Arabian subsidiary of Chevron-Texaco. "It was a big shock to everyone, and immediately people started getting e-mail from family and friends, what the heck are you still doing in the Kingdom, remember the Jews of Germany, that kind of thing." There were a few incidents in which Americans and Europeans mistaken for Americans were jostled or harassed by Saudi youths, he said, but "the people I knew took it on themselves to express profound sadness and embarrassment that Saudis were involved."[20]

"We don't travel to certain areas of the Kingdom as freely as we did, nor do we venture out on Friday afternoons when there is the possibility of an Arab gathering," said Bechtel's Terry Valenzano. "This is much like I would behave in a U.S. city like New York where I wouldn't venture into certain areas of the city at night. That's the thing that has changed—we never were shy about going anywhere and feeling safe. Now we know better than to go to certain areas at certain times. As far as feeling threatened, my family and I do not. As to there being a need to be watchful, there is, and it is much more evident than ever before."[21]

"On a personal level, there is a heightened awareness of security concerns among the American community," said Brad Bourland, chief economist of Saudi American Bank. "We look under our cars and do a few of the other things the embassy advises us to do. On a people-to-people level, there is a dislike of American policy that is translated into a lack of desire to deal with Americans. There's a boycott of American products. There's just not the same level of warmth. The country's full of nice people, but there's an erosion."

Bourland, who had been in Saudi Arabia ten years when I met him, said the "special relationship" between the United States and Saudi Arabia had been permanently undermined by the September 11 attacks because of the media scrutiny and American repugnance at some of the facts they learned about Saudi Arabia when compelled to pay closer attention. "It was more like the relationship between a man and his mistress than between a man and his wife," he said, "because both sides preferred to conduct that relationship quietly, even in some cases covertly. Metaphorically the sex was great—big money, big deals, exciting covert programs like Afghanistan. Whenever that kind of relationship gets exposed in the media and the ugly aspects of it revealed, you can never expect your mistress to defend you in public like your wife would."[22]

As the first anniversary of the September 11 attacks approached, Crown Prince Abdullah sent a message of sympathy and solidarity to the American people. "It was the perverted hope of the perpetrators of this heinous crime that they could bring humiliation to and terrorize the American nation," it said. "But the brave people of the United States of America, whose greatness lies in the strength of its brave sons and daughters in facing adversity, and which is enriched by their remarkable achievements, all of this will make them ever stronger than the designs of the evildoers. Instead of being terrorized by this catastrophe, they became more steadfast and determined." He denounced the attacks as "pure evil, condemned and abhorred by all religions and cultures."

He explicitly acknowledged that Saudi citizens were among the perpetrators. "We in Saudi Arabia felt an especially great pain at the realization that a number of young Saudi citizens had been enticed and deluded and their reasoning subverted to the degree of denying the tolerance that their religion embraced, and turning their backs on their homeland, which always stood for understanding and moderation." He vowed that terrorists would not be allowed to damage the "historic and strong" relationship between his country and the United States, and pledged "our continued will and determination to do our utmost to combat this malignant evil and uproot it from the world."[23]

It is tempting to snicker at Abdullah's assertion that Saudi Arabia, where only Islam is permitted and apostasy is punishable by beheading, has "always stood for understanding and moderation," but the crown prince had a point. Saudi Arabia has never since unification been a violent society. Intolerant and reactionary, perhaps, but not violent. The excesses committed in the name of Islam in such countries as Algeria and Sudan are alien to modern Saudi Arab culture and history. This is what made Osama bin Laden an aberrational figure in his homeland. Abdullah and his fellow princes understand that they are bin Laden's true target. That is why they supported U.S. military action in Afghanistan against the Taliban militia, who were sheltering bin Laden and his al-Qaeda fighters. Saudi leaders may have been slow to grasp the extent to which bin Laden's ideas had taken root in Saudi Arabia and the extent to which Saudi citizens were financing al-Qaeda, but they are by no means complicit in al-Qaeda's campaign. It took some courage for Abdullah to proclaim solidarity with the American people when that very solidarity is the weapon used most effectively against the House of Saud by its most committed opponents.

Abdullah's anniversary statement was reciprocated by U.S. Ambassador Robert Jordan, who published an article in the Saudi press acknowledging that the attacks had strained the relationship. "In both countries, for some segments of the population, rational thought has been replaced by emotion fed by ignorance, fear and misinformation and, sometimes, outright lies," he wrote. "This has led many to a state of anger that is harmful to both countries. This must not be permitted to continue. We cannot allow demagogues to define our relationship. . . . Nor can we allow perverters of religion to separate the world and provoke a clash of civilizations."[24]

At this official level, in commerce and in the military training missions, the bilateral relationship forged on undeterred by the September 11 attacks and their aftermath. Yet within three months of the attacks, reports began to appear in major American newspapers that the United States was contemplating the withdrawal of its remaining combat troops from Saudi Arabia and the Saudis were not asking them to stay. The problem was that pulling out the troops would be seen all over the world as capitulation to Osama bin Laden. The war on Iraq in the spring of 2003 changed the equation.

Leading an international coalition into war against Iraq for the second time in twelve years, U.S. forces rolled northward from Kuwait against surprisingly weak resistance and seized Baghdad on April 9, 2003. The regime of Saddam Hussein collapsed, and with it the rationale for stationing U.S. combat air units in Saudi Arabia to enforce

United Nations sanctions against Iraq. It was now possible to withdraw the troops without appearing to be doing so to placate the terrorists, and the announcement was not long in coming. On April 29, Defense Secretary Donald H. Rumsfeld and his Saudi counterpart, Prince Sultan, announced at a joint news conference that the troops would be redeployed outside Saudi Arabia by midsummer. The two hundred airplanes based at Prince Sultan Air Base, near al-Kharj, would leave with them. The only U.S. military personnel remaining in the Kingdom would be those of the Military Training Mission and the National Guard team, fewer than five hundred troops.

This development eliminated al-Qaeda's biggest complaint against the Saudi government, but hope that the terrorist organization would be placated was quickly dispelled. On the night of May 12, suicide truck bombers attacked three Riyadh housing compounds after overpowering gate guards. At least thirty people were killed, including eight Americans. The massive detonations ripped entire walls out of apartment buildings, hurled diners at an outdoor barbecue into a swimming pool, shattered windows hundreds of yards away, and blew apart the bodies of some victims.

There was no mistaking the intention of the attackers: It was to strike at the very heart of the House of Saud's cooperation with the West. The compounds were among about thirty in the capital that provide Western-style living for expatriates, complete with coed swimming pools, women in short sleeves, and alcohol for those who wanted it. The high walls of these compounds sequester the inhabitants from the religious police, just as the gates of Aramco's Dhahran community had done for decades. One of the devastated compounds housed the British school. Another was home to most of the Vinnell Corporation team training the Saudi National Guard.

One of the dead Americans, a Vinnell employee named Obadiah Y. Abdullah, was a former U.S. Army sergeant who had converted to Islam and made the pilgrimage to Mecca.[25] Some Saudis were also among those killed. This meant that the attackers had not only committed mass murder, they had deliberately killed Muslims, and they had done so in the royal capital of the House of Saud. The blasts shattered the illusion of safety that had comforted Western families in Saudi Arabia for nearly seventy years, and some headed for the exits. This could not be shrugged off or explained away.

In a message to friends back in the States, John Qualls described it as "a wake-up call to the Saudis that lets them know that they are in a fight to the finish with the terrorists who threaten their society—just as 9/11 was our wake-up call in the US. . . . We really need to work in unity with them to defeat this awful scourge." Qualls, a former employee of the U.S.–Saudi Arabian Joint Economic Commission who stayed on after it was disbanded to work directly for the Ministry of Finance, said that when he went to work the morning after the blasts, "there was a sense of both anger and sorrow among my Saudi friends and acquaintances, mixed with a feeling of apprehension. 'What are we going to do?' was a frequent comment/lament. Believe me, they now understand, perhaps for the very first time, that they have a gigantic problem, one that is not going to disappear by just ignoring it and going about life as normal. I get the real feeling that they recognize, perhaps for the first time, that we are all in this together."[26]

The passionate and enraged response of Crown Prince Abdullah seemed to confirm Qualls's assessment. "The tragic, bloody and painful events that took place in the heart of our dear capital, Riyadh, last night, in which innocent citizens and residents were killed or injured, prove once again that terrorists are criminals and murderers with total disregard for any Islamic and human values or decency. They are no different from vicious animals whose only concern is to shed blood and bring terror to those innocents under God's protection," his statement said. "There can be no acceptance or justification for terrorism. Nor is there a place for any ideology which promotes it, or beliefs which condone it. We specifically warn anyone who tries to justify these crimes in the name of religion. And we say that anyone who tried to so will be considered a full partner to the terrorists and will share their fate." Citing Koranic passages that prohibit killing Muslims, Abdullah said, "These messages, which do not require any interpretation, provide clear evidence that the fate of these murderers is damnation on earth and fury of Hell in the hereafter."[27]

Abdullah's statement was certainly unequivocal, and it put the extremists on notice. If, as Gregory Dowling speculated, the terrorists struck out of desperation because their message was not gaining traction with the Saudi populace; and if Abdullah and his government are now fully energized in the struggle against terrorism; and if the withdrawal of the U.S. troops quells popular resentment, it is possible that the atmosphere will stabilize and the threat will recede. Nevertheless, these early years of the twenty-first century are a time of profound uncertainty for the House of Saud and all of Saudi Arabia.

Externally, the future of Iraq remains to be determined. The menace of Saddam Hussein has been removed, along with the threat of invasion, but the emergence of a liberal, democratic government in Iraq could present Saudi Arabia with a new challenge—the challenge of ideas. If an important Arab neighbor were to become an open society, with a free press, liberated women, and a vigorous intellectual class, the retrograde nature of the Saudi political system would stand exposed. Conversely, the emergence of a Shiite theocracy in Iraq could threaten Saudi Arabia from the right instead of the left.

Across the Gulf in Iran, the theocratic regime's apparent determination to acquire nuclear weapons is causing concern in Riyadh. Saudi Arabia and the Iranian mullahs have largely reached a political *modus vivendi* since the open hostility of the 1980s, but an Iran with nuclear weapons could prompt Saudi Arabia to reconsider its own 1988 decision to forswear the nuclear option, especially if the Saudis were no longer confident that Uncle Sam would protect them.

Saudi Arabia's near-term future is also unsettled internally, even assuming that the threat of terrorism is contained. The incapacitated King Fahd's designated successor, Crown Prince Abdullah, reached the age of eighty in 2003 and the next in line, Prince Sultan, is only a year younger. The line of succession after that is undetermined, and a power struggle that splits the Kingdom, while unlikely, cannot be ruled out. Whoever comes after Abdullah and Sultan will preside over a fractious country in which the population is growing far faster than jobs are being created and the standard of living is declining; per capita income is about a quarter of what it was two decades ago because the population has exploded and oil revenue has stagnated. Difficult decisions can no longer be deferred. To cite just one example, Saudi Arabia can no longer afford to pay hundreds of thousands of foreign men to serve as chauffeurs for Saudi women, but neither can it afford the social consequences of sending them home.

Chas Freeman's quip that Moscow was a third-world city populated by first-world people, whereas Riyadh was the opposite, goes back to the good old days, about fifteen years ago, when Saudi Arabia's cities still looked new and gleaming. Now there are as many decrepit and shabby neighborhoods as new and gleaming ones. Shantytowns have sprung up in outlying areas, and beggars can be seen on some street corners. This is not the poverty of dignified bedouin subsistence that Americans respected in the 1930s; it is the poverty of urban privation. Combating it will require a vigor and flexibility that the Saudis have not so far demonstrated; failure to combat it will open the door for radical anti-Western Islamic groups to claim the allegiance of the Saudi public through social welfare programs, as has happened in other Muslim countries. The Saudis are counting on the development of a vigorous private sector to stimulate economic growth and provide job opportunities; but in a globalized economy, private sector companies are difficult to control politically and, in any case, private companies value efficiency above job creation. They want to operate with as few workers as possible.

Whatever the outcome of these issues, a steady decline in the American presence and a steady diminution of American influence are probably inevitable. Many of the Americans who departed after the housing compound attacks of May 2003 said they do not plan to return. The withdrawal of American combat military units and the termination of the Joint Economic Commission have already eliminated many points of interaction between Saudis and Americans. The top management of Saudi Aramco is almost entirely Saudi. Fewer Americans are working in Saudi Arabia's hospitals, and fewer Saudis are being educated in American universities. Americans are still competing vigorously for big capital project contracts, but fewer such contracts are being awarded, partly because of Saudi Arabia's fiscal squeeze and partly because the major infrastructure projects that drew in the likes of Bechtel have largely been completed. Lucent Technologies, for example, is nearing completion of a $4-billion upgrade of the telephone system; once it is finished, Lucent's contract will end. The high-water mark of U.S. involvement in Saudi Arabia was reached in the late 1970s and early 1980s; it is unlikely to recur. The marriage of convenience continues, helpful to both partners, but they are now spending more of their time in separate bedrooms.

As for the future of Saudi Arabia itself, it would be foolish to make predictions. The tension inherent in a society that is fully modernized in a physical sense and is part of the larger world, yet clings to cherished norms and traditions rooted in ancient ways, is readily apparent. It is the task of the Saudi monarch to manage that tension. The only one who failed conspicuously to do so, Saud, was removed by his brothers. Whether Fahd's successors will do so is an open question. We should take in the wisdom of Abu Othman, a character in Munif's *Cities of Salt* who says at the novel's end, "God only knows. Hope for the best. No one can read the future."

AFTERWORD TO
THE PAPERBACK EDITION

By THE TIME PRESIDENT GEORGE W. BUSH was sworn in for his second term as president in January 2005, events in Saudi Arabia and elsewhere in the Middle East had transformed the once unique relationship between the United States and the desert kingdom.

No longer is Saudi Arabia a peaceful outpost of American strategic policy and economic influence. The U.S. invasion of Iraq, which Saudi Arabia opposed, drove a wedge between the United States and all Arabs, inflaming mistrust that was always just beneath the surface. Americans throughout the Kingdom are the targets of terrorists, as was dramatically illustrated by an armed assault on the U.S. Consulate in Jeddah in December 2004. More than 10,000 American residents left Saudi Arabia in 2003 and 2004, and no wonder—the Web site of the U.S. Embassy in Riyadh is replete with dire warnings, urging U.S. citizens to leave the Kingdom and not come back. The State Department has declared Saudi Arabia an "unaccompanied post" for American diplomats, meaning that their families cannot accompany them when they are assigned there.

"Due to such targeted attacks against American facilities and citizens, resulting in deaths, injuries, and kidnappings, and the continuing serious threat to their safety while in Saudi Arabia, the Department of State

continues to warn U.S. citizens to defer travel to Saudi Arabia," said a notice posted after the Jeddah consulate attack. "Although counter-terrorism
efforts have succeeded in diminishing terrorist capabilities in Saudi Arabia,
terrorist groups continue to target housing compounds, hotels, methods
of transportation, and commercial establishments where Westerners can
be found."

This warning notice advised Americans who insisted on going to
Saudi Arabia anyway to stay only in secure hotels or housing compounds with armed guards and a "hardened security perimeter" to prevent suicide car bombers from approaching. When I returned to Saudi
Arabia in the late spring of 2004, the transformation of international
hotels into security bunkers, with driveways closed to vehicles and
ground-floor windows bricked up, was the most visible sign of the
plague of domestic terrorism that broke out the previous year. While I
was there, a German man was gunned down as he withdrew cash from
a bank machine, just because he was not a Muslim; hearing the com-
motion, our escorts hustled us back to the relative safety of the Marriott
Hotel. I had often experienced such incidents in other capitals but
never in Saudi Arabia.

Americans and other foreigners in Saudi Arabia are understandably
fearful after nearly two years of sporadic violence directed at them and
police shootouts with Islamic extremists allied with al-Qaeda; an American businessman who has lived in Saudi Arabia for years told me at
Christmastime 2004 that the only Americans still there were those "too
desperate, too stubborn, or too dumb" to bail out. Saudi Arabia's domestic terrorism, however, poses no near- or medium-term threat to the
rule of the al-Saud family. The security forces, better trained now and
more experienced at dealing with the threat, win their gun battles with
the militants, but the more important force that constrains the violence
is that it is not supported by the majority of the Saudi population. The
extremists have gained little political traction because they offer no political program, only nihilistic violence thinly disguised as religion, and
thus they have been unwelcome to the citizenry.

The fact that the people of Saudi Arabia have not embraced anti-
American violence, however, does not mean that Americans are again

in favor there. On the contrary, the war in Iraq has exacerbated anti-American sentiments that were already running high because of U.S. support for Israel in its long-running battle with the Palestinians.

The estrangement between the Saudi public and the United States was aggravated on the U.S. side by soaring oil prices and on the Saudi side by the rhetorical excesses of Democratic presidential nominee John F. Kerry, who spoke of Saudi Arabia as if it were a longstanding foe, and by the hostile depictions of the Kingdom in Michael Moore's film *Fahrenheit 9/11*. Paradoxically, official relations between the two governments have improved over the past two years as the Saudi authorities have increasingly cooperated with the American struggle against global terrorism. Senior officials from the State, Justice, and Treasury Departments have testified repeatedly before Congress that the Saudis, galvanized at last by the terrorism in their own country, have moved forcefully to cut off the flow of money to suspect organizations and to silence hate-mongering clerics, clean up their textbooks, and arrest individuals who carry out or espouse acts of violence.

The Saudis were gratified by the findings of the bipartisan National Commission on Terrorist Attacks upon the United States, known as the 9/11 Commission, which said their cooperation in combating terrorism, already good, improved further after the outbreak of bombings and slayings in Riyadh and other cities in 2003. "The Kingdom openly discussed the problem of radicalism, criticized the terrorists as religiously deviant, reduced official support for religious activity overseas, closed suspect charitable foundations, and publicized arrests—very public moves for a government that has preferred to keep internal problems quiet," the commission found.

The commission also absolved the Saudi government—but not individual Saudis—of providing funds to al-Qaeda's worldwide network of terror. "Saudi Arabia has long been considered the primary source of al-Qaeda funding, but we have found no evidence that the Saudi government as an institution or senior Saudi officials individually funded the organization," the commission reported.

Saudi Arabia ran advertisements in American media to publicize the commission's findings, but the fissures in the relationship between the two societies cannot be repaired by public relations. Eventually U.S. troops will withdraw from Iraq and the violence inside Saudi Arabia will subside, but even then the relationship can never again be what it was, for many reasons.

One reason is that because of terrorism fears in the United States and anti-American sentiment in Saudi Arabia, fewer young Saudis are coming to the United States for their post-secondary education. The intellectual influence of America upon Saudi Arabia's future leaders will be far less than it was in the past. In addition, the Saudis have come to terms with Iran and have distanced themselves from U.S. strategic objectives in the Gulf, which they were not in a position to do during the Cold War.

The most important reason is that Saudi Arabia is no longer economically or technologically dependent upon the United States. The Saudis no longer need Americans to show them how to fly their planes, irrigate their crops, manage their money, take their census, operate their broadcast networks, desalinate their water, or produce their oil and gas. (In the most recent round of bidding for contracts to develop Saudi Arabia's natural gas resources, American oil firms lost out to companies from Russia, China, and Europe.) In effect, the Americans have worked their way out of all of these jobs by training Saudis to do them, just as King Abdul Aziz envisioned seven decades ago.

This is as it should be. It was proper and inevitable that the United States and Saudi Arabia would move beyond their tutor-pupil relationship into a new arrangement more like that between the United States and other countries. Saudi Arabia is a maturing society, far better educated and better informed than in times past, coming to grips with the societal problems that accompany urbanization and economic development, and understandably eager to make new choices for new times.

During my travels around Saudi Arabia in 2004, I was struck by a willingness I encountered to discuss—openly in conversation, and in the media—such troubling topics as spousal and child abuse, birth defects attributable to inbreeding, drug addiction, and even AIDS. The Saudis no longer pretend that theirs is a perfect society, in harmony with God's dictates.

In the long term, there is no reason why the United States cannot maintain a constructive relationship with an evolving Saudi Arabia. Cultural differences need not preclude strong economic and strategic ties, as we have seen in Japan for six decades.

The Saudis face serious and potentially destabilizing domestic challenges—too many young people, not enough jobs, education that fails to prepare students adequately to compete in the global marketplace, narrow habits of thinking that preclude the embrace of new ideas, uncertainty about the future of the monarchy, and the inevitable decline of oil resources over the next century. These are problems for which they must find their own solutions.

One of the most thoughtful commentaries on current conditions in Saudi Arabia was "Can Saudi Arabia Reform Itself?", a report issued in July 2004 by the Brussels-based International Crisis Group. It said that the House of Saud, "which faces an unprecedented array of social, economic, political, foreign policy and security problems, has typically been guided by conservative instincts, which is why many observers, and not a few Saudi dissidents, are sceptical that the royal family will be, at least in the short term, the engine of its own modernization." This report and several others noted that the surge in oil prices in 2003 and 2004 gave the royal family enough of a cash cushion to maintain the status quo and try to buy its way out of the pressures building up around it.

The outcome of Saudi Arabia's evolution is not knowable, and there is not much the United States can do to influence it. With a bit of luck and careful management by both countries, what is becoming an arm's-length relationship can survive the current strains, and a new generation of Saudis can emerge as reliable partners for the future.

Thomas W. Lippman
January 4, 2005

NOTES

PROLOGUE

1. David E. Long, *The United States and Saudi Arabia: Ambivalent Allies* (Boulder: Westview Press, 1985), 135.

CHAPTER 1: THE PIONEERS

1. The story of the Saudi Arabian oil concession has been recounted in several publications. See Daniel Yergin, *The Prize: The Epic Quest for Oil, Money and Power* (New York: Simon & Schuster, 1991); Anthony Cave Brown, *Oil, God and Gold: The Story of Aramco and the Saudi Kings* (Boston: Houghton Mifflin, 1999); Ismail Nawwab et al., eds., *Aramco and Its World: Arabia and the Middle East* (Dhahran, Saudi Arabia: Arabian American Oil Co., 1980).

2. For a full account of the work of the mission doctors in Saudi Arabia, see Paul I. Armerding, *Doctors for the Kingdom: The Work of the American Mission Hospitals in the Kingdom of Saudi Arabia, 1913–1955* (Grand Rapids, Mich.: William B. Eerdmans Publishing Co., 2003), passim. This work includes extensive excerpts from previously unpublished journals and memoirs of the Reformed Church medical team.

3. For the text of the King-Crane Commission's report, see Appendix H in George Antonius, *The Arab Awakening* (New York: G. P. Putnam's Sons, 1946).

4. Robert Lacey, *The Kingdom: Arabia and the House of Saud* (New York: Harcourt Brace Jovanovich, 1981), 226.

5. Brown, *Oil, God and Gold*, 22ff; Lacey, *The Kingdom*, 228ff.

6. Karl S. Twitchell, *Saudi Arabia* (Princeton: Princeton University Press, 1947), 140ff.

7. Nawwab et al., *Aramco and Its World*, 192.

8. Twitchell, *Saudi Arabia*, 139.

9. J. B. Kelly, *Arabia, the Gulf and the West* (New York: Basic Books, 1980), 253.

10. David Holden and Richard Johns, *The House of Saud: The Rise and Rule of the Most Powerful Dynasty in the Arab World* (New York: Holt Rinehart and Winston, 1981), 119.

11. Thomas C. Barger, *Out in the Blue: Letters from Arabia, 1937 to 1940* (Vista, Calif.: Selwa Press, 2000), xv. This compilation of Barger's letters to his wife is the most complete personal account of life in the early days of the oil camp.

12. Wallace Stegner, *Discovery! The Search for Arabian Oil* (Beirut: Middle East Export Press, 1971), 81.

13. Barger, *Out in the Blue,* 8.

14. Ibid., 29–30.

15. Ibid., 235.

16. Ibid., 85.

17. Ibid., 118.

18. Ibid., 199.

19. This profile can be found in box 9, folder 10, of the papers of William E. Mulligan, an Aramco historian and public relations executive who collected thousands of documents relating to the oil company and Saudi Arabia. The Mulligan Papers are in the Special Collections Department of the Lauinger Library at Georgetown University, Washington, D.C. Henceforth cited as Mulligan Papers.

20. Ibid.

21. Ismail Nawwab et al., eds., *Saudi Aramco and Its World: Arabia and the Middle East* (Dhahran, Saudi Arabia: Saudi Arabian Oil Company, 1995), 199. This work is a revision of the work cited in Note 1, published after nationalization of the oil company.

22. Philip C. McConnell, *The Hundred Men* (Peterborough, N.H.: Currier Press, 1985), 148.

23. Brown, *Oil, God and Gold,* 107.

24. Mulligan Papers, box 1, folder 18.

25. William A. Eddy, *F.D.R. Meets Ibn Saud* (New York: American Friends of the Middle East, 1954).

26. Hart's comments are from *Frontline Diplomacy: The U.S. Foreign Affairs Oral History Collection,* an extensive collection of interviews with American diplomats compiled by the Association for Diplomatic Studies and Training, Arlington, Va., and published as a CD-ROM disk. See http://www.adst.org. Henceforth cited as ADST oral history.

27. Mulligan Papers, box 8, folder 9.

28. Ibid.

29. Stegner, *Discovery!* 103.

30. J. Rives Childs, *Foreign Service Farewell: My Years in the Near East* (Charlottesville, Va.: University Press of Virginia, 1969), 137–139.

31. Parker T. Hart, *Saudi Arabia and the United States: Birth of a Security Partnership* (Bloomington, Ind.: Indiana University Press, 1998), 17ff. See also *Foreign Relations of the United States,* 1943, vol. IV, 830ff. *Foreign Relations of the United States* is a compilation of declassified diplomatic documents published by the U.S. Department of State. Henceforth cited as FRUS.

32. Kay Hardy Campbell, *The History of the United States Consulate General, Dhahran, Saudi Arabia* (privately printed, 1988), 3.

33. Hart, *Saudi Arabia,* 31.

34. Mulligan Papers, box 7, folder 7.

35. Parker Hart recollections, ADST oral history.

36. Mulligan Papers, box 7, folder 23.

37. Ibid.

38. Barger, *Out in the Blue,* 102.

39. Rep. Bolton's oral report of 1945 is printed in *Problems of World War II and Its Aftermath, Part 2,* a report by the Committee on International Relations, U.S. House of Representatives, 1976.

40. Author's interview, March 27, 2002.

41. Ibid.

Chapter 2: Into the Wilderness

1. The Arnots' story is found in *American Perspectives of Aramco, the Saudi Arabian Oil-Producing Company, 1930s to 1980s,* a compilation of interviews published in 1995 by the Regional Oral History Office, Bancroft Library, University of California, Berkeley. Henceforth cited as Berkeley oral history.

2. Ismail Nawwab et al., eds., *Aramco and Its World: Arabia and the Middle East* (Dhahran, Saudi Arabia: Arabian American Oil Co., 1980), 201.

3. Berkeley oral history, 182.

4. See "The Impact of Aramco on Transportation in Saudi Arabia," an undated typescript by William E. Mulligan, Mulligan Papers, box 9, folder 10.

5. Nawwab et al., *Aramco and Its World,* 206.

6. See *Aramco Handbook,* an early version of the work cited in note 2, published in 1968 by the Arabian American Oil Company, 148.

7. Wallace Stegner, *Discovery! The Search for Arabian Oil* (Beirut: Middle East Export Press, 1971), 100.

8. Laton McCartney, *Friends in High Places: The Bechtel Story* (New York: Ballantine Books, 1989), 85–86.

9. "Over 50 Years of Service to the Kingdom," *Middle East Insight,* vol. XI, no. 6 (1995): 114ff.

10. Michael Sheldon Cheney, *Big Oil Man from Arabia* (New York: Ballantine Books, 1958), 107.

11. Ibid., 110.

12. Berkeley oral history, 475ff.

13. *Aramco Handbook* (see note 6), 152.

14. Production figures published by Aramco, various documents.

15. FRUS 1951, vol. VI, 1027ff.

16. ADST oral history.

17. Ibid.

18. Stegner, *Discovery!* 76.

19. Mulligan Papers, box 2, folder 56, and box 5, folder 10.

20. Stegner, *Discovery!* 171.

21. Mulligan Papers, box 2, folder 18.

22. Ibid., box 2, folder 56.

23. Berkeley oral history, 484.

24. Mulligan Papers, box 2, folder 56.

25. Ibid.

26. Mulligan Papers, box 5, folder 10.

27. Ibid., box 2, folder 18.

28. A copy of this letter, dated April 14, 1951, is in box 9 of Glen Brown's Papers, which are in the Special Collections Department of the Lauinger Library, Georgetown University, Washington, D.C. Henceforth cited as Brown Papers.

29. Brown Papers, box 9.

30. Lou Searcy Nelson, *Arabian Days* (Philadelphia: Dorrance & Co., 1979), 35ff.

CHAPTER 3: LITTLE AMERICA

1. Evadna Cochrane Burba, *Seasoned With Sand: An American Housewife in Saudi Arabia, 1948–1966* (Phoenix, Ariz.: Adne Press, 1981), 105.

2. The letters Mary Elizabeth Hartzell wrote to her parents from 1952 to 1965 are collected in the Mulligan Papers, box 11, folders 8 and 9.

3. Nora Johnson, *You Can Go Home Again: An Intimate Journey* (Garden City, N.Y.: Doubleday, 1982), 39.

4. Ibid., 41.

5. Ibid.

6. "Walkin' with Eula," *Al Ayyam Al Jamilah* (summer 2002): 41.

7. Paul J. Nance, *The Nance Museum: A Journey Into Traditional Saudi Arabia* (Lone Jack, Mo.: Nance Museum Publishing, 1999), 7–11.

8. Mulligan Papers, box 2, folder 6.

9. Berkeley oral history, 192.

10. Ismail Nawwab et al., eds., *Aramco and Its World: Arabia and the Middle East* (Dhahran, Saudi Arabia: Arabian American Oil Co., 1980), 244–245.

11. Berkeley oral history, 453–454.

12. Ibid., 275.

13. Thomas A. Pledge, *Saudi Aramco and Its People: A History of Training* (Dhahran, Saudi Arabia: Saudi Arabian Oil Company, 1998), 126–128.

14. Burba, *Seasoned With Sand*, 2.

15. Letter dated December 17, 1952, Mulligan Papers, box 11, folder 8.

16. Berkeley oral history, 558.

17. *Radcliffe Quarterly* (March 1977): 8ff.

18. Solon T. Kimball, "American Culture in Saudi Arabia," a paper presented to the anthropology section of the New York Academy of Sciences, February 27, 1956.

19. Berkeley oral history, 278.

20. Grant C. Butler, *Kings and Camels* (New York: Devin Adair, 1960), 24ff.

21. Kimball, "American Culture."

22. Ibid.

23. ADST oral history.

24. Burba, *Seasoned With Sand*, 129ff.

Chapter 4: Arabs and Attitudes

1. Thomas C. Barger, *Out in the Blue: Letters from Arabia, 1937 to 1940* (Vista, Calif.: Selwa Press, 2000), 168.

2. A copy of this handbook is in the Mulligan Papers, box 5, folder 24.

3. Philip C. McConnell, *The Hundred Men* (Peterborough, N.H.: Currier Press, 1985), 8.

4. U.S. Military Training Mission in Saudi Arabia, *Handbook for Newcomers* (1961), 14–15.

5. Nora Johnson, *You Can Go Home Again: An Intimate Journey* (Garden City, N.Y.: Doubleday, 1982), 42.

6. Berkeley oral history, 506.

7. Ibid., 560.

8. Wallace Stegner, *Discovery! The Search for Arabian Oil* (Beirut: Middle East Export Press, 1971), 136.

9. Letter to Peter A. Iseman, September 10, 1978, Mulligan Papers, box 11, folder 27.

10. Johnson, *You Can Go Home Again,* 66–67.

11. Michael Sheldon Cheney, *Big Oil Man from Arabia* (New York: Ballantine Books, 1958), 176.

12. Ibid., 25–26.

13. Grant C. Butler, *Kings and Camels* (New York: Devin Adair, 1960), 41.

14. McConnell, *The Hundred Men,* 164.

15. Abdelrahman Munif, *Cities of Salt* (New York: Random House, 1987), 69.

16. Ibid., 199.

17. Cheney, *Big Oil Man,* 39.

18. McConnell, *The Hundred Men,* 6.

19. Seymour Gray, *Beyond the Veil: The Adventures of an American Doctor in Saudi Arabia* (New York: Harper & Row, 1983), 218.

20. Mulligan Papers, box 7, folder 1.

21. Thomas A. Pledge, *Saudi Aramco and Its People: A History of Training* (Dhahran, Saudi Arabia: Saudi Arabian Oil Company, 1998), 42.

22. Mulligan Papers, box 2, folder 38.

23. Pledge, *Saudi Aramco,* 2.

24. Berkeley oral history, 19.

25. Ibid., 505–506.

26. Ibid., 207.

27. B. C. Nelson, *Special Labor Relations Report: The Boys in the Back Room,* 1958, Mulligan Papers, box 6, folder 22.

28. William A. Eddy, "Our Faith and Your Iron," *Middle East Journal* (summer 1963): 257ff.

29. Stegner, *Discovery!* 35.

30. Pledge, *Saudi Aramco,* 28; Anthony Cave Brown, *Oil, God and Gold: The Story of Aramco and the Saudi Kings* (Boston: Houghton Mifflin, 1999), 149.

31. Mulligan Papers, box 5, folder 25.

32. Ibid.

33. Ibid., box 3, folder 5.

34. Ibid.

35. Ismail Nawwab et al., eds., *Saudi Aramco and Its World: Arabia and the Middle East* (Dhahran, Saudi Arabia: Saudi Arabian Oil Company, 1995), 252.

36. Cheney, *Big Oil Man,* 125.

37. Ibid., 126.

38. Pledge, *Saudi Aramco,* 248; see also Nathan J. Citino, *From Arab Nationalism to OPEC: Eisenhower, King Saud and the Making of U.S.-Saudi Relations* (Bloomington, Ind.: Indiana University Press, 2002), 58.

39. George Lenczowski, *Oil and State in the Middle East* (Ithaca, N.Y.: Cornell University Press, 1960), 269.

40. Cheney, *Big Oil Man,* 220–236; Citino, *From Arab Nationalism to OPEC,* 58–60; Lenczowski, *Oil and State,* 269–270.

41. Cheney, *Big Oil Man,* 236.

42. Berkeley oral history, 37.

43. Mulligan Papers, box 8, folder 8.

44. Ibid., box 4, folder 18.

45. Ibid., box 3, folder 21.

46. Berkeley oral history, 424ff.

47. Ibid., 502.

48. FRUS 1964–1968, vol. XXI, 557.

49. David Holden and Richard Johns, *The House of Saud: The Rise and Rule of the Most Powerful Dynasty in the Arab World* (New York: Holt, Rinehart and Winston, 1981), 252. The Arabic word *jihad,* usually translated in the American media as "holy war," means utmost effort or struggle in support or defense of Islam. It seldom connotes violent action.

50. Brown, *Oil, God and Gold,* 280.

51. Mulligan Papers, box 7, folder 4.

52. Nawwab et al., *Saudi Aramco and Its World,* 250.

53. Author's interview.

Chapter 5: Funny Money

1. Thomas C. Barger, *Out in the Blue: Letters from Arabia, 1937 to 1940* (Vista, Calif.: Selwa Press, 2000), 104.

2. Kiren Aziz Chaudhry, *The Price of Wealth: Economies and Institutions in the Middle East* (Ithaca, N.Y.: Cornell University Press, 1997), 65.

3. Barger, *Out in the Blue,* 136.

4. Daniel Yergin, *The Prize: The Epic Quest for Oil, Money and Power* (New York: Simon & Schuster, 1991), 291; Wallace Stegner, *Discovery! The Search for Arabian Oil* (Beirut: Middle East Export Press, 1971), 22.

5. Aaron D. Miller, *Search for Security: Saudi Arabian Oil and American Foreign Policy, 1939–1949* (Chapel Hill, N.C.: University of North Carolina Press, 1980), 84–85.

6. FRUS 1943, vol. V, 830ff.

7. ADST oral history.

8. *Life,* March 28, 1949.

9. Berkeley oral history, 226.

10. Irvine H. Anderson, *Aramco: the United States and Saudi Arabia* (Princeton: Princeton University Press, 1981), 188.

11. Joe Stork, *Middle East Oil and the Energy Crisis* (New York: Monthly Review Press, 1975), 48.

12. Anderson, *Aramco,* 194–195.

13. David Holden and Richard Johns, *The House of Saud: The Rise and Rule of the Most Powerful Dynasty in the Arab World* (New York: Holt Rinehart and Winston, 1981), 165.

14. The English text of this decree was included in *The Organization of the Government of Saudi Arabia,* an unclassified report prepared in 1948 by Rodger P. Davies, then third secretary of the U.S. Legation in Jeddah. A copy of the Davies report is in the library of the Middle East Institute in Washington, D.C.

15. J. Rives Childs, *Foreign Service Farewell: My Years in the Near East* (Charlottesville, Va.: University Press of Virginia, 1969), 156.

16. Ibid., 157.

17. U.S. Department of State, *Comprehensive Statement of U.S. Policy Toward the Kingdom,* FRUS 1951, vol. V, 1027ff. Henceforth cited as 1951 Comprehensive Statement.

18. FRUS 1951, vol. V, 1051ff.

19. ADST oral history.

20. Robert Lacey, *The Kingdom: Arabia and the House of Saud* (New York: Harcourt Brace Jovanovich, 1981), 299–302.

21. ADST oral history.

22. Holden and Johns, *House of Saud,* 183.

23. FRUS 1961–1963, vol. XVII, 470ff.

24. Nathan J. Citino, *From Arab Nationalism to OPEC: Eisenhower, King Saud and the Making of U.S.-Saudi Relations* (Bloomington, Ind.: Indiana University Press, 2002), 138.

25. ADST oral history.

26. Anthony Cave Brown, *Oil, God and Gold: The Story of Aramco and the Saudi Kings* (Boston: Houghton Mifflin, 1999), 243; Lacey, *The Kingdom,* 323.

27. Lacey, *The Kingdom,* 324.

28. Arthur Young recounted his experience in a memoir, *Saudi Arabia: The Making of a Financial Giant* (New York University Press: 1983), and in an oral history interview at the Truman presidential library in Independence, Mo., http://www.truman library.org/oralhist/young/htm.

29. Davies, *Organization of the Government of Saudi Arabia* (see Note 14), 14.

30. Recollections of George Bennsky, ADST oral history project.

31. Ibid.

32. Berkeley oral history, 227.

33. Ibid.

34. David E. Long, *The Kingdom of Saudi Arabia* (Gainesville, Fla.: University Press of Florida, 1997), 82.

35. Letter dated August 23, 1953, Mulligan Papers, box 11, folder 8.

36. Author's interview, August 7, 2002.

37. Brad Bourland, "Saudi Banks: Sound, Strong, Modern, and Profitable," *The Gulf View* (April 2002): 4ff.

CHAPTER 6: THE LITTLE SCREEN

1. ADST oral history.

2. FRUS 1961–1963, vol. XVIII, 199ff.

3. Ibid.

4. Recollections of Isa K. Sabbagh, ADST oral history.

5. Parker Hart, *Saudi Arabia and the United States: Birth of a Security Partnership* (Bloomington, Ind.: Indiana University Press, 1998), 172.

6. ADST oral history.

7. Ibid.

8. U.S. Department of State, *United States Treaties and Other International Agreements*, vol. 15, part 2 (1964), 1864ff.

9. FRUS 1964–1968, vol. XXI, 439.

10. *Aramco Handbook*, 168.

11. Paul J. Nance, *The Nance Museum: A Journey Into Traditional Saudi Arabia* (Lone Jack, Mo.: Nance Museum Publishing, 1999), 12.

12. *Radcliffe Quarterly* (March 1977).

13. Mulligan Papers, box 4, folder 18.

14. Douglas A. Boyd, *Broadcasting in the Arab World: A Survey of Radio and Television in the Middle East* (Philadelphia: Temple University Press, 1982), 121–122.

15. Author's interview, April 12, 2002.

16. Boyd, *Broadcasting in the Arab World*, 126.

17. Ibid., 134–136.

18. Author's interview.

19. Madawi al-Rasheed, *A History of Saudi Arabia* (Cambridge: Cambridge University Press, 2002), 123.

20. Thomas W. Lippman, *Understanding Islam*, 3d. ed. (New York: Plume Books, 2002), 168.

21. Robert Lacey, *The Kingdom: Arabia and the House of Saud* (New York: Harcourt Brace Jovanovich, 1981), 369; David Holden and Richard Johns, *The House of Saud: The Rise and Rule of the Most Powerful Dynasty in the Arab World* (New York: Holt Rinehart and Winston, 1981), 261.

22. Author's interview, October 18, 2002.

23. Lacey, *The Kingdom,* 370–371; Holden and Johns, *House of Saud,* 262.

24. Ray Vicker, *The Kingdom of Oil* (New York: Scribner, 1974), 117.

CHAPTER 7: COME FLY WITH ME

1. J. E. Frankum et al., *Legacy of Leadership* (Marceline, Mo.: Walsworth Publishing Co., 1971), 139.

2. Author's interview, May 3, 2002.

3. Robert Serling, *Howard Hughes' Airline: An Informal History of TWA* (New York: St. Martin's/Marek, 1983), 300.

4. Robert Lacey, *The Kingdom: Arabia and the House of Saud* (New York: Harcourt Brace Jovanovich, 1981), 126.

5. Serling, *Howard Hughes' Airline,* 299.

6. FRUS 1947, vol. VII, 745.

7. Mulligan Papers, box 7, folder 13.

8. FRUS 1946, vol. VII, 745.

9. 1951 Comprehensive Statement.

10. J. Rives Childs, *Foreign Service Farewell: My Years in the Near East* (Charlottesville, Va.: University Press of Virginia, 1969), 145.

11. Author's interview, May 3, 2002.

12. Ibid.

13. Archives of the Ford Foundation, New York, folder 005468.

14. Author's interview, March 12, 2002.

15. See http://www.arabview.com/article.asp?artID=87.

16. Author's interview.

17. Serling, *Howard Hughes' Airline,* 300.

18. Author's interview, June 16, 2003.

19. "Saudi Arabian Airlines in the New Milennium," a position statement distributed by the corporate headquarters in Jeddah.

20. R.E.G. Davies, *Saudia: An Illustrated History of the Largest Airline in the Middle East* (McLean, Va.: Paladwr Press, 1995), 57.

21. Ibid., 54.

CHAPTER 8: A FORD IN THEIR PAST

1. Rodger Davies, *The Organization of the Government of Saudi Arabia,* unclassified report, 1948 (see Note 17, Chapter 5).

2. *A Progress Report: The Administrative Reform Program,* January 1973, Ford Foundation archives, New York, folder 005210.

3. Roy Jumper, "Ford Foundation Assistance to the Institute of Public Administration," October 1970, memo, Ford Foundation archives, folder 003835.

4. Ibid.

5. Ibid.

6. Undated memo, Ford Foundation archives, folder 005464.

7. Jumper, "Ford Foundation Assistance."

8. Ibid.

9. Ibid.

10. Conrad C. Stucky, *The Saudi Arabian Experience: A Cooperative Effort for Achieving Development,* undated report, ca. 1971, Ford Foundation archives, folder 009819.

11. *The Administrative Reform Program, Kingdom of Saudi Arabia, Purposes, Accomplishments and Future Plans,* unsigned staff report, December 17, 1966, Ford Foundation archives, folder 005198.

12. Stucky, *Saudi Arabian Experience.*

13. Ford Foundation archives, folder 005197.

14. Stucky, *Saudi Arabian Experience.*

15. Ibid.

16. Ibid.

17. Ford Foundation archives, folder 005219.

18. Internal briefing paper, February 1969, Ford Foundation archives, folder 005216.

19. David Holden and Richard Johns, *The House of Saud: The Rise and Rule of the Most Powerful Dynasty in the Arab World* (New York: Holt Rinehart and Winston, 1981), 394.

20. "A Review of Administrative Reform in Saudi Arabia," April 1972, Ford Foundation archives, folder 005557.

21. *Administrative Reform Program,* December 17, 1966, Ford Foundation archives, folder 005198.

22. Stucky, *Saudi Arabian Experience.*

23. Jumper, "Ford Foundation Assistance."

24. "Interim Plan," Ford Foundation archives, folder 005196.

25. Stucky, *Saudi Arabian Experience.*

26. Ibid.

27. *Public Personnel Administration in Saudi Arabia,* September 1968, staff report, Ford Foundation archives, folder 005400.

28. "Proposed Personnel Law for the Kingdom of Saudi Arabia," Ford Foundation archives, folder 005391.

29. "A Review of Administrative Reform in Saudi Arabia," April 1972, Ford Foundation Archives, folder 005557.

30. Leo C. Pritchard, *Administrative Reform in Operations and Management in the Kingdom of Saudi Arabia and the Ford Foundation's Participation,* November 1968, staff report, Ford Foundation Archives, folder 005213.

31. David E. Long, *The Kingdom of Saudi Arabia* (Gainesville, Fla.: University Press of Florida, 1997), 36.

32. Jumper, "Ford Foundation Assistance."

33. Mulligan Papers, box 3, folder 5.

34. Long, *Kingdom of Saudi Arabia,* 85.

35. Thomas W. Lippman, "Saudi Census Confirms Fears About Population," *Washington Post,* May 22, 1977.

36. Author's interview.

37. Author's interview.

38. Robert D. Crane, "Planning Saudi Style," *Fortune,* July 31, 1978.

39. Stucky, *Saudi Arabian Experience.*

40. Ibid.

41. Memo from Courtney A. Nelson to Robert H. Edwards, February 6, 1974, Ford Foundation archives, folder 008894.

42. Memo from Robert H. Edwards to McGeorge Bundy, March 7, 1977, Ford Foundation archives folder 011051.

Chapter 9: The American Way

1. Daniel Yergin, *The Prize: The Epic Quest for Oil, Money and Power* (New York: Simon & Schuster, 1991), 606.

2. Berkeley oral history, 134.

3. David Holden and Richard Johns, *The House of Saud: The Rise and Rule of the Most Powerful Dynasty in the Arab World* (New York: Holt Rinehart and Winston, 1981), 359.

4. Berkeley oral history, 432.

5. Projects Research Inc., "A Survey of Selected Projects in Saudi Arabia" (Falls Church, Va.: Projects Research Inc., 1983).

6. Berkeley oral history, 242.

7. Ibid., 243.

8. *Washington Post,* January 29, 1978.

9. Author's interview, January 27, 2003.

10. U.S. Department of Commerce, International Trade Administration, "Foreign Corrupt Practices Act Antibribery Provisions," online briefing paper, http://www.bisnis.doc.gov/bisnis/fcp1.htm.

11. U.S. House of Representatives, Committee on Government Operations, sub-committee on Commerce, Consumer and Monetary Affairs, proceedings of April 6, 1982; see also *Washington Post,* April 7, 1982.

12. William B. Quandt, *Saudi Arabia in the 1980s* (Washington, D.C.: The Brookings Institution, 1981), 148.

13. U.S. Department of State, *United States Treaties and Other International Obligations,* vol. 25, part 3 (1974), 3116ff.

14. Author's interview, March 17, 2002.

15. Ibid.

16. General Accounting Office, *U.S. Role as Contracting Agent for the U.S.-Saudi Arabian Joint Economic Commission,* May 14, 1984.

17. Author's interview.

18. ADST oral history.

19. Author's interview, ca. September 2002.

20. Author's interview, July 15, 2002.

21. Kiren Aziz Chaudhry, *The Price of Wealth: Economies and Institutions in the Middle East* (Ithaca: Cornell University Press, 1997), 153.

22. Author's interview.

23. ADST oral history.

24. Author's interview, September 30, 2002.

25. General Accounting Office, *Critical Factors Affecting Saudi Arabia's Oil Decisions,* May 12, 1978.

26. David K. Harbinson, "The U.S.-Saudi Arabian Joint Commission on Economic Cooperation: A Critical Appraisal," *Middle East Journal,* vol. 44, no. 2 (spring 1990).

27. Author's interview.

CHAPTER 10: DOWN ON THE FARM

1. Mildred Logan recalled her experiences in Saudi Arabia in two articles in *The Cattleman* ("The Arabs Call Me Madam Sam," January 1952, and "I Like Being the Garden of Eden's First Lady," October 1957), and in an interview with the author in 2003.

2. Thomas C. Barger, *Out in the Blue: Letters from Arabia, 1937 to 1940* (Vista, Calif.: Selwa Press, 2000), 102.

3. Karl S. Twitchell, *Report of the United States Agricultural Mission to Saudi Arabia* (Cairo 1943), 100.

4. Wallace Stegner, *Discovery! The Search for Arabian Oil* (Beirut, Lebanon: Middle East Export Press, 1971), 163.

5. Parker T. Hart, *Saudi Arabia and the United States: Birth of a Security Partnership* (Bloomington, Ind.: Indiana University Press, 1998), 29ff.

6. ADST oral history.

7. Author's interview, March 27, 2000.

8. William A. Rugh, *Riyadh, History and Guide* (Dammam, Saudi Arabia: Al-Mutawa Press, 1969), 103.

9. ADST oral history.

10. Douglas D. Crary, "Recent Agricultural Developments in Saudi Arabia," *Geographical Review* (July 1951).

11. Berkeley oral history, 474.

12. This message was sent on November 18, 1949. A copy is in the Brown Papers, box 9.

13. Glen Brown, "Résumé of U.S. Geological Survey Work in Saudi Arabia, 1944–79." This is a typed manuscript dated June 19, 1989. A copy was provided to the author by Glen Brown's daughter.

14. Brown Papers, box 9.

15. Mulligan Papers, box 1, folder 2.

16. William A. Eddy, "Our Faith and Your Iron," *Middle East Journal* (summer 1963): 260.

17. Mulligan Papers, box 8, folder 10.

18. Eugene Bird memo, Mulligan Papers, box 3, folder 18.

19. Kiren Aziz Chaudhry, *The Price of Wealth: Economies and Institutions in the Middle East* (Ithaca: Cornell University Press, 1997), 173.

20. Harold F. Heady, *Report to the Government of Saudi Arabia on Grazing Resources and Problems,* Rome, 1963. A copy is in the Mulligan Papers, box 10, folder 13.

21. Peter Wilson and Douglas Graham, *Saudi Arabia: The Coming Storm* (Armonk, N.Y.: M. E. Sharpe, 1994), 222ff.

22. Chaudhry, *Price of Wealth,* 176.

23. Aramco, "Bedouin Settlement in Saudi Arabia: Its Effect on Company Operations," Mulligan Papers, box 7, folder 16.

24. Ford Foundation archives, folder 008894.

25. Martha Kirk recorded her experience in a memoir, *Green Sands: My Five Years in the Saudi Desert* (Lubbock, Tex.: Texas Tech University Press, 1994); Terry Kirk's comments are from an interview with the author in 2002.

26. Martha Kirk, *Green Sands,* 149.

27. Ibid., 202.

28. Ibid., 209.

29. Mulligan Papers, box 9, folder 3.

30. Ford Foundation archives, folder 005210.

31. Wilson and Graham, *Saudi Arabia,* 223.

32. Anthony Cordesman, *Saudi Arabia: Guarding the Desert Kingdom* (Boulder: Westview Press, 1997), 69.

33. Thomas W. Lippman, "U.S. Gives Saudis No-Embargo Pledge," *Washington Post,* May 10, 1983.

34. *Bi-Weekly Bulletin,* Market Analysis Division, Marketing Policy Directorate, Strategic Policy Branch, Agriculture and Agri-Food Canada, Winnipeg, Manitoba, vol. 14, no. 11 (June 29, 2001), http://www.agr.gc.ca/mad-dam/e/bulletine/v14e/v14n11e.txt.

35. Wilson and Graham, *Saudi Arabia,* 222ff; Cordesman, *Saudi Arabia,* 51, 69.

36. Craig S. Smith, "Saudis Worry as They Waste Their Scarce Water," *New York Times,* January 26, 2003.

37. *Bi-Weekly Bulletin;* see also *Saudi Arabia 2002 Economic Trends,* report from the U.S. Embassy, http://www.usembassy.state.gov/riyadh/wwwhet02.html.

38. Ibid.

39. *Bi-Weekly Bulletin.*

40. U.S.-Saudi Arabian Business Council, *A Business Guide to Saudi Arabia,* 4th ed. (Washington, D.C.: U.S.-Saudi Arabian Business Council, 2002), 49.

41. See "Making the Desert Come Alive," *Saudi Arabia Magazine* (spring 2001), a publication of the Saudi Arabian embassy in Washington, http://www.saudi embassy.net/publications/Magazine-Spring-01/Agriculture.htm.

Chapter 11: Christians and Jews

1. Madawi al-Rasheed, *A History of Saudi Arabia* (Cambridge: Cambridge University Press, 2002), 91.

2. Sura, or chapter, 105.

3. Mulligan Papers, box 7, folder 21.

4. Evadna Cochrane Burba, *Seasoned With Sand: An American Housewife in Saudi Arabia, 1948–1966* (Phoenix, Ariz.: Adne Press, 1981), 28, 29.

5. Paul J. Nance, *The Nance Museum: A Journey Into Traditional Saudi Arabia* (Lone Jack, Mo.: Nance Museum Publishing, 1999), 12.

6. Berkeley oral history, 279.

7. Mulligan Papers, box 8, folder 19.

8. See 1979 paper by the Rev. Timon Costello, Mulligan Papers, box 7, folder 21.

9. Berkeley oral history, 497.

10. Ibid., 564.

11. "A Desert Christmas," *Ladies Home Journal* (December 1957).

12. J. Rives Childs, *Foreign Service Farewell: My Years in the Near East* (Charlottesville, Va.: University Press of Virginia, 1969), 154.

13. Mulligan Papers, box 7, folder 21.

14. 1951 Comprehensive Statement.

15. Nora Johnson, *You Can Go Home Again: An Intimate Journey* (Garden City, N.Y.: Doubleday, 1982), 62.

16. Mulligan Papers, box 7, folder 21.

17. Ibid.

18. Author's interview, March 12, 2002.

19. Author's interview, July 9, 2002.

20. Berkeley oral history, 60ff.

21. James P. Piscatori, "The Roles of Islam in Saudi Arabia's Political Development," in *Islam and Development: Religion and Sociopolitical Change,* ed. John L. Esposito (Syracuse, N.Y.: Syracuse University Press, 1980), 137.

22. Author's interview, July 9, 2002.

23. Berkeley oral history, 280.

24. See Anthony Cordesman, "Saudi Arabia: Opposition, Islamic Extremism, and Terrorism," in *Saudi Arabia Enters the 21st Century: Politics, Economics, and Energy,* final review draft (Washington, D.C.: Center for Strategic and International Studies, 2002), 15. Available online at http://www.csis.org/burke/Saudi21/index.htm#reports.

25. Al-Rasheed, *History of Saudi Arabia,* 154.

26. Mulligan Papers, box 7, folder 4.

27. Ibid., box 7, folder 21.

28. Available at http://www.state.gov, in the Publications section.

29. Author's interview, March 26, 2002.

30. Anthony Cave Brown, *Oil, God and Gold: The Story of Aramco and the Saudi Kings* (Boston: Houghton Mifflin, 1999), 182.

31. Ahmed Ali, translator, *Al-Quran, A Contemporary Translation* (Karachi, Pakistan, Akrash Publishing, 1984), sura 5, verse 82.

32. 1951 Comprehensive Statement.

33. Ibid.

34. FRUS 1952–1954, vol. X, 2415.

35. Ibid., vol. IX, 2428.

36. Ibid., 2429.

37. Proceedings of the Senate Foreign Relations Committee, July 20, 1956.

38. Ibid.

39. See "The Arab Campaign Against American Jews," a pamphlet published by the American Jewish Congress in 1956.

40. Ibid.

41. *In the Matter of American Jewish Congress, respondent, v. Elmer A. Carter, et al.,* Court of Appeals of the State of New York, March 2, 1961 (9 N.Y. 2d 223). See especially the dissenting opinion by Judge Froessel.

42. Author's interview, November 4, 2002.

43. FRUS 1961–1963, vol. XVII, 470ff.

44. Ibid.

45. Ibid., 758.

46. Ibid.

47. ADST oral history.

48. Ibid.

49. Berkeley oral history, 127–128.

50. Author's interview.

51. Henry A. Kissinger, *Years of Upheaval* (Boston: Little Brown & Co., 1982), 660 ff.

52. Ibid.

53. Robert H. Edwards memo, Ford Foundation archives, folder 011495.

54. U.S. House of Representatives, Committee on International Relations, Subcommittee on International Trade and Commerce, proceedings of March 6, 1975.

55. My father was Jewish but my mother was Catholic and I was baptized into the church as an infant. As the *Washington Post*'s correspondent in the Arab world in the 1970s, I carried my baptismal certificate stapled into my passport. No one ever asked to see it.

56. General Accounting Office, *U.S. Role as Contracting Agency for the U.S.-Saudi Arabian Joint Economic Commission* (Washington, D.C.: GAO, May 14, 1984), 5.

57. Laton McCartney, *Friends in High Places: The Bechtel Story* (New York: Ballantine Books, 1989), 189–193.

58. *Lawrence R. Abrams MD v. Baylor College of Medicine,* 805 F 2d 528 (5th Cir. 1986).

59. Statement by the Cooperation Council of the Arab States of the Gulf on the Cancellation of the Secondary/Tertiary Boycott of Israel, October 1, 1994.

60. Author's interview, January 27, 2003.

61. *Washington Post,* January 23, 1992.

62. Author's interview, June 21, 2002.

CHAPTER 12: GO DIRECTLY TO JAIL

1. This diplomatic cable and many others concerning James Smrkovski and Scott Nelson are included in the voluminous records compiled by their lawyers during

court proceedings and congressional hearings and in support of a "Petition for Redress" addressed to the Saudi Arabian government. The documents include affidavits, transcripts of sworn testimony, corporate personnel records, and internal administrative memoranda. All were made available to the author by attorneys for Smrkovski and Nelson, and are the basis for this narrative. Unless otherwise noted, quotations concerning the Smrkovski and Nelson cases are from those files. Their authenticity, and the facts of the cases, are not in dispute.

2. *Saudi Arabia v. Nelson,* 507 US 349 (1993).

3. Affidavit of November 18, 1986, included in record of House Foreign Affairs Committee, Subcommittee on Europe and the Middle East, proceedings of June 15, 1987.

4. *International Herald Tribune,* October 29, 1996.

5. Thomas W. Lippman, "Workers' Tales of Torture Strain U.S.-Saudi Ties," *Washington Post,* May 24, 1992.

6. Department of State, ninth annual *Report to Congress on Americans Incarcerated Abroad* (Washington, D.C., 1986).

7. Undated document entered into record of House Foreign Affairs Committee proceedings, June 15, 1987.

8. Author's interview, June 5, 2002.

9. ADST oral history.

10. Anders Jerichow, *The Saudi File: People, Power, Politics* (New York: St. Martin's Press, 1998), 262.

11. David E. Long, *The Kingdom of Saudi Arabia* (Gainesville, Fla.: University Press of Florida, 1997), 77–78.

12. Ibid.

13. Gene Lindsey, *Saudi Arabia* (New York: Hippocrene Books, 1991), 332

14. Ibid., 343.

15. Author's interview.

16. John D. McDonald, *Flight from Dhahran* (Englewood Cliffs, N.J.: Prentice-Hall, 1981), 28.

17. Ibid., 129.

18. Ibid., 153.

19. Ibid., 156.

20. Kiren Aziz Chaudhry, *The Price of Wealth: Economies and Institutions in the Middle East* (Ithaca: Cornell University Press, 1997), 153.

21. ADST oral history.

22. Ibid.

23. Proceedings of House Foreign Affairs Committee, Subcommittee on the Middle East, May 19, 1992.

24. Jerichow, *The Saudi File,* 102.

CHAPTER 13: THE CULTURAL DIVIDE

1. *Aramco World* (September-October 1987): 34ff; see also *Albuquerque Journal,* September 7, 1990, and Thomas W. Lippman, "Saudi Arabia's Vanishing Act," *Washington Post,* February 5, 1983.

2. John Topham et al., introduction to *Traditional Crafts of Saudi Arabia* (London: Stacey International, 1981).

3. Paul J. Nance, *The Nance Museum: A Journey Into Traditional Saudi Arabia* (Lone Jack, Mo.: Nance Museum Publishing, 1999), 7.

4. Ibid., 11.

5. Ibid., 102.

6. Author's interview, July 2002.

7. Author's interview, May 1977.

8. Author's interview, July 19, 2002.

9. Author's interview, July 2, 2002.

10. *Houston Post,* December 23, 1991.

11. Mulligan Papers, box 1, folder 1.

12. Author's interview, July 11, 2002.

13. Frances Meade, *Honey and Onions: A Memoir of Saudi Arabia in the Sixties* (Riyadh: Sands Books, 1996), 67.

14. ADST oral history.

15. Seymour Gray, *Beyond the Veil: The Adventures of an American Doctor in Saudi Arabia* (New York: Harper & Row, 1983), 9.

16. Ibid., 24.

17. Ibid., 37.

18. Ibid., 71–83.

19. Ibid., 109.

20. Ibid., 293.

21. Ibid., 328.

22. Author's interview, April 16, 2002.

23. Author's interview, April 10, 2002.

24. Meade, *Honey and Onions,* 77–78.

25. ADST oral history.

26. Daryle Russ, e-mail message to author, July 17, 2002.

27. Thomas A. Pledge, *Saudi Aramco and Its People: A History of Training* (Dhahran, Saudi Arabia: Saudi Arabian Oil Company, 1998), 143.

28. ADST oral history.

29. Susan Becker, e-mail message to author, June 1, 2003.

30. Susan Becker, "Treating the American Expatriate in Saudi Arabia," *International Journal of Mental Health* 20, no. 2 (summer 1991): 86ff.

31. Ibid.

32. Becker, e-mail.

33. Ibid.

Chapter 14: From Swords to Missiles

1. FRUS 1947, vol. V, 1335ff; see also FRUS 1951, vol. V, 1061ff.

2. FRUS 1947, vol. V, 1335ff.

3. Ibid., 1342.

4. FRUS 1952–1954, vol. IX, 2438.

5. FRUS 1964–1968, vol. XX, 1440.

6. *United States Military Training Mission Saudi Arabia,* descriptive booklet (Washington, D.C.: United States Military Training Mission, 1961). (No author named.)

7. FRUS 1951, vol. V, 1027ff. Italics added.

8. See documents in FRUS 1951, vol. V, section on Saudi Arabia.

9. Mulligan Papers, box 7, folder 23.

10. FRUS 1951, vol. V, 1060ff.

11. Mulligan Papers, box 7, folder 23.

12. William H. Riley Jr., "Leading From Behind," supplement to *Newcomer's Handbook* for Americans participating in the Saudi Arabian National Guard training program. Available at http://www.opmsang.sppn.af.mil/Newcomer's Handbook/NOC25a.htm.

13. Recollections of Eugene Bird, ADST oral history.

14. *United States Military Training Mission Saudi Arabia.*

15. Author's interview.

16. Author's interview, October 2, 2002.

17. Available at the OPM-SANG Web site, http://www.globalsecurity/agency/dod/opm-sang.htm

18. Author's interview.

19. Author's interview.

20. Peter Wilson and Douglas Graham, *Saudi Arabia: The Coming Storm* (Armonk, N.Y.: M. E. Sharpe, 1994), 158.

21. These comments came from a former adviser to the National Guard who agreed to be interviewed only on condition that he not be identified by name.

22. Riley, "Leading From Behind."

23. Hart, *Saudi Arabia and the United States,* 250.

24. Proceedings of U.S. House of Representatives, Committee on Foreign Affairs, Subcommittee on Europe and the Middle East, June 25, 1979.

25. FRUS 1964–1968, vol. XXI, 458–459.

26. Recollections of Talcott W. Seelye, ADST oral history project; see also Robert Lacey, *The Kingdom: Arabia and the House of Saud* (New York: Harcourt Brace Jovanovich, 1981), 467ff.

27. Author's interview.

28. Federation of American Scientists, *Arms Sales Monitoring Project,* 1966 report (reprinted in Anders Jerichow, *The Saudi File: People, Power, Politics* (New York: St. Martin's Press, 1998), 275ff); see also Alfred B. Prados, "Saudi Arabia: Current Issues and U.S. Relations," Congressional Research Service Issue Brief for Congress, July 8, 2002.

29. Prados, "Saudi Arabia."

Chapter 15: Desert Storms

1. ADST oral history.

2. H. Norman Schwarzkopf, *It Doesn't Take a Hero* (New York: Bantam Books, 1992), 302–306; Peter Wilson and Douglas Graham, *Saudi Arabia: The Coming Storm* (Armonk, N.Y.: M. E. Sharpe, 1994), 108–115.

3. ADST oral history.

4. Author's interview, May 6, 2002.

5. Schwarzkopf, *It Doesn't Take a Hero,* 386.

6. Nawaf E. Obaid, "The Power of Saudi Arabia's Islamic Leaders," *Middle East Quarterly* (September 1999).

7. ADST oral history.

8. Author's interview.

9. Khaled bin Sultan, *Desert Warrior* (New York: HarperCollins, 1995), 216

10. Author's interview.

11. Schwarzkopf, *It Doesn't Take a Hero,* 346.

12. ADST oral history.

13. Schwarzkopf, *It Doesn't Take a Hero,* 387.

14. Bin Sultan, *Desert Warrior,* 461ff.

15. Schwarzkopf, *It Doesn't Take a Hero,* 388.

16. ADST oral history.

17. Schwarzkopf, *It Doesn't Take a Hero,* 390–391.

18. ADST oral history.

19. Mamoun Fandy, *Saudi Arabia and the Politics of Dissent* (New York: St. Martin's Press, 1999), 49.

20. Brad Bourland, "The Saudi Economy at Mid-Year 2002" (Riyadh: Saudi American Bank, 2002).

21. ADST oral history.

22. Author's interview.

23. Madawi al-Rasheed, *A History of Saudi Arabia* (Cambridge: Cambridge University Press, 2002), 171.

24. ADST oral history.

25. Fouad Ajami, "The Sentry's Solitude," *Foreign Affairs* 80, no. 6 (November/December 2001): 6.

26. ADST oral history.

27. Jane Corbin, *Al-Qaeda: The Terror Network That Threatens the World* (New York: Nation Books, 2002), 27; see also Douglas Jehl, "Holy War Lured Saudis as Rulers Looked Away," *New York Times,* December 27, 2001, B-4.

28. Anders Jerichow, *The Saudi File: People, Power, Politics* (New York: St. Martin's Press, 1998), 10–12.

29. Eleanor Abdella Doumato, "A Dialogue: Saudi Arabia," *SAIS Review* 22, no. 2 (summer-fall 2002): 204.

30. Jerichow, *The Saudi File: People,* 93–94.

31. Ibid., 72.

32. Author's interview, July 15, 2002.

33. Embassy of the United States of America, *Saudi Arabia 2002 Economic Trends,* http://usembassy.state.gov/riyadh/wwwhet02.html.

34. Gene Lindsey, *Saudi Arabia* (New York: Hippocrene Books, 1991), 288.

35. Terry Valenzano, e-mail message to author, April 29, 2002.

36. Author's interview, July 9, 2002.

37. Louis J. Freeh, "American Justice for Our Khobar Heroes," *Wall Street Journal,* May 20, 2003.

38. Jerichow, *The Saudi File: People,* 258.

CHAPTER 16: AFTER SEPTEMBER 11

1. Neil Macfarquar, "Anti-Western and Extremist Views Pervade Saudi Schools," *New York Times,* October 19, 2001.

2. The web site is http://www.ain-al-yaqeen.com.

3. Hawali's remarks were translated and posted on the Web site http://www.memri.org by an Israel-based organization that monitors what it considers inflammatory or hate-inspiring rhetoric in the Muslim world.

4. Also posted on http://www.memri.org.

5. This item appeared in the newspaper *al-Riyadh* in June 2002; a translation was posted on the Web site of the English-language *Arab News,* http://www.arabnews.com.

6. Douglas Jehl, "Once Trusting, Saudis Are Now Leery of U.S.," *New York Times,* December 6, 2001.

7. Author's interview, October 5, 2002.

8. Translated by *Arab News,* posted at http://www.arabnews.com.

9. Author's interview, October 1, 2002.

10. Author's interview, October 3, 2002.

11. Jack Shafer, "The PowerPoint That Rocked the Pentagon," *Slate,* August 7, 2002, http://www.slate.msn.com.

12. Translated by the Foreign Broadcast Information Service, August 19, 2002.

13. For a useful explanation of the issues in this case, see Christopher H. Johnson, "Terrorism as Mass Tort: Responsibility for 9/11"; Johnson is a Washington lawyer who practiced in Saudi Arabia for several years. Available at http://www.arabialink.com/SAF/Newsletters/SAF_Essay_03.htm.

14. Sulaiman al-Hattlan, "Homegrown Fanatics," *New York Times,* May 15, 2003.

15. Author's interview.

16. Kevin R. Taecker, "A Post-Sept. 11 Assessment of the Financial Markets of Saudi Arabia," a paper prepared for private clients and made available to the author.

17. See "Initiatives and Actions Taken by the Kingdom of Saudi Arabia in the Financial Area to Combat Terrorism," a paper distributed by the Saudi Arabian Embassy in Washington, D.C., March 2003, http://www.Saudiembassy.net.

18. See the Reuters news agency account by Carol Giacomo, June 12, 2003.

19. Gregory J. H. Dowling, "Imagined Kingdoms: Islamic Militancy and Opposition in Saudi Arabia," distributed by the Saudi-American Forum, an online news and information service at http://www.saudi-american-forum.org.

20. Author's interview, May 3, 2002.

21. E-mail message to author, April 25, 2002.

22. Author's interview, September 29, 2002.

23. Available at http://www.saudiembassy.net.

24. Robert Jordan, *Arab News* (Jeddah), September 11, 2002.

25. Amy Goldstein, "Work, Faith, Family Needs Drew Bomb Victims to Riyadh," *Washington Post,* May 15, 2003.

26. Qualls sent his report to the National Association for Business Economics, which posted it on the Internet at http://www.nabe.com/publib/qualls.html.

27. See http://www.saudiembassy.net/pressrelease/releases/03-pr-0513-abdullah-terrorism.htm.

BIBLIOGRAPHY

Ajami, Fouad. *The Arab Predicament: Arab Political Thought and Practice Since 1967.* New York: Cambridge University Press, 1981.

Anderson, Irvine H. *Aramco, the United States and Saudi Arabia.* Princeton: Princeton University Press, 1981.

Anderson, Norman A., et al. *The Kingdom of Saudi Arabia.* London: Stacey International, 1977.

Armerding, Paul I. *Doctors for the Kingdom: The Work of the American Mission Hospitals in the Kingdom of Saudi Arabia, 1913–1955.* Grand Rapids, Mich.: William B. Eerdmans Publishing Co., 2003.

Barger, Thomas C. *Out in the Blue: Letters from Arabia—1937 to 1940.* Vista, Calif.: Selwa Press, 2000.

Bin Sultan, Khaled. *Desert Warrior: A Personal View of the Gulf War By the Joint Forces Commander.* New York: HarperCollins, 1995.

Boyd, Douglas A. *Broadcasting in the Arab World: A Survey of Radio and Television in the Middle East.* Philadelphia: Temple University Press, 1982.

Brown, Anthony Cave. *Oil, God and Gold: The Story of Aramco and the Saudi Kings.* Boston: Houghton Mifflin, 1999.

Burba, Evadna Cochrane. *Seasoned With Sand: An American Housewife in Saudi Arabia, 1948–1966.* Phoenix, Ariz.: Adne Press, 1981.

Butler, Grant C. *Kings and Camels.* New York: Devin Adair, 1960.

Chaudhry, Kiren Aziz. *The Price of Wealth: Economies and Institutions in the Middle East.* Ithaca: Cornell University Press, 1997.

Cheney, Michael Sheldon. *Big Oil Man From Arabia.* New York: Ballantine Books, 1958.

Childs, J. Rives. *Foreign Service Farewell: My Years in the Near East.* Charlottesville, Va.: University Press of Virginia, 1969.

Citino, Nathan J. *From Arab Nationalism to OPEC: Eisenhower, King Saud, and the Making of U.S.-Saudi Relations.* Bloomington, Ind.: Indiana University Press, 2002.

Corbin, Jane. *Al-Qaeda: The Terror Network That Threatens the World.* New York: Nation Books, 2002.

Cordesman, Anthony. *Saudi Arabia: Guarding the Desert Kingdom.* Boulder: Westview Press, 1997.

Davies, R.E.G. *Saudia: An Illustrated History of the Largest Airline in the Middle East.* McLean, Va.: Paladwr Press, 1995.

Dekmejian, R. Hrair. *Islam in Revolution: Fundamentalism in the Arab World.* Syracuse, N.Y.: Syracuse University Press, 1985.

Eddy, William A. *F.D.R. Meets Ibn Saud.* New York: American Friends of the Middle East, 1954.

Emerson, Steven. *The American House of Saud: The Secret Petrodollar Connection.* New York: Franklin Watts, 1985.

Esposito, John L., ed. *Islam and Development: Religion and Sociopolitical Change.* Syracuse, N.Y.: Syracuse University Press, 1980.

Fandy, Mamoun. *Saudi Arabia and the Politics of Dissent.* New York: St. Martin's Press, 1999.

Gray, Seymour. *Beyond the Veil: The Adventures of an American Doctor in Saudi Arabia.* New York: Harper & Row, 1983.

Grayson, Benson L. *Saudi-American Relations.* Washington, D.C.: University Press of America, 1982.

Hart, Parker T. *Saudi Arabia and the United States: Birth of a Security Partnership.* Bloomington, Ind.: Indiana University Press, 1998.

Hiro, Dilip. *War Without End: The Rise of Islamist Terrorism and the Global Response.* London: Routledge, 2002.

Holden, David, and Richard Johns. *The House of Saud: The Rise and Rule of the Most Powerful Dynasty in the Arab World.* New York: Holt, Rinehart and Winston, 1981.

Jerichow, Anders. *The Saudi File: People, Power, Politics.* New York: St. Martin's Press, 1998.

Johnson, Nora. *You Can Go Home Again: An Intimate Journey.* Garden City, N.Y.: Doubleday, 1982.

Kaplan, Robert D. *The Arabists: The Romance of an American Elite.* New York: Free Press, 1993.

Kelly, J. B. *Arabia, The Gulf and the West.* New York: Basic Books, 1980.

Kirk, Martha. *Green Sands: My Five Years in the Saudi Desert.* Lubbock, Tex.: Texas Tech University Press, 1994.

Lacey, Robert. *The Kingdom: Arabia and the House of Saud.* New York: Harcourt Brace Jovanovich, 1981.

Lapidus, Ira M. *A History of Islamic Societies.* Cambridge: Cambridge University Press, 1988.

Lee, Eve. *The American in Saudi Arabia.* Chicago: Intercultural Press, 1980.

Lenczowski, George. *Oil and State in the Middle East.* Ithaca: Cornell University Press, 1960.

Lindsey, Gene. *Saudi Arabia.* New York: Hippocrene Books, 1991.

Lippman, Thomas W. *Understanding Islam: An Introduction to the Muslim World.* 3d ed. New York: Plume, 2002.

Long, David E. *The Kingdom of Saudi Arabia.* Gainesville, Fla.: University Press of Florida, 1997.

————. *The United States and Saudi Arabia: Ambivalent Allies.* Boulder: Westview Press, 1985.

McCartney, Laton. *Friends in High Places: The Bechtel Story.* New York: Ballantine Books, 1989.

McConnell, Philip C. *The Hundred Men.* Peterborough, N.H.: Currier Press, 1985.

McDonald, John D. *Flight From Dhahran: The True Experience of an American Businessman Held Hostage in Saudi Arabia.* Englewood Cliffs, N.J.: Prentice-Hall, 1981.

Meade, Frances. *Honey and Onions: A Memoir of Saudi Arabia in the Sixties.* Riyadh, Saudi Arabia: Sands Books, 1996.

Miller, Aaron D. *Search for Security: Saudi Arabian Oil and American Foreign Policy 1939–1949.* Chapel Hill, N.C.: University of North Carolina Press, 1980.

Munif, Abdelrahman. *Cities of Salt.* New York: Random House, 1987.

Nance, Paul J. *The Nance Museum: A Journey Into Traditional Saudi Arabia.* Lone Jack, Mo.: Nance Museum Publishing, 1999.

Nawwab, Ismail, et al., eds. *Aramco and Its World: Arabia and the Middle East.* Dhahran, Saudi Arabia: Arabian American Oil Co., 1980.

_____. *Saudi Aramco and Its World: Arabia and the Middle East.* Dhahran, Saudi Arabia: Saudi Arabian Oil Company, 1995.

Nelson, Lou Searcy. *Arabian Days.* Philadelphia: Dorrance & Co., 1979.

Nyrop, Richard F., et al. *Area Handbook for Saudi Arabia.* 3d ed. Washington, D.C.: U.S. Government Printing Office, 1977.

Pledge, Thomas A. *Saudi Aramco and Its People: A History of Training.* Dhahran, Saudi Arabia: Saudi Arabian Oil Company, 1998.

Pollack, Kenneth M. *Arabs at War: Military Effectiveness, 1948–1991.* Lincoln, Neb.: University of Nebraska Press, 1992.

Quandt, William B. *Saudi Arabia in the 1980s: Foreign Policy, Security and Oil.* Washington, D.C.: Brookings Institution, 1981.

Rand, Christopher T. *Making Democracy Safe for Oil: Oilmen and the Islamic East.* Boston: Atlantic–Little, Brown, 1975.

Rasheed, Madawi al-. *A History of Saudi Arabia.* Cambridge: Cambridge University Press, 2002.

Rubin, Barry, and Judith C. Rubin. *Anti-American Terrorism and the Middle East: A Documentary Record.* New York: Oxford University Press, 2002.

Rugh, William A. *Riyadh, History and Guide.* Dammam, Saudi Arabia: Al-Mutawa Press, 1969.

Safran, Nadav. *Saudi Arabia: The Ceaseless Quest for Security.* Cambridge, Mass.: Harvard University Press, 1985.

Schwarzkopf, H. Norman. *It Doesn't Take a Hero.* New York: Bantam Books, 1992.

Serling, Robert. *Howard Hughes' Airline: An Informal History of TWA.* New York: St. Martin's/Marek, 1983.

Stegner, Wallace. *Discovery! The Search for Arabian Oil.* Beirut, Lebanon: Middle East Export Press, 1971.

Stork, Joe. *Middle East Oil and the Energy Crisis.* New York: Monthly Review Press, 1975.

Terzian, Pierre. *OPEC: The Inside Story.* London: Zed Books, 1985.

Topham, John, et al. *Traditional Crafts of Saudi Arabia.* London: Stacey International, 1981.

Twitchell, Karl S. *Saudi Arabia.* Princeton: Princeton University Press, 1947.

Vicker, Ray. *The Kingdom of Oil: The Middle East: Its People and Its Power.* New York: Scribner, 1974.

Wilson, Peter, and Douglas Graham. *Saudi Arabia: The Coming Storm.* Armonk, N.Y.: M. E. Sharpe, 1994.

Yergin, Daniel: *The Prize: The Epic Quest for Oil, Money and Power.* New York: Simon & Schuster, 1991.

Young, Arthur N. *Saudi Arabia: The Making of a Financial Giant.* New York: New York University Press, 1983.

INDEX